Model Driven Architecture for Reverse Engineering Technologies:

Strategic Directions and System Evolution

Liliana Favre
Universidad Nacional de Centro de la Proviencia de Buenos Aires, Argentina

T0320490

A volume in the Advances in Computer and Electrical Engineering (ACEE) Book Series

Director of Editorial Content:	Kristin Klinger
Director of Book Publications:	Julia Mosemann
Acquisitions Editor:	Lindsay Johnston
Development Editor:	Julia Mosemann
Publishing Assistant:	Michael Brehm
Typesetter:	Michael Brehm
Quality control:	Jamie Snavely
Cover Design:	Lisa Tosheff

Published in the United States of America by
Engineering Science Reference (an imprint of IGI Global)
701 E. Chocolate Avenue
Hershey PA 17033
Tel: 717-533-8845
Fax: 717-533-8661
E-mail: cust@igi-global.com
Web site: http://www.igi-global.com

Library of Congress Cataloging-in-Publication Data

Favre, Liliana.
 Model driven architecture for reverse engineering technologies : strategic directions and system evolution / by Liliana Favre.
 p. cm.
 Includes bibliographical references and index.
 Summary: "This book proposes an integration of classical compiler techniques, metamodeling techniques and algebraic specification techniques to make a significant impact on the automation of MDA-based reverse engineering processes"-- Provided by publisher.
 ISBN 978-1-61520-649-0 (hardcover) -- ISBN 978-1-61520-650-6 (ebook) 1. Model-driven software architecture. 2. Reverse engineering. I. Title.
 QA76.76.D47F385 2010
 005.1--dc22
                                                2009047588

This book is published in the IGI Global book series Advances in Computer and Electrical Engineering (ACEE) Book Series (ISSN: 2327-039X; eISSN: 2327-0403)

British Cataloguing in Publication Data
A Cataloguing in Publication record for this book is available from the British Library.

All work contributed to this book is new, previously-unpublished material. The views expressed in this book are those of the authors, but not necessarily of the publisher.

Advances in Computer and Electrical Engineering (ACEE) Book Series

Srikanta Patnaik
SOA University, India

ISSN: 2327-039X
EISSN: 2327-0403

MISSION

The fields of computer engineering and electrical engineering encompass a broad range of interdisciplinary topics allowing for expansive research developments across multiple fields. Research in these areas continues to develop and become increasingly important as computer and electrical systems have become an integral part of everyday life.

The **Advances in Computer and Electrical Engineering (ACEE) Book Series** aims to publish research on diverse topics pertaining to computer engineering and electrical engineering. **ACEE** encourages scholarly discourse on the latest applications, tools, and methodologies being implemented in the field for the design and development of computer and electrical systems.

COVERAGE

- Algorithms
- Applied Electromagnetics
- Chip Design
- Circuit Analysis
- Digital Electronics
- Electrical Power Conversion
- Optical Electronics
- Power Electronics
- Programming
- Qualitative Methods

IGI Global is currently accepting manuscripts for publication within this series. To submit a proposal for a volume in this series, please contact our Acquisition Editors at Acquisitions@igi-global.com or visit: http://www.igi-global.com/publish/.

Titles in this Series

For a list of additional titles in this series, please visit: www.igi-global.com

Agile and Lean Service-Oriented Development Foundations, Theory, and Practice
Xiaofeng Wang (Free University of Bozen/Bolzano, Italy) Nour Ali (Lero- The Irish Software Engineering Research Centre, University of Limerick, Ireland) Isidro Ramos (Valencia University of Technology) and Richard Vidgen (Hull University Business School, UK)
Information Science Reference • copyright 2013 • 312pp • H/C (ISBN: 9781466625037) • US $195.00 (our price)

Electromagnetic Transients in Transformer and Rotating Machine Windings
Editor, Charles Q. Su (Charling Technology, Australia)
Engineering Science Reference • copyright 2013 • 586pp • H/C (ISBN: 9781466619210) • US $195.00 (our price)

Design and Test Technology for Dependable Systems-on-Chip
Raimund Ubar (Tallinn University of Technology, Estonia) Jaan Raik (Tallinn University of Technology, Estonia) and Heinrich Theodor Vierhaus (Brandenburg University of Technology Cottbus, Germany)
Information Science Reference • copyright 2011 • 578pp • H/C (ISBN: 9781609602123) • US $180.00 (our price)

Kansei Engineering and Soft Computing Theory and Practice
Ying Dai (Iwate Pref. University, Japan) Basabi Chakraborty (Iwate Prefectural University, Japan) and Minghui Shi (Xiamen University, China)
Engineering Science Reference • copyright 2011 • 436pp • H/C (ISBN: 9781616927974) • US $180.00 (our price)

Model Driven Architecture for Reverse Engineering Technologies Strategic Directions and System Evolution
Liliana Favre (Universidad Nacional de Centro de la Proviencia de Buenos Aires, Argentina)
Engineering Science Reference • copyright 2010 • 460pp • H/C (ISBN: 9781615206490) • US $180.00 (our price)

www.igi-global.com

701 E. Chocolate Ave., Hershey, PA 17033
Order online at www.igi-global.com or call 717-533-8845 x100
To place a standing order for titles released in this series, contact: cust@igi-global.com
Mon-Fri 8:00 am - 5:00 pm (est) or fax 24 hours a day 717-533-8661

Table of Contents

Preface x

Acknowledgment xvi

Section 1
Basics

Chapter 1
Reverse Engineering and MDA: An Introduction 1
Introduction 1
Reverse Engineering in the Last 20 Years 4
Reverse Engineering and MDA 6
References 13

Chapter 2
Model Driven Architecture (MDA) 15
Introduction 15
The Basic Concepts 17
UML Metamodel 20
The Meta Object Facility (MOF) 25
Four-Layer Architecture 27
Profiles vs. Metamodels 30
References 31

Chapter 3
MDA, Metamodeling and Transformation 34
Introduction 34
MOF Constructs 35
Examples 37
Common Concepts on Transformations 45
References 47

Section 2
Formalization of MOF-Based Processes

Chapter 4

Formalization of MOF-Based Metamodels 49
Introduction.. 49
Object-Orientation, Metamodeling and Formal Languages 50
MDA Infrastructure.. 52
NEREUS: A Metamodeling Language.. 54
Example 4-1: OCL Collections in NEREUS... 60
Example 4-2: Bidirectional Associations in NEREUS... 67
Example 4-3: Aggregation/Composition in NEREUS.. 69
Example 4-4: State Diagram Metamodel 71
Example 4-5: QVT Core Formalization... 73
References... 76

Chapter 5

MOF-Metamodels and Formal Languages 80
A Bridge Between MOF-Metamodels and NEREUS.. 80
Transformation of Associations 83
Transformation of OCL Specification into NEREUS.. 83
Example 5-1: Class Diagram Specified in OCL 85
References... 97

Chapter 6

Mappings of MOF Metamodels and Algebraic Languages 98
Introduction.. 98
Translating Basic Specifications... 99
Translating Associations.. 102
Example 6-1: Translating P&M Class Diagram into CASL................................... 102
References.. 106

Chapter 7

Mappings of MOF Metamodels and Object-Oriented Languages........................... 107
Introduction.. 107
Mapping Classes and Associations.. 107
Constructing Object-Oriented Contracts and Implementations............................ 111
References.. 112

Section 3
Techniques Underlying MDA-Based Reverse Engineering

Chapter 8

Software Evolution, MDA and Design Pattern Components.. 115

Introduction.. 115

Related Work.. 116

A Megamodel for Defining MDA Reusable Components.. 117

Specifying MDA Design Pattern Components... 119

The Observer Component.. 120

PIM-Metamodel of the Observer Pattern... 121

PSM-Metamodel of the Observer Pattern... 136

ISM-Metamodel of the Observer Pattern.. 140

Specifying Metamodel-Based Transformations.. 143

Formalization of Megamodel Instances.. 150

References... 156

Chapter 9

Evolution of Models and MDA-Based Refactoring 158

Introduction.. 158

Related Work.. 159

MDA-Based Refactoring.. 160

Specifying MDA Refactoring 161

Refactoring at Metamodel Level.. 161

Refactoring at Model Level.. 182

Refactoring at Formal Language Level.. 185

Example 9-1: State Machine Diagram Refactoring.. 190

References... 196

Chapter 10

MDA-Based Object-Oriented Reverse Engineering.. 199

Introduction.. 199

Related Work.. 200

CASE Tools 201

A Framework for Reverse Engineering 204

Code-to-Model Transformations.. 206

Code-to-Model Transformations: The Bases for Recovering Class Diagram............................... 214

Code-to-Model Transformations: The Bases for Recovering State Diagram................................ 215

MOF-Based Formalization: Reverse Engineering UML Class Diagram 218

MOF-Based Formalization: Reverse Engineering UML State Diagram 221

Specifying Anti-Refinements in NEREUS.. 224

References... 226

Section 4
Conclusions

Chapter 11

Summing Up the Parts 231

    Reverse Engineering: A Different Point of View.. 231

    Challenges on MDA-Based Reverse Engineering 234

Chapter 12

Towards MDA Software Evolution 236

    Introduction.. 236

    Challenges on MDA-Based Software Evolution.. 237

    References.. 239

Section 5
Selected Readings

Chapter 13

Foundations for MDA Case Tools 242

    Liliana Favre, Universidad Nacional del Centro de la Pcia. de Buenos Aires, Argentina

    Claudia Teresa Pereira, Universidad Nacional del Centro de la Pcia. de Buenos Aires, Argentina

    Liliana Inés Martinez, Universidad Nacional del Centro de la Pcia. de Buenos Aires, Argentina

Chapter 14

A Rigorous Framework for Model-Driven Development.. 253

    Liliana Favre, Universidad Nacional del Centro de la Provincia de Buenos Aires, Argentina

Section 6
Appendices

Appendix A

Platform Specific Metamodels and Language Metamodels.. 278

A.1. PSM Metamodel: Eiffel Platform 278

A.2. PSM Metamodel: Java Platform.. 284

A.3. ISM Metamodel: Eiffel Language 294

A.4. ISM Metamodel: Java Language.. 305

A.5. ISM Metamodel: C++ Language 316

Appendix B

OCL and NEREUS: Type System...332

B.1. Primitive Types 332

B.2. Collection Types 348

B.3. Enumeration Signature..355

B.4. Type Constructors...355

Appendix C

Transformation Rule System 381

The Object Constraint Language: An Overview..381

From OCL to NEREUS: A System of Transformation Rules 386

Appendix D

Design Pattern Metamodels 396

D.1. Eiffel–PSM Observer Metamodel 396

D.2. Java–PSM Observer Metamodel 406

D.3. Java–ISM Observer Metamodel..420

About the Author 437

Index...438

Preface

The software industry has evolved to tackle new approaches aligned with the Internet, object-orientation, distributed components and new platforms. However, the majority of the large information systems running today in many organizations were developed many years ago with technologies that are now obsolete. These old systems, known as legacy systems, include software, hardware, business processes and organizational strategies and policies. Many are still business-critical and their complete replacement is dangerous and their maintenance is increasingly expensive. The amount of code in legacy systems is immense; there are billions upon billions of lines of code in existence that must be maintained.

The demand for modernization of legacy systems created the need for new architectural frameworks for information integration and tool interoperation that allow managing new platform technologies, design techniques and processes. The Object Management Group (OMG) adopted the Model Driven Architecture (MDA) that is an evolving conceptual architecture aligned with this demand.

Beyond interoperability reasons, there are other benefits to using MDA such as improving productivity, process quality and maintenance costs. MDA itself is not a technology specification, but it represents an evolving plan to achieve cohesive model-driven technology specifications.

All artifacts, such as requirement specifications, architecture descriptions, design descriptions and code are regarded as models. MDA distinguishes at least the following ones:

- **Computation Independent Model (CIM):** a model that describes a system from the computation independent viewpoint that focuses on the environment of and the requirements for the system. In general, it is called domain model.
- **Platform Independent Model (PIM):** a model with a high level of abstraction that is independent of any implementation technology.
- **Platform Specific Model (PSM):** a tailored model to specify the system in terms of the implementation constructs available in one specific platform.
- **Implementation Specific Model (ISM):** a description (specification) of the system in source code.

The idea behind MDA is to manage the evolution from CIMs to PIMs and PSMs that can be used to generate executable components and applications. In MDA, it is crucial to define, manage, and maintain traces and relationships between different models and automatically transform them and produce code that is complete and executable.

We can distinguish three main transformations in MDA processes: refinements, anti-refinements and refactorings. A refinement is the process of building a more detailed specification that conforms to another that is more abstract. On the other hand, an anti-refinement is the process of extracting from a more detailed specification (or code) another, more abstract specification that is conformed by the more detailed specification. Refactoring means changing a model, leaving its behavior unchanged, but enhancing some non-functionality quality factors such as simplicity, flexibility, understandability and performance.

The initial diffusion of MDA was focused on its relation with the Unified Modeling Language (UML) as modeling language. However, there are UML users who do not use MDA, and MDA users who use other modeling languages such as Domain Specific Languages (DSLs).

MDA requires the ability to understand different languages such as general purpose languages, domain specific languages, modeling languages or programming languages. An underlying concept of MDA for integrating such languages semantically in a unified and interoperable way is metamodeling.

The essence of MDA is the Meta-Object-Facility (MOF) metamodel that allows different kinds of artifacts from multiple vendors to be used together in the same project.

MOF (latest revision 2.0) defines a common way to capture all the diversity of modeling standards and interchange constructs. It provides a metadata management framework where models can be, for instance, exported from one application, imported into another, stored in a repository and then retrieved, transformed, and used to generate code. The MOF 2.0 Query, View, Transformation (QVT) metamodel addresses queries on models, views on metamodels and transformations of models.

With the emergence of MDA, new approaches should be developed in order to reverse engineering, both platform independent and platform specific models, from object oriented code.

This book is a contribution for the demand of system modernization. In particular, the objective of this book is to analyze the integration of MDA with reverse engineering techniques to control the evolution of systems towards object oriented technologies.

A central problem is how to correctly define metamodels and align them with MOF. Inconsistencies in a metamodel specification will affect models and their implementations. MOF-metamodels are expressed as a combination of UML, the Object Constraint Language (OCL) and natural language. MOF has no built-in semantics apart from the well-formedness rules in OCL and what can deduced from them. This form of specification does not make it possible to validate that specific metamodels like UML metamodel conform to MOF (in the sense of each metaclass of the metamodel conforms a MOF meta-metaclass). A combination of MOF metamodeling and formal specification can help us to address MDA. A formal specification allows us to produce a precise and analyzable software specification and clarifies the intended meaning of metamodels. It also helps to validate model transformations, and provides reference for implementations.

In light of this, the book proposes an integration of classical compiler techniques, metamodeling techniques and algebraic specification techniques to make a significant impact on the automation of MDA-based reverse engineering processes.

The proposed approach has two main advantages linked to automation and interoperability. On the one hand, our approach shows how to automatically generate formal specifications from MOF metamodels. Due to scalability problems, this is an essential requisite. On the other hand, it focuses on interoperability of formal languages.

Reverse engineering and software evolution are crucial and complex research domains in software engineering. This book intends to increase the consciousness of the advantages of defining MDA-based reverse engineering and software evolution processes. It emphasizes techniques that are the foundations of innovative MDA processes and inspires research to open new frontiers with the power of MDA Case tools.

To date, most model-driven development research emphasizes on "Software Language Engineering." Perhaps in the coming years, the focus will be on "Software Engineering Processes." This book intends to shorten the path to this goal by providing an overview of several techniques that can be adopted in MDA-based processes.

This book was written for a broad audience of researchers, advanced students, professionals and those people that have adopted reverse engineering practices or are about to invest in system modernization. It encourages software professionals to explore the use of MDA for innovative projects that involve reverse engineering efforts combined with software evolution. It can also be used in advanced undergraduate courses to teach reverse engineering as an integral part of software design processes.

We assume that readers have a general knowledge of object oriented modeling, in particular UML models. A self-contained discussion of the principles of reverse engineering in a novel context including topics such as MDA, OCL, MOF, UML metamodel and QVT is presented.

ORGANIZATION AND STRUCTURE

The book is divided into six sections:

- **Section 1: Basics**
- **Section 2 : Formalization of MDA Processes**
- **Section 3: Techniques Underlying MDA-Based Reverse Engineering**
- **Section 4: Conclusions**
- **Section 5: Selected Readings**
- **Section 6: Appendices**

Section 1 includes a discussion of the fundamentals of reverse engineering and MDA. It also includes a description of the main OMG standards involved in MDA processes. It introduces the main concepts of MOF-based metamodeling techniques for specifying platforms, models and metamodel-based transformations. It includes three chapters:

- **Chapter 1:** Reverse Engineering and MDA: An Introduction
- **Chapter 2:** Model Driven Architecture (MDA)
- **Chapter 3:** MDA, Metamodeling and Transformation

Section 2 describes foundations for metamodeling. It shows how to specify a metamodel by using formal specifications and how to generate formal specifications in an automatic way. Also, this section show how different formalization styles can be integrated. It includes four chapters:

- **Chapter 4:** Formalization of MOF-Based Metamodels
- **Chapter 5:** MOF-Metamodels and Formal Languages
- **Chapter 6:** Mappings of MOF Metamodels and Algebraic Languages
- **Chapter 7:** Mappings of MOF Metamodels and Object-Oriented Languages

Section 3 is a central part of this book. It describes underlying techniques in MDA processes, in particular in reverse engineering and software evolution. It describes how to adapt crucial techniques such as design patterns, model refactoring and pattern recovery in a way that fits with MDA. It includes the description of a framework for reverse engineering object oriented code. It includes three chapters:

- **Chapter 8:** Software Evolution, MDA and Design Pattern Components
- **Chapter 9:** Evolution of Models and MDA-Based Refactoring
- **Chapter 10:** MDA-Based Object-Oriented Reverse Engineering

Section 4 summarizes the main contributions and includes strategic directions and challenges in MDA reverse engineering and software evolution. It includes two chapters:

- **Chapter 11:** Summing Up the Parts
- **Chapter 12:** Towards MDA Software Evolution

Finally, the book also includes appendixes and selected readings that provide complementary information about metamodels, platforms, languages and formalisms.

Next, we describe contents of the different sections.

Section 1: Basics

Chapter 1: Reverse Engineering and MDA: An Introduction

This chapter gives an overview of state-of-the-practices in reverse engineering techniques and motivates the interest that Model Driven Reverse Engineering has gained in different application areas related to the evolution of existing software.

Chapter 2: Model Driven Architecture (MDA)

Chapter 2 explains MDA and its main concepts such as model, metamodel and transformations. It introduces the main OMG standards related to MDA such as UML Infrastructure, UML Superstructure, MOF, QVT and XMI (XML Metadata Interchange). Besides, it includes a comparison of UML Profiles, metamodels and DSL (Domain Specific Languages).

Chapter 3: MDA, Metamodeling and Transformation

Chapter 3 explains the main MOF modeling concepts and MOF-based transformations. It also provides UML/OCL notation for specifying metamodels and transformations. It includes MOF-based metamodels for object oriented languages such as Java, C++ and Eiffel and examples of transformations.

Section 2: Formalization of MOF-Based Processes

Chapter 4: Formalization of MOF-Based Metamodels

This chapter proposes a combination of metamodeling and formal specification techniques to address MDA-based processes involved in software evolution. It introduces an MDA Infrastructure, a minimal subset of packages of OMG standards to formalize MDA process. It describes an algebraic language called NEREUS which is suited for specifying metamodels, and particularly the MDA Infrastructure. The chapter also includes several examples of specifications such as OCL Collection and the QVT Core package.

Chapter 5: MOF-Metamodels and Formal Languages

The chapter explains how to integrate MOF metamodels with formal specification. It describes a bridge between MOF and NEREUS that is supported by reusable schemes and a system of transformation rules for translating OCL specifications into NEREUS. The chapter exemplifies the different steps of the transformation process.

Chapter 6: Mappings of MOF Metamodels and Algebraic Languages

The chapter analyzes mapping between MOF metamodels and traditional formal languages. In particular, it examines the relation between NEREUS and CASL (Common Algebraic Specification Language) as a common algebraic language. It proposes a transformation process that could be automated.

Chapter 7: Mappings of MOF Metamodels and Object-Oriented Languages

The chapter analyzes mapping between MOF metamodels and traditional object oriented languages. In particular, it examines the relation between NEREUS and the Eiffel language. It proposes a transformation process and a set of heuristics for integrating OCL specification and Eiffel contracts.

Section 3: Techniques Underlying MDA-Based Reverse Engineering

Chapter 8: Software Evolution, MDA and Design Pattern Components

This chapter describes how to define MDA-based reusable components. It defines a megamodel for defining MDA components at different abstraction levels (PIM, PSM and ISM). Considering the relevant role that design patterns have in software evolution, this chapter exemplifies MDA components for classical design patterns. Besides, it shows how to integrate design patterns components with MDA-based processes and also introduces formalization of metamodels and metamodel-based transformation. This chapter is used to exemplify the specification of refinements.

Chapter 9: Evolution of Models and MDA-Based Refactoring

The chapter analyzes MDA-based refactoring techniques. It explains an MDA framework for refactoring that is structured at three different levels of abstraction linked to models, metamodels and formal specification. The main contributions of this chapter are the definition of refactorings as metamodel-based transformations that are expressed as OCL contracts, a technique for identifying refactoring patterns and an algebraic formalization of refactorings. The chapter proposes a uniform treatment of refactoring at level of PIM, PSM and code.

Chapter 10: MDA-Based Object-Oriented Reverse Engineering

This chapter describes a reverse engineering approach that fits with MDA. It explains a framework to integrate different techniques that come from compiler theory, metamodeling and formal specification. It emphasizes the use of static and dynamic analysis for generating MDA models. The chapter also shows how MOF and QVT metamodels can be used to drive model recovery processes. It also describes how metamodels and transformations can be integrated with formal specifications in an interoperable way. The reverse engineering of class diagram and state diagram at PSM level from Java code is exemplified. This chapter is used to exemplify the specification of anti-refinements.

Section 4: Conclusions

Chapter 11: Summing Up the Parts

This chapter summarizes the main results described in the book and challenges in MDA reverse engineering.

Chapter 12: Towards MDA Software Evolution

This chapter discusses software evolution, challenges and strategic directions in the context of MDA.

Section 5: Selected Readings contains two previously published chapters. For Section 6: Appendices, contains four appendices. Appendix A: Platform Specific Metamodels and Language Metamodels; Appendix B: OCL and NEREUS: Type System; Appendix C: Transformation Rule System; and Appendix D: Design Pattern Metamodels.

Acknowledgment

I am very grateful to all the staff at IGI Global, whose contributions throughout the whole process from the inception of the initial idea to final publication have been invaluable. I would also like to thank all members of the publishing team at IGI Global. I am very grateful to Julia Mosemann for a huge amount of help in preparing this book. I gratefully acknowledge the useful comments and suggestions made by the anonymous reviewers whose feedback helped me improve the book. In closing, I would like to express my gratitude to Mehdi Khosrow-Pour at IGI Global.

Liliana Favre
Universidad Nacional del Centro de la Provincia de Buenos Aires
Comisión de Investigaciones Científicas de la Provincia de Buenos Aires
Argentina

Section 1
Basics

Chapter 1
Reverse Engineering and MDA:
An Introduction

INTRODUCTION

Reverse Engineering is the process of analyzing available software artifacts such as requirements, design, architectures, code or byte code, with the objective of extracting information and providing high-level views on the underlying system.

A common idea in reverse engineering is to exploit the source code as the most reliable description both of the behavior of a software system and of the organization and its business rules. However, reverse engineering is immersed in a variety of tasks related to comprehending and modifying software such as re-documentation of programs and relational databases, recovering of architectures, recovering of alternative design views, recovering of design patterns, building traceability between code and designs, modernization of interfaces or extracting the source code or high level abstractions from byte code when the source code is not available.

Reverse engineering is hardly associated with modernization of legacy systems that were developed many years ago with technology that is now obsolete. These systems include software, hardware, business processes and organizational strategies and politics. Many of them remain in use after more than 20 years; they may be written for technology which is expensive to maintain and which may not be aligned with current organizational politics. Legacy systems resume key knowledge acquired over the life of an organization. Changes are motivated for multiple reasons, for instance the way in which we do business and create value. Important business rules are embedded in the software and may not be documented elsewhere. The way in which the legacy system operates is not explicit (Brodie and Stonebraker, 1995) (Sommerville, 2004).

On the one hand, there are billions upon billions of lines of legacy code in existence, which must be maintained with a high cost and, on the other hand, there is a high risk in replacing legacy systems

DOI: 10.4018/978-1-61520-649-0.ch001

that are still business-critical. The cost of reengineering should be significantly less than the cost of a new developing.

Reverse engineering does not involve changing the source legacy systems, but understanding them to help reengineering processes that are concerned with their re-implementing. Software reengineering starts from an existing implementation and requires an evaluation of every part of the system that could be transformed or implemented anew from scratch. This definition distinguishes the following main phases:

the examination and the alteration of a subject system to reconstitute it in a new form

and

the subsequent implementation in a new form. (Demeyer, Ducasse and Nierstrasz, 2002)

In other words, reengineering includes some form of reverse engineering followed by some form of forward engineering. Reverse engineering is the process of examination, not the process of change. Chikofsky and Cross (1990) define reverse engineering and forward engineering:

- **Reverse engineering:** "the process of analyzing a subject system to (i) identify the system's components and their interrelationships and (ii) create representations of the system in another form or at a higher level of abstraction"
- **Forward engineering:** "the traditional process of moving from high-level abstractions and logical, implementation-independent designs to the physical implementation of a system"

Reverse engineering and related processes are using only three life-cycle phases: requirements specifications (including objectives, constraints and business rules), design of the solution and implementation (coding, testing, and delivery of the operational system) (Chikofsky & Cross, 1990).

Figure 1 depicts the relationship between tasks related to reverse engineering expressing transformations between or within abstraction levels linked to lifecycle phases. It also shows three processes related to reverse engineering: re-documentation, design recovery and restructuring.

Re-documentation is the creation of a representation of software artifacts that existed or should have existed within the same relative abstraction level. The resulting forms of representation are usually considered alternate views (for example dataflow, Abstract Syntax Tree, Patterns).

Design recovery rebuilds design abstractions from an integration of code, existing design documentation (if available), personal experience, and general knowledge about problem and application domains.

Restructuring is the transformation of a software artifact from one representation form to another at the same relative abstraction level, while preserving the artifact external behavior.

Reverse engineering has been used with two essential goals: design recovering and abstraction; however, it can be used to obtain more abstract representations with other purposes, for example testing, quality assurance, reuse and security.

Reverse engineering has been related with software evolution and maintenance. Software evolution is the process of initial development of a software artifact, followed by its maintenance. The ANSI/IEEE standard 729-1983 (Ansi/IEEE, 1884) defines software maintenance "as the modification of a software product after delivery to correct faults, to improve performance or other attributes, or to adapt

Figure 1. Reverse engineering and related process

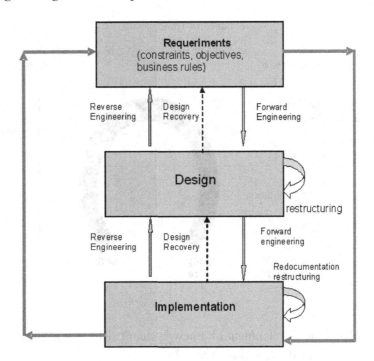

the product to a changed environment". This definition focuses on modification after delivery however maintenance lasts a long time than the initial development. This definition does not cover implementation of new functionality and it is not aligned with modern developments that require characterizing the implementation of changes in response to change request with reference to the whole life cycle.

Reverse engineering techniques can be used as a mean to design software systems by evolving existing ones based on new requirements or technologies. It involves extracting higher-level design abstractions from an existing operational system, but this is not a requirement. On the one hand, it can start from any level of abstraction or at any stage of the life cycle. On the other hand a system must be continuously reverse engineered during its life cycle and integrated with the evolution of software artifacts. Changes can be related to correcting software (corrective maintenance), adapting a system to a new environment (adaptive maintenance) or implementing new functional or non-functional requirements (perfective maintenance) (IEEE, 1984).

Baxter and Mehlich (1997) argue that "reverse engineering needs the same knowledge and infrastructure as forward engineering". When the reverse engineering and forward engineering are placed within the contexts of building new systems in a more incremental and evolutionary style of development the resulting process is round-trip engineering. The goal of round-trip engineering is to provide the generation of models from source code and generation of source code from models, while it keep the two views consistent.

In particular, reengineering includes a reverse engineering phase in which an abstraction of the software artifacts to be reengineered is built, and a forward engineering phase. A reengineering process can be view as a conceptual "horseshoe" model that distinguishes different levels of analysis and provides foundations for logical transformations at different abstraction levels, especially for transformations to

Figure 2. The Horseshoe Model for architectural reengineering

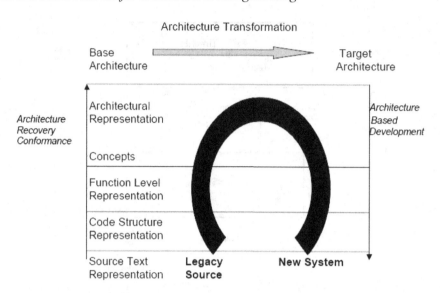

the architectural level and the development of a new system (SEI, 2009). These three processes form the basis of the "horseshoe" as illustrated in Figure 2.

REVERSE ENGINEERING IN THE LAST 20 YEARS

20 years ago, reverse engineering focused mainly on recovering high-level architectures or diagrams from procedural code to face up with problems such as comprehending data structures or databases or the Y2K problem. At that time, many different kinds of slicing techniques had been developed and several studies had been carried out to compare them. Several slicing-based tools that had to do with extractors of intermediate representations from the source code were developed.

Basically, the initial reverse engineering techniques were based on program analysis and the concept of abstract interpretation, which amounts the program computations using value descriptions or abstract values in place of actual computed values. Abstract interpretation allows obtaining information about run time behavior without actually having to run programs on all input data. Reverse engineering was affected by practical concerns, such as the target programming language and the available libraries of reusable components.

A general framework for reverse engineering based on compiler theory and abstract interpretation included at least the steps shown in Figure 3.

The source code is parsed to obtain an abstract syntax tree (AST) associated with the source programming language grammar. Information about software at the source code level is represented by metamodels. The information represented according to the metamodel allows building the data-flow graph for a given source code, as well as conducting all other analyses that do not depend on the graph. The basic idea is that information is derived statically by performing a propagation of data. Different kinds of analysis propagate different kinds of information in the data-flow graph. During this phase, the analysis, that is called static analysis, is assisted by automated tools.

Figure 3. Reverse engineering: Static analysis based on compiler techniques

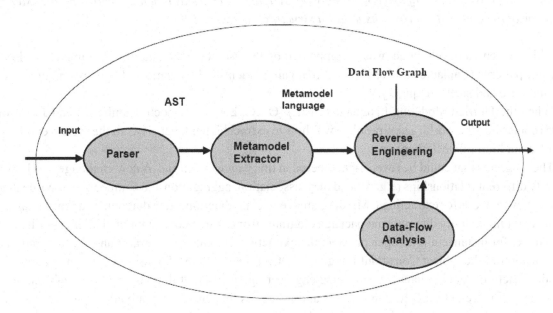

When the object oriented languages emerged, a growing demand for reengineering object oriented systems appeared on the stage. New approaches were developed to identify objects into legacy code (e.g. legacy code in COBOL) and translate this code into an object oriented language. Many object-oriented languages allow for high dynamicity loading classes at run-time and supporting the concept of reflection. The first results showed shortcomings about comprehensibility and maintainability of object oriented target code, for instance, design of classes and interrelations do not adhere to the object-oriented philosophy.

The compiler techniques were adapted to perform a propagation of proper data in a graph representation of the object flows occurring in an execution (Aho, Sethi and Ullman, 1985). In this context, the data flow is called the Object Flow Graph (Tonella & Potrich, 2005). It allows tracking the lifetime of the objects from their creation along their life-cycle.

Object-oriented programs are essentially dynamic and present particular problems linked to polymorphism and late binding, abstract classes and dynamically typed languages. For example, some object oriented languages introduce concepts such as the reflection and the possibility of loading dynamically classes, although these are powerful mechanisms, they affect reverse engineering techniques. The object oriented features such as method redefinition, dynamic method resolution and dynamic associations between classes require capturing system states through dynamic analysis.

Then, during the time of object-oriented programming the focus of software analysis moved from static analysis to dynamic one, more precisely static analysis was complemented with dynamic one. Correspondingly, reverse engineering techniques had to be customized to address these aspects.

At time of object orientation, a new generation of tracer tools assisting in dynamic analysis appeared on the marketplace. The term refactoring was introduced by Martin Fowler for defining a special kind of restructuring in object-oriented code (Fowler, 1999):

"Refactoring is the process of changing a software system in such a way that it does not alter the external behavior of the code yet improves its internal structure" (Fowler, 1999).

Object-oriented development was accompanied by the use of design patterns (Gamma et al., 1990) and anti-patterns (Laplante and Neill, 2005) that can be identified by static and dynamic analysis promoting reuse and software quality.

When the Unified Modeling Language (UML) (OMG, 2009-a) (Booch, Rumbaugh and Jacobson, 2005) comes into the world, a new problem was how to extract higher level views of the system expressed by different kind of UML diagrams.

The diagrams that could be reverse-engineered in this way were partial. A new challenge was how to identify different relationships (e.g. dependency, association, aggregation and composition). While there exists relevant work for extracting UML diagrams (e.g. class diagram, state diagram, sequence diagram, object diagram, activity diagram and package diagram) from source code, a lot of challenges still needs to be done, for instance it is an open problem the extraction of dynamic diagrams and the integration of specification in the Object Constraint Language (OCL) (OCL, 2006). Software environments provide a wide variety of tools to handle the reverse engineering at different dimensions. Although, there are tools for slicing, refactoring, design patterns and test cases, in general they are not integrated with one other in order that software evolves consistently.

REVERSE ENGINEERING AND MDA

Nowadays, software and system engineering industry evolves to manage new platform technologies, design techniques and processes. A new technical framework for information integration and tool interoperation such as the Model Driven Development (MDD) had created the need to develop new analysis tools and specific techniques. MDD refers to a range of development approaches that are based on the use of software models as first class entities. The most well-known is the OMG standard Model Driven Architecture (MDA), i.e., MDA is a realization of MDD (MDA, 2003) (MDA, 2005).

MDA is an evolution of OMG (Object Management Group) (OMG, 2009-a) standards to support model centric development increasing the degree of automation of processes such as source code translation, reverse engineering, forward engineering and data reengineering. The scope of MDA is not restricted to software systems and many kinds of domains, from system engineering, business and manufacturing can be benefited from the concepts underlying MDA.

The outstanding ideas behind MDA are separating the specification of the system functionality from its implementation on specific platforms, managing the software evolution from abstract models to implementations increasing the degree of automation and achieving interoperability with multiple platforms, programming languages and formal languages.

Models play a major role in MDA, which distinguishes at least the following ones:

- **Computation Independent Model (CIM):** a model that describes a system from the computation independent viewpoint that focuses on the environment of and the requirements for the system. In general it is called domain model.
- **Platform Independent Model (PIM):** a model with a high level of abstraction that is independent of any implementation technology.

Figure 4. MDA-based reverse and forward engineering: Models and metamodels

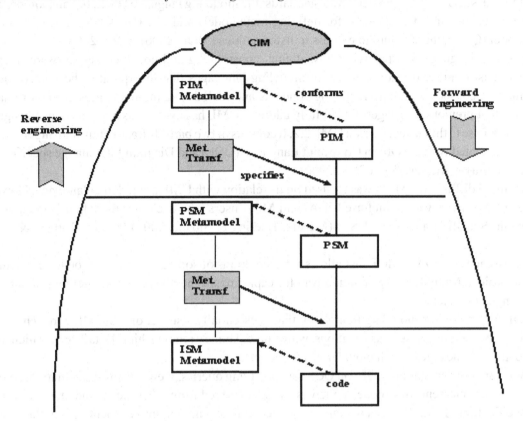

- **Platform Specific Model (PSM):** a tailored model to specify the system in terms of the implementation constructs available in one specific platform.
- **Implementation Specific Model (ISM):** a description (specification) of the system in source code.

MDA is carried out as a sequence of model transformations. We can distinguish three main transformations: refinements, anti-refinements and refactorings. A refinement is the process of building a more detailed specification that conforms to another that is more abstract. On the other hand, an anti-refinement is the process of extracting from a more detailed specification (or code) another one, more abstract, that is conformed by the more detailed one. Refactoring means changing a model leaving its behavior unchanged, but enhancing some non-functionality quality factors such as simplicity, flexibility, understandability and performance.

One of the main issues behind MDA is that all artifacts generated during software development are represented using common metamodeling languages. Metamodels integrate semantically different languages, platforms and technologies in a unified way. Figure 4 shows interrelationships between models, metamodels and transformations.

MDA is associated with popular OMG standards: the modeling language UML, the metamodel MOF (Meta Object Facility), the standard for defining metamodels and, the Query, View, Transformation Metamodel (QVT), the standard to express transformations (MOF, 2006) (QVT, 2008).

UML is a language for specifying, visualizing, constructing and documenting software intensive systems. It is a unifier of proven software modeling languages that incorporates the object-oriented community's consensus on core modeling concepts and includes additional expressiveness to handle problems that previous languages did not fully address. UML has evolved as a result of insights gained through their use to the current version UML 2.2. It consists of two parts: Infrastructure and Superstructure that are associated with the Object Constraint Language (OCL) and Diagram Interchange specifications (UML, 2009-a) (UML, 2009-b) (OCL, 2006).

The initial diffusion of MDA was focused on its relation with UML as modeling language. However, there are UML users who do not use MDA, and MDA users who use other modeling languages such as Domain Specific Languages (DSL) (Mernik, Heering & Sloane, 2005) (Krahn, Rumpe, & Volkel, 2008).

The essence of MDA is MOF that allows different kinds of software artifacts to be used together in a single project. MOF defines a common way for capturing all the diversity of modeling standards and interchange constructs.

MOF uses an object modeling framework that is essentially a subset of the UML core. The 4 main modeling concepts are classes, associations, which model binary relationships, Data Types, which model other data, and Packages which modularize the models.

QVT standard depends on MOF and OCL for specifying queries, views, and transformations. A query selects specific elements of a model, a view is a model derived from other model and, a transformation is a specification of a mechanism to convert the elements of a model, into elements of another model.

A PIM-metamodel is related to more than one PSM-metamodels, each one suited for different platforms, e.g. .NET, J2EE or relational. The PSM-metamodel corresponds to ISM-metamodels. A metamodel is a description of all the concepts that can be used in the respective level. For instance, a metamodel linked to a relational platform refers to concepts of table, foreign key and column. An ISM-metamodel includes concepts of programming languages such as constructor and method.

Metamodel transformations are a specific type of model transformations that impose relations between pairs of metamodels. A metamodel-based transformation is a specification of a mechanism to convert the elements of a model that conform to a particular metamodel, into elements of another model which can be confirmed by the same or different metamodels. Model transformations are specified as OCL contracts between metamodel.

The following types of transformations can be distinguished:

- **PIM to PSM Refinement:** It describes how a PIM that conforms to a MOF-metamodel is transformed into a PSM that conforms to a specialized MOF-metamodel for a specific platform.
- **PSM to ISM Refinement:** It describes how a PSM (which conforms to a MOF-metamodel for specific platform) is transformed into code (which conforms to a MOF-metamodel for a specific object-oriented language).
- **ISM to PSM Anti-refinement:** It describes how a code that conforms to an ISM metamodel is transformed into a PSM that conforms to a specialized MOF metamodel for a specific platform.
- **PSM to PIM Anti-refinement:** It describes how a PSM that conforms to a PSM metamodel is transformed into a PIM.

Figure 5. MDA transformations: Refinements, anti-refinements and refactoring

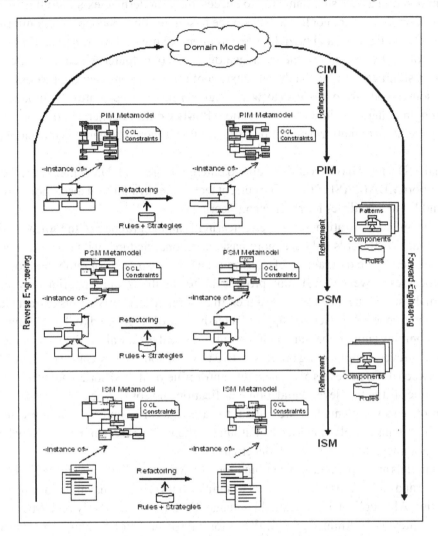

- **Refactoring:** It specifies how a model in a given level is transformed into a new restructured model in the same level (for instance, PIM to PIM, PSM to PSM, ISM to ISM). The source and target models conform to the same MOF-metamodel.

Figure 5 shows the different correspondences that may be held between several metamodel, instances of metamodels and their interrelations via refinements, anti-refinements and refactorings in a reengineering process. It can be viewed as an MDA "horseshoe" model that describes the phases of architecture recovery and architecture based development, MDA is the underlying architectural framework. It shows how reengineering proceeds at different levels of abstraction: code representation, platform dependent models, platform independent models and computation independent models. In particular, reengineering includes a reverse engineering phase in which an abstraction of the software models to be reengineered is expressed in terms of MDA models, and a forward engineering phase.

OMG is involved in a series of standards to successfully modernize existing information systems. Modernization supports, but are not limited to, source to source conversion, platform migration, service oriented architecture migration and model driven architecture migration (ADM, 2007).

The success of MDA depends on the existence of CASE (Computer Aided Software Engineering) tools that make a significant impact on the automation of round-trip engineering processes that provide generation of source code from models (forward engineering) and generation of models from source code (reverse engineering). For instance, one or more PSMs would be generated from a PIM using tools for automatic generation of platform details or, different PSMs would be generated from object-oriented code.

Commercial MDA tools have recently begun to emerge. In general, UML preexisting tools are been extended to support MDA (CASE, 2009). The current techniques available in these tools provide forward engineering and limited facilities for reverse engineering.

In legacy system modernization, reverse engineering is an integral part of the software development cycle. The existing CASE tools only use more basic notational features with a direct code representation and produce very large diagrams. Refactoring is an important step for evolving models in reverse engineering processes; however CASE tools provide limited facilities for refactoring only on source code through an explicit selection made for the designer. In general, MDA CASE tools extract class diagrams from object oriented code, while lacking support for recovering different kinds of UML diagrams. Reverse engineering is complex enough that human intervention is still essential for the time being.

With respect to reverse engineering processes, two types of consistency can be distinguished, vertical consistency between different levels of refinements/anti-refinements and horizontal consistency between models at the same abstraction level. Validation, verification and consistency are crucial activities in the modernization of legacy systems that are critical to safety, security and economic profits. Reasoning about models of systems is well supported by automated theorem provers and model checkers, however these tools are not integrated into CASE tools environments.

MOF-metamodels are expressed as a combination of UML class diagrams and OCL. UML and OCL are too imprecise and ambiguous when it comes to simulation, verification, validation and forecasting of system properties. Although OCL is a textual language, OCL expressions rely on UML class diagrams, i.e., the syntax context is determined graphically. A formal specification technique must provide at least syntax, some semantics and an inference system. The inference system can help to automate testing, prototyping or verification. However, OCL does not support logic deductions in the style of solid formal languages.

One of the most important features for a rigorous development is the combination of tests and proofs. When artifacts at different levels of abstraction are available, a continuous consistency check between them could be help to reduce development mistakes, for example checking whether the code is consistent with the design or complies with the pre- and post-conditions.

With the emergence of MDA, the static analysis and dynamic analysis must be integrated with metamodeling techniques. We propose an approach for MDA-based reverse engineering that integrates classical compiler techniques, metamodeling techniques and formal specification.

Reverse engineering involves processes with different degrees of automation, which can go from totally automatic static analysis to human intervention requiring processes to dynamically analyze the resultant models. We propose to combine static and dynamic analysis to generate models (PSMs, and PIMs) from code and, to analyze the consistency of these transformations by integrating metamodeling and formal specification.

Figure 6. MDA and interoperability at level of formal languages

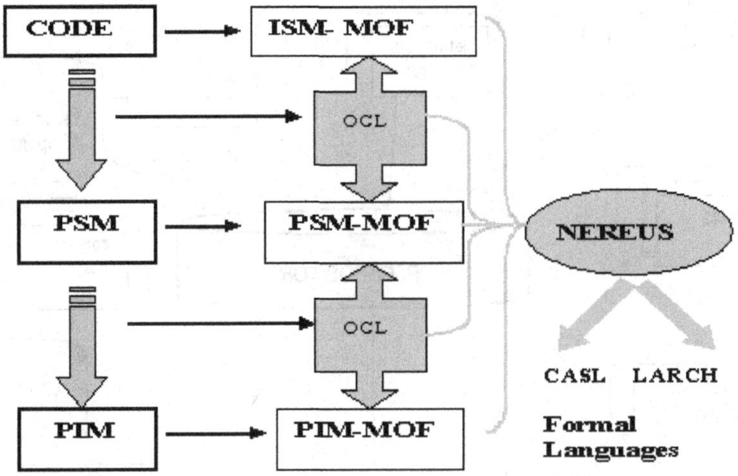

This book proposes a framework for reverse engineering that distinguishes three different abstraction levels linked to models, metamodels and formal specifications.

The model level includes code, PSMs and PIMs. Transformations at this level are based on classical static and dynamic analysis techniques.

The metamodel level includes MOF-metamodels that describe families of ISMs, PSMs and PIMs. Every ISM, PSM and PIM conforms to a MOF-metamodel. Metamodel transformations are based on a minimal subset of OMG standard metamodels that we called MDA Infrastructure.

The level of formal specification includes specifications of MOF-metamodels and metamodel transformations by using the metamodeling language NEREUS that can be viewed as an intermediate formal-language independent notation. It focuses on interoperability of formal languages in MDD and would eliminate the need to define formalizations and specific transformations for each different formal language.

We define a bridge between MOF-metamodels and NEREUS consisting of a system of transformation rules to convert automatically MOF into NEREUS. Figure 6 shows the relation between metamodel specifications and NEREUS. Relevant techniques of software evolution, such as reuse and refactoring ones have been integrated in a way that fits with MDA.

It is worth considering that although, we use as an intermediate notation NEREUS and specific transformation rule systems, the ideas underlying this approach are independent of particular notations. The bases of our approach are:

- The integration of compiler techniques, metamodeling and formal specification.
- The formalization of an MDA Infrastructure.
- The definition of a formal Domain Specific Language (DSL) for defining metamodels and transformations.
- The automation of bridges between MOF metamodels and the DSL.
- The definition of MDA-based reuse and refactoring techniques.

Figure 7. MDA reverse engineering environments

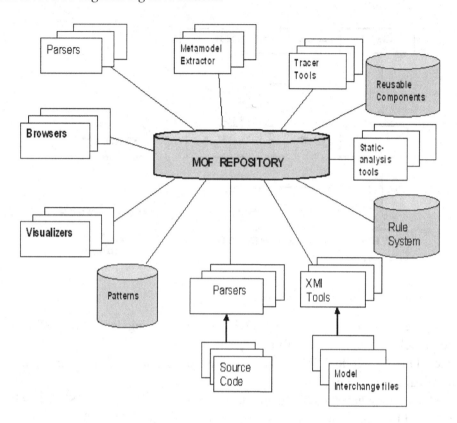

MDA-based reverse engineering environments are structured in the way depicted in Figure 7. There is a common repository to store data of the system; in MDA is a MOF- metadata repository. This repository attempts to address the problem of sharing models between different software tools. There are parsers, to extract information from source code, metamodel tools to extract metamodel representations and model interchange tools. These tools focus on static analysis. Other tracer tools focus on dynamic analysis. Traditional tools such as visualizers, analyzers, browsers and debuggers, use the repository as their base information. Other tools that focus on formal specification and formal transformation also need the MOF- repository and basic facilities for import/export. Libraries of pattern and components must fit with MDA.

The following chapters include background, foundations of innovative MDA processes and challenges and strategic directions that can be adopted in the field of MDA-based reverse engineering and software evolution. We analyze principles of reverse engineering within system evolution and, show how to recover MDA-based designs and architectures. Different principles of reverse engineering are covered, with special emphasis on consistency, traceability, testing and verification of systems that are critical to safety, security and economic profits.

The main strength of our approach is to detect a common conceptual foundation for what we do in MDA processes. From making these foundations explicit, better tools should emerge.

REFERENCES

ADM (2007). *ADM Task Force. Architecture Driven Modernization Roadmap.* Retrieved on July 20, 2009 from adm.omg.org

Aho, A., Sethi, R., & Ullman, J. (1985). *Compilers: Principles, Techniques, and Tools* (2nd ed.). Reading: Addison-Wesley.

ANSI-IEEE. (1984). ANSI/IEEE Software Engineering Standards: Std 729-1983, Std 730-1884, Std 828-1983, 829-1984, 830-1984. Los Alamitos: IEEE/Wiley.

Baxter, I., & Mehlich, M. (1997). Reverse Engineering is Reverse Forward Engineering. In *Proceedings of Fourth Working Conference on Reverse Engineering, Amsterdam, The Netherlands.* Retrieved on July 20, 2009 from www.semdesigns.com/Company/Publications/WCRE97.pdf

Booch, G., Rumbaugh, J., & Jacobson, I. (2005). *The Unified Modeling Language. User Guide* (2nd ed.). Reading: Addison-Wesley.

Brodie, M., & Stonebraker, M. (1995). *Migration Legacy Systems: Gateways, Interfaces, and Incremental Approach.* Morgan Kauffman.

CASE. (2009). *CASE Tools.* Retrieved on July 20, 2009 from www.objectsbydesign.com/tools/uml-tools_byCompany.html

Chikofsky, E., & Cross, J. (1990). Reverse engineering and design recovery: A taxonomy. *IEEE Software, 7*(1), 13–17. doi:10.1109/52.43044

Demeyer, S., Ducasse, S., & Nierstrasz, O. (2002). *Object-Oriented Reengineering Patterns.* Amsterdam: Morgan Kaufmann.

Fowler, M. (1999). *Refactoring: Improving the Design of Existing Programs.* Reading: Addison-Wesley.

Gamma, E., Helm, R., Johnson, R., & Vlissides, J. (1995). Design Patterns. Elements of Reusable Object-Oriented Software. Reading: Addison-Wesley.

Krahn, H., Rumpe, B., & Volkel, S. (2008). MontiCore: Modular development of Textual Domain Specific Languages. In *Proceedings of TOOLS (46), Lecture Notes in Business information Processing 11* (pp. 297-315). Heidelberg: Springer-Verlag.

Laplante, P., & Neill, C. (2005). *Antipatterns: Identification, Refactoring and Management.* Auerbach Publications.

MDA. (2003). MDA Guide Version 1.0.1. In J. Miller & J. Mukerji (Eds.). Document omg/2003-06-01. Retrieved on July 20, 2009 from www.omg.org/mda

MDA. (2005). *The Model Driven Architecture.* Retrieved on July 20, 2009 from www.omg.org/mda.

Mernik, M., Heering, J., & Sloane, A. (2005). When and how to develop domain-specific languages. *ACM Computing Surveys, 37*(4), 316–344. doi:10.1145/1118890.1118892

MOF. (2006). *MOF: Meta Object facility (MOF ™) 2.0.* OMG Specification formal/2006-01-01. Retrieved on July 20, 2009 from www.omg.org/mof

OCL. (2006). *OCL: Object Constraint Language. Version 2.0.* OMG: formal/06-05-01.Retrieved on July 20, 2009 from www.omg.org

OMG. (2009a). *The Object Management Group Consortium.* Retrieved on July 20, 2009 from www.omg.org

QVT. (2008). *QVT: MOF 2.0 Query, View, Transformation.* Formal/2008-04-03. Retrieved on July 20, 2009 from www.omg.org

SEI. (2009) Carnegie Mellon- Software Engineering Institute. *Reengineering: The Horseshoe Model.* Retrieved on July 20, 2009 from http://www.sei.cmu.edu/reengineering/Horseshoe_model.html

Sommerville, I. (2004). *Software Engineering* (7th ed.). Reading: Addison Wesley.

Tonella, P., & Potrich, A. (2005). Reverse Engineering of Object Oriented Code. *Monographs in Computer Science.* Heidelberg: Springer-Verlag.

UML. (2009a). *Unified Modeling Language: Infrastructure.* Version 2.2. OMG Specification formal/2009-02-04. Retrieved on July 20, 2009 from www.omg.org.

UML. (2009b). *UML: Unified Modeling Language: Superstructure.* Version 2.2. OMG Specification: formal/2009-02-02. Retrieved on July 20, 2009 from www.omg.org

Chapter 2
Model Driven Architecture (MDA)

INTRODUCTION

The architecture of a system is a specification of software components, interrelationships, and rules for component interactions and evolution over time.

In 2001 OMG, adopted an architecture standard, the Model Driven Architecture (MDA). MDA is an architectural framework for improving portability, interoperability and reusability through separation of concerns (MDA, 2003) (MDA, 2005). It is not itself a technology specification but it represents an evolving plan to achieve cohesive model-driven technology specifications. MDA is built on OMG standards including the Unified Modeling Language (UML), the XML Metadata Interchange (XMI) (XMI, 2007) and CORBA (CORBA, 1992) (CORBA, 2002) a major middleware standard.

MDA is model-driven because it uses models to direct the complete lifecycle of a system. All artifacts such as requirement specifications, architecture descriptions, design descriptions and code, are regarded as models. MDA provides an approach for specifying a system independently of the platforms that it supports, specifying platforms, selecting a particular platform for the system, and transforming the system specification into one implementation for the selected particular platform.

Why MDA? OMG has focused on the creation of open specifications to encourage application interoperability. It was defined to solve enterprise application integration. A middleware describes a piece of software that connects two or more software applications, allowing them to exchange data. To achieve this, it must be implemented for all different languages and platforms that need linking.

DOI: 10.4018/978-1-61520-649-0.ch002

With the emergence of internet applications, the interoperability problem moved from the integration of platforms and programming languages on a company intranet to the integration of different middleware on Internet. In this situation, the middleware is part of the problem itself. The original inspiration around the definition of MDA had to do with this internet middleware integration problem. Apart from interoperability reasons, there are other good benefits to use MDA such as to improve the productivity, code and processes quality and, software maintenance costs.

MDA defines a framework that separates the specification of the system functionality from its implementation on a specific platform. It distinguishes different kinds of models:

- **Computation Independent Model (CIM),** a model that describes a system from the computation independent viewpoint.
- **Platform Independent Model (PIM),** a model with a high level of abstraction that is independent of any implementation technology.
- **Platform Specific Model (PSM),** a tailored model to specify the system in terms of the implementation constructs available in one specific platform.
- **Implementation Specific Model (ISM),** a description (specification) of the system in source code.

The Unified Modeling Language (UML) (UML, 2009a) (UML, 2009b) combined with the Object Constraint Language (OCL) (OCL, 2006) is the most widely used way for writing either PIMs or PSMs.

Model Driven Development (MDD) refers to a range of development approaches that are based on the use of software models as first class entities. (Sztipanovits and Karsai, 1997) and (Kulkarni and Reddy, 2005) describe approaches for MDD. Selic (2006) positions UML 2 as a model driven development tool. Hailpern & Tarr (2006) illustrate "the good, the bad and the ugly" of MDD and improvements to meet major challenges at all stages of the software life cycle. France and Rumpe (2007) describe a research roadmap of MDD of complex software.

MDA is the specific realization of MDD proposed by OMG. It is carried out as a sequence of model transformations: the process of converting one model into another one of the same system preserving some kind of equivalence relation between them.

The idea behind MDA is to manage the evolution from CIMs to PIMs and PSMs that can be used to generated executable components and applications. The high level models that are developed independently of a particular platform are gradually transformed into models and code for specific platforms.

The transformation for one PIM to several PSMs is at the core of MDA. A model-driven forward engineering process is carried out as a sequence of model transformations that includes, at least, the following steps: construct a CIM; transform the CIM into a PIM that provides a computing architecture independent of specific platforms; transform the PIM into one or more PSMs, and derive code directly from the PSMs.

The concept of formal metamodel has contributed significantly to some of the core principles of the emerging MDA. The Meta Object Facility (MOF), an adopted OMG standard, (latest revision MOF 2.0) provides a metadata management framework, and a set of metadata services to enable the development and interoperability of model and metadata driven systems (MOF, 2006).

A metamodel is an abstract language for describing different types of models and data. The framework for metamodeling is based on architectures with four meta-layers: meta-metamodel, metamodel, model and object model layers. The primary responsibility of these layers is to define languages that describe metamodels, models, semantic domains and run-time instances of model elements respectively.

Related OMG standard metamodels and meta-metamodels such as Meta Object Facility (MOF) (MOF, 2006), Software Process Engineering Metamodel (SPEM) (SPEM, 2008) and Common Warehouse Metamodel (CWM) (CWM, 2003) share a common design philosophy. All of them, including MOF, are expressed using MOF. It defines a common way for capturing all the diversity of modeling standards and interchange constructs that are used in MDA. Its goal is to define languages in a same way and hence integrate them semantically.

MOF and the core of the UML metamodel are closely aligned with their modeling concepts. The UML metamodel can be viewed as an "instance-of" the MOF metamodel in the sense of each UML metaclasses conforms to an instance of a MOF metaclass.

OMG adopted the MOF 2.0 Query, View and Transformation (QVT) metamodel (QVT) for expressing transformations (QVT, 2008). A "query" selects specific elements of a model, a "view" is a model derived from other model, and a "transformation" is a specification of a mechanism to convert the elements of a model, into elements of another model, which conform the same or different metamodel.

MDA reverse engineering can be used to recover architectural models of legacy systems that will be later used in forward engineering processes to produce new versions of the systems. OMG is involved in a series of standards to successfully modernize existing information systems. Modernization supports, but are not limited to, source to source conversion, platform migration, service oriented architecture migration and model driven architecture migration. Architecture-Driven Modernization (ADM) is an OMG initiative related to extending the modeling approach to the existing software systems and to the concept of reverse engineering (ADM, 2007).

A lot of work has been conducted within the diffusion of MDA. (Kleppe & Warner, 2003) and (Mellor, Scott, Uhl & Weise, 2003) are the first books that introduced the MDA approach. Other books provide a set of readings on the state-of-the-art and the state-of-the-practice of MDA (Byededa, Book & Gruhn, 2005). (Raistrick, Francis & Wright, 2004) analyzes the automatic executable code generation directly from model specifications using Executable UML (XUML).

Arlow and Neustad (2003) propose a practical guide to applying MDA and patterns in order to create business applications more easily. It provides a proven catalog of archetype patterns to understand and model a specific part of an enterprise system. (Hruby, 2006) shows how to apply the pattern ideas in business applications and presents more than 20 structural and behavioral business patterns.

Guttman and Parodi (2006) describe six case studies of real companies illustrating the variety of MDA approaches.

(Pastor & Molina, 2007) includes a software process based on model transformation technology introducing information required to put MDA into the industrial practice.

THE BASIC CONCEPTS

MDA initiative is an evolving conceptual architecture for a set of industry-wide technology specifications that will support a model-driven approach to software development. This section presents the concepts that are at the core of MDA.

Models, Metamodels and Transformations

Models

A model is a simplified view of a (part of) system and its environments. Models are expressed in a well-defined modeling language. They are centered in a set of diagrams and textual notations that allow specifying, visualizing and documenting systems.

For instance, a model could be a set of UML diagrams, OCL specifications and text. MDA distinguishes different kinds of models which go from abstract ones that specify the system functionality to platform-dependent and concrete ones linked to specific platforms, technologies and implementations. Figure 1 shows models at different abstraction levels. MDA distinguishes at least the following ones:

- Computation Independent Model (CIM)
- Platform Independent Model (PIM)
- Platform Specific Model (PSM)
- Implementation Specific Model (ISM)

A CIM describes a system from the computation independent viewpoint that focuses on the environment of and the requirements for the system. It is independent of how the system is implemented. In general, it is called domain model and may be expressed using business models. The CIM helps to bridge the gap between the experts about the domain and the software engineer. A CIM could consist of UML models and other models of requirements.

In the context of MDA, a platform "is a set of subsystems and technologies that provides a coherent set of functionality through interfaces and specified usage patterns, which any application supported by that platform can use without concern for the details of how the functionality provided by the platform is implemented" (MDA, 2003, pp. 2-3). An application refers to a functionality being developed. A system can be described in terms of one or more applications supported by one or more platforms. MDA is based on platform models expressed in UML, OCL, and stored in a repository aligned with MOF.

A PIM is a view of the system that focuses on the operation of a system from the platform independent viewpoint. Analysis and logical models are typically independent of implementation and specific platforms and can be considered PIMs.

A PIM is defined as a set of components and functionalities, which are defined independently of any specific platforms, and which can be realized in platform specific models. A PIM can be viewed as a system model for a technology-neutral virtual machine that includes parts and services defined independently of any specific platform. It can be viewed as an abstraction of a system that can be realized by different platform-specific ways on which the virtual machine can be implemented.

A PSM describes a system in the terms of the final implementation platform e.g., .NET or J2EE. A PSM is a view of the system from the platform specific viewpoint that combines a PIM with the details specifying how that system uses a particular type of platform. It includes a set of technical concepts representing the different parts and services provided by the platform.

An ISM is a specification, which provides all the information needed to construct an executable system.

Figure 1. MDA models: From abstract levels to implementations

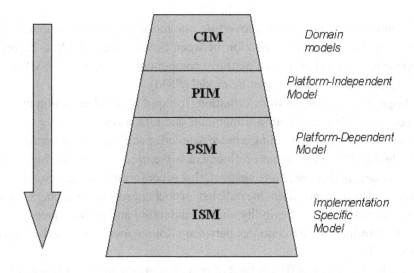

Although there is a structural gap between CIM and PIM, a CIM should be traceable to PIM. In the same way, a PIM should be traceable to PSMs which in turn should be traceable to ISMs.

Metamodels

Metamodeling is a powerful technique to specify families of models. A metamodel is a model that defines the language for expressing a model, i.e. "a model of models". A metamodel is an explicit model of the constructs and rules needed to build specific models. It is a description of all the concepts that can be used in a model.

A meta-metamodel defines a language to write metamodels. Since a metamodel itself is a model, it can be usually defined using a reflexive definition in a modeling language. A metamodel can be viewed as a model of a modeling language.

Metamodeling has become an essential technique in MDA. In particular, MDA is based on the use of a language to write metamodels called the Meta Object Facility (MOF). MOF uses an object modeling framework that is essentially a subset of the UML 2.2 core. The four main modeling concepts are classes, which model MOF metaobjects; associations, which model binary relations between metaobjects; Data Types, which model other data; and Packages, which modularize the models (MOF, 2006) (MOF, 2002).

The UML itself is defined using a metamodeling approach. The metamodeling framework for the UML is based on a modeling architecture with four layers: meta-metamodel, metamodel, model and user objects. A model is expressed in the language of one specific metamodel. A metamodel is an explicit model of the constructs and rules needed to construct specific models. Meta-metamodel are usually self-defined using a reflexive definition that is based at least on three concepts (entity, association and package) and a set of primitive types. Languages for expressing MOF-based metamodels are based on UML class diagrams and OCL constraints to rule out illegal models.

Transformations

Model transformation is the process of converting one model into another model of the same system preserving some kind of equivalence relation between both of these models. Figure 2 shows how a platform independent model (PIM) and a platform component description (PDM) are combined by the transformation to produce a platform specific model (PSM).

We can distinguish three types of transformations to support model evolution in forward and reverse engineering processes: refinements, anti-refinements and refactorings.

A refinement is the process of building a more detailed specification that conforms to another that is more abstract. On the other hand, an anti-refinement is the process of extracting from a more detailed specification (or code) another one, more abstract, that is conformed by the more detailed specification. Refactoring means changing a model leaving its behavior unchanged, but enhancing some non-functionality quality factors such as simplicity, flexibility, understandability and performance.

Metamodel transformations are contracts between a source metamodel and a target metamodel and describe families of transformations.

Figure 3 partially depicts the different kind of transformations and the relationships between models and metamodels.

UML METAMODEL

UML have emerged as a de-facto standard for expressing object-oriented models. It is a graphical language for visualizing, specifying, constructing and, documenting the artifacts of software intensive systems that can be used with all major object and component methods, and can be applied to a large and diverse set of domains (e.g. healthcare, finance, telecom, aerospace) and implementation platforms

Figure 2. Metamodel-based transformations

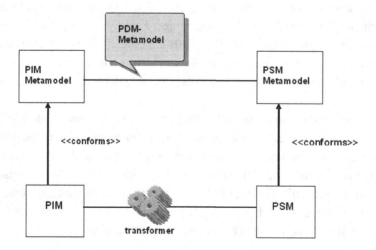

(e.g. .NET, relational or different Java platforms) (Rumbaugh, Jacobson, & Booch, 1998) (Booch, Rumbaugh & Jacobson, 2005).

Although UML does not prescribe any particular development process, various companies are working on processes to provide advice on the use of UML in the software development life cycle.

The OMG presents the "Software Process Engineering Metamodel" (SPEM) (SPEM, 2008). This metamodel is used to describe a concrete software development process or a family of related software development process. Several processes enact SPEM. The most popular is Rational Unified Process (RUP), developed and marketed by Rational Software. It is a software development process based on UML that is a use-driven, architecture –centered, iterative and risk driven. It provides a disciplined approach to assigning tasks and responsibilities within a development organization. RUP is organized around four phases (inception, elaboration, construction and transition) and core workflows (require-

Figure 3. MDA transformations: Metamodel-based transformations

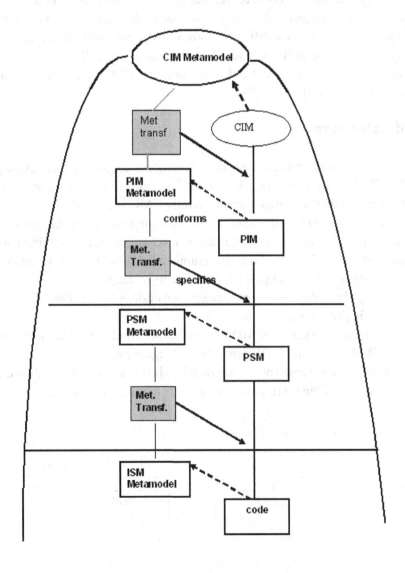

Table 1. Different UML diagrams: Static diagrams and behavioral diagrams

Static Diagrams	Behavioral Diagrams
Class Diagram	Use case Diagram
Object Diagram	State Diagram
Component Diagram	Communication Diagram
Composite Structure Diagram	Sequence Diagram
Package Diagram	Activity Diagram
Deployment Diagram	Timing Diagram
	Interaction Diagrams

ments, capture, analysis, design, implementation and test). Various industry sectors around the world use RUP in different applications: telecommunications, transportation, aerospace, defense, manufacturing and financial services (Jacobson, Booch, & Rumbaugh, 1999) (Kruchten, 2000).

UML supports different diagrams that can be used for modeling different views of the system under development. Table 1 summarizes the different kinds of UML static and behavioral diagrams. A detailed analysis of them may be found at (Booch, Rumbaugh & Jacobson, 2005).

The latest version 2.2 of UML is defined in terms of the UML 2. 2. Infrastructure and UML 2. 2 Superstructure (UML, 2009a) (UML, 2009b).

The UML Infrastructure

The UML Infrastructure specification defines the foundational language constructs required for UML 2. 2. (UML, 2009a). The UML Infrastructure defines the foundational language constructs that are required to be used in other metamodel and aligns architecturally UML and MOF.

Figure 4 shows the package InfrastructureLibrary containing core concepts used when metamodeling. It includes the packages Core and Profiles that define mechanisms for customizing metamodels.

The Core package can be viewed as an architectural kernel of MDA. It is a complete metamodel that is reused by other metamodels that import or specialize its metaclasses.

The Profile package depends on the Core package, and defines the mechanisms used to adapt existing metamodels to specific platforms or domains.

Core can be considered the kernel of MDA since the metamodels that are at the heart of MDA such as UML, CWM (CWM, 2003) and MOF depend on it (Figure 5).

The UML infrastructure is reused at several metalevels in various specifications, e.g. the UML Superstructure uses it to model the UML models and MOF, to model metamodels.

Figure 4. The InfrastructureLibrary package

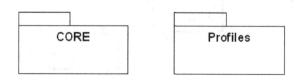

Figure 5. Core and related metamodels

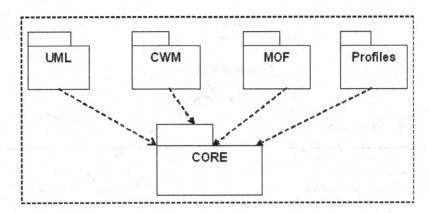

Core package is composed by four main packages: PrimitiveTypes, Abstractions, Basic, and Constructs as shown in Figure 6.

The package PrimitiveTypes contains the primitive types that are used when metamodeling in the context of UML and MOF. In order to facilitate reuse, the package Abstractions contains abstract metaclasses commonly reused or specialized by many metamodel. The package Constructs contains concrete metaclasses linked to object-oriented modeling and reflects a central part of the alignment of UML and MOF. The package Basic defines constructs that are used as the basis for the produced XMI for metamodels based on the InfrastructureLibrary. While instantiation of metaclasses is carried out through MOF, the InfrastructureLibrary defines the actual metaclasses that are used to instantiate the elements of metamodels such as UML, and indeed the elements of the InfrastructureLibrary itself. Then, it is reflective. All of the UML metamodel is instantiated from meta-metaclasses that are defined in the InfrastructureLibrary.

The Profiles Package depends on the Core package and define the mechanisms that allow metaclasses from existing metamodel to be extended to adapt for different purpose languages/platforms such as C++,

Figure 6. The Core packages

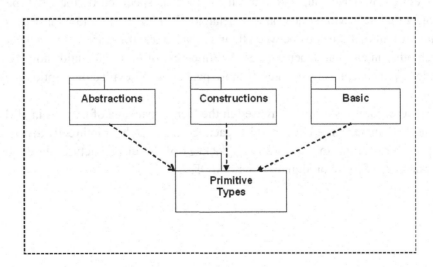

Figure 7. Metalevels of UML and MOF

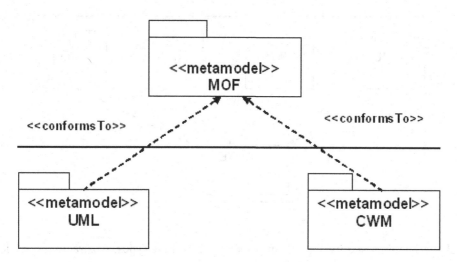

CORBA (CORBA, 2002), or EJB (EJB, 2004); or domains such as real-time, business objects, or software process modeling. In general, profiles are associated to UML, but it is possible to define profiles in terms of a metamodel that is based on the common core (see Figure 5).

The Infrastructure has aligned architecturally UML and MOF. Figure 7 shows UML and MOF at different metalevels. UML is defined as a model based on MOF in which each UML metaclass is an instance of a MOF metaclass. Also, MOF is the metamodel of other OMG standards e.g. CWM and SPEM.

The UML Superstructure

The UML Infrastructure is complemented by UML Superstructure (UMLb, 2009), which defines the user level constructs required for UML 2.2. The two complementary specifications constitute a complete specification for the UML 2 modeling language.

The UML Superstructure metamodel includes a number of packages that deal with structural and behavioral modeling. The UML Superstructure metamodel is specified by the UML package, which includes packages that deal with structural and behavioral modeling as shown in Figure 8. Due to it shows a summary of all relationships between their subpackages, there are some packages that are dependent on each other in circular dependencies. A refinement of Figure 8 could show that there are no circular dependencies between subpackages of those packages. A detailed description may be found at (UML, 2009b).

The InfrastructureLibrary is primarily reused in the Kernel package of Classes in UML 2.2. Superstructure and the UML metaclasses of every other package are directly or indirectly dependent on it. The Kernel package is very similar to the Constructs package of the InfrastructureLibrary, but adds more constructs for purposes of reuse or alignment with MOF.

Figure 8. The top level package structure of the UML Superstructure 2.1.2

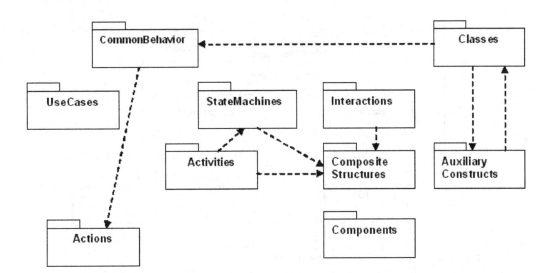

UML Semantics

UML semantic specification is defined using a metamodeling approach that combines MOF-based meta-models, OCL specification and text. The metamodel is described in a semi-formal way using abstract syntax, well-formed rules and semantics. The abstract syntax is provided as a model expressed by UML class diagram and a natural language description. The class diagram shows the metaclasses defining the constructs and their relationships. The well-formed rules are expressed in OCL and natural language.

THE META OBJECT FACILITY (MOF)

The Meta Object Facility (MOF) defines a framework for specifying, constructing and managing meta-models (MOF, 2002) (MOF, 2006). A meta-metamodel and a metamodel are abstract languages for some kind of metadata. The term metadata is used to refer to data whose purpose is to describe other data.

MOF provides "a metadata management framework and a set of metadata services to enable the development and interoperability of models and metadata driven systems" (MOF, 2006, pp. 5). MOF facilitates interoperability among modeling and development tools, data warehouse systems and meta-data repositories. A number of OMG standards, including UML, MOF, various UML profiles and XMI are aligned with MOF.

In the UML version 2.0 the concepts of MOF and the UML superstructure are based on the concepts of the UML Infrastructure. MOF provides two metamodels: EMOF (Essential MOF) and CMOF (Complete MOF). The former favors simplicity of implementation over expressiveness, while the latter is more expressive, but more complex. Figure 9 shows the dependencies between them. EMOF merges the Reflection, Identifiers, and Extension capability packages to provide services for discovering, manipulating, identifying, and extending metadata. CMOF is the metamodel used to specify other metamodels such as UML 2. It is built from EMOF and the Core::Constructs of UML Infrastructure. The Model package

Figure 9. MOF and UML Core

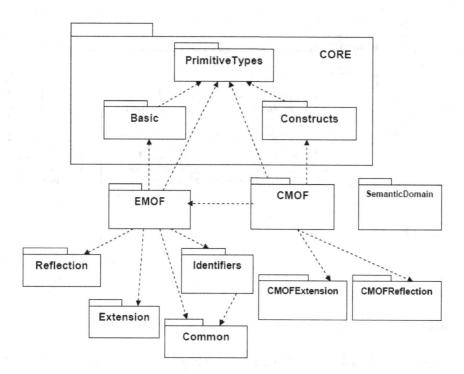

does not define any classes of its own. Rather, it merges packages with its extensions that together define basic metamodeling capabilities.

The four modeling concepts in MOF are:

- Classes, which model MOF metaobjects
- Associations, which model binary relationships between metaobjects
- Data types, which model other data such primitive types or external types
- Packages, which modularize the models.

The traditional metamodel architecture is four-layer metadata architecture however this hierarchy could be based on more levels. Strength of metamodels is the possibility to define more abstraction levels. Besides, a model (a collection of metadata) is not necessarily limited to one meta-level. For instance a reverse engineering process that requires code transformations could describe an ISM by four layers. The topmost layer M3 is an EBNF (the meta-metamodel), the M2 layer is a specific grammar (the meta-model), the M1 layer a Java program and M0 an execution model, the entity in the real world.

The MOF model is self-describing, that is to say it is formally defined using its own metamodeling constructs. This provides a uniform semantic treatment between artifacts that represent models and metamodels.

Figure 10. MOF four layer architecture

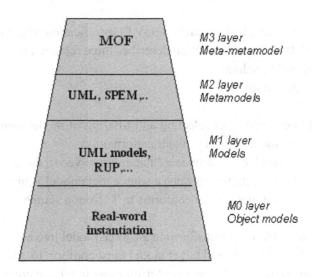

FOUR-LAYER ARCHITECTURE

The MDA is based on four meta-layer architectures. The layers are conventionally identified as M3, M2, M1 and M0 layers. Figure 10 exemplifies the MOF metadata architecture based on four layers.

The M3 layer is the meta-metamodel and MOF is an example of meta-metamodel. MOF is a framework for specifying, constructing, and managing independent metamodels. It is the basis to define modeling languages such as UML or MOF itself. A meta-metamodel describes a family of metamodels. In general, metamodels and meta-metamodels share a common design philosophies and constructs. However, each layer can be viewed independently of others layers

All metamodels that conform to a meta-metamodel are placed in the M2 layer. UML and SPEM metamodel (SPEM, 2008) are examples of metamodel that conforms to MOF. The metamodels of this layer describe families of models of the real world, which are represented in the M1 level. A model is an instance of a metamodel. M1 is a model layer that defines languages. UML models, that conform to UML metamodel, and the IBM Rational Unified Process (RUP) that conforms to SPEM are in M1 (Krutchen, 2000) (SPEM, 2008). A user model is an instance of the UML metamodel. M1 contains both model elements and snapshots of instances of these model elements.

The bottom most layer is the instance layer M0 that contains run-time instances of the concepts defined in M1 layer.

The information layer includes the data that we wish to describe; the data in the information layer are described in the model layer; the metamodel layer is comprised of the descriptions that define the structure and semantics of metadata and, the meta-metamodel layer is comprised of the description of the structure and semantics of meta-metadata.

MOF 2.0 Query, View, Transformation

The MOF 2.0 Query, View, Transformation (QVT) specification is the OMG standard for model transformations (QVT, 2008). This specification describes three related transformational languages: Relations, Core and Operational Matching.

The acronym QVT refers to:

- **Query:** ad-hoc "query" for selecting and filtering of model element. In general, a query selects elements of the source model of the transformation
- **View:** "views" of MOF metamodels (that are involved in the transformation)
- **Transformation:** a relation between a source metamodel S and a target metamodel T that is used to generate a target model (that conforms to T) from a source model (that conforms to S).

QVT defines a standard for transforming a source model into a target model. One of the underlying ideas in QVT is that the source and target model must conform to arbitrary MOF metamodels. Another one is that the transformation is considered itself as a model that conforms to a MOF metamodel.

The QVT specification includes three main packages: QVTCore, QVTRelation and QVTOperations. These packages depends on another intermediate QVT packages (QVTBase, QVTTemplate and ImperativeOCL), EMOF and EssentialOCL. Figure 11 shows dependencies of packages in the QVT specification (QVT, 2008, pp. 12). EMOF is a subset of MOF that allows simple metamodels to be defined using simple concepts while supporting extensions for more sophisticated metamodeling using CMOF (see Figure 9). Essential-OCL (OCL, 2006, pp. 171) is a package exposing the minimal OCL required to work with EMOF (MOF, 2006, pp. 31).

A transformation defines how one set of models can be transformed into another. It is composed by a set of rules that specify its execution behavior. Also, it includes a set of typed model parameters associated with the transformation. Syntactically, a transformation is a subclass of both a Package and a Class. A transformation can extend another transformation. A rule domain is the set of model elements

Figure 11. Packages and dependencies in QVT

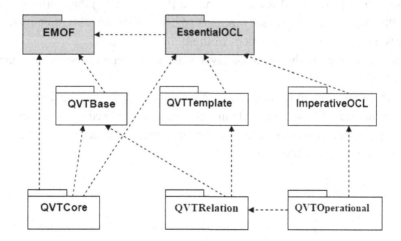

of a typed model that are of interest to it. A domain may be marked as checkable or enforceable. "A checkable domain declares that the owning rule is only required to check whether the model elements specified by the domain exist in the target model and report errors when they do not. An enforceable domain declares the owning rule must ensure that the model elements specified by the domain exist in the target model" (QVT, 2008, pp. 27).

The QVT specification has a hybrid declarative/imperative nature. Figure 11 shows the relationships between the QVT metamodel.

The declarative part of this specification is structured in two layers:

- A user-friendly Relations metamodel and language which supports the creation of object template, complex object pattern matching and the creation of traces between model elements involved in a transformation.
- A Core metamodel and language defined using minimal extensions to EMOF and OCL. All trace classes are explicitly defined as MOF models, and trace instance creation and deletion in the same way as the creation and deletion of any other object.

Relations metamodel includes a declarative specification of the relationships between MOF models. The Relations language supports complex object pattern matching, and implicitly creates trace classes and their instances to record what occurred during a transformation execution. Relations can assert that other relations also hold between particular model elements matched by their patterns.

Core is a small model/language which only supports pattern matching over a flat set of variables by evaluating conditions over those variables against a set of models. It treats all of the model elements of source, target and trace models symmetrically. It is equally powerful to the Relations language, and because of its relative simplicity, its semantics can be defined more simply, although transformation descriptions described using the Core and therefore more verbose. In addition, the trace models must be explicitly defined, and are not deduced from the transformation description, as is the case with Relations.

The core model may be implemented directly, or simply used as a reference for the semantics of Relations, which are mapped to the Core, using the transformation language itself.

The Relational language has a textual and graphical concrete syntax. Figure 12 shows the relationships between the QVT metamodel. A transformation between source models is specified as a set of relations that must be hold for the transformation to be successful. Source models are named, and the types of elements they can contain are restricted to those within a set of referenced packages. A transformation can be invoked either to check two models for consistency or to modify one model to enforce consistency.

In addition to the declarative Relations and Core languages which embody the same semantics at two different levels of abstraction, there are two mechanisms for invoking imperative implementations of transformations: one standard language, Operational mappings, as well as non-standard Black-box MOF Operation implementations.

The first is an imperative language whose syntax provides constructs commonly found in imperative languages. The latter allows invoking transformation facilities expressed in other languages. It is a crucial mechanism for integrating non-QVT libraries with QVT transformations.

At this time QVT standard only addresses model to model transformations. In this context a model means some entity conforming to any MOF 2.0 metamodel.

Figure 12. QVT metamodel

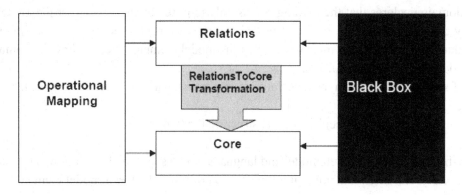

The XML Metadata Interchange (XMI)

The XML Metadata Interchange (XMI) is an OMG standard for defining, interchanging, manipulating and integrating XML data and objects. A detailed description may be found at (XMI, 2007). XML is an open standard of the World Wide Web Consortium (W3C) designed as a data format for document interchange on the web. It is intended to give developers working with MDA and object technology the ability to exchange programming data over the Internet in a standardized way.

XMI defines mappings of meta-metamodels, metamodels and models onto XML documents and XML schemes. It can be viewed as a "stream" format that can either be stored in a file system or streamed across the Internet from a repository.

XMI combines XML, MOF and UML for integrating tools, repositories, applications and data warehouses in distributed heterogeneous environments.

XMI can be used as an interchange format for both UML models and serialization of MOF metamodels.

XMI is an international standard ISO/IEC 19503:2005 (XMI) that provides a set of rules by which a schema can be generated for any valid XMI-transmissible MOF-based metamodel, a mapping from MOF to XML and design principles for XMI-based schemas and XML documents.

PROFILES VS. METAMODELS

A profile in the UML provides a generic extension mechanism for customizing models. Profiles are defined using mechanisms that allow metaclasses from existing metamodels to be extend to adapt them for particular domains (e.g., aerospace, healthcare, financial, telecommunications), platforms (e.g., J2EE, .NET) or methods (e.g. Unified Process, Agile methods). A Profile is an extension mechanism that preserves the semantics of UML being consistent with MOF.

A profile definition extends a language at the metamodel level in such a way that the specialized semantics does not contradict the semantics of the reference metamodel. It is defined as a UML Package using stereotypes, tag, and constraints. The UML 2.2 infrastructure and superstructure specifications defining stereotypes are specific metaclasses, tagged values are standard meta-attributes, and profiles are specific kinds of packages. A stereotype can be viewed as a metatype, because it allows creating new elements of UML metamodel. A tag definition can be attached to model elements. They can be viewed as metadata definitions, because they extend the properties of a UML element, creating new information in the element metaclass. The actual values of the properties of particular elements are called tagged values. A constraint extends the semantics of a UML element, adding new constraints or modifying existing ones.

More detail of the extension mechanisms may be found at (Booch, Rumbaugh & Jacobson, 2005) and (UML, 2009b).

(EJB, 2004) describes the Enterprise JavaBeans metamodel and the Java metamodel and shows how each metamodel element can be mapped to profile representations. Many profiles have been adopted by OMG, such as the UML Profile for CORBA (CORBA, 2002) and EJB. Other profiles have been accepted by the software community such as the UML profile for Web applications (Conallen, 2002).

MOF supports first-class extensibility that allows adding and removing metaclasses and relationships. The mechanisms for first-class extensibility and profiles start fusing when methodology restrictions that prevent to modify existing metamodel are applied.

There are multiple factors that determine when we should create a new metamodel and when we instead should create a profile. Tools that implement MOF 2.0 will allow users to define entirely new languages via metamodel or profiles. For instance Domain Specific Language (DSL) may be defined by using a standard MOF foundation (Mernik, Heering & Sloane, 2005).

A domain-specific language (DSL) allows us to solve problems in a particular domain and is not intended to be able to solve problems outside it. DSLs can be based on the profiles mechanisms or new metamodel. In both cases, MOF foundation brings the benefits of metamodeling tool standards. As examples of these situations, we can mention OMG standards System Modeling Language (SysML) (SysML, 2008) and the Semantics of Business Vocabulary and Business Rules (SBVR) (SBVR, 2008).

On the one hand, SysML is a DSL for systems engineering. It supports the specification, analysis, design, verification and validation of complex systems that include hardware, software, information and processes. SysML is defined as an extension of a subset of UML diagrams by using the UML profile mechanism.

On the other hand, SBVR is an adopted standard of OMG for representing business rules. It has its own notation to formalize complex compliance rules, such as operational rules for an enterprise, security policy, standard compliance, or regulatory compliance rules. It was defined as a MOF metamodel.

REFERENCES

ADM (2007). *ADM Task Force. Architecture Driven Modernization Roadmap.* Retrieved on July 20, 2009 from adm.omg.org

Arlow, J., & Neustad, I. (2003). *Enterprise Patterns and MDA: Building Better Software with Archetype Patterns and UML.* Reading: Addison-Wesley.

Beydeda, S., Book, M., & Gruhn, V. (2005). *Model Driven Software Development.* Heildelberg: Springer-Verlag.

Booch, G., Rumbaugh, J., & Jacobson, I. (2005). *The Unified Modeling Language. User Guide* (2nd ed.). Reading: Addison-Wesley.

Conallen, J. (2002). *Building Web Applications with UML* (2nd ed). Reading: Addison-Wesley.

CORBA. (1992). *Common Object Request Broker Architecture (CORBA) V. 1.1*. Retrieved on July 20, 2009 from www.corba.org

CORBA. (2002). *UML Profile for Corba, version 1.0*. Document: formal/02-04-01. Retrieved on July 20, 2009 from www.omg.org

CWM. (2003).*Common Warehouse Metamodel, v. 1.1 formal/2003-03-02*. Retrieved on July 20, 2009 from www.omg.org/spec/cwm

EJB. (2004). *Metamodel and UML Profile for Java and EJB Specification*. Document: formal/04-02-02. Retrieved on July 20, 2009 from www.omg.org

France, R., & Rumpe, B. (2007). Model-driven Development of Complex software: A Research Roadmap. In *Proceedings of the Future of Software Engineering (FOSE 2007)* (pp. 37-54). Los Alamitos: IEEE Computer Society.

Guttman, M., & Parodi, J. (2006). *Real-Life MDA: Solving Business Problems with Model-Driven Architecture*. Morgan Kaufmann OMG Press.

Hailpern, B., & Tarr, P. (2006). Model-driven development: The good, the bad, and the ugly. *IBM Systems Journal, 45*(3), 451–461.

Hruby, P. (2006). *Model Driven Design using Business Patterns*. Heidelberg: Springer.

Jacobson, I., Booch, G., & Rumbaugh, J. (1999). *The Unified Software Development Process*. Reading: Addison-Wesley.

Kleppe, A., Warmer, J., & Bast, W. (2003). *MDA Explained: The Model Driven Architecture: Practice and Promise*. Reading: Addison-Wesley.

Kruchten, P. (2000). *The Rational Unified Process: An Introduction* (2nd Ed.). Reading: Addison Wesley Professional.

Kulkarni, V., & Reddy, S. (2005). Model Driven Development of Enterprise Applications (LNCS 3297, pp. 118-128). Heidelberg: Springer-Verlag.

MDA. (2003). MDA Guide Version 1.0.1. In J. Miller & J. Mukerji (Eds.). Document omg/2003-06-01. Retrieved on July 20, 2009 from www.omg.org/mda

MDA. (2005). *The Model Driven Architecture*. Retrieved on July 20, 2009 from www.omg.org/mda.

Mellor, S., Scott, K., Uhl, A., & Weise, D. (2003). *MDA Distilled: Principles of Model Driven Architecture*. Addison-Wesley.

Mernik, M., Heering, J., & Sloane, A. (2005). When and how to develop domain-specific languages. *ACM Computing Surveys, 37*(4), 316–344. doi:10.1145/1118890.1118892

MOF. (2002). *Meta Object Facility (MOF) Specification version 1.4*. Document formal/01-11-02. Retrieved on July 20, 2009 from www.omg.org

MOF. (2006). *MOF: Meta Object facility (MOF ™) 2.0*. OMG Specification formal/2006-01-01. Retrieved on July 20, 2009 from www.omg.org/mof

OCL. (2006). *OCL: Object Constraint Language. Version 2.0*. OMG: formal/06-05-01.Retrieved on July 20, 2009 from www.omg.org

Pastor, O., & Molina, J. (2007). *Model-Driven Architecture in Practice: A Software production Environment Based on Conceptual Modeling*. Heidelberg: Springer-Verlag.

QVT. (2008). *QVT: MOF 2.0 Query, View, Transformation*. Formal/2008-04-03. Retrieved on July 20, 2009 from www.omg.org

Raistrick, C., Francis, P., & Wright, J. (2004). *Model Driven Architecture with Executable UML*. Cambridge University Press.

Rumbaugh, J., Jacobson, I., & Booch, G. (1998). *The Unified Modeling Language Reference Manual*. Reading: Addison-Wesley.

SBVR. (2008). *Semantics of Business Vocabulary and Business Rules (SBVR), v1.0*. Document: formal/2008-01-02. Retrieved on July 20, 2009 from http://www.omg.org/spec/SBVR/1.0/PDF

Selic, B. (2006). UML 2: A model-driven development tool. *IBM Systems Journal*, *45*(3), 607–620.

SPEM. (2008). *Software & Systems Process Engineering Meta-Model Specification (SPEM) version 2.0*. Document: formal/2008-04-01. Retrieved on July 20, 2009 from http://www.omg.org/spec/SPEM/2.0/PDF

SysML (2008) *OMG System Modeling Language*. version 1.1.Document: formal/2008-11-01. Retrieved on July 20, 2009 from http://www.omg.org/spec/SysML/1.1/.

Sztipanovits, J., & Karsai, G. (1997). Model Integrated Computing. *IEEE Computer*, *30*(4), 110–112.

UML. (2009a). *Unified Modeling Language: Infrastructure*. Version 2.2. OMG Specification formal/2009-02-04. Retrieved on July 20, 2009 from www.omg.org.

UML. (2009b). *UML: Unified Modeling Language: Superstructure*. Version 2.2. OMG Specification: formal/2009-02-02. Retrieved on July 20, 2009 from www.omg.org

XMI. (2007). *MOF 2.0 / XMI Mapping, Version 2.1.1*. Document: formal/2007-12-01. Retrieved on July 20, 2009 from http://www.omg.org/spec/XMI/2.1/PDF

Chapter 3
MDA, Metamodeling and Transformation

INTRODUCTION

MDA requires the ability to understand different languages such as general purpose languages, domain specific languages, modeling languages or programming languages. An underlying principle of MDA for integrating semantically in a unified and interoperable way such languages is using metamodeling techniques.

A metamodel describes a family of models whose elements are instances of the metaclasses of the respective metamodel. The kind of entities and relations defines the kind of metamodel, for instance:

- An ISM-Java metamodel includes entities (metaclasses) for classes, fields, operations, methods, constructors, parameters and interfaces. Methods and constructors are subtypes of operations. Interfaces are associated with classes.
- A PSM-Java metamodel distinguishes entities such as Java-metamodel entities and another entities such as associations.
- A RDBMS metamodel includes entities for schema, table, column, key and foreign key.

The OMG standard for defining models is the Meta-Object-Facility (MOF) metamodel (MOF, 2006). MOF is essential to define different modeling languages and metamodeling languages such as UML or MOF itself. It allows capturing all the diversity of modeling standards and interchange constructs that are used in MDA. A MOF-aware modeling tool can capture UML diagram elements in machine readable form allowing tools from multiple vendors to be used together on a single project.

DOI: 10.4018/978-1-61520-649-0.ch003

The initial diffusion of MDA was focused on its relation with UML as modeling language. However, there are UML users who do not use MDA, and MDA users who use other modeling languages such as Domain Specific Languages (DSL).

The essence of MDA is MOF that allows different kinds of software artifacts to be used together in a single project. It allows capturing all the diversity of modeling standards and interchange constructs that are used in MDA. MOF provides a metadata management framework, and a set of metadata services to enable the development and interoperability of models and metadata driven systems.

MOF CONSTRUCTS

The MOF modeling concepts are "classes, which model MOF meta-objects; associations, which model binary relations between meta-objects; Data Types, which model other data; and Packages, which modularize the models" (MOF, 2006, pp. 2-6). OCL can be used to attach consistency rules to metamodel components.

Next, we describe these constructs in detail.

Classes

Classes are type descriptions of "first class instance" MOF meta-objects. Instances of classes have object identity, state, and behavior. Classes can have three kinds of features which are attribute, operation and reference. They can also contain exceptions, constants, data types, constraints and other elements.

An attribute has properties such as type, name and multiplicity. Besides, it can contain flags such as "isChangeable" and "isDerived". The first determines whether the client is provided with an explicit operation to set the attribute values and the latter, determines whether the contents of the notational value holder is derived from other state.

Operations are "hooks" for describing the class behavior. They simply specify the name, the type signatures by which the behavior is invoked. Operations have the following properties: name, a sequence of parameters including name, type and multiplicity, an optional return type and, a list of Exceptions that can be raised by an invocation. An attribute may be an optional-valued, single-valued, or multi-valued depending on its multiplicity specification. The multiplicity can also include the flags "is-Ordered" for indicating ordered attributes and "is-unique" for indicating whether instances with equal value are allowed in the given attribute or parameter.

Like UML, MOF provides class generalization. However, MOF imposes restrictions on generalization to ensure that it can be transformed into a range of implementation technologies:

- A class cannot generalize itself, either directly or indirectly
- A class cannot generalize another class if the subclass contains a model element with the same name as a model element contained or inherited by the superclass (i.e. no over-riding is allowed)
- When a class has multiple superclasses, no model elements contained or inherited by superclasses can have the same name.

MOF uses "abstract class" in the same sense as UML and other object-oriented programming languages.

A class may be defined as "leaf" or "root". Declaring a class as a leaf prevents the existence of sub-classes. Declaring a class as a root prevents the declaration of any superclasses.

Binary Associations

Like UML, MOF provides associations, although there are no association classes and only binary associations are allowed. Each MOF association contains precisely two association-ends that include properties such as name, type, multiplicity, navigability, changeability and, aggregation specification.

MOF supports two kinds of aggregation for relationships between instances: "composite" and "non-aggregate". The semantic of shared-aggregation is not supported in MOF.

A non-aggregate relationship has the following properties:

- There are no special restrictions on the multiplicity.
- There are no special restrictions on the origin of the instances in the relationship.
- The association does not impact on the lifecycle of related instances.

On the contrary, a composite aggregation is a stronger link between instances with the following properties (MOF, 2006):

- A composite relationship is asymmetrical, with one end denoting the role of whole in the relationship ("composite") and the other one denoting the parts ("components")
- An instance cannot be a component of more than one composite at a time, under any composite relationship.
- The relationships impacts on the lifecycle of the whole and its parts. When a composite instance is deleted, all of its components under any composite relationship (directly or transitively) are also deleted.
- The Composition Closure rule: The composite and component instances in a composition along with any links that form the composition must all belong to the same outermost Package extent.

The effective semantics for an attribute depends on the type of attribute. A "non-aggregate" semantics correspond to an attribute whose type is expressed as a data Type. On the other hand, an attribute whose type is expressed as a Class has a composite semantics.

Data Types

Metamodels often requires using attribute and operation parameter values that have types whose values do not have object identity. Considering this, MOF provides the metamodeling concept of Data Type. Data Types can represent two kinds of data type:

- Primitive data types such as Boolean, Integer, and String.
- DataType constructors that allow meta-designers to define more complex data types.

They are enumeration types, structure types, collection types, and alias types.

Packages

The package is the MOF mechanism for grouping elements into a metamodel. A package can contain different model elements such as packages, classes, associations and data types. It provides four structuring mechanisms: generalization, nesting, importing and clustering.

Generalization is similar to class generalization in MOF. However, packages may be defined as "root" or "leaf" packages, but "abstract" packages are not supported.

A nested package is a component of its enclosing package. There are some restrictions on nesting relationships, nested packages do not admit generalization, importing or clustering relations with other packages. Conceptually, a nested package instance is a component of an instance of the containing package and, they can not be directly instantiated.

When one package imports another, the importing package is allowed to make use of elements defined in the imported one package. Package clustering can be viewed as a stronger form of package import that links imported packages into a "cluster".

EXAMPLES

In order to illustrate the use of MOF language, this section includes MOF-based metamodels for three popular object oriented languages JAVA, C++ and Eiffel. Although, these examples only specify a part of MOF metamodel, we introduce now the notation used in the following chapters of this book for describing metamodels.

Metamodel Notation

Metamodels are specified by using the UML notation including an abstract syntax and metaclass descriptions.

The abstract syntax consists of one or more UML class diagrams that show the package including metaclasses, their constructs and interrelationships. A number of metaclasses from the UML Infrastructure are imported. These metaclasses are shown in the models with a transparent fill color.

The description of a metaclass starts with an informal definition of the metaclass that sets the context for the definition. This description is followed by a description of generalizations, attributes and associations. Each of them is enumerated together with a short explanation. The multiplicity of attributes and associations is enclosed in square brackets.

The description includes well-formedness rules expressed in OCL. These rules are defined as a (possibly empty) set of invariants for the metaclass, which must be satisfied by all instances of that metaclass for the model to be meaningful The OCL expressions thus specify constraints over attributes and associations defined in the metamodel. The statement 'No additional constraints' means that all well-formedness rules are expressed in the superclasses together with the multiplicity and type information expressed in the diagrams. Constraints are specified in EssentialOCL (OCL, 2006).

In many cases, additional operations on the classes are needed for the OCL expressions. These are then defined in a separate subsection after the constraint section using comments followed by the OCL expression defining the operation.

Metamodels are specified in the style proposed in the OMG documentation for the different standards. The structure of the text describing a metaclass is as follows:

```
<className>
Description
< text>
Generalizations
< generalizationList>
Attributes
< attributeList>
Associations
<associationList>
Constraints
<constraintList>
Additional Operations
<additionalOperationList>
```

Appendix C includes an overview of OCL, in particular EssentialOCL (OCL, 2006, pp. 171-176). A detailed description may be found at (OCL, 2006)

Example 3-1: Eiffel Metamodel

The Package Eiffel-Class specifies the basic entities for specifying classes such as metaclasses for classes, attributes, features, routines, parameters and assertions (Meyer, 1997). Figure 1 shows the static diagram of the package. Next follows a specification of the metaclass EiffelClass (Meyer, 1992). The complete specification of the Eiffel metamodel may be found at Appendix-A.

EiffelClass Specification

Description

An Eiffel class describes a set of objects sharing the same feature specifications, restrictions and semantics.

Generalizations

• Class (from Kernel), Classifier (from Templates)

Attributes

• isDeferred: Boolean [1] It specifies whether a class is deferred, i.e., it includes one or more features that are specified but no implemented. It redefines *Classifier::isAbstract*.
• isExpanded: Boolean [1] It specifies whether the class is flattened, i.e. its instances are objects but no references to objects.
• isObsolete: Boolean [1] It specifies whether the class is obsolete.

Figure 1. ISM Eiffel metamodel. Diagram of classes

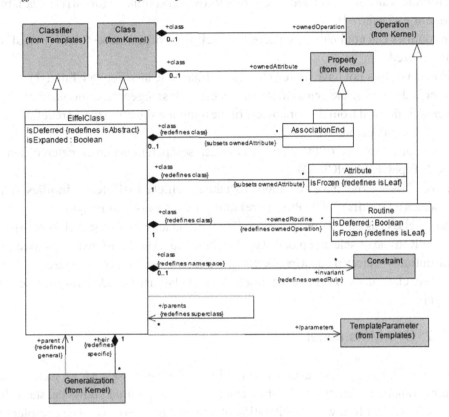

Associations

- attribute: Attribute [*] It refers to the own attributes of the Eiffel class. It redefines Class::ownedAttribute.
- eiffelFeatures: EiffelFeature [*] It refers to the features of which this class is client.
- generalization: Generalization [*] It specifies the generalization for this class.
- invariant: Assertion [*] It refers to invariants of the class. It redefines NameSpace::ownedRule.
- ownedRoutine: Routine [*] It refers to the own routines of the class. It redefines Class::ownedOperation.
- /parameters: EiffelParameter [*] It refers to the set of parameters of the class. It is derived.
- /parent: EiffelClass [*] It refers to the parent class of an Eiffel class. It redefines *Class::superClass*. It is derived.

Constraints

[1]   A class having a deferred routine must be declared deferred. self.ownedRoutine -> exists (r | r.isDeferred) **implies** self. isDeferred

[2] Secret routines can not be declared deferred. self.ownedRoutine -> forAll (r | r.availability = #secret **implies not** r.isDeferred)

[3] Frozen routines can not be declared deferred. self.ownedRoutine -> forAll (r | r.isFrozen **implies not** r.isDeferred)

[4] An Eiffel class does not have nested classes. self.nestedClassifier -> isEmpty()

[5] *ancestors* is derived of the generalization. ancestors = self.generalization.parent

[6] *parameters* is derived from the parameters of the template signature that is redefinable. parameters = ownedSignature.parameter

[7] Parameters of a class are of the type Eiffel class. self.parameters.parameteredElement -> forAll (p | p.oclIsTypeOf (EiffelClass))

[8] A deferred class does not have a creation procedure. self.class.isDeferred **implies** self.ownedRoutine -> select(p | p.oclIsTypOf (Procedure) **and** p.isCreator) -> isEmpty()

[9] A flattened class has only a creation procedure without arguments. self.class.isExpanded **implies** self.ownedRoutine -> select(p| p.oclIsTypeOf (Procedure) **and** p.isCreator) -> size() = 1 **and** self.ownedRoutine -> select(p | p.isCreator and p.argument -> isEmpty()) -> size() = 1

[10] A flattened class does not have parameters. self.class.isExpanded **implies** self.parameter -> isEmpty()

Example 3-2: C++ Metamodel

The Package C++-Class specifies the basic entities for specifying classes in C++ such as metaclasses for classes, member functions, functions, variables and parameters. Figure 2 shows the static diagram of the Package C++-Class. Next follows a specification of a metaclass C++Class. The complete specification of the C++ metamodel may be found at Appendix-A.

C++ Class Specification

Description
A C++ class describes a set of objects that share the same specifications of features, restrictions and semantics.

Generalizations

• Class (from Kernel), Classifier (from Templates)

Attributes

• class-key: Class-Key [1] It specifies the type of the class, i.e., if it is a class, structure or union.
• isFinal: Boolean [1] It specifies whether the class has subclasses. It redefines *RedefinableElement::isLeaf.*
• /isGeneric: Boolean It specifies whether the class is generic. It is a derived attribute.

Figure 2. ISM C++ metamodel. Diagram of classes

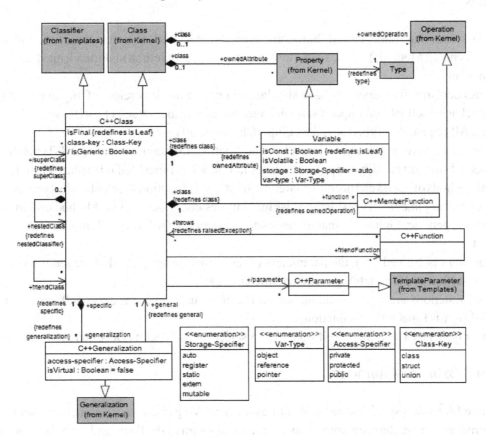

Associations

- variable: Variable [*] It refers to the own variables of the C++ class. It redefines *Class::ownedAttribute*.

- nestedClass: C++Class [*] It refers to the C++ classes that are declared within the body of a C++ class (nested classes). It is a subset of *Class::nestedClassifier*.

- /superClass: C++Class [*] It refers to the superclasses of a C++ class. It redefines *Class::superClass*. It is derived.

- function: C++MemberFunction [*] It refers to the own functions of the class. It redefines *Class::ownedOperation*.

- generalization: C++Generalization [*] It refers to the generalizations of the class. It redefines *Class::Generalization*.

- friendClass: C++Class [*] It refers to the friend classes of the class.

- friendFunction: C++Function [*] It refers to the friend functions of the class.

- /parameters: C++Parameter [*] It refers to the set of parameters of the class. It is derived.

Constraints

[1]   A class that has pure virtual functions must be declared abstract. self.function -> select (oclIsTypeOf(Method)) -> exists (m | m.oclAsType (Method).isPureVirtual) implies self. isAbstract

[2]   A class declared final does not have subclasses, i.e, it is not superclass of any class belonging to the package. self.isFinal implies self.package.ownedMember -> select (oclIsTypeOf(C++Class)) -> forAll (c | c.oclAsType(C++Class).superClass <> self)

[3]   Private functions of a class can not be declared abstract. self.function -> select (oclIsTypeOf(Method)) -> forAll (m | m.visibility = #private implies not m.oclAsType(Method).isPureVirtual)

[4]   Final methods of a class can not be declared abstracts. self.function -> select (oclIsTypeOf(Method)) -> forAll (m | m.oclAsType(Method).isFinal implies not m.oclAsType(Method).isVirtual)

[5]   A class is generic if it has a signature template. isGeneric = (self.ownedTemplateSignature -> size () =1)

[6]   *parameters* is derived from the parameters of the signature template that are redefinable. /parameters= self.ownedTemplateSignature.parameter

[7]   Friend functions are C++ functions but no member functions of a class. self.friendFunction -> forAll (f | f.isTypeOf (C++Function))

[8]   A class only has a destructor. self.function -> select (oclIsTypeOf (Destructor)) -> size () <= 1

Example 3-3: Java Metamodel

The Package Java-Class specifies the basic entities for specifying classes such as metaclasses for classes, fields, operations, parameters. Figure 3 shows the static diagram of the Package Java-Class. Next follows the specification of the metaclass JavaClass.

JavaClass Specification

Description
A Java class as is defined in the Java language.

Generalizations

•   Class (from Kernel), Classifier (from Templates), BehavioredClassifier (from Interfaces)

Attributes

•   isFinal: Boolean It specifies whether the class can have subclasses. It redefines *RedefinableElement::isLeaf.*
•   /isGeneric: Boolean It specifies whether the class is generic. It is a derived attribute.
•   isStatic: Boolean It specifies whether the class is static.

Figure 3. ISM Java metamodel. Diagram of classes

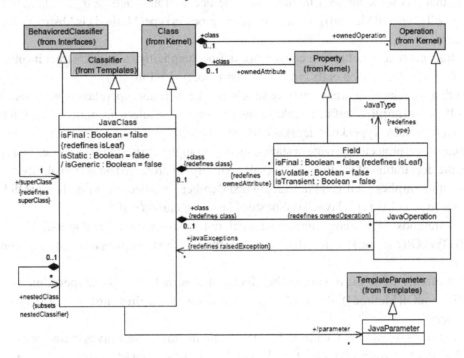

Associations

- field: Field [*] It refers to the own variables of the Java class. It redefines *Class::ownedAttribute*.
- /implement: It refers to the Java interfaces that are implemented by this class. It is derived.
- javaOperation: JavaOperation [*] It refers the own operations of the class. It redefines *Class::ownedOperation*.
- javaPackage: JavaPackage [0..1] It refers to the package in which is declared. It redefines *Type::package*.
- nestedClass: JavaClass [*] It refers to the Java classes that are declared within the body of a Java class (nested classes). It is a subset of *Class::nestedClassifier*.
- nestedInterface: JavaInterface [*] It refers to the Java interfaces that are declared within the body of a JavaClass (nested interfaces). It is a subset of *Class::nestedClassifier*.
- /parameters: JavaParameters [*] It refers to the set of parameters of a class. It is derived.
- /superClass: JavaClass [1] It refers to a superclass of a Java class. It redefines *Class::superClass*. It is derived.

Constraints

[1] Nested classifiers belonging to a class or interface can only be of type JavaClass or JavaInterface. self. nestedClassifier -> forAll (c | c.oclIsTypeOf (JavaClass) **or** c.oclIsTypeOf (JavaInterface))

[2] The implemented interfaces are those referred through the interface realization. implement = self. interfaceRealization.contract

[3] A class that has some abstract method must be declared abstract. self.javaOperation -> select (op| op.oclIsTypeOf(Method)) -> exists (m | m.oclAsType(Method).isAbstract) **implies** self. isAbstract

[4] An abstract class does not have a constructor defined explicitly. self.isAbstract **implies** self.java-Operation -> select(op| op.oclIsTypeOf (Constructor)) -> isEmpty()

[5] A class that is declared final can not have subclasses, i.e., it is not superclass of any class in the package. self.isFinal **implies** self.javaPackage.ownedMember -> select(m| m.oclIsTypeOf(JavaClass)) -> forAll (c| c.oclAsType(JavaClass).superClass <> self)

[6] The access level protected, private or static can only be applied to nested classes, i.e., that are declared within the declaration of another class. (self.visibility = #protected **or** self.visibility = #private **or** self.isStatic) **implies** self.javaPackage.ownedMember -> select(m| m.oclIsTypeOf(JavaClass)) -> exists (c | c.oclAsType(JavaClass).nestedClass -> includes(self))

[7] Private methods of a class cannot be declared abstract. self.javaOperation -> select(op| op.oclIsTypeOf(Method)) -> forAll (m | m.visibility = #private **implies not** m.oclAsType(Method). isAbstract)

[8] Static methods of a class cannot be declared abstract. self.javaOperation -> select(op| op.oclIsTypeOf(Method)) -> forAll (m | m.isStatic **implies not** m.oclAsType(Method). isAbstract)

[9] Final methods of a class cannot be declared abstract. self.javaOperation -> select(op| op.oclIsTypeOf(Method)) -> forAll (m | m.oclAsType(Method).isFinal **implies not** m.oclAsType(Method).isAbstract)

[10] A class is generic if it has a signature template. isGeneric = (self.ownedTemplateSignature -> size () =1)

[11] *Parameters* is derived from the parameters of the signature template. /parameters= self.ownedTemplateSignature.parameter

[12] A class is concrete, if its methods have associated an implementation. **not** self.isAbstract **implies** self.allMethod () -> forAll (m | self.allBody() -> exist (b| b.signature = m))

[13] Elements, that can be actual parameters of a formal parameter, are of type Java. self.parameters. parameteredElement -> forAll (p| p.oclIsTypeOf (JavaType))

Additional Operations

[1] allMethod is the set of all methods, i.e., the methods that are own, inherited and, the methods of the interfaces implemented. allMethod (): Set(Method) allMethod () = self.allClassMethod() -> union(self.implement.allInterfaceMethod ()) allClassMethod (): Set (Method) allClassMethod () = self.javaOperation -> select(o |o.oclIsType(Method)) -> union(self.superClass.allClassMethod()) allInterfaceMethod (): Set(Method) allInterfaceMethod () = self.method -> union(self. superInterface.allInterfaceMethod ())

[2] *allBody* is the set of all method implementations of a class, i.e., both own and inherited. allBody(): Set (Implementation) allBody = self.allMethod ().body

COMMON CONCEPTS ON TRANSFORMATIONS

In the following chapters we will refer to different kind of transformations: refinements, refactoring and anti-refinements. This section shows common concepts and notation for all of them.

We propose to define transformations as OCL contracts between MOF-based metamodels. OCL contracts are based on the EssentialOCL (OCL, 2006, pp. 171-176) that is an adaptation of OCL for defining simple MOF metamodels. Our approach is aligned with QVT or, more precisely, with the CORE of QVT (QVT, 2008) due to we express transformations as basic contract in EssentialOCL without using the Relational language.

EssentialOCL is the package exposing the minimal OCL required to work with EMOF (MOF, 2006). Particularly, it depends on the EMOF Package referring explicitly the following EMOF classes: Property, Operation, Parameter, TypedElement, Type, Class, DataType, Enumeration, PrimitiveType, and EnumerationLiteral. The following metaclasses defined in complete OCL are not part of BasicOCL (and EssentialOCL): MessageType, ElementType, AssociationClassCallExp, MessageExp, StateExp, UnspecifiedValueExp. Moreover, any well-formedness rules defined for these classes are consequently not part of the definition of the EssentialOCL. Figure4 shows a metamodel for transformations

Transformation AtoB could be a refinement, an anti-refinement or a refactoring. A transformation is associated to a source metamodel and a target metamodel and is composed by preconditions and postconditions.

The classes Metamodel_A and Metamodel_B describe families of MOF metamodels. The class Transformation_AtoB describes families of transformations between Metamodel_A and Metamodel_B.

There is an association between the class Metamodel_A and the class Transformation_AtoB specifying that for every instance of Metamodel_A are zero or more instances of Transformation_AtoB. Besides, there is an association between the class Metamodel_B and the class Transformation_AtoB specifying that for every instance of Metamodel_B are zero or more instances of Transformation_AtoB.

The syntax for expressing metamodel-based transformation is the following:

```
Transformation transformationName
{parameter source: metamodelName target: metamodelName precondit
ions <preconditionList> postconditions <postconditionList> local
```

Figure 4. Formalization of metamodel transformations

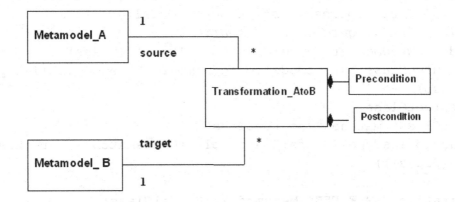

```
operations<localOperationsList>
}
```

The parameters are a source and a target metamodel that are instances of Metamodel_A and Metamodel_B. The section *local operations* includes a set of operations that are used many times in this transformation. Preconditions state relations between the metaclasses of the source metamodel. Postconditions deal with the state of models after transformation.

Below, we show a part a transformation of a PIM to a PSM based in the Eiffel platform. It refers to concrete instances of metamodels and transformations and links between them. Links connect an instance of a transformation with an instance of a metamodel.

Postconditions specify how classes and interfaces of the source model are related with classes in the target model, guaranteeing, for instance, that for each class in the source exists a class in the target so that: the source class and the target class have the same name, visibility, abstraction degree, restrictions and parameters (if any), attributes and operations both in, the source and target, must match and so on

```
Transformation PIM-UML to PSM-EIFFEL {parameters
sourceModel: PIM-Metamodel:: Package
targetModel: PSM-EIFFEL-Metamodel:: Package
preconditions--postconditions-- sourceModel and targetModel have the
same number of classifiers.
targetModel.ownedMember -> select(oclIsTypeOf (EiffelClass)) ->
size() =
sourceModel.ownedMember -> select(oclIsTypeOf(Class) -> size () +
sourceModel.ownedMember -> select(oclIsTypeOf(Interface)) -> size ()
-- for each 'sourceInterface' in sourceModel exists a 'targetClass'
in targetModel so that:
sourceModel.ownedMember -> select(oclIsTypeOf(Interface))->
forAll (sourceInterface| targetModelownedMember -> select (oclIsTy-
peOf (EiffelClass)) ->
exists (targetClass|
-- 'targetClass' matches 'sourceInterface'.
targetClass.oclAsType (EiffelClass).
classInterfaceMatch (sourceInterface.oclAsType (interface))))
-- for each class 'sourceClass' in sourceModel exists a
'targetClass'in 'targetModel' so that:
sourceModel.ownedMember -> select (oclIsTypeOf (Class)) ->
forAll (sourceClass targetModel.ownedMember -> select(oclIsTypeOf
(EiffelClass)) ->
exists (targetClass |
-- 'targetClass' matches 'sourceClass'.
targetClass.oclAsType (EiffelClass).classClassMatch (sourceClass.
oclAsType(Class))))

local operationsPSM-EIFFEL-Metamodel::EiffelClass::
```

```
classClassMatch(aClass: PIM-Metamodel::Class): Boolean
classClassMatch (aClass) =
--The class to which operation is applied (self) matches the param-
eter ´aClass´ if both have
-- the same name
self.name = aClass.name and
-- the same abstraction degree
self.isDeferred = aClass.isAbstract and
-- the same visibility,
self.visibility = aClass.visibility and
-- the same restrictions
self.invariant = aClass.ownedRule and
-- the same parameters
self.parameters = aClass.ownedTemplateSignature.parameter
and...
```

REFERENCES

Meyer, B. (1992). *Eiffel: The Language*. Prentice Hall.

Meyer, B. (1997). *Object-Oriented software Construction*. Prentice Hall.

MOF. (2006). *MOF: Meta Object facility (MOF ™) 2.0*. OMG Specification formal/2006-01-01. Retrieved on July 20, 2009 from www.omg.org/mof

OCL. (2006). *OCL: Object Constraint Language. Version 2.0*. OMG: formal/06-05-01.Retrieved on July 20, 2009 from www.omg.org

QVT. (2008). *QVT: MOF 2.0 Query, View, Transformation*. Formal/2008-04-03. Retrieved on July 20, 2009 from www.omg.org

Section 2
Formalization of MOF–Based Processes

Chapter 4
Formalization of MOF–Based Metamodels

INTRODUCTION

Formal and semiformal techniques can play complementary roles in MDA-based software development processes. We consider it beneficial for both semiformal and formal specification techniques. On the one hand, semiformal techniques lack a precise semantics; however, they have the ability to visualize language constructions, allowing a great difference in the productivity of the specification process, especially when the graphical view is supported by means of good tools. On the other hand, formal specification allows us to produce a precise and analyzable software specification and clarifies the intended meaning of metamodels, helps to validate model transformations, and provides reference for implementations; however, they require familiarity with formal notations that most designers and implementers do not currently have and the learning curve for the application of these techniques requires considerable time.

A combination of metamodeling and formal specification techniques can help us to address MDA-based processes such as reverse engineering, forward engineering and round-trip engineering. In light of this, we propose to use the algebraic metamodeling language, called NEREUS which can be viewed as an intermediate notation. NEREUS can be integrated with different formal languages and object-oriented languages. It is particularly suited for specifying metamodels based on the concepts of entity, relation and system. Most of the MOF metamodel concepts can be mapped directly to NEREUS.

In terms of NEREUS we will explain a reusable infrastructure for more efficient development of evolution system techniques and high quality of the results. In the following sections we summarize the main specification languages linked to object-orientation approaches such as UML and MDA and, motivate the use of NEREUS as a metamodeling language.

DOI: 10.4018/978-1-61520-649-0.ch004

OBJECT-ORIENTATION, METAMODELING AND FORMAL LANGUAGES

In the early 1980s, new specification languages or extensions of formal languages to support object-oriented concepts began to develop. Among them the different extensions of the Z language, for example Z++ (Lano, 1991), OBJECT-Z (Smith, 2000) (Kim, & Carrington, 1999) or OOZE (Alencar & Goguen, 1991) can be mentioned. Another language with object-oriented characteristics is FOOPS (Rappanotti & Socorro, 1992).

Larch/Smalltalk was the first language with subtype and inheritance specification. Larch/C++ is another language with similar characteristics. JML is a behavioral interface specification language for formally specifying the behavior and interfaces of Java classes and functions (Leavens, 1996) (Leavens et al., 2002).

CASL-LTL, an extension of CASL (Bidoit & Mosses, 2004), has been provided to deal with reactivity (Reggio, Cerioli & Astesiano, 2001).

BON is an object-oriented method possessing graphical and textual languages for specifying classes, their relations and assertions, written in first-order predicate logic (Paige, Kaminskaya & Ostroff, 2002).

Various works analyzed the integration of semiformal techniques and object-oriented designs with formal techniques. (Bordeau, 1995) introduces a method to derive Larch specifications from class diagrams. France, Bruel and Larrondo-Prieti (1997) describe the formalization of FUSION models in Z.

A lot of work has been carried out dealing with the semantics for UML/OCL models. ThePreciseUML Group, pUML, was created in 1997 with the goal of giving precision to UML (France, Evans, Lano & Rumpe, 1998).

Considering that OCL has merely a denotational semantics that can be implemented by dynamic validation of snapshots, several works propose UML formalization by using traditional formal languages. These formal languages provide at least syntax, some semantics and an inference system. The syntax defines the structure of the text of a formal specification including properties that are expressed as axioms, formulas of some logic. The semantics describes the models linked to a given specification; in the formal specification context, a model is a mathematical object that defines behavior of the realizations of the specifications. The inference system allows defining deductions that can be made from a formal specification. These deductions allow new formulas to be derived and checked. So, the inference system can help to automate testing, prototyping or verification.

Bruel and France (1998) describe how to formalize UML models using Z. Gogolla and Ritcher (1997) do this by transforming UML to TROLL and Overgaard (1998) achieves it by using operational semantics. U2B (Snook & Butler, 2002) transforms UML models to B (Abrial, 1996). (Kim & Carrington, 1999) (Kim and Carrington, 2002) formalize UML by using OBJECT-Z.

Borger, Cavarra and Riccobene (2000) provide a rigorous semantics for one of the central diagram types which are used in UML for the description of dynamical system behavior, namely activity diagrams.

Reggio, Cerioli and Astesiano (2001) present a general framework of the semantics of UML, where an individual semantics is given to the different kinds of UML diagrams within a UML model, and next, such semantics are composed to get the semantics on the overall model.

Gerber et al. (2002) explores the state-of-the-art of model-to-model transformation. Strengths and weakness of different technologies such as Common Warehouse Metamodel (CWM) transformations (CWM, 2003) and graph transformations (Mens et al., 2006) are remarked.

Gogolla and Henderson-Seller (2002) analyze the UML metamodel part dealing with stereotypes, and make various suggestions for improving the definition and use of stereotypes. Barbier, Henderson-Sellers, Le Parc-Lacayrelle and Bruel (2003) introduce a formal definition for the semantics of the Whole-Part relation that had been incorporated into version 2.0 of UML. Kuske, Gogolla, Kollmann and Kreowski (2002) describe an integrated semantics for UML class, object and state diagrams based on graph transformation.

Graph transformation theory has been developed over the last three decades as a suite of techniques and tools for formal modeling and very high-level visual programming (Rozenberg, 1997). AGG is a rule-based visual programming environment supporting an algebraic approach to graph transformation that is used for modeling and software validation (Taentzer, 2004).

UML CASE tools could be enhanced with functionality for formal specification, deductive verification; however, only research tools provide support for advanced analysis. For example, the main task of USE tool (Gogolla, Bohling and Ritchers, 2005) is to validate and verify specifications consisting of UML/OCL class diagrams. Key (Ahrendt et al., 2005) is a tool based on Together enhanced with functionality for formal specification and deductive verification (CASE, 2009) (Ahrent, Baar, Beckert, Bubel, Giese, Hahnle, Menzel, Mostowski, Roth, Schlager, & Smith, 2005) (Ahrent, Baar, Beckert, Giese, Hahnle, Menzel, Mostowski, & Smith, 2005).

It is difficult to compare the existing results and to see how to integrate them in order to define a standard semantics since they specify different UML subsets and they are based on different formalisms. For instance, the books (Siau, & Halpin, 2001) and (Favre, 2003) describe different approaches.

With the emergence of MDA, the emphasis moved from UML formalization to MOF-based meta-model formalization.

MCumber and Cheng (2001) propose a general framework for formalizing UML diagrams in terms of different formal languages using a mapping from UML metamodels and formal languages.

Akehurst, Kent and Patrascoiu (2003) describe how to formalize metamodels and model transformations by using relational algebras. They propose an approach that uses metamodeling patterns capturing the essence of mathematical relations. The proposed technique is to adopt a pattern that models a transformation relationship as a relation or collections of relations, and encode this as an object model. Hausmann (2003) defined an extension of a metamodeling language to specify mappings between metamodels based on concepts presented in Akehurst, Kent and Patrascoiu (2003). Kuster, Sendall and Wahler (2004) compare and contrast two approaches to model transformations: one is graph transformation and the other is a relational approach. Buttner and Gogolla (2004) analyze UML metamodel transformations using a specific graph transformation tool, AGG. Czarnecki and Helsen (2003) describe taxonomy with a feature model to compare several existing and proposed model-to-model transformation approaches.

To date, there is no way to integrate semantically formal languages and their related tools with Model-Driven Development.

Poernomo (2004) proposes a formalization of MOF metamodels within the constructive type theory. Joualt & Kurtev (2006) describe ATL that is a transformation language that implements the MOF-metamodel *Query, View, Transformation* (QVT).

More recently, (Boronat, & Meseguer, 2007) and (Boronat, & Messeger, 2008) present a formal, algebraic semantics of the MOF standard in membership equational logic (MEL). An executable framework for MOF has been integrated within the Eclipse Modeling framework (Eclipse, 2009).

MDA INFRASTRUCTURE

Our goal is to formalize MDA processes in terms of MOF-based metamodels and QVT-based transformations. Both, MOF and QVT, depend on UML metamodel, which in turn depends on OCL. That is to say, the formalization of MDA processes depends on various OMG standards. Some of them, such as OCL and QVT, involve imperative constructions that are hard to formalize. To avoid this inconvenient, we analyzed the graph of package dependencies to select a minimal set of packages that allows us to precisely define the semantics of MDA process in a way independent of imperative constructions. Next, we describe the package dependencies involve in this analysis.

The Infrastructure::Core package is a complete metamodel that is reused by other metamodels that import or specialize its metaclasses.

MOF 2.0 reuses and integrates the UML Infrastructure::Core and provides two metamodels EMOF (Essential MOF) and CMOF (Complete MOF). EMOF favors simplicity of implementation over expressiveness. CMOF is the metamodel used to specify more sophisticated metamodels such as UML 2.2 Superstructure. It is built from EMOF and the Core::Constructs of UML 2.2 (see Chapter 2 Figure 9).

MOF, like all metamodels in the MOF and UML family, is described as a CMOF model. However, EMOF can be described in itself. This results in a complete, standalone model of EMOF that has no dependencies on any other packages, or metamodeling capabilities that are not supported by EMOF itself.

Other important consideration is that MOF and QVT depends only on UML Core::Basic package which at the same time only depends on EssentialOCL, a subset of the complete OCL, exposing the minimal OCL required to work with EMOF (see Chapter 2 Figures 9 and 11). It references explicitly the EMOF classes: Property, Operation, Parameter, TypedElement, Type, Class, DataType, Enumeration, PrimitiveType, and EnumerationLiteral. The following metaclasses defined in complete OCL are not part of EssentialOCL: MessageType, ElementType, AssociationClassCallExp, MessageExp, StateExp, UnspecifiedValueExp. Moreover, any well-formedness rules defined for these classes are consequently not part of the definition of Essential OCL. Then, EssentialOCL does not depend on imperative constructions (OCL, 2006).

On the other hand, QVT has a hybrid declarative/imperative nature. The declarative part includes two metamodels/languages layers: Relation and Core. The latter is defined using Essential OCL and EMOF. The Core language is equally powerful to the Relation language and can be implemented directly or used as a reference for defining the semantics of relations, which are mapped to Core using the transformation language itself (see Chapter 2 Figure 11). Then, we can formalize QVT transformations via the formalization of the QVT::Core and QVT::Base. We can reason about transformations by reasoning about the corresponding core transformation.

Considering the above, we select a minimal subset of packages of OMG standards to formalize MDA process. This subset constitutes an MDA Infrastructure that can be reused by different MDA processes. Figure 1 shows the components of the MDA Infrastructure.

To formalize metamodels, we use a special-purpose language NEREUS. It takes advantage of all the existing theoretical background on formal methods, for instance, the notions of refinement, implementation correctness, observable equivalences and behavioral equivalences that play an essential role in model-to-model transformations (Astesiano, Kreowski, & Krieg-Bruckner, 1999) (Cardelli, & Wegner, 1985). The system type of NEREUS was defined rigorously in the algebraic framework. Considering that MOF supports only binary associations, NEREUS typifies a hierarchy of type constructor for binary

Figure 1. MDA Infrastructure

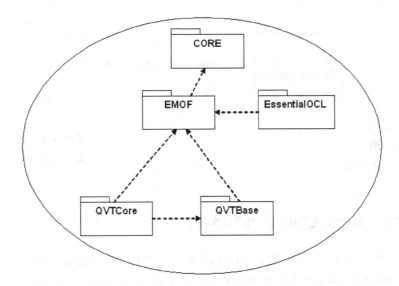

associations and provides rigorous specification of them. The semantics of MOF metamodels (that is specified in OCL) can be enriched and refined by integrating it with NEREUS. This integration facilitates proofs and tests of models and model transformations via the formal specification of metamodels and metamodel transformations. Some properties can be deduced from the formal specification and could be re-injected into the MOF specification without wasting the advantages of semi-formal languages of being more intuitive and pragmatic for most implementers and practitioners.

In contrast to the works mentioned above, our approach has two main advantages linked to automation and interoperability. On the one hand, we show how to generate automatically formal specifications from MOF metamodels. Due to scalability problems, this is an essential requisite. We define a system of transformation rules for translating MOF metamodels specified in OCL into algebraic languages. On the other hand, our approach focuses on interoperability of formal languages. Languages that are defined in terms of NEREUS metamodels can be related to each other because they are defined in the same way through a textual syntax. Any number of source languages such as different Domain Specific Languages (DSLs) and target languages (different formal language) could be connected without having to define explicit metamodel transformations for each language pair (Figure 2). Such as MOF is a DSL to define semi-formal metamodels, NEREUS can be viewed as a DSL for defining formal metamodels.

Another advantage of our approach is linked to pragmatic aspects. NEREUS is a formal notation closed to MOF metamodels that allows meta-designers who must manipulate metamodels to understand their formal specification.

Rather than requiring developers to manipulate formal specifications, the idea is to provide rigorous foundations for MDD in order to develop tools that, on the one hand, take advantage of the power of formal languages and, on the other hand, allow developers to directly manipulate MDA models; however meta-designers need to understand MOF metamodels and NEREUS specifications.

Experiments and tool support related to the NEREUS approach may be found at (Favre, 2001) (Favre, 2005) (Favre, 2006) and (Favre, 2009). However, we would like remark that here NEREUS is used as an intermediate formal notation to communicate the essential of an MDA reverse engineering approach.

Figure 2. Interoperability and NEREUS

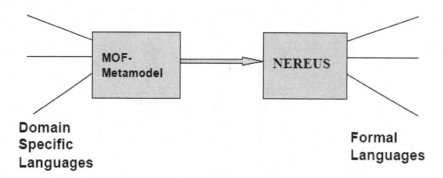

NEREUS: A METAMODELING LANGUAGE

The definition of NEREUS was inspired in MOF. Like MOF, NEREUS provides mechanisms for specifying classes, relations and packages. The outstanding characteristic with respect other algebraic languages is that it expresses different kinds of relations (dependency, binary association, aggregation, composition) as primitives to develop specifications. Next, a description of the NEREUS constructs is included.

Classes

Classes may declare types, operations and, axioms that are formulas of first-order logic. They are structured by three different kinds of relations: importing, inheritance and subtyping. The syntax of a class is as follows:

```
CLASS className
IMPORTS<importList>IS-SUBTYPE-OF<subtypeList>INHERITS<inheritList>GE
NERATED-BY<constructorList>
DEFERRED
TYPES<sortList>ATTRIBUTES<attributeList>OPERATIONS<operationList>
EFFECTIVE
TYPES<sortList>ATTRIBUTES<attributeList>OPERATIONS<operationList>AXI
OMS<varList> <axiomList>
END-CLASS
```

The clauses IMPORT, INHERITS, IS-SUBTYPE-OF, DEFERRED and EFFECTIVE are optional and there is no order between them, except the lineal order imposed by the visibility: each symbol has to be declared before being used.

Types, attributes and operations can be declared as DEFERRED or EFFECTIVE. The DEFERRED clause declares elements that are incompletely defined due to there are not enough axioms to define the behavior of the new operations or, there are not enough operations to generate all values of a sort. The EFFECTIVE clause either declares new types, operations or attributes that are completely defined or completes the definition of some inherited type, attribute or operation.

The IMPORTS, INHERITS and IS-SUBTYPE-OF Clauses

The IMPORTS clause expresses dependency relations. The specification of a new class is based on the imported specifications declared in *<importsList>* and their public operations may be used in the new specification.

The INHERITS clause specifies that a new class is built starting from the union of classes appearing in *<inheritsList>*. The component of these classes will be components of the new class, and their own types, attributes and operations will be elements of the new class.

In contrast to the module reuse viewpoint of the INHERITS clause, the IS-SUBTYPE-OF clause relies on the inheritance of behavior viewpoint. A notion closely related with subtyping is polymorphism, which satisfies the property that each object of a subclass is at the same time an object of its superclasses.

The components of the class that do not come from INHERITS, IS-SUBTYPE and IMPORTS clauses are named the "own part" of the class.

The TYPES Clause

The declaration of types (sorts) has the following form:

```
TYPES s1,s2,…,sn
```

This clause can declare types as EFFECTIVE or DEFERRED.

The ATTRIBUTES and OPERATIONS Clauses

The ATTRIBUTES and OPERATIONS clauses declare functionalities of attributes and operations respectively with the traditional syntax of signatures. Operations can be declared as total or partial. Partial operations must specify its domain by means of the PRE clause that indicates what conditions the function arguments must satisfy to belong to the function domain.

Constructors, DEFERRED/INHERITED OPERATIONS

The GENERATED-BY clause refers to the basic constructor operations of the class. NEREUS allows us to specify operation signatures in an incomplete way by using the underscore notation "_". An underscore in the domain of functionality expresses that the subclasses can extend the inherited functionality with the Cartesian product of other types. An incomplete operation has the following syntax:

```
Operation: Type₁ x Type₂ x .. x Typeₙ x _ -> RType
```

The "*" notation in a functionality refers to the functionality inherited from the base class. This notation precedes the Cartesian product of own domains:

```
Operation: * x Type₁ x Type₂ x….-> RType
```

Higher Order Simulation

NEREUS supports higher order operations (a function f is higher order if functional sorts appear in a parameter sort or the result sort of f). In the context of OCL Collection formalization, second-order operations are required.

Axioms

The AXIOMS clause declares pairs *v: C* where v is a universal quantified variable of type C. Following this clause, axioms are included to specify the class semantics. As for many-sorted specifications, axioms are formulas in first-order logic.

A term is a typed variable, a constant or a well-formed operation application. Formulas may be atomic or compound. An atomic formula is an equivalence equation between two terms of the same type. Equations of the form *term=True* can be abbreviated by *term*. All operations are strict, if one of its arguments is undefined, the result too. A compound formula (or predicate) is built by using the logic operators *not*, *and*, *implies* and *equivalence*.

To facilitate the use of conditionals, the class Boolean provides the operation IF-THEN-ELSE whose signature is:

```
IF-THEN-ELSE: Boolean x S x S -> S
```

and the axioms related are:

```
IF-THEN-ELSE (True, x, y) = x
IF-THEN-ELSE (False, x, y) = y
2 PARAMETERIZED CLASSES
```

NEREUS distinguishes variable parts in a specification by means of explicit parameterization. The elements of *<parameterList>* are pairs C1:C2 where C1 is the formal generic parameter constrained by an existing class C2 (only subclasses of C2 will be actual parameters). The syntax of a parameterized class is as follows:

```
CLASS className [<parameterList>]IMPORTS<importList>IS-SUBTYPE-OF<su
btypeList>INHERITS<inheritList>GENERATED-BY<constructorList>
DEFERRED
TYPES<sortList>FUNCTIONS<functionList>
EFFECTIVE
TYPES<sortList>FUNCTIONS<functionList>AXIOMS<varList>
<axiomList>
END-CLASS
```

Local Instances of Classes

NEREUS allows to define local instances of a class in the IMPORTS, INHERITS and IS-SUBTYPE-OF clauses by the syntax

```
className [<parameterList>] [<bindingList>]
```

where the elements of *<bindingList>* can be pairs of sorts s1:s2 and/or pairs of operations o1:o2 with o2 and s2 belonging to the "own part" of ClassName. References to parameterized specifications instantiate always the parameters. The sort of interest of a class (if any) is also implicitly renamed each time the class is substituted or renamed.

Axioms can introduce local names whether for referring common sub-terms or for defining axioms that involve second order functions. NEREUS provides the construction LET...IN to limit the scope of the declarations of auxiliary symbols by using local symbols.

The following expressions are equivalent, and exemplifies the use of the LET...IN construct in the construction of axioms over second order functions:

```
LET
OPERATIONS
f: Elem -> Boolean
AXIOMS v: Elem
f (v) = …
IN
expression-with-operation (c, f)
END-LET
```

NEREUS includes a concise notation that is closed to the OCL notation. The syntax F_x (c, [g(x_1, x_2, ..., x_i, x, x_{i+1}, ...)] where c is a collection, is equivalent to

```
LET
OPERATIONS
h: T_x -> T_g
AXIOMS x: T_x; …
h (x) = g (x_1, x_2, ...., x_i, x, x_{i+1}, ....)
IN
…F (c, h)…
END-LET
```

In a similar way, the above expression may be written by using the WHERE notation:

```
expression-with-operation (c, f)
WHERE f: Elem -> Boolean
AXIOMS v: Elem
f (v) = …
```

Primitive and Constructor Types

Several useful predefined types are offered in NEREUS. It provides primitive types (Boolean, Integer, Real and String), enumerated types and tuple. Besides, it provides a hierarchy of collections including Set, Bag, Sequence and OrderedSet. Appendix-B includes their specification.

Association Definition

NEREUS provides a taxonomy of constructor types that classifies binary association according to kind (ordinary association, aggregation and composition), degree (unary, binary), navigability (unidirectional, bidirectional), and connectivity (e.g. one-to-one, one-to-many and many-to-many). Figure 3 partially depicts the hierarchy of constructor types.

Generic relations can be used in the definition of concrete relations by instantiation. New associations can be defined as follows:

```
ASSOCIATION <relationName>
IS <constructorTypeName> [...:class1;...:class2;...:role1;...:role2;
...:mult1;...:mult2;...:visibility1;...:visibility2]
CONSTRAINED-BY <constraintList>
END
```

Figure 3. Hierarchy of constructor types for associations

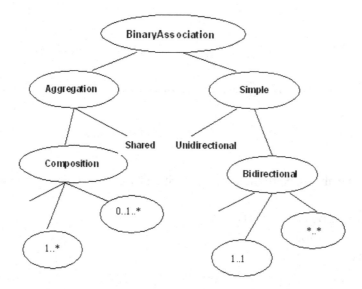

The IS paragraph expresses the instantiation of *<constructorTypeName>* with classes, roles, visibility and multiplicity. The CONSTRAINED-BY clause allows the specification of predefined constraints (ordered, changeable, addOnly, Frozen, xor, subset) and specific static constraints in first-order logic.

Associations are defined in a class by means of the ASSOCIATES clause:

```
CLASS className
...
ASSOCIATES <<associationName>>
...
END-CLASS
```

Package Definition

The package is the mechanism provided by NEREUS for grouping classes and associations and controlling its visibility. The syntax of a package is as follows:

```
PACKAGE packageName
IMPORTING <importsList>
GENERALIZATION <inheritsList>
NESTING <nestingList>
CLUSTERING <clusteringList>
<elements>
END-PACKAGE
```

Like MOF, NEREUS provides mechanisms for metamodel composition and reuse (importing, generalization, nesting and clustering) (MOF, 2002, pp. 2-14) The IMPORTING clause lists the imported packages (*<importsList>*); the GENERALIZATION clause lists the inherited packages in *<inheritList>*; NESTING clause lists the nested packages (*<nestingList>*) and CLUSTERING clause lists the clustering ones (*<clusteringList>*).

Comments

A comment is a line preceded by "- -"

```
-- <texto>
```

The "::" Notation

The "::" notation allows expressing the name of an element as an ordered list of another elements in which it is contained. The syntax for using it is:

```
Package::Class::roleName
```

Next, we show examples of NEREUS specifications.

EXAMPLE 4-1: OCL COLLECTIONS IN NEREUS

Following we show the predefined type Collection in OCL and NEREUS. Collection is a superclass of all collection types in OCL: Set, Bag, Sequence and OrderedSet (OCL, 2006). In Appendix-B we present the complete specification of this hierarchy both in OCL and NEREUS.

Collection in OCL

size (): Integer
The number of elements in the collection *self*.

```
post: result = self -> iterate (elem; acc: Integer = 0 | acc + 1)
```

includes (object: T): Boolean
True if *object* is an element of *self*, false otherwise.

```
post: result = (self -> count (object) > 0)
```

excludes (object: T): Boolean
True if *object* is not an element of *self*, false otherwise.

```
post: result = (self -> count (object) = 0)
```

count (object: T): Integer
The number of times that *object* occurs in the collection *self*.

```
post: result = self -> iterate (elem; acc: Integer = 0 | if elem =
object then acc + 1 else acc endif)
```

includesAll (c2: Collection (T)): Boolean
Does *self* contain all the elements of *c2* ?

```
post: result = c2 -> forAll (elem | self -> includes (elem))
```

excludesAll (c2: Collection (T)): Boolean
Does *self* contain none of the elements of *c2* ?

```
post: result = c2 -> forAll(elem | self -> excludes (elem))
```

isEmpty(): Boolean
Is *self* the empty collection?

```
post: result = (self -> size () = 0)
```

notEmpty (): Boolean
Is *self* not the empty collection?

```
post: result = (self -> size () <> 0)
```

sum (): T
The addition of all elements in *self*. Elements must be of a type supporting the + operation. The + operation must take one parameter of type T and be both associative: $(a + b) + c = a + (b + c)$, and commutative: $a + b = b + a$.

Integer and Real fulfill this condition.

```
post: result = self -> iterate (elem; acc: T = 0 | acc + elem)
```

product (c2: Collection (T2)): Set (Tuple (first: T, second: T2))
The cartesian product operation of *self* and *c2*.

```
post: result = self -> iterate (e1; acc: Set (Tuple (first: T, sec-
ond: T2)) = Set {} | c2 -> iterate (e2; acc2: Set (Tuple (first: T,
second: T2)) = acc | acc2 -> including (Tuple {first = e1, second =
e2})))
```

Collection in NEREUS

Following we show the predefined type OCL-Collection in NEREUS (Favre, 2001). Collection is a parameterized class. It imports Boolean and Nat specifications. Its basic constructor operations are *create* and *add*. The sort Collection and the operations *create, add*, *count* and *collect* are defined as deferred. For instance, the *count* operation determines the number of times that an element occurs in the Collection. Due to the collection Set does not admit more than one occurrence, the semantics of count can only be completed in the subclasses. The rest of its operations are effective. Some of them are second-order operations (*forAll*, *select*, *exists* and *iterate*). The semantic specification of count exemplifies how to use local definitions by using the WHERE paragraph. The *includes* and *excludes* operations exemplify the use of the if-then-else notation.

```
CLASS Collection [Elem]
IMPORTS Boolean, Nat
GENERATED-BY create, add DEFERREDTYPES
Collection
OPERATIONS
create: → Collection
add: Collection x Elem → Collection
count: Collection x Elem → Nat
collect: Collection x (Elem -> Elem1: ANY) -> Collection
EFFECTIVEOPERATIONS
isEmpty: Collection -> Boolean
```

```
size: Collection → Nat
includes: Collection x Elem -> Boolean
excludes: Collection x Elem -> Boolean
includesAll: Collection x Collection -> Boolean
forAll: Collection x (Elem -> Boolean) -> Boolean
exists: Collection x (Elem -> Boolean) -> Boolean
select: Collection x (Elem -> Boolean) -> Collection
reject: Collection x (Elem -> Boolean) -> Collection
iterate: Collection x (Elem x Acc: ANY) x (-> Acc) -> Acc
AXIOMS c, c1: Collection; e: Elem; f: Elem -> Boolean;
g: Elem x Acc -> Acc; base: -> Acc
isEmpty (c) = (size (c) = 0)
iterate (create, g, base) = base
iterate (add (c, e), g, base) = g (e, iterate (c, g, base))
count (c, e) = iterate (c, f1, 0)
    WHEREOPERATIONS f1: Elem x Nat ->Nat
    AXIOMS e1: Elem; i: Nat
    f1 (e1, i) = if e = e1 then i+1 else i
    END-WHERE
size (create) = 0
size (add (c, e)) = 1 + size (c)
includes (create, e) = False
includes (add (c, e), e1) = if e = e1 then True
else includes (c, e1)
excludes (create, e) = True
excludes (add (c, e), e1) = if e = e1 then False else excludes (c,
e1)
includesAll (create, c) = True
includesAll (add (c, e), c1) = includesAll (c, c1) and includes (e,
c1)
excludesAll (create, c) = True
excludesAll (add (c, e), c1) = excludesAll (c, c1) and excludes (e,
c1)
forAll (create, f) = True
forAll (add (c, e), f) = f (e) and forAll (c, f)
exists (create, f) = False
exists (add (c, e)) = f (e) or exists (c, f)
select (create, f) = create
select (add (c, e), f) = if f (e) then add (select (c, f), e) else
select (c, f)
reject (create, f) = create
reject (add (c, e), f) = if not f (e) then add (reject (c, f), e)
   else reject (c, f)
END-CLASS
```

Set in OCL

union (s: Set (T)): Set (T)

```
The union of self and s.
post: result -> forAll (elem | self -> includes (elem) or s -> in-
cludes (elem))
post: self -> forAll (elem | result -> includes(elem))
post: s -> forAll (elem | result -> includes (elem))
```

union(bag: Bag(T)): Bag(T)

```
The union of self and bag.
post: result -> forAll (elem |
result -> count (elem) = self -> count (elem) + bag -> count (elem))
post: self -> forAll (elem | result -> includes (elem))
post: bag -> forAll (elem | result -> includes (elem))
```

= (s: Set (T)): Boolean

```
Evaluates to true if self and s contain the same elements.
post: result = (self -> forAll (elem |
s -> includes (elem)) and s -> forAll (elem | self -> includes
(elem)))
```

intersection (s: Set (T)): Set (T)

```
The intersection of self and s (i.e., the set of all elements that
are in both self and s).
post: result -> forAll (elem | self -> includes (elem) and s -> in-
cludes (elem))
post: self -> forAll (elem | s -> includes (elem) = result -> in-
cludes (elem))
post: s -> forAll (elem | self -> includes (elem) = result -> in-
cludes (elem))
```

intersection (bag: Bag(T)): Set(T)

```
The intersection of self and bag.post: result = self ->
intersection(bag -> asSet)
```

ñ (s: Set (T)): Set(T)

The elements of *self*, which are not in *s*.
post: result -> forAll (elem | self -> includes (elem) and s -> excludes (elem))
post: self -> forAll (elem | result -> includes (elem) = s -> excludes (elem))

including (object: T): Set(T)

The set containing all elements of *self* plus *object*.
post: result-> forAll (elem | self -> includes (elem) or (elem = object))
post: self -> forAll (elem | result -> includes (elem))
post: result -> includes (object)

excluding (object: T): Set(T)

The set containing all elements of *self* without *object*.
post: result -> forAll (elem | self -> includes (elem) and (elem <> object))
post: self - > forAll (elem | result -> includes (elem) = (object <> elem))
post: result -> excludes (object)

symmetricDifference (s: Set (T)): Set (T)

The sets containing all the elements that are in *self* or *s*, but not in both.
post: result -> forAll (elem | self -> includes (elem) xor s -> includes (elem))
post: self -> forAll (elem | result -> includes (elem) = s -> excludes (elem))
post: s -> forAll (elem | result -> includes (elem) = self -> excludes (elem))

count (object: T): Integer
The number of occurrences of object in *self*.

post: result <= 1

flatten (): Set (T2)
If the element type is not a collection type, this results is the same *self*. If the element type is a collection type, the result is the set containing all the elements of all the elements of *self*.

```
post: result = if self.type.elementType.oclIsKindOf (CollectionType)
then
self -> iterate (c; acc: Set () = Set {} | acc -> union (c -> asSet
())) else self endif
```

asSet (): Set (T)
A Set identical to *self.*

```
post: result = self
```

asOrderedSet (): OrderedSet (T)
An OrderedSet that contains all the elements from *self*, in undefined order.

```
post: result -> forAll (elem | self -> includes (elem))
```

asSequence (): Sequence (T)
A Sequence that contains all the elements from *self*, in undefined order.

```
post: result -> forAll (elem | self -> includes (elem))
post: self -> forAll (elem | result -> count (elem) = 1)
```

asBag (): Bag (T)
The Bag that contains all the elements from *self.*

```
post: result -> forAll (elem | self -> includes (elem))
post: self -> forAll (elem | result -> count (elem) = 1)
```

Set in NEREUS

The class Set is a subtype of Collection. The IS-SUBTYPE-OF clause exemplifies the definition of a local instance of Collection that renames the operations *create* and add by *createSet* and *including* respectively. All operations are defined as effective. In AXIOMS, a concise notation for second-order operations is exemplified. For instance, forAll(v) (s, [includes (union (s, s2), v)]) refers to an operation *forAll* over an index *v*, and collection *s* and the logical expression *includes (union (s, s2), v)*.

```
CLASS Set [T]
IS-SUBTYPE-OF Collection [T] [create: createSet; add: including]
IMPORTS Sequence, Bag [create: createBag; including: includingBag],
OrderedSet EFFECTIVETYPES
Set
OPERATIONS
createSet, including, count
equal: Set x Set -> Boolean
union: Set x Set → Set
```

```
union: Set x Bag → Bag
intersection: Set x Set → Set
intersection: Set x Bag → Set
-: Set x Set → Set
excluding: Set x T → Set
symmetricDifference: Set x Set → Set
collect: Set x (T → T1: ANY) → Bag [T1]
flatten: Set -> Set[T1:ANY]
asSet: Set -> Set
asOrderedSet: Set -> OrderedSet
asSequence: Set → Sequence
asBag: Set → Bag
```

AXIOMS s, s2: Set; b: Bag; b1: Bag[T1] ; e, e1: T; g: T1 -> Boolean

```
collect (createSet, g) = createBag
collect (including (s, e), g) = includingBag (collect (excluding (s,
e), g(e))
count (s, e) <= 1
forAll (v) (union (s, s2), [includes (s, v) or includes (s2, v)])
forAll (v) (s, [ includes (union (s, s2), v) ])
forAll (v) (s2, [includes (union (s, s2), v) ])
forAll (v) (s, [includes (union (s, b), v) ])
forAll (v) (b, [includes (union (s, b), v)])
forAll (v) (union (s, b), [count (union (s, b), v) = count(s, v) +
count (b, v)])
equal (s, s2) =
forAll (v) (s, [includes (s2, v)) and forAll (v1) (s2, [includes (s,
v1)]) ])
forAll (v) (intersection (s, s2), [includes (s, v) and includes (s2,
v)]
forAll (v) (s, [includes (s2, v)) = includes (intersection (s, s2),
v)])
forAll (v) (s2, [includes (s, v)) = includes (intersection (s, s2),
v)])
intersection (s, b) = intersection (s, asSet (b))
forAll (v) (s - s2, [includes (s,v) and excludes (s2,v) ])
forAll (v)(s, [includes (s - s2, v) = excludes (s2,v) ])
forAll (v) (including (s, e), [includes (s,v) or equal (v,e)]
forAll (v)(s, [includes (including (s, e), v) ])
includes (including (s, e), e)
forAll (v) (excluding (s, e), [includes (s, v) and not equal (v,e)])
forAll (v) (s, [includes (excluding (s, e), v) = not equal (e,v)])
excludes (excluding (s, e), e)
forAll (v) (symmetricDifference (s, s2), [includes (s, v) xor in-
cludes (s2, v)])
```

```
forAll (v) (s, [includes (symmetricDifference (s, s2), v) = excludes
(s2, v)])
forAll (v) [includes (symmetricDifference (s, s2), v) = excludes (s,
v)])
flatten (s)= if oclIsKindOf (elementType (type (s)), CollectionType)
   then iterate (v) (s, [union (acc, asSet (v))], [acc = createSet])
else s
asSet(s) = s
forAll (v) (asOrderedSet (s), [includes (asOrderedSet (s), v)])
forAll (v) (asSequence (s), includes (s, v))
forAll (v) (s, count (asSequence (s), v) = 1)
forAll (v) (asBag (s), [includes (s, v)])
forAll (v)(s, [count (asBag (s), v) = 1])
forAll (v) (asOrderedSet (b), [includes(b,v)])
forAll (v) (b, [includes (asOrdered (b), v))
forAll(v) (b, [count (asOrderedSet (b), v) = 1])
```
END-CLASS

EXAMPLE 4-2: BIDIRECTIONAL ASSOCIATIONS IN NEREUS

Figure 4 shows a bidirectional association between the classes A and B whose association-end multiplicity is *. Next, we show the scheme in NEREUS related to this bidirectional association. The elements that have to be instantiated are shown in italics. The scheme must be instantiated with classes (Class1, Class2), roles (role1, role2), multiplicities and properties.

An association is specified as a set of links, each link is added by applying the addlink operation. isRightLinked operation determines whether or not an instance of Class1 belongs to a link. isLeftLinked operation determines whether or not an instance of Class2 belongs to a link. rightCardinality gives the cardinality associated with instances of Class1. get_role1 gives the collection[Class2] associated with an instance of Class1. isRelated determines whether or not two instances are related and so on.

addLink, get_role1, get_role2 and remove are partial operations that restrict their domains by preconditions. Various axioms must be instantiated according to the properties of the association. The parts that must be instantiated are shown in italics. A complete specification may be found at Appendix-B.

Figure 4. Bidirectional association in NEREUS

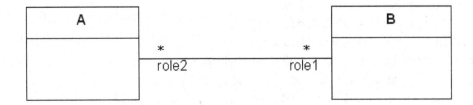

RELATION SCHEME Bidirectional-3
IMPORTS Collection-C1: *Collection* [*Class1*], Collection-C2: *Collection* [*Class2*]
IS-SUBTYPE-OF BinaryAssociation
GENERATED-BY create, addLink
EFFECTIVEOPERATIONS
name, frozen, changeable, addOnly, get_*role1,* get_*role2,* getMult1, getMult2, getVisibility1, getVisibility2
create: Typename → Bidirectional-3
addLink: Bidirectional-3 (a) x *Class1* (c1) x *Class2* (c2) → Bidirectional-3
pre: not isRelated (a, c1, c2)
isEmpty: Bidirectional-3 → Boolean
isRightLinked: Bidirectional-3 x *Class1* → Boolean
isLeftLinked: Bidirectional-3 x *Class2* → Boolean
rightCardinality: Bidirectional-3 x *Class1* → Nat
leftCardinality: Bidirectional-3 x *Class2* → Nat
get_*role1*: Bidirectional-3 (a) x *Class1*(c1) → Collection-C2
pre: isRightLinked (a, c1)
get_*role2*: Bidirectional-3 (a) x *Class2* (c2) → Collection-C1
pre: isLeftLinked (a, c2)
remove: Bidirectional-3 (a) x *Class1* (c1) x *Class2* (c2) → Bidirectional-3
pre: isRelated (a, c1, c2)
isRelated: Bidirectional-3 x *Class1* (c1) x *Class2* (c2) → Boolean
AXIOMS a: Bidirectional-3; c1, cc1: *Class1*; c2, cc2: *Class2*; t:
TypeName
name (create (t)) = t
name (add (a, c1, c2)) = name (a)
isEmpty (create (t)) = True
isEmpty (addLink (a, c1, c2)) = False
frozen (a) = <*True or False*>
changeable (a) = <*True or False*>
addOnly (a) = <*True or False*>
get_*role1* (a) = <*role name*>
get_*role2* (a) = <*role name*>
getMult1 (a) = <*multiplicity*>
getMult2 (a) = <*multiplicity*>
getVisibility1 (a) = <*visibility*>
getVisibility2 (a) = <*visibility*>
isRelated (create (t), c1, c2) = False
isRelated (addLink (a, c1, c2), cc1, cc2) =
(c1= cc1 and c2 = cc2) or isRelated (a, cc1, cc2)
isRightLinked (create (t), c1) = False

```
isRightLinked (addLink (a, c1, c2), cc1) =
if c1 = cc1 then True else isRightLinked (a, cc1)
isLeftLinked (create (t), c2) = False
isLeftLinked (addLink (a, c1, c2), cc2) =
if c2 = cc2 then True else isLeftLinked (a, cc2)
rightCardinality (create (t), c1) = 0
rightCardinality (addLink(a, c1, c2), cc1) =
if c1= cc1 then 1 + rightCardinality (a, cc1) else rightCardinality
(a, cc1)
leftCardinality (create (t), c2) = 0
leftCardinality (addLink (a, c1, c2), cc2) =
if c2 = cc2 then 1 + leftCardinality (a, cc2) else leftCardinality
(a, cc2)
getClass2 (addLink (a, c1, c2), cc1) =
if c1= cc1 then add (getClass2 (a, cc1), c2) else getClass2 (a, cc1)
getClass1 (addLink (a, c1, c2), cc2) =
if c2 = cc2 then add (getClass1 (a, cc2), c2) else getClass1 (a,
cc2)
remove (addLink (a, c1, c2), cc1, cc2) =
if (c1= cc1 and c2 = cc2) then a else remove (a, cc1, cc2)
```
END-RELATION

EXAMPLE 4-3: AGGREGATION / COMPOSITION IN NEREUS

This example shows the specification of a composition between two classes A (composite) and B (component) (Figure 5)

Next, we show the scheme for a composition (1.. n1..n2) in NEREUS. This scheme expresses a subtype relationship between Composition and Aggregation (which in turn is a subtype of BinaryAssociation) as shows Figure 6.

RELATION SCHEME AggregationIS-SUBTYPE-OF BinaryAssociation [*Whole:* Class1, *Part:* Class2]
DEFERREDOPERATIONS
is*Part*: Aggregation x *Whole* x *Part*→ Boolean

Figure 5. Composition in NEREUS

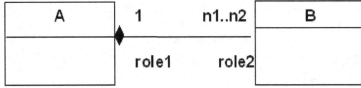

Figure 6. Relationships between composition, aggregation and binary associations

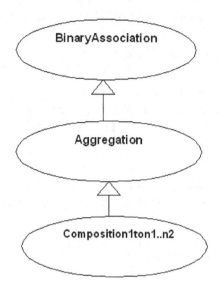

```
isEmpty: Aggregation → Boolean
isLinkedWhole: Aggregation x Whole → Boolean
isLinkedPart: Aggregation x Part → Boolean
```
END-RELATIONRELATION SCHEME Composition-2
```
--0..1 to n1..n2
```
IMPORTS C-*Part*: *Collection* [*Part*] [create-s: create]
IS-SUBTYPE-OF Aggregation [C-*Part*: *Part*]
GENERATED-BY create, add*Part***EFFECTIVEOPERATIONS**
```
name, frozen, changeable, addOnly, get_role1, get_role2, getMult1,
getMult2, getVisibility1, getVisibility2, isPart, isEmpty, isLinked-
Whole, isLinkedPart
create: TypeName → Aggregation-7
```
add*Part*: Composition-2 (a) x C-*Part* (cp) x *Whole* (w) → Composition-2
pre:`<n1>` ≤ size(cp) ≤ `<n2>` and not isLinkedWhole (a, w)
```
rightCardinality: Composition-2 x Whole → Nat
leftCardinality: Composition-2 x Part → Nat
getPart: Aggregation (a) x Whole (w) → C-Part (p)
```
pre: isLinkedWhole (a, w)
getWhole: Aggregation (a) x *Part* (p) → *Whole***pre:** isLinkedPart (a, p)
AXIOMS a: Composition-2; p, p1: *Part*; w, w: *Whole*; t: TypeName; cp:
C-Part
```
name (create (t)) = t
```
name (add*Part* (a, cp, w)) = name (a)
```
frozen (a) = True
changeable (a) = False
```

```
addOnly (a) = True
getMult1 (a) = 1
getMult2 (a) = <n1> .. <n2>
rightCardinality (create (t), w) = 0
rightCardinality (addPart (a, cp, w), w1) =
if includes (cp, w1) then 1 else leftCardinality (a, w1)
rightCardinality (create (t), w) = 0
leftCardinality (addPart (a, cp, w), p1) =
if includes (cp, p1) then 1 else leftCardinality (a, p1)
get_role1 (a) = <name-role1>
get_role2 (a) = <name-role2>
getVisibility1 = <visibility>
getVisibility2 = <visibility>
getPart (addPart (a, cp, w), w1) = if (w = w1) then cp else getPart
(a, w1)
getWhole (addPart (a, cp, w), p)=
if includes (cp, p) then w else getWhole (a, p)
isPart (create (t), p) = False
isPart(addPart (a, cp, w), p1, w1) =
(includes (cp, p1) and w = w1) or isPart (a, p1, w1)
isLinkedWhole(create (t), w) = False
isLinkedWhole (addPart (a, cp, w), w1) = (w = w1) or isLinkedWhole
(a, w1)
isLinkedPart (create(t), w) = False
isLinkedPart (addPart (a, cp, w), p) = includes (cp, p) or isLinked-
Part (a, p)
END-RELATION
```

EXAMPLE 4-4: STATE DIAGRAM METAMODEL

The State Diagram Metamodel (Figure 7) defines a set of concepts than can be used for modeling discrete behavior through finite state transition systems such as state machines, state and transitions. OCL can be reused to attach consistency rules to metamodel components. For instance the following rules may be attached to State-Diagram metamodel.

```
Context Statemachine
--The connection points of a state machine are pseudostates of kind
entry point
--or exit point.
conectionPoint -> forAll (c | c.kind = #entryPoint or c.kind = #ex-
itPoint)
Context PseudoState
-An initial vertex can have at most one ongoing transition
```

Figure 7. State Diagram metamodel

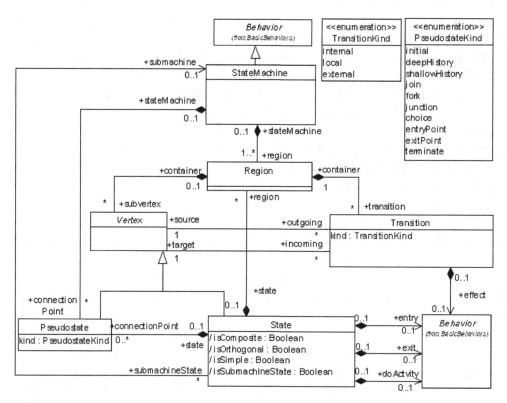

```
(self.kind = #initial) implies (self.outgoing -> size <= 1)
Context Region
--A region can have at most one initial vertex.
self.subvertex -> select (v| v.oclIsKindOf (Pseudostate)) ->
   select (p: Pseudostate|p.kind = #initial) -> size () <= 1
```

Next, we show partially the specification in NEREUS of Figure 5. The shaded specification is linked to OCL axioms.

```
PACKAGE StateDiagramMetamodel
IMPORTS TransitionKind, PseudoStateKind
CLASS StateMachine
IS-SUBTYPE-OF UML::CommonBehaviors::BasicBehaviors::Behavior
ASSOCIATES
<< StateMachine-State>>
<< StateMachine-PseudoState >>…
AXIOMS a: StateMachine-PseudoState; sm:StateMachine
forAll (c) (get_connectionPoint (a, sm),
[kind(c) = #entryPoint or kind(c) = #exitPoint]) …
END-CLASSCLASS Region
```

IS-SUBTYPE-OFUML::Classes::Kernel::Namespace
ASSOCIATES
<< State-Region>>
<< StateMachine-Region>>
<< Region-Vertex >>…
AXIOMS a: Region-Vertex; r: Region
size (select (p) (select (v) (get_subvertex (a, r),
oclIsKinfOf (v, PseudoState)]), [kind(p) = #initial])) <= 1
END-CLASSCLASS PseudoState
IS-SUBTYPE-OF Vertex, NameElement
ASSOCIATES
<<Vertex-Transition-1>>
<<Vertex-Transition-2>>
<< StateMachine-PseudoState>>

…
OPERATIONS
kind: PseudoState -> PseudoStateKind
AXIOMS ps: PseudoState; a: Vertex-Transition-1
kind (ps) = #initial implies
    size (get_outgoing (a,ps)) <=1…
END-CLASSASSOCIATION stateMachine-PseudoState
IS Composition-2 [StateMachine: class1; PseudoState: class2;
stateMachine: role1; conectionPoint: role2; 0..1: mult1; *: mult2;
+: visibility1;+: visibility2]
CONSTRAINED-BY StateMachine: subsets namespace; PseudoState: subsets
ownedMember
ENDASSOCIATION Region-Vertex
IS Composition-2 [Region: class1; Vertex: class2; container: role1;
subvertex: role2; 0..1: mult1; *: mult2; +: visibility1; +: visibil-
ity2]
CONSTRAINED-BY Region: subsets namespace; Vertex: subsets ownedMember
END

…

END-PACKAGE

EXAMPLE 4-5: QVT CORE FORMALIZATION

We show the formalization of the QVT Core metamodel. The Core language is as powerful as the Relation language and may be used as a reference for the semantics of relations, which are mapped to Core.
Figure 8 shows two metaclasses of the QVT-BASE package and their interrelationships. The complete
diagram may be found at (QVT, 2008, pp.15). A transformation defines how one set of models can be
transformed into another. It is composed by a set of rules that specify its execution behavior. The fol-

Figure 8. Transformation and rules in QVT

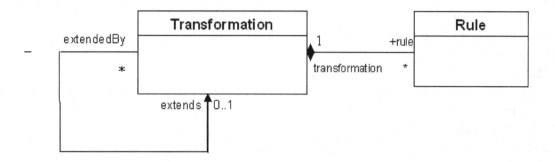

lowing constraints (extendingRule and transitiveRule) may be attached to the package specifying that the rules of the extended transformation are included in the extending transformation and the extension is transitive:

```
extendingRule =
Transformation.allInstances -> forAll (t|
t.extends.size = 1 implies t.extends.rule -> include (t.rule))

transitiveRule =
Transformation.allInstances ->
forAll (t1, t2, t3 | t1.extends.size = 1 and t2.extends.size = 1 and
t3.extends.size = 1
and (t1.extends.rule -> includes (t2.rule) and
t2.extends.rule -> includes (t3.rules)) implies t1.extends.rule ->
includes (t3.rule)
```

A rule domain is the set of model elements of a typed model that are of interest to it. A domain may be marked as checkable or enforceable

An analogy between a virtual machine-based architecture and QVT is described in (QVT, 2008 pp. 10). The Core language is like JAVA byte code and the Core semantics is like the behavior specification for the Java Virtual Machine (JVM). The Relation language is like the Java language, and the standard transformation from Relations to Core is like the Java compiler which produces byte code. We can go beyond that showing an analogy between the semantics of the JVM byte code and the core of QVT. The semantics of Java, that includes object-oriented features, is hard to formalize. However, JVM byte code is defined more precisely. Liu and Moore (2004) proved that Java program verification via a deep embedding of the JVM into the logic of ACL2 (Kaufman & Moore, 2009) is a viable approach. Analogously, the semantics of QVT, that includes mechanisms for involving imperative implementations of transformations, is hard to formalize. The Core package that is based on QVT Base package, EMOF and Essential OCL (see Chapter 2 Figure 11) is more simply and more precisely defined. Then, we decided to formalize QVT transformations via the QVT core and QVT base formalization.

We can reason about transformations by reasoning about the corresponding core transformation. Following, we include a partial specification in NEREUS of the QVT-BASE package.

As an example, the OCL specification, extendingRule and transformationRule can be translated into the shaded axioms.

```
PACKAGE QVTBase
CLASS Transformation
IMPORTS EMOF::Tag
INHERITS EMOF::MetaClass, EMOF::Package
ASSOCIATES
<<Transformation-Tag>>
<<Transformation-Transformation>>
<<Transformation-Rule>>,
<<Transformation-TypeModel>>
AXIOMS ass1: <<Transformation-Transformation>>;
ass2: <<Transformation-Rule>> ; t: Transformation ;…
size (get_extends (ass1, t)) = 1 implies
includes (get_rule (ass2, get_extends (ass1, t)), get_rule (ass1,
t))
END-CLASSCLASS TypedModel
IMPORTS EMOF::Package
IS-SUBTYPE-OF EMOF::NamedElement
ASSOCIATES
<<Transformation-TypeModel>>
<<TypeModel-Package>>
<<Domain-TypeModel>>
<<TypeModel-TypeModel>>
END-CLASSCLASS Domain
IS-SUBTYPE-OF EMOF::NamedElement
ASSOCIATES
<<Rule-Domain>>
<<Domain-TypeModel>>
DEFERREDATTRIBUTES
isCheckable: Domain -> Boolean
isEnforceable: Domain -> Boolean
END-CLASSCLASS Rule
IS-SUBTYPE-OF EMOF::NamedElement
ASSOCIATES
<<Rule-Domain>>
<<Rule-Rule>>
<<Transformation-Rule>>
END-CLASSASSOCIATION Transformation-Transformation
IS Unidirectional-2 [Transformation: class1; Transformation: class2;
extendedBy: role1; extends: role2; *: mult1; 0..1: mult2; +: vis-
ibility1; +: visibility2]
```

```
END-ASSOCIATIONASSOCIATION Transformation-Rule
IS Composition-2 [Transformation: class1; Rule: class2; transfor-
mation: role1; rule: role2; 1: mult1; *: mult2; +: visibility1; +:
visibility2]
END-ASSOCIATIONASSOCIATION Transformation-TypedModel
...
END-PACKAGE
```

REFERENCES

Abrial, J. (1996). *The B Book: Assigning Programs to Meanings*. Cambridge: Cambridge University Press.

Ahrendt, W., Baar, T., Beckert, B., Bubel, R., Giese, M., & Hähnle, R. (2005). The Key Tool. *Software and Systems Modeling, 4*, 32–54. doi:10.1007/s10270-004-0058-x

Akehurst, D., Kent, S., & Patrascoiu, O. (2003). A relational approach to defining and implementing transformations between metamodels. *Software and System Modeling, 2*(4), 215–239. doi:10.1007/s10270-003-0032-z

Alencar, A., & Goguen, J. (1991). OOZE: An Object-oriented Z Environment. In *Proceedings of the European Conference on Object-oriented Programming, ECOOP 91* (LNCS 512, pp. 180-199. Heidelberg: Springer-Verlag.

Astesiano, E., Kreowski, H., & Krieg-Bruckner, B. (Eds.). (1999). *Algebraic Foundations of System Specification*. Heidelberg: Springer-Verlag.

Barbier, F., Henderson-Sellers, B., Le Parc-Lacayrelle, A., & Bruel, J. (2003). Formalization of the Whole-Part Relationship in the Unified Modeling Language. *IEEE Transactions on Software Engineering, 29*(5), 450–470. doi:10.1109/TSE.2003.1199074

Bidoit, M., & Mosses, P. (2004). CASL User Manual- Introduction to Using the Common Algebraic Specification Language (LNCS 2900). Heidelberg: Springer-Verlag.

Bordeau, R., & Cheng, B. (1995). A Formal Semantic for Object Model Diagrams. *IEEE Transactions on Software Engineering, 21*(10).

Borger, E., Cavarra, A., & Riccobene, E. (2000). An ASM Semantics for UML Activity Diagrams. In T. Rus (Ed.), *Proceedings AMAST 2000* (LNCS 1816, pp. 293-308). Heidelberg: Springer-Verlag.

Boronat, A., & Meseguer, J. (2007). *Algebraic semantics of EMOF/OCL metamodels* (Technical Report UIUCDCS-R-2007-2904, CS Dept., University of Illinois at Urbana-Champaign). Retrieved on July 20, 2009 from https://www.ideals.uiuc.edu/handle/2142/11398

Boronat, A., & Messeger, J. (2008). An algebraic semantics for MOF. In J. Fiadiero & P. Inverardi (Eds.), *FASE 2008* (LNCS 4961, pp. 377- 391). Heilderberg: Springer-Verlag.

Bruel, J., & France, R. (1998). *Transforming UML Models to Formal Specifications*. CiteSearX. Retrieved on July, 20 from http://www.oblog.pt/Download/P7.ps

Büttner, F., & Gogolla, M. (2004). Realizing UML Metamodel Transformations with AGG. In: R. Heckel (Ed.). In *Proceedings of ETAPS Workshop Graph Transformation and Visual Modeling Techniques (GT-VMT 2004)*. Retrieved on July 20, 2009 from wwwcs.uni-paderborn.de/cs/ag-engels/GT-VMT04.

Cardelli, L., & Wegner, P. (1985). On understanding Types, Data Abstraction and Polymorphism. *ACM Computing Surveys, 17*(4), 471–522. doi:10.1145/6041.6042

CASE. (2009). *CASE Tools*. Retrieved on July 20, 2009 from www.objectsbydesign.com/tools/umltools_by-Company.html

CWM. (2003). *Common Warehouse Metamodel, v. 1.1 formal/2003-03-02*. Retrieved on July 20, 2009 from www.omg.org/spec/cwm

Czarnecki, K., & Helsen, S. (2003). Classification of Model Transformation Approaches. In J. Bettin et al. (Eds), *Proceedings of OOSPLA 2003 Workshop on Generative Techniques in the Context of Model-Driven Architecture*. Retrieved on July 20, 2009 from www.swen.uwaterloo.ca/~kczarnec/ECE750T7/czarnecki_helsen.pdf

Eclipse (2009). *The eclipse modeling framework*. Retrieved from July 20, 2009 from http://www.eclipse.org/emf/

Favre, L. (2001). A Formal Mapping between UML Static Models and Algebraic Specifications. Lecture Notes in Informatics (p. 7) Evans, A. France, R., Moreira, A., & Rumpe, B.(Eds) SEW Practical UML-Based Rigorous Development Methods- Countering or Integrating the eXtremists. (pp. 113 - 127) Bonn: GI Edition, Bonner Kollen-Verlag.

Favre, L. (Ed.). (2003). *UML and the Unified Process*. Hershey, PA: IRM Press.

Favre, L. (2005). Foundations for MDA-based Forward Engineering. *Journal of Object Technology (JOT), 4*(1), 129-153). Retrieved on July 20, 2009 from www.jot.fm

Favre, L. (2006). A Rigorous Framework for Model Driven Development. In K. Siau (Ed.), *Advanced Topics in Database Research, Vol. 5* (pp. 1-27). Hershey, PA: Idea Group Publishing.

Favre, L. (2009) A Formal Foundation for Metamodeling (LNCS 5570, pp. 177-191). Heilderberg: Springer-Verlag. France, R., Bruel, J., & Larrondo-Petrie, M. (1997). An Integrated Object-Oriented and Formal Modeling Environment. *JOOP*, November-December.

France, R., Evans, A., Lano, K., & Rumpe, B. (1998). The UML as a Formal Modeling Notation. *Computer Standards & Interfaces, 19*(7), 325–334. doi:10.1016/S0920-5489(98)00020-8

France, R., Bruel, J., & Larrondo-Petrie, M. (1997). An Integrated Object-Oriented and Formal Modeling Environment", JOOP, November-December.

Gerber, A., Lawley, M., & Raymond, K. Steel, J., & Wood, A. (2002) Transformation: The Missing Link of MDA. In *Proceedings of Graph Transformation- First International Conference, ICCT 2002* (LNCS 2505, pp. 90-105). Heidelberg: Springer-Verlag.

Gogolla, M., Bohling, J., & Richters, M. (2005). Validating UML and OCL Models in USE by Automatic Snapshot Generation. *Journal on Software and System Modeling, 4*(4), 386–398. doi:10.1007/s10270-005-0089-y

Gogolla, M., & Henderson-Sellers, B. (2002). Formal Analysis of UML Stereotypes within the UML Metamodel. In *Proceedings of <<UML>> 2002, 5th Int.Conf. Unified Modeling Language* (LNCS 2460, pp. 84-92). Heidelberg: Springer-Verlag

Gogolla, M., & Richters, M. (1998). On Constraints and Queries in UML. *The Unified Modeling Language – Technical Aspects and Applications, Physica-Verlag.* Retrieved on July 20, 2009 from http://www.db.informatik.uni-bremen.de/publications/Gogolla_1997_UMLWS.ps

Haussmann, J. (2003). Relations-Relating metamodels. In A. Evans, P. Sammut, & J. Williams (Eds.), *Proceedings of Metamodeling for MDA. First International Workshop York, UK* (pp. 147-161).

Joualt, F., & Kurtev, I. (2006). On the Architectural Alignment of ATL and QVT. In *Proceedings of 2006 ACM Symposium on Applied Computing (SAC 2006) Chapter Model Transformation* (pp. 1188- 1195). ACM.

Kaufman, M., & Moore, J. S. (2009). *ACL2 version 3.5.* Retrieved on July 20, 2009 from http://www.cs.utexas.edu/~moore/acl2/

Kim, S., & Carrington, D. (1999). Formalizing the UML Class Diagram using OBJECT-Z. In *Proceedings of UML 99* (LNCS 1723, pp. 83-98). Heidelberg: Springer-Verlag.

Kim, S., & Carrington, D. (2002). A Formal Model of the UML Metamodel: The UML State Machine and Its Integrity Constraints (LNCS 2272, pp. 477- 496). Heidelberg: Springer-Verlag.

Kuske, S., Gogolla, M., Kollmann, R., & Kreowski, H. (2002). An Integrated Semantics for UML Class, Object and State Diagrams based on Graph Transformation. In *Proceedings 3rd Int. Conf. Integrated Formal Methods (IFM 02)*. Heidelberg: Springer-Verlag.

Kuster, J., Sendall, S., & Wahler, M. (2004). Comparing Two Model Transformation Approaches. In J. Bezivin et al (Eds.), *Proceedings of OCL and Model Driven Engineering Workshop. Lisboa, Portugal.* Retrieved on July 20, 2009 from http://www.cs.kent.ac.uk/projects/ocl/oclmdewsuml04/

Lano, K. (1991). *Z++, An Object-Oriented Extension to Z. Z User Workshop* (pp. 151-172). Heidelberg: Springer.

Leavens, G. (1996). An Overview of Larch/C++: Behavioral Specification for C++ Modules. *Specification of Behavioral Semantics in Object-Oriented Information Modeling* (pp. 121-142). Kluwer Academic Publishers.

Leavens, G., Poll, E., Clifton, C., Cheon, Y., & Ruby, C. (2002). *JML Reference.* Manual Draft Revision 1.1. Retrieved on July 20, 2009 from www.cs.iastate.edu/~leavens

Liu, H., & Strother Moore, J. (2004). Java Program verification via JVM Deep Embedding in ACL2. Lecture Notes in Computer Science 3223 (pp.184 - 200). Heildelberg: Springer-Verlag.

McUmber, W., & Cheng, B. (2001). A General Framework for Formalizing UML with Formal Languages. In *Proceedings of the IEEE International Conference on Software Engineering (ICSE01).*

Mens, T., Van Gorp, P., Varró, D., & Karsai, G. (2006). Applying a Model Transformation Taxonomy to Graph Transformation Technology. *Electronic Notes in Theoretical Computer Science, 152,* 143–159. doi:10.1016/j.entcs.2005.10.022

MOF. (2002). *Meta Object Facility (MOF) Specification version 1.4*. Document formal/01-11-02. Retrieved on July 20, 2009 from www.omg.org

OCL. (2006). *OCL: Object Constraint Language. Version 2.0*. OMG: formal/06-05-01.Retrieved on July 20, 2009 from www.omg.org

Overgaard, G. (1998). A Formal Approach to Relationships in the Unified Modeling Language. In *Proceedings of Workshop on Precise Semantic of Modeling Notations, International Conference on Software Engineering, ICSE 98, Japan*. Retrieved on July 20, 2009 from http://www.it.kth.se/~gunnaro/pub/psmt98.rev.ps

Paige, R., Kaminskaya, L., & Ostroff, J. (2002). BON-CASE: An Extensible CASE Tool for Formal Specification and Reasoning. *Journal of Object Technology (JOT) 1*(3), 77-96. Retrieved on July 20, 2009 from www.jot.fm

Poernomo, I. (2006). The meta-Object facility Typed. In *Proceedings of the 2006 ACM Symposium on Applied Computing (SAC)* (pp. 1845-1849). Dijon, France. ACM.

QVT. (2008). *QVT: MOF 2.0 Query, View, Transformation*. Formal/2008-04-03. Retrieved on July 20, 2009 from www.omg.org

Rapanotti, L., & Socorro, A. (1992). *Introducing FOOPS*. Report PRG-TR-28-92, Programming Research Group, Oxford University Computing Laboratory.

Reggio, G., Cerioli, M., & Astesiano, E. (2001). Towards a Rigorous Semantics of UML Supporting its Multiview Approach. In *Proceedings of Fundamental Approaches to Software Engineering (FASE 2001)* (LNCS 2029, pp. 171-186). Heidelberg: Springer-Verlag.

Rozenberg, G. (Ed.). (1997). *Handbook of Graph Grammars and Computing by Graph Transformation* (Vol. 1). World Scientific.

Siau, S., & Halpin, T. (Eds.). (2001). *Unified Modeling Language: Systems, Analysis, Design and Development Issues*. Hershey, PA: Idea Group Publishing.

Smith, G. (2000). The Object-Z Specification Language. *Advances in Formal Methods*. Kluwer Academic Publishers.

Snook, C., & Butler, M. (2002). *Tool-Supported Use of UML for Constructing B Specifications*. Technical Report, Department of Electronics and Computer Science, University of Southampton, United Kingdom.

Taentzer, G. (2004) AGG: A Graph Transformation Environment for Modeling and Validation of Software. In *Proceedings of Applications of Graph Transformations with Industrial relevance (AGTIVE)* (LNCS 3062, pp. 446-453). Heidelberg: Springer-Verlag.

Chapter 5
MOF–Metamodels and Formal Languages

A BRIDGE BETWEEN MOF-METAMODELS AND NEREUS

This chapter describes how to automatically translate MOF metamodels into NEREUS (Favre, 2005) (Favre, Martinez, & Pereira, 2005). We describe a bridge between MOF metamodels and NEREUS based on reusable schemes and a system of transformation rules. We consider MOF metamodels that are expressed by UML class diagrams, packages diagrams and OCL specifications.

The text of a NEREUS specification is completed gradually. Figure 1 shows the main steps of this transformation. First, the signature and axioms are obtained by instantiating the reusable scheme BOX_. Next, associations are transformed by instantiating reusable schemes that exist in the component Association. Finally, OCL specifications are transformed using a set of transformation rules. Then, a specification that reflects all the information of UML diagrams is constructed.

Following we describe the transformation of a basic package (that does not depend on others) including only classes and relationships. Following sections describe how to transform basic classes and associations. The transformation processes is supported by reusable schemes and a system of transformation rules for translating OCL specifications into NEREUS.

DOI: 10.4018/978-1-61520-649-0.ch005

Figure 1. Transforming MOF metamodels into NEREUS

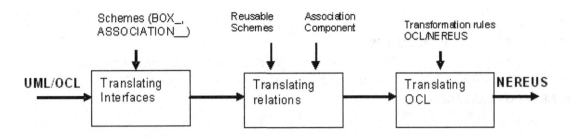

Figure 2 depicts the different ways in which a class A may be related in a MOF metamodel: generalization, dependency, aggregation, composition and binary associations. Figure 2 shows in an only box several relations, for instance, the class A is associated with the classes D1, D2, ..D_k or is composed by the classes C_1, C_2,...C_k. It can be transformed in part of a NEREUS specification by instantiating the following scheme Class_:

```
CLASS __
IMPORTS F1, F2,.., Fk
INHERITS B1, B2,...Bk
Box_ [...:attr1;...:attri;...:meth1;..:methi,..]
ASSOCIATES <<Aggregation-E1>>
ASSOCIATES <<Aggregation-E2>> …
ASSOCIATES <<Composition-C1>>
ASSOCIATES <<Composition-C2>>...
ASSOCIATES <<Association-D1>>
ASSOCIATES <<Association-D2>>
AXIOMSEND-CLASS
```

Figure 2. MOF relationships

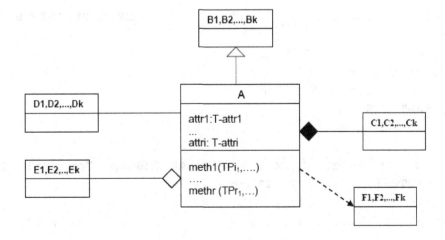

CLASS__ refers to other scheme called BOX_:

CLASS Box_
IMPORTS TP$_1$ ..,TP$_m$**INHERITS**
Cartes-Prod [T-attr$_1$: T1; T- attr$_2$: T2;..; get-1: select-1 ;
get-2:select-2,..., set-1:modif-1,..., set-n: modif-n]
DEFERREDOPERATIONS
meth$_1$:Box_ x TPi$_1$ x TPi$_2$ x .....TPi$_n$→TPi$_j$
....
meth$_r$: Box_ x TPr$_1$ xTPr$_2$.....x TPr$_p$→ TPr$_k$
END-CLASS

The Box_ scheme refines the following scheme CartesProd:

CLASS Cartes-Prod_
IMPORTS T1,...,Tn
EFFECTIVETYPES
Cartes-Prod
OPERATIONS
create: T1 x ... x Tn→ Cartes-Prod
modif-i: Cartes-Prod x Ti → Cartes-Prod
select-i: Cartes-Prod → Ti 1 ≤ i ≤ n
AXIOMS cp: Cartes-Prod; t1: T1; ti, ti´:Ti...tn:Tn
select-i (create (t1, t2,..., tn)) = ti
modif-i(create (t1, t2,....tn),ti´) = create(t1, t2,.., ti´,.. tn) 1
≤ i ≤ n
END-CLASS

Flattening the class CartesProd in the scheme BOX_ results the following Box_ scheme:

CLASS Box_
IMPORTS TP1,.., TPm, T-attr$_1$, T-attr$_{2,...,}$ T-attr$_n$**EFFECTIVETYPES** Box_
OPERATIONS
create_: T-attr$_1$ x ... x T-attr$_n$→ Box_
set-i: Box_ x T-attr$_i$→ Box_
get-i: Box_ → T-attr$_i$ 1 ≤ i ≤ n
DEFERREDOPERATIONS
meth$_1$: Box_ x TPi$_1$ x TPi$_2$ x .....TPi$_n$→TPi$_j$
...
*meth$_r$: Box_ x TPr$_1$ xTPr$_2$.....x TPr$_p$→ TPr$_k$***AXIOMS cp: Box_; t1: T-ATTR1;**
ti, ti´: T-ATTR-i,...,tn: T-ATTR-n
get-i (create_(t1,t2,...,tn)) = ti
set-i(create_(t1,t2,....tn),ti´) = create(t1,t2,..,ti´,..tn) 1 ≤ i ≤
n

END-CLASS

The mapping of attributes requires two operations: an access operation and a modifier. The access operation takes no arguments and returns the object to which the receiver is mapped to. The modifier takes no argument and changes the mapping of the receiver to that argument. In NEREUS no standard convention exists, but frequently we use names such as get_ and set_ for them.

In the instantiation, the underscore _ is followed by the name of the sort of interest.

TRANSFORMATION OF ASSOCIATIONS

Association specification is constructed by instantiating the scheme ASSOCIATION_:

ASSOCIATION __IS __[_:Class1; _: Class2; _: Role1; _: Role2; _: Mult1; _: Mult2; _: Visibility1; _: Visibility2]
CONSTRAINED BY __END

Besides, the specification of the association is generated by instantiating the respective scheme in the hierarchy of binary associations (Chapter 4 Figure 3).

TRANSFORMATION OF OCL SPECIFICATION INTO NEREUS

In the context of MOF metamodels, OCL can appear linked to class invariants, pre-and post-conditions of operations, attribute constraints and association constraints.

Analyzing OCL specifications we can derive axioms that will be included in the NEREUS specifications. Preconditions written in OCL are used to generate preconditions in NEREUS. Postconditions and invariants allow generating axioms in NEREUS.

An operation can be specified in OCL by means of preconditions and postconditions by the following syntax:

Typename:: OperationName (parameter1:Type1,...): ReturnTypepre:_
some expression of self and parameter1
post: Result = _ some function of self and parameter1

self can be used in the expression to refer to the object on which an operation was called, and the name Result is the name of the returned object, if there is any. The names of the parameter (parameter1,...) can also be used in the expression.

The value of a property in a postcondition is the value upon completion of the operation. To refer to the value of a property at the start of the operation, the property name has to postfix with "@" followed by the keyword "pre".

Other predefined constraints can appear: changeable, addOnly and frozen in attributes and, ordered, changeable, addOnly, frozen, xor and subset in associations.

Table 1. Rules for transforming operation signature

OCL NEREUS
Type -> operationName (paramater1: Type1, parameter2: Type2,...): ReturnType operationName: Type x Type1 x. Type2 x ...-> ReturnType
Type::operationName (parameter1: Type1, parameter2: Type2,...): ReturnType operationName: Type x Type1 x Type2 X ...-> ReturnType collection -> operationName (expr: OCLBooleanExpr, parameter1: Type1,...): ReturnType operationName: Collection x (*Elem* -> Boolean) x Type1 x ...-> ReturnType
collection -> operationName (expr: OCLExprType, parameter1: Type1,...): ReturnType operationName: Collection x (*Elem* -> Type) x Type1 x ...-> ReturnType
collection -> operationName (expr: OCLExprType, parameter1: Type1,...): ReturnType operationName: Collection x (*Elem* -> Type) x Type1 x ...-> ReturnType

The following section describes how to integrate OCL with NEREUS by using a system of transformation rules

From OCL to NEREUS

The OCL basic types Boolean, Integer, Real and String are associated with NEREUS basic types with the same name. Like OCL, NEREUS provides enumeration types that are aligned to the OCL semantics. NEREUS provides classes for collection type hierarchies. The types Set, Bag and Sequence are subtypes of Collection(x). Collection(Type1) conforms to Collection(Type2) when Type1 conforms to Type2. This is also true for Set(Type1), Bag(Type1) and Sequence(Type1), each one with Collection(Type2). Type1 conforms to Type2 both, when they are identical or Type1 is subtype of Type2.

The transformation process of OCL specifications to NEREUS is supported by a system of transformation rules. By analyzing OCL specifications we can derive axioms that will be included in the NEREUS specifications. Preconditions written in OCL are used to generate preconditions in NEREUS.

Table 2. Rules for transforming operation body

OCL NEREUS
v. operationName (parameters) operationName (*Translate*$_{NEREUS}$ (v),*Translate*$_{NEREUS}$ (parameters))
self.operationName (parameters) operationName (c, *Translate*$_{NEREUS}$ *(parameters)*) *with* [c| ->*self*]
Type::operationName (parameters): ReturnType operationName = expression operationName (c, *Translate*$_{NEREUS}$ (parameters)) = *Translate*$_{NEREUS}$(expression)) *with [c|->self]*
V -> operationName (parameters) operationName (*Translate*$_{NEREUS}$ (v), *Translate*$_{NEREUS}$ (parameters))

Table 3. Attribute rule

OCL NEREUS
v.attributeName attributeName (v)

Table 4. Role rule

OCL NEREUS
context AssociationName object.roleName **AXIOMS** a: AssociationName get_roleName (a, object) *with [a | ->Assoc]*

Postconditions and invariants allow us to generate axioms in NEREUS. We define a system of transformation rules that only considers expressions based on Essential OCL. The following metaclasses defined in complete OCL are not part of the EssentialOCL: MessageType, StateExp, ElementType, AssociationClassCallExp, MessageExp, and UnspecifiedValueExp. Any well-formed rules defined for these classes are consequently not part of the definition of the transformation rule system.

The following tables show some rules for translating OCL expressions into NEREUS. Each rule is a pair of an OCL expression (the shaded expression at the top) and a NEREUS expression. An introduction to OCL constructs and the transformation rule system may be found at Appendix-C.

The system includes a small set with around fifty rules. It was built by means of an iterative approach through successive refinements. The set of rules was validated by analyzing the different OCL expression attached to the UML metamodels (UMLa, 2007) (UMLb, 2007), MOF (MOF, 2006) and QVT (QVT, 2007).

EXAMPLE 5-1: CLASS DIAGRAM SPECIFIED IN OCL

Figure 3 shows a simple class diagram P&M. It introduces two classes (Person and Meeting) and a bidirectional association between them (Participates). We have meetings in which persons may participate. This example was analyzed in (Hussmann, Cerioli, Reggio and Tort, 1999), (Padawitz, 2000), and (Favre, 2005). Although this package is a model at M2 level, it shows the main problem in the translation process and is self-contained.

The following OCL constraints are attached to the diagram P&M (Figure 3):

```
context Meeting::checkDate (): Bool
post: result = self.participants -> collect (meetings) ->
forAll (m | m<> self and m.isConfirmed implies
(after (self.end, m.start) or after (m.end,self.start)))
```

Table 5. Rules for basic OCL expressions

OCL NEREUS
Expression.operationName operationName (*Translate*$_{Nereus}$ (expression))
Expression1 binaryOperator expression2 *Translate*$_{Nereus}$ (expression1)*Translate*$_{Nereus}$ (binaryOperator) *Translate*$_{Nereus}$ (expression2) *Translate*$_{Nereus}$ (binaryOperator) (*Translate*$_{Nereus}$ (expression1), *Translate*$_{Nereus}$(expression2))
unaryOperator expression *Translate*$_{Nereus}$ (unaryOperator) *Translate*$_{Nereus}$ (expression)
if booleanExpression **then** expression1 **else** expression2 **endif** **IF***Translate*$_{Nereus}$ (booleanExpression) **THEN***Translate*$_{Nereus}$ (expression1) **ELSE***Translate*$_{Nereus}$(expression2)
let v: Type = expression1 **in** expression2-with-v **LET** v =*Translate*$_{Nereus}$ (expression1) **IN** *Translate*$_{Nereus}$ (expression2-with -v) **END-LET** *Translate*$_{Nereus}$(expression2-with -v) **WHERE** v =*Translate*$_{Nereus}$ (expression1) **END-WHERE**

```
context Meeting::isConfirmed ()
post: result = self.checkdate () and self.numConfirmedParticipants
>= 2


context Person::numMeeting (): Nat
post: result = self.meetings -> size


context Person::numConfirmedMeeting (): Nat
post: result = self.meetings -> select (isConfirmed) -> size


context Meeting::isConfirmed (): Bool
post: result = self.checkdate () and self.numConfirmedParticipants
>= 2


context Meeting::duration (): Time
post: result = timeDifference (self.end, self.start)


context Meeting:: checkDate():Bool
post: result = self.participants-> collect(meetings) ->
```

Table 6. Rules for transforming forAll and exist operations

OCL
NEREUS
Collection -> operationName (v:Element| boolean-expr-with-v)   operationName::= forAll | exists   **OPERATIONS**   operationName: Collection x (Element -> Boolean) -> Boolean   **AXIOMS**   …   **LET**   **OPERATIONS**   f: Element -> Boolean   **AXIOMS v: Element**   f (v)= *Translate* _{NEREUS} (boolean-expr-with-v)   **IN**   operationName (collection, f)   **END-LET**   Collection -> operationName (v:Element| boolean-expr-with-v)   operationName::= forAll | exists   operationName (collection, f)   **WHERE**   **OPERATIONS**   f: Element -> Boolean   **AXIOMS v: Element**   f (v)= *Translate* _{NEREUS} (boolean-expr-with-v)   **END-WHERE**   Collection -> operationName (v:Element| boolean-expr-with-v)   operationName::= forAll | exists   *Shorthand notation*   operationName (v) (collection, [f (v)])
Collection -> operationName (v |boolean-expr-with-v)   operationName::= forAll | exists   *Collection [Element]*   **OPERATIONS**   operationName: Collection x (Element-> Boolean) -> Boolean   **AXIOMS…**   **LET**   **OPERATIONS**   f: Element -> Boolean   **AXIOMS v: Element**   f (v)= *Translate* _{NEREUS} (boolean-expr-with-v)   **IN**   operationName (collection, f)   **END-LET**   Collection -> operationName (v |boolean-expr-with-v)   operationName::= forAll | exists   *Collection [Element]*   operationName (collection, f)   **WHERE**   **OPERATIONS**   f: Element -> Boolean   **AXIOMS v: Element**   f(v)= *Translate* _{NEREUS} (boolean-expr-with-v)   **END-WHERE**   Collection -> operationName (v |boolean-expr-with-v)   operationName::= forAll | exists   *Collection [Element]*   *Shorthand notation*   operationName (v) (collection, [f (v)])

continued on following page

Table 6. continued

Collection -> operationName (v |boolean-expr-with-v)
operationName::= forAll │ exists
Collection [Element]
OPERATIONS
operationName: Collection x (Element-> Boolean) -> Boolean
AXIOMS...
LET
OPERATIONS
f: Element -> Boolean
AXIOMS v: Element
f (v)= *Translate $_{NEREUS}$* (boolean-expr-with-v)
IN
operationName (collection, f)
END-LET
Collection -> operationName (v |boolean-expr-with-v)
operationName::= forAll │ exists
Collection [Element]
operationName (collection, f)
WHERE
OPERATIONS
f: Element -> Boolean
AXIOMS v: Element
f(v)= *Translate $_{NEREUS}$* (boolean-expr-with-v)
END-WHERE
Collection -> operationName (v |boolean-expr-with-v)
operationName::= forAll │ exists
Collection [Element]
Shorthand notation
operationName (v) (collection, [f (v)])

Collection -> operationName (v |boolean-expr)
operationName::= forAll │ exists
Collection [Element]
OPERATIONS
operationName: Collection x (Element-> Boolean)-> Boolean
AXIOMS...
LET
OPERATIONS
f: Element -> Boolean
AXIOMS v: Elem
f(v)= *Translate $_{NEREUS}$* (boolean-expr)
IN
operationName (collection, f)
END-LET
Collection -> operationName (v |boolean-expr)
operationName::= forAll │ exists
Collection [Element]
operationName (collection, f)
WHERE
OPERATIONS
f: Element -> Boolean
AXIOMS v: Elem
f (v)= *Translate $_{NEREUS}$* (boolean-expr)
END-WHERE
Collection -> operationName (v |boolean-expr)
operationName::= forAll │ exists
Collection [Element]
Shorthand notation
operationName (v) (collection, [f (v)])

Table 7. Rules for collection operations (select, reject, collect, iterate)

OCL
NEREUS
Collection -> operationName (v: Element | boolean-expr-with-v) operationName::= select | reject **OPERATIONS** operationName: Collection x (Element -> Boolean) -> Collection **AXIOMS** **LET OPERATIONS** f: Element -> Boolean **AXIOMS v: Element** f (v)= *Translate$_{NEREUS}$* (boolean-expr-with-v) **IN** operationName (collection, f) **END-LET** Collection -> operationName (v: Element | boolean-expr-with-v) operationName::= select | reject operationName (collection, f) **WHERE** **OPERATIONS** f: Element -> Boolean **AXIOMS v: Element** f (v)= *Translate$_{NEREUS}$* (boolean-expr-with-v) **END-WHERE** Collection -> operationName (v: Element | boolean-expr-with-v) operationName::= select | reject *Shorthand notation* operationName (v) (collection, [f (v)])
Collection -> collect (v: Element | expression-with-v) *Let Type(expression-with-v) be S* **OPERATIONS** collect: Collection x (Element ->Boolean) -> Collection **AXIOMS** **LET** **OPERATIONS** f: Element -> S **AXIOMS v: Element** f (v)= *Translate $_{NEREUS}$* (expr-with-v) **IN** collect (collection, f) **END-LET** Collection -> collect (v: Element | expression-with-v) *Let Type(expression-with-v) be S* collect (collection, f) **WHERE** **OPERATIONS** f: Element -> S **AXIOMS v: Element** f (v)= *Translate NEREUS* (expr-with-v) **END-WHERE** Collection -> collect (v: Element | expression-with-v) *Let Type(expression-with-v) be S* *Shorthand notation* Collect (v) (collection, [f (v)])

continued on following page

Table 7. continued

```
collection -> iterate (v: Element; acc: Type = exp |
expression-with-v-and-acc)
OPERATIONS
iterate: Collection x (Element x Acc: ANY) x -> Acc) -> Acc
AXIOMS
LET
OPERATIONS
f: Element x Type -> Type
base: -> Type
AXIOMS v: Element; acc: Type
f (v, acc)=Translate_NEREUS(expr-with-v-and-acc)
base = Translate_NEREUS (exp)
IN
iterate (collection, f, base)
END-LET
collection -> iterate (v: Element; acc: Type = exp |
expression-with-v-and-acc)
iterate (collection, f, base)
WHERE
OPERATIONS
f: Element x Type -> Type
base: -> Type
AXIOMS v: Element; acc: Type
f (v, acc)=Translate_NEREUS (expr-with-v-and-acc)
base = Translate_NEREUS (exp)
END-WHERE
```

Table 8. Precondition Rule

OCL
NEREUS
Type::operationName (par1: Type1,…): ReturnType
pre: expression-with-self - or-attribute-or--par1..pari
operationName: Type (t) x Type1(t1) x...x TypeI (ti)-> ReturnType
pre: *Translate_NEREUS* (expression-with-self -or-attribute-or--par1..pari)
with [self| -> t; attribute| -> attribute(t); par1| ->t1;...pari| ->ti]

```
forAll (m1 | m1<> self and m1.isConfirmed implies
(after (self.end, m1.start) or after(m1.end, self.start)))
```

We can built a specification of the diagram of Figure 3 by instantiating the scheme BOX_ and the scheme ASSOCIATION_ and, applying rules of the transformation system . The classes Person and Meeting are built by instantiating the BOX_ scheme.

Next, we show the partial specification in NEREUS of the classes Person and Meeting.

```
CLASS Person
IMPORTS String, Nat
INHERITS Box_ Person [Box_Person: Person]
```

Table 9. Rules for transforming postconditions

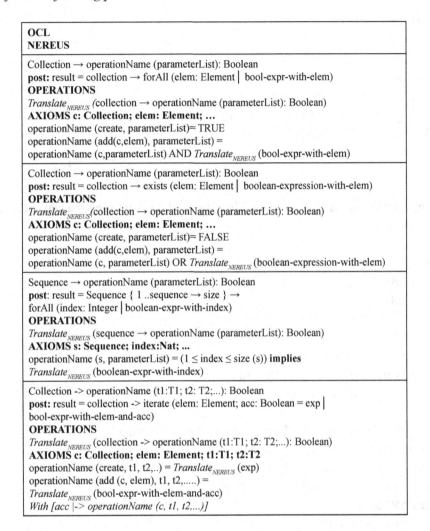

OCL NEREUS
Collection → operationName (parameterList): Boolean **post:** result = collection → forAll (elem: Element | bool-expr-with-elem) **OPERATIONS** *Translate$_{NEREUS}$* (collection → operationName (parameterList): Boolean) **AXIOMS c: Collection; elem: Element; …** operationName (create, parameterList)= TRUE operationName (add(c,elem), parameterList) = operationName (c,parameterList) AND *Translate$_{NEREUS}$* (bool-expr-with-elem)
Collection → operationName (parameterList): Boolean **post:** result = collection → exists (elem: Element | boolean-expression-with-elem) **OPERATIONS** *Translate$_{NEREUS}$*(collection → operationName (parameterList): Boolean) **AXIOMS c: Collection; elem: Element; …** operationName (create, parameterList)= FALSE operationName (add(c,elem), parameterList) = operationName (c, parameterList) OR *Translate$_{NEREUS}$* (boolean-expression-with-elem)
Sequence → operationName (parameterList): Boolean **post:** result = Sequence { 1 ..sequence → size } → forAll (index: Integer | boolean-expr-with-index) **OPERATIONS** *Translate$_{NEREUS}$* (sequence → operationName (parameterList): Boolean) **AXIOMS s: Sequence; index:Nat; …** operationName (s, parameterList) = (1 ≤ index ≤ size (s)) **implies** *Translate$_{NEREUS}$* (boolean-expr-with-index)
Collection -> operationName (t1:T1; t2: T2;...): Boolean **post:** result = collection -> iterate (elem: Element; acc: Boolean = exp | bool-expr-with-elem-and-acc) **OPERATIONS** *Translate$_{NEREUS}$* (collection -> operationName (t1:T1; t2: T2;...): Boolean) **AXIOMS c: Collection; elem: Element; t1:T1; t2:T2** operationName (create, t1, t2,..) = *Translate$_{NEREUS}$* (exp) operationName (add (c, elem), t1, t2,.....) = *Translate$_{NEREUS}$* (bool-expr-with-elem-and-acc) *With [acc |-> operationName (c, t1, t2,...)]*

Figure 3. P&M Class Diagram

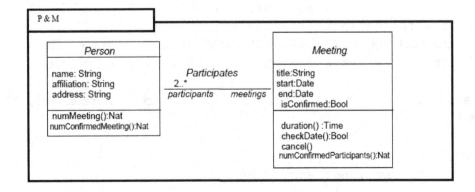

ASSOCIATES
<<Participates>>
END-CLASS

CLASS Meeting
IMPORTS String, Date, Boolean, Time
INHERITS Box_ Meeting [Box_Meeting: Meeting]
ASSOCIATES <<Participates>>
AXIOMS
END-CLASS

The following specifications of Person and Meeting result by flattening the classes Box_Person and Box_Meeting respectively.

CLASS Person
IMPORTS Nat, String
EFFECTIVETYPES
Person
ATTRIBUTES
get_name: Person → String
get_affiliation: Person → String
get_address: Person → String
OPERATIONS
createPerson: String x String x String → Person
set_name: Person x String → Person
set_affiliation: Person x String → Person
set_address: Person x String → Person
DEFERREDOPERATIONS
numMeeting: Person → Nat
numConfirmedMeeting: Person → Nat
AXIOMS cp: Person; t1, t2, t3, tp1, tp2, tp3: String
get_name (createPerson (t1, t2, t3)) = t1
get_affiliation (createPerson (t1, t2, t3)) = t2
get_address (createPerson (t1, t2, t3)) = t3
set_name (createPerson (t1, t2, t3), tp2) = createPerson (tp1, t2, t3)
set_affiliation (createPerson (t1, t2, t3), tp2) = createPerson (t1, tp2, t3)
set_address (createPerson (t1, t2, t3), tp3) = createPerson (t1, t2, tp3)
END-CLASS

CLASS Meeting
IMPORTS String, Date, Boolean, Time

```
EFFECTIVETYPES Meeting
GENERATED-BY createMeeting
OPERATIONS
createMeeting: String x Date x Date x Boolean -> Meeting
title: Meeting -> String
start: Meeting -> Date
end: Meeting -> Date
isConfirmed: Meeting -> Boolean
set_title: Meeting x String -> Meeting
set_start: Meeting x Date -> Meeting
set_end: Meeting x Date -> Meeting
set_isConfirmed: Meeting x Boolean -> Boolean
AXIOMS s: String; d, d1: Date; b: Boolean; …
title (createMeeting (s, d, d1, b)) = s
start (createMeeting (s, d, d1, b)) = d
end (createMeeting (s, d, d1, b)) = d1
isConfirmed (createMeeting (s, d, d1, b)) = b
...
END-CLASS
```

The association Participates can be built by instantiating the scheme ASSOCIATION_:

```
ASSOCIATION Participates
IS Bidirectional-Set [Person: Class1; Meeting: Class2; participants:
role1; meetings: role2; *: mult1; *: mult2; +: visibility1; +: vis-
ibility2]
END
```

The Association Participates refers to Bidirectional-Set, a scheme belonging to the reusable component Association:

```
RELATION SCHEME Bidirectional-Set
-- Bidirectional /* to */ as Set
IS-SUBTYPE-OF BinaryAssociation [Person: Class1; Meeting: Class2]
IMPORTS Set_Person: Set [Person], Set_Meeting: Set [Meeting]
GENERATED-BY create, addLink
name, frozen, changeable, addOnly, getRole1, getRole2,
getMult1,getMult2, getVisibility1, getVisibility2, isRelated, isEmp-
ty, rightCardinality, leftCardinality
EFFECTIVEOPERATIONS create: Typename -> Participates
addLink:Participates (b) x Person (p) x Meeting (m)-> Participates
 pre: not isRelated (a, p, m)
```

```
isRightLinked: Participates x Person -> Boolean
isLeftLinked: Participates x Meeting -> Boolean
getMeetings: Participates (a) x Person (p) -> Set_Meeting
 pre: isRightLinked (a, p)
getParticipants: Participates (a) x Meeting (m)-> Set_Person
 pre: isLeftLinked (a, m)
remove: Participates (a) x Person (p) x Meeting (m) -> Participates
 pre: isRelated (a, p, m)
```

AXIOMS a: Participates; p, p1: Person; m, m1: Meeting; t: TypeName

```
Name (create (t)) = t
Name (add (a, p, m)) = name (a)
isEmpty (create (t))= True
isEmpty (addLink (a, p, m)) = False
frozen (a) = False
changeable (a) = True
addOnly (a) = False
getRole1 (a) = " participants"
getRole2 (a) = "meetings"
getMult1 (a) = *
getMult2 (a) = *
getVisibility1 (a) = +
getVisibility2 (a) = +
isRelated (create (t), p, m) = False
isRelated (addLink (a, p, m), p1, m1) =
(p = p1 and m = m1) or isRelated (a, p1, m1)
isRightLinked (create (t), p) = False
isRightLinked (addLink (a, p, m), p1) =
if p = p1 then True else isRightLinked (a, p1)
isLeftLinked (create (t), m) = False
isLeftLinked (addLink (a, p, m), m1) =
if m = m1 then True else isLeftLinked (a, m1)
rightCardinality (create (t), p) = 0
rightCardinality (addLink (a, p, m), p1) =
if p = p1 then 1 + rightCardinality (a, p1) else rightCardinality
(a, p1)
leftCardinality (create (t), m) = 0
leftCardinality (addLink (a, p, m), m1) =
if m = m1 then 1+ leftCardinality (a, m1) else leftCardinality (a,
m1)
getMeetings (addLink (a, p, m), p1) =
if p = p1 then including (getMeetings (a, p1), m) else getMeetings
(a, p1)
```

```
getParticipants (addLink (a, p, m), m1) =
if m = m1 then including (getParticipants (a, m1), m)
   else getParticipants (a, m1)
remove (addLink (a, p, m), p1, m1) =
if (p = p1 and m = m1) then a else remove (a, p1, m1)
```
END-RELATION

Next, we show the specifications of Person and Meeting constructed by using the system of transformation rules. In this transformation the main rules used are shown in Table 10.

CLASS Person
IMPORTS String, Nat
ASSOCIATES <<Participates>>
GENERATED-BY create_Person
. . .
AXIOMS p: Person; s, sp: String; Pa: Participates
name (create_Person (s)) = s
set-name (create_Person (s), sp) = create_Person (sp)
numConfirmedMeetings (p) =
size (select (m) (getMeetings (Pa, p), [isConfirmed (m)]) **--Rules 1, 2**
numMeetings (p) = size (getMeetings (Pa, p)) **--Rule 1**
END-CLASS

CLASS Meeting
IMPORTS String, Date, Boolean, Time
ASSOCIATES <<Participates>>
GENERATED-BY create_Meeting
AXIOMS m, m1: Meeting; s, sp: String; d, dp, d1, d1p: Date; b, bp:

Table 10. Transformation rules

RULE	OCL NEREUS
1	$T \rightarrow$ operationName (parameterList): returnType **post**: expression **OPERATIONS** $Translate_{NEREUS}$ ($T \rightarrow$ operationName (parameterList): returnType) **AXIOMS** $Translate_{NEREUS}$ (expression)
2	T-> operationName (v:Type | bool-expr-with-v) OperationName::= forAll | exists | select | reject T::= Collection|Set|OrderedSet|Bag operationName (v) ($Translate_{NEREUS}$ (T), [$Translate_{NEREUS}$ (bool-expr-with-v)])
3	T -> collect (v: type | v.property) collect (v)($Translate_{NEREUS}$ (T), [$Translate_{NEREUS}$ (v.property)])

```
Boolean; Pa:Participates
title (create_Meeting (s, d, d1, b)) = s
start (create_Meeting (s, d, d1, b)) = d
end (create_Meeting (s, d, d1, b)) = d1
set-tittle (create_Meeting (s, d, d1, b), sp) = create_Meeting (sp,
d, d1, b)
set-start (create_Meeting (s, d, d1, b), dp) = create_Meeting (s,
dp, d1, b)
set-end (create_Meeting (s, d, d1, b), d1p) = create_Meeting (s, d,
d1p, b)
duration (m) = timeDifference (end (m), start (m))
isConfirmed (cancel (m)) = False
isConfirmed (m) = checkDate (m) and NumConfirmedParticipants (m) >= 2
 --Rule 1
checkDate (m) = forAll (me) (collect (p) (getParticipants (Pa, m),
[getMeetings (Pa, p)]), [consistent (m, me]) --Rule 1
Consistent (m, m1)=
not (isConfirmed (m1)) or (end (m) < start (m1) or end (m1) < start
(m))
NumConfirmedParticipants (m) = size (getParticipants (Participates, m))
   --Rules 1, 2, 3
END-CLASS
```

For example, the following OCL specification:

```
context Person:: numMeetingConfirmed (): Nat
post: result= self.meetings -> select (isConfirmed) -> size
```

is translated into:

```
AXIOMS p: Person;...
NumConfirmedMeeting (p) =
Translate_Nereus (self.meetings -> select (isConfirmed) -> size)
Translate_Nereus (self.meetings -> select (isConfirmed) -> size) =
Size (Translate_NEREUS (self.meetings-> select (isConfirmed)))
numConfirmedMeetings (p) = size(select (m) (getMeetings (Pa, p),
[isConfirmed(m)])
```

Figure 4 summarizes the phases of the translation of P&M.

Figure 4. From P&M diagram to NEREUS

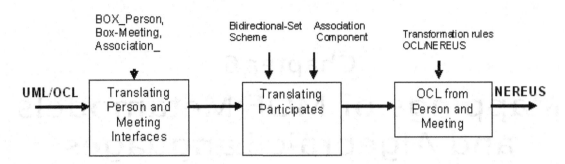

REFERENCES

Favre, L. (2005). Foundations for MDA-based Forward Engineering. *Journal of Object Technology (JOT), 4*(1), 129-153). Retrieved on July 20, 2009 from www.jot.fm

Favre, L., Martinez, L., & Pereira, C. (2005). Forward Engineering of UML Static Models. In M. Khosrow-Pour (Ed.), *Encyclopedia of Information Science and Technology* (pp. 1212-1217). Hershey, PA: Idea Group Publishing.

Hussmann, H., Cerioli, M., Reggio, G., & Tort, F. (1999). *Abstract Data Types and UML Models*. Report DISI-TR-99-15. University of Genova.

MOF. (2006). *MOF: Meta Object facility (MOF ™) 2.0*. OMG Specification formal/2006-01-01. Retrieved on July 20, 2009 from www.omg.org/mof

Padawitz, P. (2000). Swinging UML: How to make class diagrams and state machines amenable to constraint solving and proving. In A. Evans & S. Kent (Eds.) (LNCS, pp. 265-277). Heidelberg: Springer-Verlag.

QVT. (2008). *QVT: MOF 2.0 Query, View, Transformation*. Formal/2008-04-03. Retrieved on July 20, 2009 from www.omg.org

UML. (2009a). *Unified Modeling Language: Infrastructure*. Version 2.2. OMG Specification formal/2009-02-04. Retrieved on July 20, 2009 from www.omg.org.

UML. (2009b). *UML: Unified Modeling Language: Superstructure*. Version 2.2. OMG Specification: formal/2009-02-02. Retrieved on July 20, 2009 from www.omg.org

Chapter 6
Mappings of MOF Metamodels and Algebraic Languages

INTRODUCTION

In this chapter we examine the relation between NEREUS and formal specification using CASL (Common Algebraic Specification Language) as a common algebraic language (Bidoit & Mosses, 2004).

CASL is an expressive and simple language based on a critical selection of known constructs such as subsorts, partial functions, first-order logic, and structured and architectural specifications. A basic specification declares sorts, subsorts, operations and predicates, and gives axioms and constraints. Specifications are structured by means of specification building operators for renaming, extension and combining. Architectural specifications impose structure on implementations, whereas structured specifications only structure the text of specifications.

CASL allows loose, free and generated specifications. The models of a loose specification include all those where the declared functions have the specified properties, without any restrictions on the set of values corresponding to the various sorts. In models of a generated specification, in contrast, it is required that all values can be expressed by terms formed from the specified constructors, i.e. unreachable values are prohibited. In models of free specifications, it is required that values of terms are distinct except when their equality follows from the specified axioms: the possibility of unintended coincidence between their axioms is prohibited.

DOI: 10.4018/978-1-61520-649-0.ch006

CASL is at the center of a family of specification languages. It has restrictions to various sublanguages, and extensions to higher-order, state-based, concurrent, and other languages. CASL is supported by tools and facilitates interoperability of prototyping and verification tools.

Algebraic languages do not follow similar structuring mechanisms to UML or NEREUS. The graph structure of a class diagram involves cycles such as those created by bidirectional associations. However, the algebraic specifications are structured hierarchically and cyclic import structures between two specifications are avoided. In the following, we describe how to translate basic specification in NEREUS into CASL, and then we analyze how to translate associations (Favre, 2009), (Favre, 2006) (Favre, 2005).

TRANSLATING BASIC SPECIFICATIONS

In NEREUS the elements of <parameterList> are pairs C1:C2 where C1 is the formal generic parameter constrained by an existing class C2 or C1: ANY. In CASL, the first syntax is translated into [C2] and the second in [sort C1]. Next, we show two expressions in NEREUS and the CASL:

NEREUS CLASS CartesProd [E:ANY; E1: ANY]
CASL spec CARTESPROD [sort E] [sort E1]

NEREUS CLASS HASH [T:ANY; V:HASHABLE]
CASL spec HASH [sort T] [HASHABLE]

NEREUS and CASL have the similar syntax for declaring types. The sorts in the IS-SUBTYPE paragraph are linked to subsorts in CASL.

The signatures of the NEREUS operations are translated into operations or predicates in CASL. Data type declarations may be used to abbreviate declarations of types and constructors.

Any NEREUS function that includes partial functions must specify the domain of each of them. This is the role of the PRE clause that indicates what conditions the function's arguments must satisfy to belong to the function's domain. To indicate that a CASL function may be partial the notation uses ->?; the normal arrow will be reserved for total functions. The translation includes an axiom for restricting the domain. For example, a partial function remove (see Bidirectional-3 specification in Appendix-B)

```
remove: Bidirectional-3 (b) x Class1 (c1) x Class2(c2) -> Bidirec-
tional-3
pre: isRelated (b,c1,c2)
```

is translated into

```
remove: Bidirectional-3 (b) x Class1 x Class2 ->? Bidirectional-3
...
forall b:Bidirectional-3, c1:Class1; c2: Class2
def remove (b,c1,c2) ⇔ isRelated (b,c1,c2)
```

In NEREUS it is possible to specify three different levels of visibility for operations: public, protected and private. In CASL, a private visibility requires to hide the operation by means of the operator Hide. On the other hand, a protected operation in a class is included in all the subclasses of that class, and it is hided by means of the operator Hide or the use of local definitions.

The IMPORTS paragraph declares imported specifications. In CASL, the specifications are declared in the header specification after the keyword given, or, like unions of specifications. A generic specification definition SN with some parameters and some imports is expressed as follows:

```
spec SN [SP₁] [SP₂] …[SPₙ]
given SP1´, SP2´,..., SPm´= SP1´´ and SP´´ and …
then
   SP
end
```

SN refers to the specification that has parameter specifications SP1, SP2,... SPn, (if any). Parameters should be distinguished from references to fixed specifications that are not intended to be instantiated such as SP1', SP2', .., SPm'(if any). SP1", SP2", … are references to import that can be instantiated. Unions also allow us to express inheritance relations in CASL. The translation of the expression in NEREUS

```
CLASS A
INHERITS B,C
```

is translated into the following expression in CASL

```
spec A = B and C
end
```

References to generic specifications always instantiate the parameters. In NEREUS, the instantiation of parameters [C: B] where C is a class already existing in the environment and B is a component of A and C is a subclass of B, constructs an instance of A in which the component B is substituted by C. In CASL, the intended fitting of the parameter symbols to the argument symbols may have to be specified explicitly by means of a fit C|-> B.

NEREUS and CASL have the similar syntax for defining local functions. Then, this transformation is reduced to a simple translation.

NEREUS distinguishes incomplete and complete specifications. In CASL, the incomplete specifications are translated to loose specifications and complete ones to free specifications. If the specification has basic constructors, it will be translated into generated specifications. However, if it is incomplete it will be translated into loose generated specifications. Both NEREUS and CASL allow loose extensions of free specifications.

The classes that include higher order operations are translated inside parameterized first-order specifications. The main difference between higher order specifications and parameterized ones is that, in the first approach, several function-calls can be done with the same specification and parameterized specifications require the construction of several instantiations. Next, we show the translation of the Collection specification (see Class Collection in Chapter 4) to CASL. Take into account that there are as much functions f1, f2, f3, and f4 as functions select, reject, forAll and exists. There are as much functions base and g as functions iterate too.

```
spec Operation [ sort X] =
Z1 and Z2 and ... Zr
thenpred
f1_j: X →    | 1 ≤ j ≤ m
f2_j: X →    | 1 ≤ j ≤ n
f3_j: X →    | 1 ≤ j ≤ k
f4_j: X →    | 1 ≤ j ≤ l
ops
base_j: -> Z_j | 1 ≤ j ≤ r
g_j: Z_j x X -> Z_j | 1 ≤ j ≤ r
end
```

```
spec Collection [sort Elem]
given NAT= OPERATION [Elem]
thengenerated type
Collection::= create | add (Collection ; Elem)
pred
isEmpty: Collection
includes: Collection x Elem
includesAll: Collection x Collection
forAll_i: Collection |1 ≤ i ≤ k
exists_i: Collection |1 ≤ i ≤ l
iterate_i: Collection → Z_j | 1≤ i ≤ r
ops
size: Collection → Nat
select_i: Collection → Collection |1≤i ≤ m
reject_i: Collection → Collection |1≤i ≤ n
forall c, c1: Collection; e: Elem
isEmpty (create)
includes (add (c, e), e1) = if e = e1 then true else includes (c,
e1)
select_i (create) = create
select_i (add (c, e)) =
if f1_i (e) then add (select_i (c), e) else select_i (c) |1≤i ≤ m
includesAll (c, add (c1, e)) = includes(c, e) and includesAll (c, c1)
reject_i (create) = create
reject_i (add (c, e))=
if not f2_i (e) then add (reject_i (c), e) else reject_i (c) |1 ≤ i ≤ n
forAll_i (add (c, e))= f3_i (e) and for-all_i (c) |1 ≤ i ≤ k
exists_i (add (c, e))= f4_i (e) or exists_i (c) |1 ≤ i ≤ l
iterate_j (create) = base_j
```

```
iterate_j (add (c, e)) = g_j (e, iterate_j (c)) | 1 ≤ i ≤ r
localops f2: Elem x Nat ->Nat
forall e: Elem; i: Nat
f2(e, i) = i + 1
within size (c) = iterate (c, f2, 0)
end-local
end
```

TRANSLATING ASSOCIATIONS

NEREUS and UML follow similar structuring mechanisms of data abstraction and data encapsulation. The algebraic languages do not follow these structuring mechanisms in an UML style. In UML an association can be viewed as a local part of an object. This interpretation can not be mapped to classical algebraic specifications which do not admit cyclic import relations.

We propose an algebraic specification that considers associations belonging to the environment in which an actual instance of the class is embedded. Let Assoc be a bi-directional association between two classes called A and B, the following steps can be distinguished in the translation process:

- **Step1:** Regroup the operations of classes A and B distinguishing operations local to A, local to B and, local to A and B and Assoc.
- **Step 2:** Construct the specifications A' and B' from A and B where A' and B' include local operations to A and B respectively.
- **Step 3:** Construct specifications Collection[A'] and Collection[B'] by instantiating reusable schemes.
- **Step 4:** Construct a specification Assoc (with A' and B') by instantiating reusable schemes in the component Association
- **Step 5:** Construct the specification AssocA+B by extending Assoc with A', B' and the operations local to A', B' and Assoc.

Figure 1 shows the relations among the specifications built in the different steps and partially depicts the structure of CASL specifications in the shaded text.

EXAMPLE 6-1: TRANSLATING P&M CLASS DIAGRAM INTO CASL

We exemplify the previous steps with the transformation of P&M (see Chapter 5 Figure 3).

Step 1: Regroup the operations of classes Person and Meeting distinguishing operations local to Person, local to Meeting and, local to Person and Meeting and Participates. (see Table 1)

Step 2: Construct the specifications PERSON and MEETING including only local operations.

```
spec PERSON given STRING, NAT =
thengenerated type Person::= create-Person (String)
ops
```

Figure 1. Translating associations into CASL

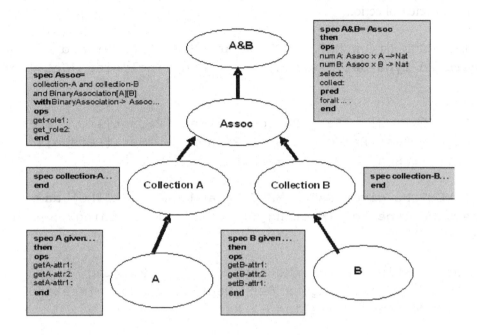

Table 1.

Local to...	Operations/Attributes
PERSON	*Name*
MEETING	*title, start, end, duration*
PERSON, MEETING, PARTICIPATES	*cancel, isConfirmed, numConfirmedMeetings, checkDate, num-Meetings, numConfirmedParticipants*

```
name:Person -> String
setName: Person x String -> Name
end

spec MEETING given STRING, DATE =
thengenerated type Meeting::= create-Meeting (String; Date;Date)
ops
title: Meeting -> String
set-title: Meeting x String -(Meeting
start: Meeting -(Date
set-start: Meeting x Date -(Meeting
isEnd: Meeting -(Date
set-end: Meeting x Date -(Meeting
end
```

Step 3: Construct specifications by instantiating reusable schemes for collections, in particular, we select Set as concrete Collection.

spec SET-PERSON given NAT = PERSON **and** BAG [PERSON] and …
thengenerated type Set [Person]::= create (including (Set [Person];
Person)
ops
union: Set [Person] x Set [Person] -> Set [Person]
intersection: Set [Person] x Set [Person] -> Set [Person]
count: Set [Person] x Person -> Nat
…

spec SET-MEETING **given** NAT = MEETING **and** BAG [MEETING] **and**…
thengenerated type Set [Meeting]::= create | including (Set [Meeting]; Meeting)
ops
union: Set [Meeting] x Set [Meeting] -> Set [Meeting]
intersection: Set [Meeting] x Set [Meeting] -> Set [Meeting]
count: Set [Meeting] x Meeting -> Nat
…

Step 4: Construct a specification Participates (with PERSON and MEETING) by instantiating reusable schemes in the component Association

spec PARTICIPATES = SET-PERSON **and** SET-MEETING **and**
BINARY-ASSOCIATION [PERSON] [MEETING]
with BinaryAssociation |-> Participates
pred
isRightLinked: Participates x Person
isLeftLinked: Participates x Meeting
isRelated: Participates x Person x Meeting
ops
addLink: Participates x Person x Meeting -> Participates
getParticipants: Participates x Meeting -> Set [Person]
getMeetings: Participates x Person -> Set [Meeting]
remove: Participates x Person x Meeting -> Participates
∀**a**: Participates; p, p1: Person; m, m1: Meeting
def addLink (a, p, m) ⇔ not isRelated (a, p, m)
def getParticipants (a, m) ⇔ isLeftLinked (a, m)
def getMeetings (a, m) ⇔ isRightLinked (a, m)
def remove (a, p, m) ⇔ isRelated (a, p, m)
endspec

Step 5: Construct the specification PERSON&MEETING by extending Participates and the operations local to PERSON, MEETING and PARTICIPATES.

```
spec PERSON&MEETING = PARTICIPATES
thenops
numMeeting: Participates x Person -> Nat
numConfirmedMeetings: Participates x Person -> Nat
isConfirmed: Participates x Meeting -> Boolean
numConfirmedParticipants: Participates x Meeting -(Nat
checkDate: Participates x Meeting -(Participates
select: Participates x Set [Meeting] -(Set [Meeting]
collect: Participates x Set [Person] -(Bag [Meeting]
pred
forall: Participates x Set [Meeting] x Meeting
(s: Set [Meeting]; m: Meeting; pa: Participates; p: Person; m: Meet-
ing; sp: Set [Person];
bm: Bag [Meeting]
forall (pa, including (s, m), m1) = isConsistent (pa, m, m1) and
forall (pa, s, m1)
select (pa, create-Meeting) = create-Meeting
select (pa, including (s, m)) = including (select (pa, s), m) when
isConfirmed (pa, m)
   else select (pa, s)
collect (pa, create-Person, s) = asBag (create-Person)
collect (pa, including (sp, p)) = asBag (including (collect (pa,
sp), p))
numMeeting (pa, p) = size (getMeetings (pa, p))
isConfirmed (pa, m) = checkDate (pa, m) and numConfirmedParticipants
(pa, m) ((2
numConfirmedMeetings (pa, p) = size (select (getMeetings (pa, p))
checkDate (pa, m) = forall (pa, collect (pa, getParticipants(pa, m),
m)
isConsistent (pa, m, m1) =
not (isConfirmed (pa, m1)) or (end (m) (start (m1) or end (m1)
(start (m))
numConfirmedParticipants (pa, m) = size (getParticipants (pa, m))
end
```

Figure 2 depicts the relations among the specifications built in the different steps.

Figure 2. Translating Participates association into CASL

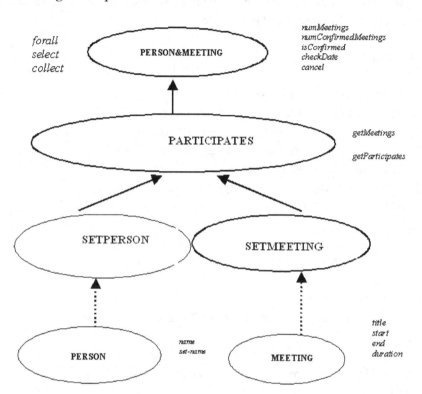

REFERENCES

Bidoit, M., & Mosses, P. (2004). CASL User Manual- Introduction to Using the Common Algebraic Specification Language (LNCS 2900). Heidelberg: Springer-Verlag.

Favre, L. (2005). Foundations for MDA-based Forward Engineering. *Journal of Object Technology (JOT), 4*(1), 129-153). Retrieved on July 20, 2009 from www.jot.fm

Favre, L. (2006). A Rigorous Framework for Model Driven Development. In K. Siau (Ed.), *Advanced Topics in Database Research, Vol. 5* (pp. 1-27). Hershey, PA: Idea Group Publishing.

Favre, L. (2009) A Formal Foundation for Metamodeling (LNCS 5570, pp. 177-191). Heilderberg: Springer-Verlag.

Chapter 7
Mappings of MOF Metamodels and Object–Oriented Languages

INTRODUCTION

This chapter discusses the main steps for transforming NEREUS constructions into object oriented languages. As an example, we use the Eiffel language that allows integrating specifications with Eiffel contracts (Meyer, 1992). Figure 1 shows the main steps.

The Eiffel code is constructed gradually. First, associations and operation signature are translated. The transformation is supported by reusable components. From OCL and NEREUS specifications it is possible to construct contracts on Eiffel and /or feature implementations by applying heuristics.

MAPPING CLASSES AND ASSOCIATIONS

For generating code from some NEREUS specification we need transformation rules. For each class in NEREUS an Eiffel class is built. If a NEREUS class is incomplete, i.e., it contains sorts and operations in the clause DEFERRED, the keyword *class* in Eiffel is preceded by the keyword *deferred*. NEREUS and Eiffel have the same syntax for declaring class parameters. Then, this transformation is reduced to a trivial translation.

The relation introduced in NEREUS using the clause IMPORTS will be translated into a client relation in Eiffel. The relation expressed through the keyword INHERITS in NEREUS will become an inheritance relation in Eiffel. This provides the mechanism to carry out modifications on the inherited classes that will allow adaptation. Also, subsortings will become inheritance relations.

Associations are transformed by instantiating schemes that exist in the reusable component Association. A component is defined in three levels of abstraction that integrate NEREUS incomplete algebraic specifications, complete algebraic specifications and object oriented code.

DOI: 10.4018/978-1-61520-649-0.ch007

Figure 1. From NEREUS to object oriented languages

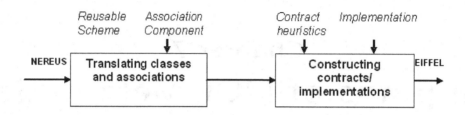

Figure 2 depicts a specific Association component including schemes for the Eiffel language. It describes taxonomy of associations classified according to kind, degree, navigability and multiplicity.

The first level describes a hierarchy of incomplete specifications of associations using NEREUS and OCL. Every leaf in this level corresponds to sub-components at the second level.

A realization sub-component is a tree of algebraic specifications: the root is the most abstract definition and the internal nodes correspond to different realizations of the root. For example, for a "binary,

Figure 2. Association component

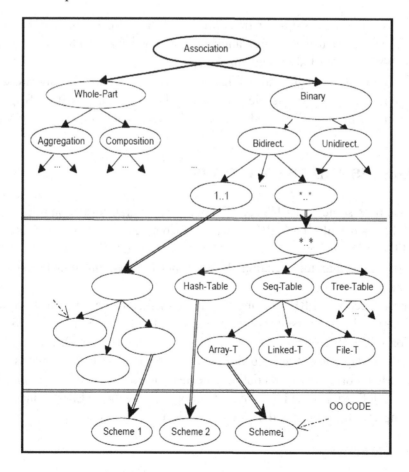

bi-directional and many-to-many" association, different realizations through hashing, sequences, or trees could be associated. These subcomponents specify realizations starting from algebraic specifications of Eiffel libraries (Meyer, 1994).

The implementation level associates each leaf of the realization level with different implementations in Eiffel. Implementation sub-components express how to implement associations and aggregations. For example, a bi-directional binary association with multiplicity "one-to-one" will be implemented as an attribute in each associated class containing a reference to the related object. On the contrary, if the association is "many-to-many", the best approach is to implement the association as a different class in which each instance represents one link and its attributes.

For every ASSOCIATES clause, a scheme in the implementation level of the association component will be selected and instantiated. In these cases, the implementation level schemes suggest including reference attributes in the classes or introducing an intermediate class or container. Notice that the transformation of an association does not necessarily imply the existence of an associated class in the generated code as an efficient implementation can suggest including reference attributes in the involved classes.

The following scheme may be used to implement bidirectional associations. It include two schemes for classes *Class1* and *Class2*

Eiffel-Bidirectional-SET Scheme

```
classClass1
...
feature {NONE}
-- data members for association Association_Name
rol2: UnboundedCollectionbyReference [Class2];
mult_rol1: MULTIPLICITY;
-- operations for association Association_Name
get_mult_rol2: MULTIPLICITY isdo
Result:= mult_rol2end;
get_frozen_rol2: BOOLEAN isdo
Result:= result_frozen1end;
add_only_rol2: BOOLEAN isdo
Result:= result_add_only1end;
changeable_rol2: BOOLEAN isdo
Result:= result_changeable1end;
cardinality_rol2: INTEGER isdo
Result:= rol2.count
end;

set_ rol2 (d:UnboundedCollectionbyReference [Class2]) isrequire
get_mult_rol2.get_upper_bound >= d.count
dorol2:= d
end;
```

```
get_ rol2:
UnboundedCollectionbyReference[Class2] isdo
Result:= rol2end;
remove_rol2 (e: Class2) isrequire
is-related_rol2 (e) and not get_frozen_rol2 and not add-only_
rol2dorol2. prune (e)
end;
add_rol2 (e: Class2) isrequire is-related_rol2 (e) and not get_fro-
zen_rol2 and cardinality_rol2get_mult_rol2.get_upper_bound
dorol2. put (e)
end;

add_rol2 (e:Class2) isrequire
is-related_rol2 (e) and
multiplicity_rol2get_mult_rol2.get_upper_bound and not get_frozen_
rol2
dorol2. put (e)
end;

is_related_rol2 (e: Class2): BOOLEAN isdo
Result:=rol2. has (e)
end;

invariant
mult_ rol2.get_lower_bound = LowerBound;
mult_ rol2.get_upper_bound = Upper Bound;
rol2.count >= LowerBound;
rol2.count <= Upper Boundend - class Class1
-------------------------------------------------------------------
classClass2
...
feature {NONE}
-- data members for association Association_Name
rol1: UnbondedCollectionby Reference [Class1];
mult_rol1: MULTIPLICITY;
-- operations for association Association_Name
...
add_rol1(e: Class1) isrequire
is-related_rol1 (e) and and not get_frozen_rol1 and multiplicity_
rol1get_mult_rol1.get_upper_bound
dorol1. put (e)
end;
```

```
is_related_roll (e: Class2): BOOLEAN isdo
Result:=roll. has (e)
end;
```

```
invariant
mult_ roll.get_lower_bound = LowerBound;
mult_ roll.get_upper_bound = Upper Bound;
roll.count >= LowerBound;
roll.count <= Upper Bound
end - class Class2
```

For the association *Participates* the following will be in the code:

- For each class there is a private attribute in the opposite class
- The type of the newly created attribute is a Set and it will have corresponding get_ and set_ operations.

Next, from the operation signatures, the interfaces for the features of the Eiffel class are generated. The translation of each operation has a different treatment according to the type of feature to which it makes reference (functions, procedures, variables, or constants). It should also be considered that of all the domains of an operation, the first one that coincides with the sort of the specified class is the object Current in Eiffel and it should be eliminated from the list of parameters of the resultant feature. Second order functionalities of collections are translated respecting the syntax of the Eiffel schemes for Collection classes. As an example, we can generate code for the P&M Class Diagram described in Example 5-1 and translated into CASL in Example 6-1 by using the following textual substitution:

```
[Class1: Person; Class2: Meeting; roll: participants; rol2: meet-
ings; UnboundedCollectionbyReference: UnboundedSetbyReference; re-
sult_frozen1: false; result_add_only1: false,LowerBound1:2; Upper-
Bound: *; ..]
```

CONSTRUCTING OBJECT ORIENTED CONTRACTS AND IMPLEMENTATIONS

Eiffel provides an assertion language. Assertions are Boolean expressions of semantic properties of the classes. They can play the following roles:

- **Precondition:** Expresses the requirements that the client must satisfy to call a routine.
- **Postcondition:** Expresses the conditions that the routine guarantees on return.
- **Class invariant:** Expresses the requirements that every object of the class must satisfy after its creation.

The expression of the form *old exp* denotes the value that an attribute or expression *exp* had on routine entry. *Current* refers to the target object itself and *Result* is the name of the returned object, if there is any.

Let *Translate*Eiffel be a function that expresses the translation of a NEREUS term to Eiffel.

*Translate*Eiffel *op(es,e2,e3,...)* (where es, e2, e3 ... are well-formed non-ground terms and es is a term of the sort of interest) can be given in the following inductive way:

```
TranslateEiffel op(es, e2, e3 ...) =
TranslateEiffel es.op (TranslateEiffele2, TranslateEiffel e3....)
```

Preconditions and axioms of a function written in NEREUS are used to generate preconditions and postconditions for routines and invariants for Eiffel classes.

A NEREUS precondition, which is a well-formed term defined over functions and constants of the global environment classes, is automatically translated to Eiffel precondition. Axioms are translated to Eiffel post-conditions, invariants and implementations. We define two heuristics to obtain postconditions and /or implementations in Eiffel:

- **Invariant heuristics:** It is possible to derive an invariant if it can establish a correspondence between the functions in an axiom A and the class attributes that only depend on the state of the object (that is to say, all the terms of the interest sort are variables). Then, *TranslateEiffel (A)* is the Eiffel invariant.

- **Postcondition / implementation heuristics:** A postcondition can automatically be generated from one axiom if a term *e(<list-of-arguments>)* which is associated to an operation *op*, can be distinguished within itself in such a way that any other term of the axiom depends upon the *<list-of-arguments>* or constants. Then, the postcondition will associate itself with the feature linked to the term and will obviously depend only upon the previous state of the method execution, upon the state after its execution and upon the method arguments. If the selected term *e* is linked with a value belonging to the sort of interest, it is associated with *Current* and the sort then it is associated to *old*. If the selected term *e* is linked with a value the different sort, it is associated with *Result*. If the resulting expression is in the form *Result* =... it is possible to generate the body of the feature. The programmer can also incorporate assertions that reflect purely implementation aspects. For simple operations the body of the feature could be generated from OCL postconditions but frequently the body of the feature must be written. In that case, generating code for the pre and post-conditions ensures that the code conforms to the specification in the UML diagrams. Next, we show some examples of heuristic application. (see Table 1)

REFERENCES

Meyer, B. (1992). *Eiffel: The Language*. Prentice Hall.

Meyer, B. (1994). *Reusable Software*: *The Base object-oriented component libraries*. Prentice Hall.

Table 1.

NEREUS	EIFFEL
CLASS Bounded-Sequence [Elem] ... **AXIOMS s: Bounded-Sequence;** **e: Elem** full (s) = (capacity (s) = count (s)) empty (s) = (count(s) =0)	**class** BOUNDED-Sequence [G] ... capacity:INTEGER count: INTEGER full: BOOLEAN empty: BOOLEAN **invariant** full = (count = capacity) empty = (count = 0)
CLASS Set [Elem] .... **AXIOMS s: Set; e: Elem** *current* has (s,e) **implies** count(extend (s, e)) =count (s) *old* **not** has (s,e) **implies** count(extend (s, e)) = count (s) + 1	**class** SET [G] ... extend (e: G) .... **ensure** **old** has (e) **implies** count = **old** count **not old** has (e) **implies** (count = **old** count + 1)
CLASS Set [Elem] .... **Axioms s: Set; e: Elem** has (s, e) => not empty (s) *result*	**class** SET[G] .... has (e: G):BOOLEAN ... **ensure** Result **implies not** empty
CLASS Meeting ... **Axioms p: Person** numMeetings (p)= size(getParticipates (p))	**class** Meeting ... numMeeting (p:PERSON) **do** Result:= meetings.size() **end**

Section 3
Techniques Underlying
MDA–Based Reverse Engineering

Chapter 8
Software Evolution, MDA and Design Pattern Components

INTRODUCTION

The success of MDA depends on the definition of model transformations and component libraries which make a significant impact on tools that provide support for MDA. MDA is a young approach and several technical issues are not adequately addressed. For instance, existing MDA-based CASE tools do not provide adequate support to deal with component-based reuse (CASE, 2009). In light of this, we propose a metamodeling technique to reach a high level of reusability and adaptability of components.

Reusability is the ability to use software elements for constructing many different applications. An ideal software reusability tehnology should facilitate a consistent system implementation, starting from the adaptation and integration of "implementation pieces" that exist in reusable components library. Software reusability has two main purposes: to increase the reliability of software and to reduce the cost of software development. Most current approaches to object oriented reusability are based on empirical methods. However the most effective forms of reuse are generally found at more abstract levels of design (Krueger, 1992).

In MDA, software reusability is difficult because it requires taking many different requirements into account, some of which are abstract and conceptual, while others, such as efficiency are concrete. A good approach for MDA reusability must reconcile models at different abstraction levels.

In this chapter, we analyze how to define reusable components in a way that fits with MDA and propose a megamodel for defining MDA components. Considering the relevant role that design patterns take in software evolution we exemplify MDA components for them.

We propose a megamodel to define families of design pattern components by means of PIM-, PSM- and ISM-metamodels and their interrelations. Instances of the megamodel are reusable components that describe specific design patterns at different levels of abstraction (PIMs, PSMs and ISMs). They can be

DOI: 10.4018/978-1-61520-649-0.ch008

viewed as megacomponents that allow defining in a concise way as many components as different pattern solutions can appear. We analyze metamodel transformations of both PIMs into PSMs, and PSMs into ISMs (Favre, & Martinez, 2006).

The traditional techniques for verification and validation are still essential to achieve software quality. We describe foundations for constructing formalizations of design pattern component. We define a megamodel based on MOF-metamodels and metamodel-based model transformations and show how to formalize them by using the metamodeling notation NEREUS. This notation, as we had said, can be viewed as an intermediate notation open to many other formal languages (Favre, 2006) (Favre, 2005). We illustrate our MDA-based approach by using the *Observer* design pattern.

Considering design patterns is a relevant technique in software development, in particular in forward and reverse engineering processes we include some references to related work and remark the contribution of an MDA approach.

RELATED WORK

This section shows the evolution of design pattern techniques and remarks the advantages of an MDA approach to define design pattern components.

In (Budinsky, Finni, Vlissides, & Yu, 1996) a tool to automatically generate code of design patterns from a small amount of information given by the user is described. This approach has two widespread problems. The user should understand "what to cut" and "where to paste" and both cannot be obvious. Once the user has incorporated pattern code in his application, any change that implies to generate the code again will force it to reinstate the pattern code in the application. The user cannot see changes in the generated code through the tool.

Florijn, Meijers, and van Winsen, (1997) describe a tool prototype that supports design pattern during the development or maintenance of object-oriented programs.

Albin-Amiot and Guéhéneuc (2001) describe how a metamodel can be used to obtain a representation of design patterns and how this representation allows both automatic generation and detection of design patterns. The contribution of this proposal is the definition of design patterns as entities of modeling of first class. The main limitation of this approach concerns the integration of the generated code with the user code.

Judson, Carver and France (2003) describe an approach to rigorous modeling of pattern-based transformations that involve specializations of the UML metamodel to characterize source and target models.

Kim, France, Ghosh, and Song (2003a) describe a metamodeling approach to specify design patterns using roles. They analyze the characteristics of object-based roles and generalize them. Based on the generalized notion of a role, they define a new notion of a model role which is played by a model element. The approach is intended to be easy to use and practical for the development of tools that incorporate patterns into UML models.

Kim, France, Ghosh, and Song (2003b) describe a metamodeling approach that uses a pattern specification language called Role-Based Modeling Language (RBML). A pattern specification defines a family of UML models in terms of roles, where a role is associated with a UML metaclass as its base. RBML uses visual notations based on the UML and textual constraints expressed in OCL to specify patterns properties. The RBML allows specifying various perspectives of design patterns such as static structure, interactions and state-based behavior.

France, Kim, Ghosh, and Song (2004) present a technique to specify pattern solutions expressed in the UML. The specifications created by this technique are metamodels that characterize UML design models of pattern solutions. The patterns specification consists of a Structural Pattern Specification (SPS) that specifies the class diagram view of pattern solutions, and a set of Interaction Pattern Specification (IPSs) that specifies interactions in pattern solutions. A UML model conforms to a pattern specification if its class diagram conforms to the SPS and the interactions described by sequence diagrams conform to the IPSs.

Component-based approaches have been proposed to reuse (D'Souza & Wills, 1999) (Szyperski, Gruntz, & Murer, 2002).

Bettin (2003) summarizes lessons from several projects related to component-based development and MDA and examines the pragmatic use of today's MDA tools.

Meyer (2003) discusses the concept of Trusted Components, a reusable software element possessing specified and guaranteed property quality and examines a first framework for a Component Quality Model. Arnout (2004) analyzes the popular Gamma's design patterns (Gamma, Helm, Johnson and Vlissides, 1995) to identify which ones can become reusable components in an Eiffel library.

In this chapter, we show how to integrate design patterns components with MDA-based processes. The following advantages between our approach and some existing ones are worth mentioning. We define a megamodel to define families of reusable design pattern components. It refers to metamodel and transformations organized in an architectural framework. A design pattern metamodel allows detecting the presence of a pattern in a family of models. If there were no metamodels, a library of models specifying each one the ways in that the design pattern can appear should be necessary (this is expensive). Also, it should be necessary to compare the model that is analyzed with the models of the library to see if matching exists. On the other hand, the specification of the metamodels in the three levels allows us to refine pattern model step-by-step in a MDA perspective.

A MEGAMODEL FOR DEFINING MDA REUSABLE COMPONENTS

We propose a metamodeling technique to define MDA components. To define families of reusable components we describe a megamodel that refers to metamodels and model transformations organized into an architectural framework (Bezivin, Jouault, & Valduriez, 2004). Figure 1 depicts a megamodel.

The megamodel associates a set of classes linked to metamodels and transformations. Metamodels are defined at three different levels of abstraction linked to PIM, PSM and ISM. Transformations describe families of refinements between a source model and a target model at a different abstraction level (PIM to PSM, PSM to ISM).

In this context, a refinement is a more detailed specification that conforms to another which is more abstract. A refinement is associated to a source metamodel and a target metamodel and is composed by parameters, preconditions and postconditions (see Figure 1). The precondition states the conditions that must be hold whenever the transformation is applied. Properties that the transformation guarantees when it was applied are stated by the postconditions. OCL contracts describe conditions that must be met for a refinement step to be consistent.

The classes PIM-Metamodel, PSM-Metamodel and the class ISM-Metamodel describe families of PIMs, PSMs and ISMs respectively. The classes Refinement PIM-PSM and Refinement PIM-PSM

Figure 1. A "megamodel" for MDA components

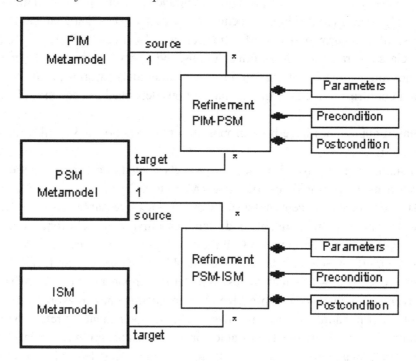

describe families of refinements both between PIM- and PSM- metamodels and PSM- and ISM- metamodels respectively.

There are associations between metamodel and refinements so that each refinement links a source metamodel and a target metamodel:

- There is an association between the class PIM-Metamodel and the class Refinement PIM-PSM specifying that each instance of PIM metamodel is connected with zero or more instances of the Refinement PIM-PSM associated.
- There is an association between the class PSM-Metamodel and the class Refinement PIM-PSM specifying that each instance of PSM metamodel is connected with zero or more instances of the Refinement PIM-PSM associated.
- There is an association between the class PSM-Metamodel and the class Refinement PSM-ISM specifying that each instance of PSM metamodel is connected with zero or more instances of the Refinement PSM-ISM associated.
- There is an association between the class ISM-Metamodel and the class Refinement PSM-ISM specifying that each instance of PSM metamodel is connected with zero or more instances of the Refinement PSM-ISM associated.

Figure 2 shows an instance of the megamodel that refers concrete instances of an *Observer* pattern metamodel, refinements and, links between metamodels and refinements. Links connect an instance of a refinement with an instance of a metamodel. The Observer pattern "defines a one-to-many dependency

Figure 2. An instance of the megamodel: The observer pattern component

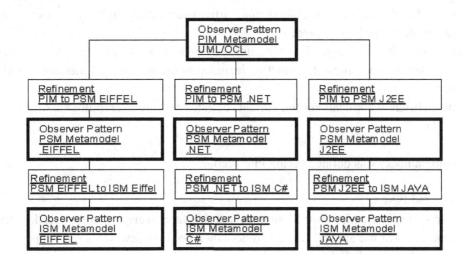

between objects so that when one object changes state, all its dependents are notified and updated automatically" (Gamma et.al, 1995, pp. 293).

This instantiation can be viewed as a megacomponent defining a family of reusable components that integrate instances of PIMs, PSMs and ISMs.

SPECIFYING MDA DESIGN PATTERN COMPONENTS

We analyze how to specify design patterns with MDA. To specify design patterns at different abstraction levels, it was necessary to build metamodels both for different platforms and programming languages. These metamodels were specified as specializations of the UML metamodel. Metamodels for Eiffel, Java and C++ at levels of PSM and ISM are shown in Appendix A.

Metamodels are defined at three levels:

- **PIM Level:** Metamodels describe design patterns in a way independent of platforms and specific technologies.
- **PSM Level:** Metamodels describe design patterns for specific platforms.
- **ISM Level:** Metamodels describe design pattern in a specific programming language.

The definition of metamodels is based on popular catalogues: Gamma et al. (1995), Alpert, Brown and Woolf (1998), Grand (1998), each one of them exemplifies design patterns by using C++, Smalltalk y Java respectively.

Metamodels were specified taking into account:

- **Structure:** Different representations of classes in the pattern, i.e. the different ways in which the design pattern can appear at PIM level, where analyzed.

- **Participants:** In view of each element that appears in the model must be specified in the respective metamodel, the classes and objects that participate in the pattern, their responsibilities and interrelationships must be analyzed.
- **Collaborations:** It was analyzed how participants collaborate to carry out their responsibilities which revealed the operations that must be included in the pattern and therefore specified in the metamodel.
- **Examples:** Different applications and variants of patterns were exemplified in order that to check metamodels.

Each PSM-metamodel was defined taking into account:

- The associated PIM
- The features of specific platform: Metamodels at this level were based on specific technologies. For instance, a Java metamodel restricts inheritance because Java does not support multiple inheritance, while not an Eiffel-metamodel.

ISM-metamodels are defined considering the grammar of the respective programming language.

THE OBSERVER COMPONENT

This section partially describes an Observer component that includes metamodels and refinements. In particular, we present one PIM-metamodel and two PSM-and ISM-metamodels linked to Eiffel and Java platforms/languages. We show how to formalize MDA components by integrating metamodels and refinements.

Metamodels are expressed as UML class diagrams following the UML 2.2 notation. Metaclasses of the UML metamodel are shown in dark gray; metaclasses of the specific platforms and programming languages are shown gray whereas the remaining metaclasses corresponds to the specialization of the UML metamodel of the pattern. The description of metaclasses is organized in alphabetical order. Next, a brief description of the Observer pattern is included.

Observer Pattern Description

The Observer pattern defines "a one-to-many dependency between objects so that when one object changes state, all its dependents are notified and updated automatically" (Gamma et al., 1995). It involves the following central participants:

- **Subject:** It can contain any number of observers. It maintains a collection of observers and is responsible for adding and removing observers of this collection (*attach* y *detach*). When state changes (i.e. the values of some attributes change) the subject will notify observers of this situation (*notify*).
- **Observer:** It can observe one or more subjects. It has the responsibility of updating itself when receives a notification of change from the subject (*update*).

- **Concrete Subject:** It stores state of interest to ConcreteObserver objects. It sends a notification to its observers when its state changes.
- **Concrete Observer:** It maintains a reference to a *ConcreteSubject* object. It stores state that should stay consistent with the subjects. It implements the Observer updating interface to keep its states consistent with the subjects (*update*).

Collaborations

- ConcreteSubject notifies its observers when there is a change that could make state of its observers inconsistent with its own.
- After being informed of a change in the concrete subject, a ConcreteObserver object may query the subject for information. ConcreteObserver uses this information to reconcile its state with that of the subject.

Consequences

The *Observer* pattern allows us to vary subjects and observers independently. It is possible to reuse subjects without reusing their observers, and vice versa. It lets us add observers without modifying the subject or other observers.

Figure 3 shows the class diagram (a) and sequence diagram (b) that model the Observer pattern.

PIM-METAMODEL OF THE OBSERVER PATTERN

The *Observer* pattern metamodel at PIM level specifies the structural and behavior views of this pattern in a platform independent pattern model, i.e., it specifies the classes that participate, their operations and attributes and the relation between classes.

There are four essential participants: *Subject*, *Observer*, *ConcreteSubject* and *ConcreteObserver*. So, these four classes must be specified in the metamodel, as well as the relation between them and their interactions. The PIM metamodel involves the following participants linked to them:

- **AbstractObserver:** This metaclass specifies the characteristics of class Observer inside the Observer pattern. It should have at least an operation with the characteristics of Update. Each instance of this metaclass can be an abstract class or an interface. If the instance is an abstract class, a concrete observer inherits its behavior and, therefore there is an inheritance relation with the concrete observer. If the instance is an interface, there is a realization relation with the concrete observer.
- **ConcreteObserver:** This metaclass specifies the characteristics of a concrete observer. It knows the subject (or the subjects), then it is associated to ConcreteSubject through a unidirectional association navigable away from that end.
- **AbstractSubject:** Each instance of this metaclass can be an abstract class or an interface and it has at least three operations specified by Attach, Detach and Notify. If the instance of this metaclass is

Figure 3. The Observer pattern

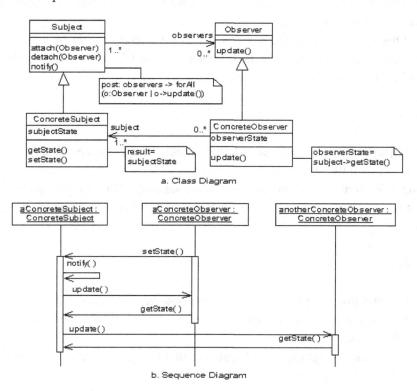

a. Class Diagram

b. Sequence Diagram

an abstract class, all concrete subjects inherit its behavior therefore there is an inheritance relation with the concrete subject. If the instance is an interface, there is a realization relation with the concrete subject. If the instance of AbstractSubject is an abstract class, it is associated to an instance of AbstractObserver through a unidirectional association navigable away from that end.

- **ConcreteSubject:** This metaclass specifies the characteristics of a concrete subject. It has at least two operations specified by GetState and SetState and its internal state is specified by the ObserverState metaclass.

The specialized UML metamodel of the *Observer* pattern is partially shown in Figures 4, 5, 6, and 7 (a,b,c,d). The shaded metaclasses correspond to metaclasses of the UML metamodel, whereas the remaining corresponds to the specialization of the UML metamodel of the *Observer* pattern.

Description of Metaclasses

Next, we describe the metaclasses of the metamodel at PIM level. For each one of them it is included a brief description, generalizations, associations and restrictions in OCL and natural language. The Observer pattern metamodel at PIM level specifies the structural and behavior views of this pattern in a platform independent pattern model. It specifies the classes that participate, its operations and attributes and the relation between classes.

Figure 4. Observer metamodel: Class diagram

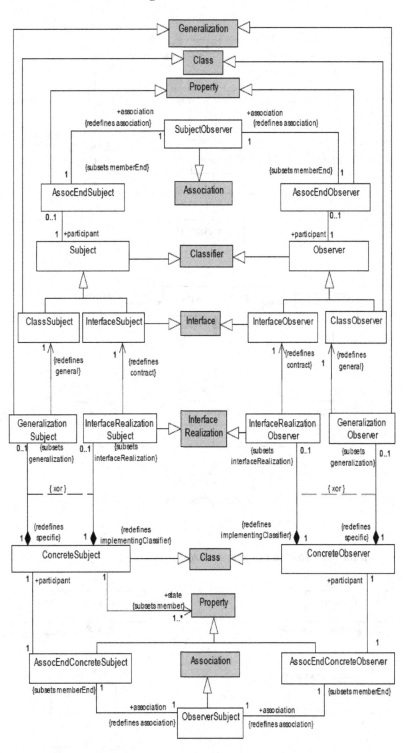

Figure 5. Observer metamodel: Abstract subject: Operations

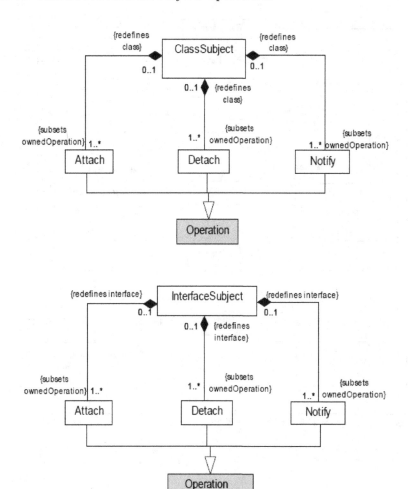

Figure 6. Observer metamodel: Abstract observer: Operations

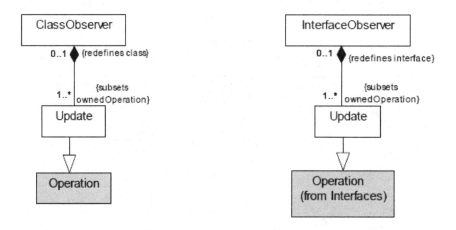

Figure 7. Observer metamodel: ConcreteSubject: Operations

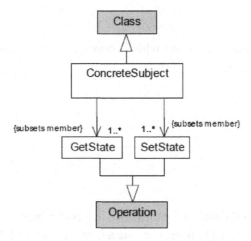

AssocEndConcreteObserver

Description
It represents the association-end that links one association ObserverSubject, of which is a member, with one ConcreteObserver.

Generalizations

- Property (from Kernel)

Associations

- participant: ConcreteObserver [1] It refers to the classifier that takes part in the association.
- association: ObserverSubject [1] It refers to the association of which this association-end is member. It redefines Property::association

Constraints

[1]   This association-end has a multiplicity n1..n2 (n1>= 0 and n2>=1) self.lower >= 0 **and** self.upper >= 1

[2]   It must be navigable self.isNavigable()

Additional Operations

[1]   The observer operation isNavigable denotes if the association-end is navigable. isNavigable = not self.class -> isEmpty ()

AssocEndObserver

Description

This property represents the association-end which connects an association SubjectObserver, of which is member, with a class Observer.

Generalizations

- Property (from Kernel)

Associations

- participant: Observer [1] It denotes the classifier that participates in the association.
- association: SubjectObserver [1] It denotes the association of which the association-end is member. It redefines Property::association.

Constraints

[1] This association-end has a multiplicity n1..n2 (n1>= 0 and n2>=1) self.lower >= 0 **and** self.upper >= 1

[2] It must be navigable. self.isNavigable ()

AssocEndSubject

Description

This property represents the association-end which connects an association SubjectObserver, of which is member, with a class Observer.

Generalizations

- Property (from Kernel)

Associations

- participant: Subject [1] It denotes the classifier that takes part in the association.
- association: SubjectObserver [1] It denotes the association of which this association-end is member. It redefines Property::association.

Constraints

[1] This association-end has a multiplicity n1..n2 (n1 >= 0 and n2 >= 1) self.lower >= 0 **and** self.upper >= 1

Attach

Description
It defines an operation that is declared by a Subject.

Generalizations

• Operation (from Kernel, Interfaces)

Associations

• classSubject: ClassSubject [0..1] It denotes the class that declares this operation. It redefines Operation::class.
• interfaceSubject: InterfaceSubject [0..1] It denotes the interface that declares this operation. It redefines Operation::interface.

Constraints

[1] This operation changes the state of the subject. **not** self.isQuery
[2] It has a nonempty set of parameters containing exactly one input parameter (direction=#in) whose type is Observer. self.ownedParameter -> notEmpty () **and** self.ownedParameter -> select (param | param.direction= #in **and** param.type = oclIsKindOf (Observer)) -> size() = 1
[3] Its visibility must be public self.visibility = #public

ClassObserver

Description
This metaclass specifies the features that a class taking the role of observer in the pattern must have.

Generalizations

• Observer, Class (from Kernel)

Associations

• update: Update [1..*] Every instance of the ClassObserver must have at least one operation that is an instance of Update. It is a subset of Class::ownedOperation.

Constraints
No additional restrictions.

ClassSubject

Description
This metaclass specifies the features that a class taking the role of subject in the pattern must have.

Generalizations

- Subject, Class (from Kernel)

Associations

- attach: Attach [1..*] Every instance of ClassSubject has at least one operation that is an instance of Attach. It is a subset of Class::ownedOperation.
- detach: Detach [1..*] Every instance of ClassSubject has at least one operation that is instance of Detach. It is a subset of Class::ownedOperation.
- notify: Notify [1..*] Every instance of ClassSubject has at least one operation that is an instance of Notify. It is a subset of Class::ownedOperation.

Constraints
No additional constraints.

ConcreteObserver

Description
This metaclass specifies the features that must be have a class taking the role of Concrete Observer in the pattern.

Generalizations

- Class (from Kernel)

Associations

- assocEndConcreteObserver: AssocEndConcreteObserver[1] It denotes the association-end of the association ObserverSubject in which this classifier participates.
- generalizationObserver: GeneralizationObserver [0..1] It designs a generalization in which ConcreteObserver takes the role of subclass (specific). It is a subset of Classifier::generalization.
- interfaceRealizationObserver: InterfaceRealizationObserver [0..1] It denotes a realization of interface where ConcreteObserver takes the role of the classifier implementing the contract (implementingClassifier).It is a subset of BehavioredClassifier::interfaceRealization.

Constraints

[1]   Instances of concrete observers should not be abstract classes. **not** self.isAbstract

[2]   If an instance of a concrete observer participates in an interface realization, then it must be a BehavioredClassifier. self.interfaceRealizationObserver -> notEmpty () **implies** self.oclIsKindOf (BehavioredClassifier))

ConcreteSubject

Description
This metaclass specifies the features that must have a class taking the role of Concrete Subject in the model of the pattern Observer.

Generalizations

*   Class (from Kernel)

Associations

*   assocEndConcreteSubject: AssocEndConcreteSubject [1] It denotes the association-end of the association ObserverSubject in which this classifier participates.
*   generalizationSubject: GeneralizationSubject [0..1] It designs a generalization where ConcreteSubject takes the role of child (specific). It is a subset of Classifier::generalización.
*   getState: GetState [1..*] Every instance of ConcreteSubject must have one or more operation instances of GetState operation. They can be own or inherited. It is a subset of NameSpace::member.
*   interfaceRealizationSubject: InterfaceRealization [0..1] It designs an interface realization where ConcreteSubject takes the role of classifier implementing the contract (implementingClassifier). It is a subset of BehavioredClassifier::InterfaceRealization.
*   setState: SetState [1..*] Every instance of ConcreteSubject must have one or more operation instances of SetState operation. They can be own or inherited. It is a subset of NameSpace::member.
*   state: Property [1..*] It specifies a non-empty set of all attributes of ConcreteSubject. They can be own or inherited. It is a subset of NameSpace::member.

Constraints

[1]   An instance of a concrete subject should not be an abstract class. **not** self.isAbstract
[2]   If an instance of the concrete subject participates in an interface realization, then it must be a BehavioredClassifier. self.interfaceRealizationSubject -> notEmpty () **implies** self.oclIsKindOf (BehavioredClassifier)
[3]   State is a set of properties that are attributes but not association-ends. self.state -> forAll (p | p.association -> isEmpty())

Detach

Description
It defines an operation that is declared by a subject.

Generalizations

•   Operation (from Kernel, Interfaces)

Associations

•   classSubject: ClassSubject [0..1] It designs the class that declares this operation. It redefines Operation::class
•   interfaceSubject: InterfaceSubject [0..1] It denotes the interface that declares this operation. It redefines Operation::interface.

Constraints

[1]   This operation changes the state of the subject. **not** self.isQuery
[2]   It has a nonempty set of parameters, one of them must be an input parameter of type *Observer*. self. ownedParameter -> notEmpty () **and** self.ownedParameter -> select (param | param.direction = #in **and** param.type = oclIsKindOf (Observer)) -> size() = 1
[3]   Its visibility must be public. self.visibility = #public

GeneralizationObserver

Description
This metaclass specifies a generalization between an observer (ClassObserver) and a concrete observer (ConcreteObserver) in the pattern.

Generalizations

•   Generalization (from Kernel)

Associations

•   classObserver: ClassObserver [1] It denotes the general element of this relation. It redefines Generalization::general.
•   concreteObserver: ConcreteObserver [1] It denotes the specific element of this relation. It redefines Generalization::specific.

Constraints
No additional constraints.

GeneralizationSubject

Description
This metaclass specifies a generalization between a subject (ClassSubject) and a concrete subject (ConcreteSubject) in the model of the Observer pattern.

Generalizations

- Generalization (from Kernel)

Associations

- classSubject: ClassSubject [1] It denotes the general element of this relation. It redefines Generalization::general.
- concreteSubject: ConcreteSubject [1] It denotes the specific element of this relation. It redefines Generalization::specific.

Constraints

No additional constraints.

GetState

Description

It defines an operation that is member of ConcreteSubject. It specifies a service that may be required by another object.

Generalizations

- Operation (from Kernel)

Associations

No additional operations.

Constraints

[1] It is an observer operation. self.isQuery
[2] Due to it must return the subject state, the set of parameter is not empty and at least, one of them must have a direction equal to out or return. self.ownedParameter -> notEmpty () **and** self.owned-Parameter ->select (par |par.direction = #return **or** par.direction = #out) -> size () >= 1
[3] Its visibility must be public. self.visibility = #public

InterfaceObserver

Description

An interface InterfaceObserver specifies the features that must have an interface taking the role of Abstract Observer in the model of the Observer pattern.

Generalizations

- Observer, Interface (from Interfaces)

Associations

- update: Update [1..*] Every instance of InterfaceObserver must have at least one operation that is an instance of Update. It is a subset of Interface::ownedOperation.

Constraints

No additional constraints.

InterfaceSubject

Description

This metaclass specifies the features that must have an interface taking the role of abstract subject in the model of the Observer pattern.

Generalizations

- Subject, Interface (from Interfaces)

Associations

- attach: Attach [1..*] Every instance of InterfaceSubject must have at least one operation that is an instance of Attach. It is subset of Interface::ownedOperation.
- detach: Detach [1..*] Every instance of InterfaceSubject must have at least one operation that is an instance of Detach. It is a subset of Interface::ownedOperation.
- notify: Notify[1..*] Every instance of InterfaceSubject must have at least one operation that is an instance of Notify. It is a subset of Interface::ownedOperation.

Constraints

No additional constraints.

InterfaceRealizationObserver

Description

This metaclass specifies an interface realization between an abstract observer (InterfaceObserver) and a concrete observer (ConcreteObserver) in the model of the pattern *Observer*.

Generalizations

- InterfaceRealization (from Kernel)

Associations

- concreteObserver: ConcreteObserver [1] It designs the element that implements the contract in this relation. It redefines InterfaceRealization::implementingClassifier.

- interfaceObserver: InterfaceObserver [1] It designs the element that defines the contract in this relation. It redefines InterfaceRealization::contract.

Constraints
No additional constraints.

InterfaceRealizationSubject

Description
This metaclass specifies an interface realization between an abstract subject (InterfaceSubject) and a concrete subject (ConcreteSubject) in the model of the pattern *Observer*.

Generalizations

- InterfaceRealization (from Kernel)

Associations

- concreteSubject: ConcreteSubject [1] It designs the element that implements the contract in this relation. It redefines InterfaceRealization::implementingClassifier.
- interfaceSubject: InterfaceSubject [1] It designs the element that defines the contract in this relation. It redefines InterfaceRealization::contract.

Constraints
No additional constraints.

Notify

Description
It defines an operation that is declared by a subject.

Generalizations

- Operation (from Kernel, Interfaces)

Associations

- classSubject: ClassSubject [0..1] It designs the class that declares this operation. It redefines Operation::class.
- interfaceSubject: InterfaceSubject [0..1] It designs the interface that declares this operation. It redefines Operation::interface.

Constraints

[1]   It is an operation that does not change the state of the subject. self.isQuery
[2]   Its visibility must be public. self.visibility = #public

Observer

Description
An Observer is a specialized classifier that specifies the features of the classifier taking the role of observer in the model of the pattern Observer. It is an abstract metaclass.

Generalizations

•   Classifier (from Kernel)

Associations

•   assocEndObserver: AssocEndObserver [0..1] It denotes the end-association of the association SubjectObserver in which this classifier participates.

Constraints
No additional constraints.

ObserverSubject

Description
This metaclass specifies a binary association between two instances of Observer y Subject respectively.

Generalizations

•   Association (from Kernel)

Associations

•   assocEndConcreteObserver: AssocEndConcreteObserver [1] It represents a connection with the classifier ConcreteObserver. It is a subset of Association::memberEnd.
•   assocEndConcreteSubject: AssocEndConcreteSubject [1] It represents a connection with the classifier ConcreteSubject. It is a subset of Association::memberEnd.

Constraints

[1]   It has two association-end. self.memberEnd -> size () = 2

SetState

Description

It defines an operation of ConcreteSubject. It specifies a service that can be required from other object.

Generalizations

- Operation (from Kernel)

Associations

There are no additional associations.

Constraints

[1] It is a non-observer operation. **not** self.isQuery

[2] The set of parameters is not empty and at least, one of them must be an input parameter. self.ownedParameter -> notEmpty () **and** self.ownedParameter -> select (param | param.direction = #in) -> size() >= 1

[3] Its visibility must be public. self.visibility = #public

Subject

Description

This metaclass is a specialized classifier that specifies the features that must have the instance taking the role of subject in the model of the Observer pattern. It is an abstract metaclass.

Generalizations

- Classifier (from Kernel)

Associations

- assocEndSubject: AssocEndSubject [0..1] It denotes the association-end of the association SubjectObserver in which this classifier participates.

Constraints

No additional constraints.

SubjectObserver

Description

This metaclass specifies a binary association between two classifiers: Subject y Observer.

Generalizations

- Association (from Kernel)

Associations

- assocEndObserver: AssocEndObserver [1] It represents a connection with the Observer classifier. It is a subset of Association::memberEnd.
- assocEndSubject: AssocEndSubject [1] It represents a connection with the Subject classifier. It is a subset of Association::memberEnd.

Constraints

[1]   There are two association-end members. self.memberEnd -> size () = 2

Update

Description
It defines an operation that is declared by Observer specifing a service that may be required from other object.

Generalizations

- Operation (from Kernel, Interfaces)

Associations

- classObserver: ClassObserver [0..1] It denotes a class that is declared by this operation. It redefines Operation::ownedOperation.
- interfaceObserver: InterfaceObserver [0..1] It denotes the interface that is declared by this operation. It redefines Operation::ownedOperation.

Constraints

[1]   This operation does not change the state of the observer. self.isQuery
[2]   Its visibility must be public. self.visibility = #public

PSM-METAMODEL OF THE OBSERVER PATTERN

For each design pattern at the PIM level there is a number of metamodels corresponding to different platforms at the PSM level. In particular, we exemplify metamodels of the Observer pattern (structural view) in the Eiffel platform and Java platform.

PSM-Metamodel of the Observer Pattern for the Eiffel Platform

Figure 8 shows the metamodel of the structural view of the Observer pattern in the Eiffel platform. This metamodel was constructed as a specialization of the PSM-Eiffel metamodel. The PSM-Eiffel metamodel is described in Appendix A.

The main difference between the PIM and the PSM-Eiffel lies in the way in which are modeled the interfaces. These can be modeled as abstract classes, so instances of metaclasses Observer and Subject

Figure 8. PSM Eiffel observer metamodel

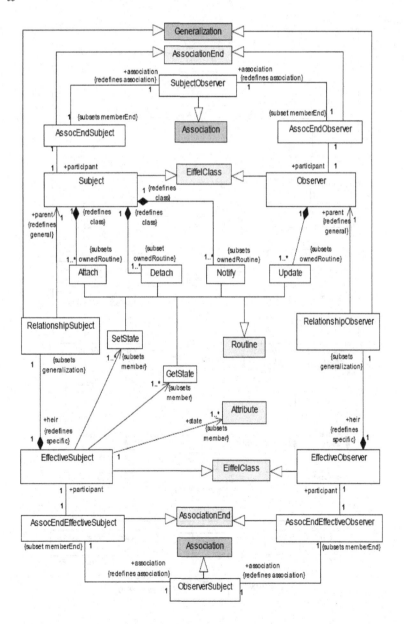

are abstract classes in Eiffel, and therefore, the relationships between instances of Observer and EffectiveObserver, and between the instances of Subject and EffectiveSubject are generalizations.

The metamodel establishes that a subject is related with an observer through a binary association to which is connected by two end-associations. In the same way, the effective observer is linked through a binary association to the effective subject.

A subject has at least three routine instances of the Attach, Detach y Notify operations. An observer has at least a routine of Update.

Figure 9. PSM Java Observer metamodel

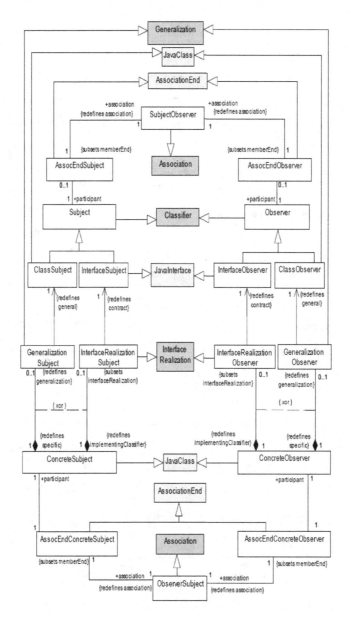

An effective subject must have a state determined by an attribute or a set of attributes, which will be objects of observation and, at least operations that allow us to obtain and modify their values. Attributes and routines can be own or inherited.

PSM-Metamodel of the Observer Pattern for the Java Platform

Figure 9 shows the Observer pattern metamodel in the Java platform. This metamodel is a specialization of the UML metamodel. Figure 10 shows the main metaclasses and their interrelations. Figure 11 and Figure 12 complete this view with methods corresponding to subjects and observers. This metamodel is a specialization of the PSM-Java metamodel (Appendix A), which in turn is a specialization of the UML metamodel (UML, 2009a, UML, 2009b).

The main difference with the PIM metamodel has to do with inheritance relationships due to Java does not have multiple inheritance. The metamodel establishes that the subject can be a Java class or a Java interface. In case that the subject is a Java class, it is linked to every concrete subject through a generalization where the subject takes the role of parent and the concrete subject the role of child.

Figure 10. PSM Java Observer metamodel: Abstract subject: Operations

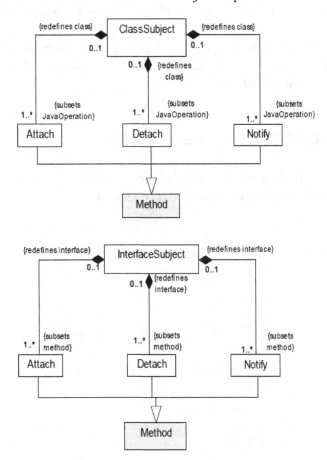

Figure 11. PSM Java Observer metamodel: Abstract observer: Operations

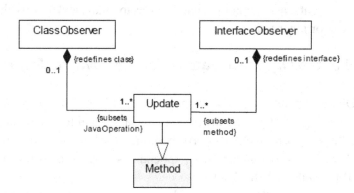

Otherwise, if the subject is an interface, it is linked to a concrete subject through a realization where the concrete subject implements the contract that is defined by the abstract subject.

Similar relations are established for the observer and the concrete observer. A subject is related with an observer through a binary association to which is connected by association-ends. In case the subject is an interface, this association can not appear. The concrete subject and the concrete object are linked in the same way through a binary association. A subject has at least three method instances of Attach, Detach y Notify.

An observer has at least an instance of Update. A concrete subject must have a state composed by one or more fields, observer object, and at least methods that allow get and modify their values. Both fields and methods, can be own or inherited.

ISM-METAMODEL OF THE OBSERVER PATTERN

Figures 13, 14, 15, 16, and 17 show the metamodel of the pattern Observer at Java level. This metamodel was built starting from the ISM-Java metamodel (Appendix A).

Figure 12. PSM Java Observer metamodel: Concrete subject: Operations

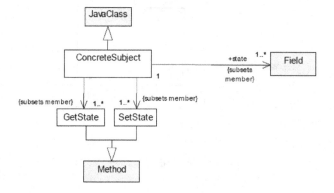

The main difference with the PSM metamodel is that at ISM level does not include association constructs and on the other hand, appear implementation constructs.

The metamodel establishes that a subject can be a class of a Java interface. If it is a class will includes at least three method instances of Attach, Detach y Notify, and a reference to its observers through an attribute which can be an instance of ObserverReference or an instance of SubjectObserverReference. In the first case, the attribute refers to the collection of observers. In the second case refers to the intermediate class that maintains the relation between subjects and observers.

Figure 13. ISM Java Observer metamodel: Class diagram

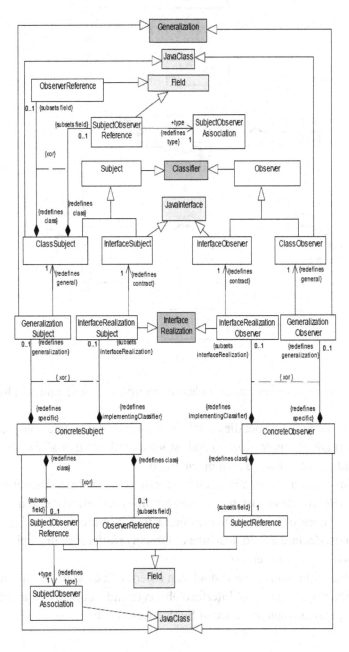

Figure 14. ISM Java Observer metamodel: Abstract subject: Operations

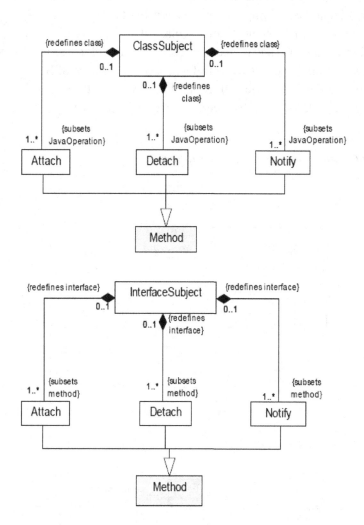

A class taking the role of observer can be a class or an interface Java and will have at least a method instance of Update.

The metaclass ConcreteSubject specifies a Java class which has a state composes by a field or a set of fields (which in turn are observer objects) and, at least methods that allow obtain and modify their values. Both fields and methods can be own or inherited.

If an instance of ConcreteSubject is heir of an instance of ClassSubject, then it will inherit a field that is instance of ObserverReference or instance of SubjectObserverReference, and hence does not need to declare any reference to their observers. On the contrary, if it implements an interface that is instance of InterfaceSubject, must declare a field, instance of ObserverReference or SubjectObserverReference, to maintain information on their observers.

ConcreteObserver specifies a Java class which can inherit of a class that is instance of ClassObserver or can implement an interface instance of InterfaceObserver and can maintain a reference to the subject that is observed through an attribute instance of SubjectReference.

Figure 15. ISM Java Observer metamodel: Abstract observer: Operations

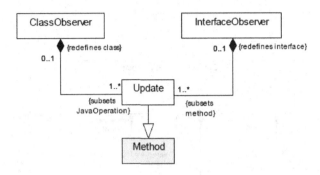

SubjectObserverAssociation specifies the Java class that maintains the relation between a subject and their observers. This class has an attribute instance of SubjectObserverMapping that stores the links between the subject and its observers. It must have methods for adding and removing such links and notify to observers of the changes in the subject.

SPECIFYING METAMODEL-BASED TRANSFORMATIONS

A model transformation is a specification of a mechanism to convert the elements of a model, that are instances of a particular metamodel, into elements of another model which can be instances of the same or different metamodels.

Metamodel transformations are a specific type of model transformations that impose relations between pairs of metamodels. They can be used in the specification stages of the MDA-based developments to check the validity of a transformation.

Figure 16. ISM Java Observer metamodel: Concrete subject: Operations

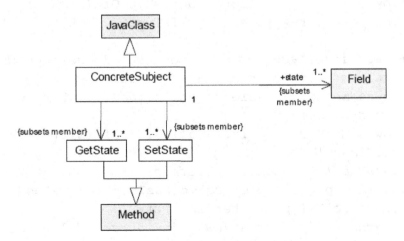

Figure 17. ISM Java Observer metamodel: SubjectObserverAssociation: Operations

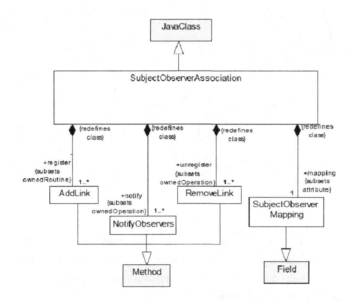

We specify metamodel-based model transformations as OCL contracts that are described by means of the notation described in Chapter 3 (see Figure 4). Below, we partially exemplify a transformation *Observer* Pattern component from a PIM to an Eiffel-based PSM.

```
Transformation PIM-UML to PSM-EIFFEL {parameters
sourceModel: Observer-PIM-Metamodel:: Package
targetModel: Observer-PSM-EIFFEL-Metamodel:: Package
preconditions-- TRUE for the general casepostconditionspost:--
sourceModel and targetModel have the same number of classifiers.
targetModel.ownedMember -> select (oclIsTypeOf (EiffelClass)) ->
size () =
sourceModel.ownedMember -> select (oclIsTypeOf (Class)) -> size () +
sourceModel.ownedMember-> select (oclIsTypeOf (Interface)) -> size
()
post:-- for each interface 'sourceInterface' in sourceModel exists a
class 'targetClass'-- in targetModel so that:
sourceModel.ownedMember -> select (oclIsTypeOf (Interface)) ->
forAll (sourceInterface |
targetModel.ownedMember -> select (oclIsTypeOf (EiffelClass)) ->
exists (targetClass |
-- 'targetClass' matches sourceInterface'.
targetClass.oclAsType (EiffelClass).classInterfaceMatch
(sourceInterface.oclAsType (Interface))))
post:-- For each class 'sourceClass' in sourceModel exists a class
'targetClass' in targetModel-- so that:
```

```
sourceModel.ownedMember -> select (oclIsTypeOf (Class)) -> forAll
(sourceClass |
targetModel.ownedMember -> select (oclIsTypeOf (EiffelClass)) ->
exists (targetClass |
-- 'targetClass' matches 'sourceClass'.
targetClass.oclAsType(EiffelClass).classClassMatch
(sourceClass.oclAsType (Class))))
```

local operationsObserver-PSM-EIFFEL -Metamodel::EiffelClass:: class-ClassMatch (aClass: Observer-PIM-Metamodel::Class): Boolean
```
classClassMatch (aClass) =
-- the class to which is applied this operation (self) matches the
class 'aClass '-- if they have the same name,
self.name = aClass.name and
-- they have the same abstraction level,
self.isDeferred = aClass.isAbstract and
-- they have the same visibility,
self.visibility = aClass.visibility and
-- they have the same restrictions,
self.invariant = aClass.ownedRule and
-- they have the same parameters,
self.parameters = aClass.ownedTemplateSignature.parameter and
-- the number of parents of self is equal to the number of parents
of aClass plus-- the number of interfaces implemented in aClass.
self.parents -> size () =
aClass.superClass -> size () + aClass.interfaceRealization.contract
-> size () and
-- for each class 'sourceParent' that is parent of aClass, exists a
class 'targetParent' in-- targetModel that is parent of self, and
'targetParent' matches sourceParent',
aClass.superClass -> forAll (sourceParent |
self.parents -> exists (targetParent |
targetParent.classClassMatch(sourceParent))) and
-- for each interface 'sourceContract' that implements aClass, ex-
ists a class-- 'targetParent' in targetModel that is the parent of
self, so that 'targetParent'-- matches 'sourceContract',
aClass.interfaceRealization.contract -> forAll (sourceContract |
self.parents -> exists (targetParent |
targetParent.classInterfaceMatch(sourceContract))) and
-- the number of routines of self is equal to the number of opera-
tions of aClass,
self.ownedRoutine -> size() = aClass.ownedOperation -> size () and
-- for each operation 'sourceOperation' of aClass which does not
return a result exists-- a procedure 'targetProcedure' in self that
```

```
matches 'sourceOperation',
aClass.ownedOperation -> select (op |
not op.ownedParameter -> exists (direction = #return)) -> forAll
(sourceOperation|
self.ownedRoutine -> exists (targetProcedure |
targetProcedure.oclIsTypeOf (Procedure) and

targetProcedure.rutineOperationMatch (sourceOperation))) and
-- for each operation 'sourceOperation' of aClass that returns a
result, exists a function 'targetFunction' in--self that matches
with the first,
aClass.ownedOperation -> select (op |
op.ownedParameter -> exists (direction = #return)) -> forAll (sour-
ceOperation|
self.ownedRoutine -> exists (targetFunction |
targetFunction.oclIsTypeOf (Function) and
targetFunction.rutineOperationMatch (sourceOperation))) and
-- the number of attributes plus the number of association-ends of
self is equal to-- the number of properties of aClass,
self.associationEnd -> size () + self.attribute -> size () = aClass.
ownedAttribute -> size () and
-- for each property 'sourceEnd' of aClass, which is an association-
end, exists-- in self an association-end 'targetEnd' that matches
'sourceEnd' and
aClass.ownedAttribute -> select (end | end.association -> size () =
1) ->
forAll (sourceEnd | self.associationEnd -> exists (targetEnd |
targetEnd.propertyMatch (sourceEnd))) and
-- for each property 'sourceAtt' of aClass, which is an attribute,
exists in self an attribute-- 'targetAtt' that matches 'sourceAtt'.
aClass.ownedAttribute -> select (att | att.association -> size () =
0) ->
forAll (sourceAtt | self.attribute -> exists (targetAtt |
targetAtt.propertyMatch (sourceAtt)))
```

**Observer-PSM-EIFFEL -Metamodel:: EiffelClass:: classInterfaceMatch
(anInterface: Observer-PIM-Metamodel::Interface): Boolean**
```
classInterfaceMatch (anInterface) =
-- the class to which this operation is applied (self) matches the
interface-- 'anInterface' if:-- they have the same name,
self.name = anInterface.name and
-- self is deferred,
self.isDeferred and
-- they have the same visibility,
```

```
self.visibility = anInterface.visibility and
-- they have the same restrictions,
self.invariant = anInterface.ownedRule and
-- they have the same parameters,
self.parameters = anInterface.ownedTemplateSignature.parameter and
-- for each interface that is parent of 'anInterface' exists a class
that is parent of self so that both-- match,
anInterface.superClass -> forAll (sourceParent |
self.parents -> exists (targetParent |
targetParent.classInterfaceMatch (sourceParent))) and
-- the number of routines of self is equal to the number of opera-
tions of ' anInterface'
self.ownedRoutine -> size () = anInterface.ownedOperation -> size ()
and
-- for each operation 'sourceOperation' of 'anInterface' which does
not return a result,-- exists a procedure 'targetProcedure' in self
that matches 'sourceOperation',
anInterface.ownedOperation -> select (op |
not op.ownedParameter ->exists (direction = #return)) -> forAll
(sourceOperation |
self.ownedRoutine -> exists (targetProcedure |
targetProcedure.oclIsTypeOf (Procedure) and
targetProcedure.routineOperationMatch (sourceOperation))) and
-- for each operation 'sourceOperation' of 'anInterface' that return
a result exists a-- function 'targetFunction' in self that matches
'sourceOperation',
anInterface.ownedOperation -> select (op |
op.ownedParameter -> exists (direction = #return)) -> forAll (sour-
ceOperation |
self.ownedRoutine -> exists (targetFunction |
targetFunction.oclIsTypeOf (Function) and
targetFunction.routineOperationMatch(sourceOperation))) and
-- the number of attributes plus the number of association-end of
self is equal to the-- number of properties of 'anInterface',
self.associationEnd -> size () + self.attribute -> size () = anIn-
terface.ownedAttribute ->size () and
-- for each property 'sourceEnd' of 'anInterface', that is an asso-
ciation-end,-- exists in self an association-end 'targetEnd 'so that
both properties match and,
anInterface.attribute -> select (end | end.association -> size () =
1) ->
forAll (sourceEnd | self.associationEnd -> exists (targetEnd |
targetEnd.propertyMatch (sourceEnd))) and
-- for each property 'sourceAtt' of 'anInterface',which is an attri-
```

bute, exists in self-- an attribute 'targetAtt' so that both properties match.
anInterface.attribute -> select (att | att.association -> size () =
0) ->
forAll (sourceAtt | self.attribute -> exists (targetAtt |
targetAtt.**propertyMatch**(sourceAtt)))

**Observer-PSM-EIFFEL -Metamodel:: Routine:: routineOperationMatch(anO
peration: Observer-PIM-Metamodel::Operation): Boolean**
routineOperationMatch (anOperation) =
-- the routine to which this operation is applied (self) matches the
operation-- 'anOperation' if:-- they have the same name,
self.name = anOperation.name and
-- they have the same visibility,
self.visibility = anOperation.visibility and
-- they have the same attribute value for isFrozen and isLeaf,
self.isFrozen = anOperation.isLeaf and
-- they have the same restrictions,
self.precondition = anOperation.precondition and
self.postcondition = anOperation.postcondition and
self.bodycondition = anOperation.bodycondition and
-- they have parameters with the same values of attributes and types
that match and,
anOperation.ownedParameter -> forAll (sourceParam |
self.ownedParameter -> exists(targetParam |
targetParam.name = sourceParam.name and
targetParam.direction = sourceParam.direction and
targetParam.defaultValue = sourceParam.defaultValue and
targetParam.isOrdered = sourceParam.isOrdered and
targetParam.upperValue = sourceParam.upperValue and
targetParam.lowerValue = sourceParam.lowerValue and
(targetParam.type = sourceParam.type or
targetParam.type.**conformsTo**(sourceParam.type)))) and
-- if 'anOperation' belongs to an interface, then it implies that
self is deferred
anOperation.interface -> size () =1 implies self.isDeferred

**Observer-PSM-EIFFEL -Metamodel:: Property::propertyMatch(aProperty:
Observer-PIM-Metamodel::Property): Boolean**
attributeMatch (aProperty) =
-- The property to which this operation is applied (self) matches
'aProperty'-- if both have attributes with the same values and
self.name = aProperty.name and
self.isDerived = aProperty.isDerived and

```
self.isReadOnly = aProperty.isReadOnly and
self.isDerivedOnly = aProperty.isDerivedOnly and
self.aggregation = aProperty.aggregation and
self.default = aProperty.default and
self.isComposite = aProperty.isComposite and
self.isStatic = aProperty.isStatic and
self.isOrdered = aProperty.isOrdered and
self.isUnique = aProperty.isUnique and
self.upper = aProperty.upper and
self.lower = aProperty.lower and
self.ownedRule = aProperty.ownedRule and
self.isFrozen = aProperty.isLeaf and
self.visibility = aProperty.visibility and
```
-- the type of self conforms to the type of 'aProperty'.
```
self.type = aProperty.type or self.type.conformsTo (aProperty.type)
```
Observer-PSM-EIFFEL -Metamodel:: Type::conformsTo (aType: Observer-PIM-Metamodel:: Type): Boolean
```
conformsTo (aType) =
```
*-- This operation determines whether the type to which this operation is applied (self)matches 'aType'.-- if 'aType' is an OCL type, self could match some of the types that are defined in Eiffel library.-- There are two cases:-- If 'aType' is an OCL primitive type, self could match some of the primitive types that are defined in the Kernel component in the Eiffel library.***if** aType.oclIsKindOf (Primitive) **then** (
```
aType.oclIsTypeOf (Integer) implies self.oclIsTypeOf (INTEGER) and
aType.oclIsTypeOf (Real) implies self.oclIsTypeOf (REAL) and
aType.oclIsTypeOf (String) implies self.oclIsTypeOf (STRING) and
aType.oclIsTypeOf (Boolean) implies self.oclIsTypeOf (BOOLEAN)
```
) **else***-- If 'aType' is an OCL Collection type, self could match some of the collection types that are defined in the -- data structures component in the Eiffel library.***if** aType.oclIsKindOf(Collection) **then** (
```
aType.oclIsTypeOf (SetType) implies self.oclIsKindOf (SET) and
aType.oclIsTypeOf (OrderedSetType) implies
self.oclIsKindOf (TWO_WAY_SORTED_SET) and
aType.oclIsTypeOf (SequenceType) implies
self.oclIsKinkOf(SEQUENCE) and
aType.oclIsTypeOf (BagType) implies self.oclIsKindOf (BAG))
```
endif
endif

The definition of the transformation from PIM to PSM uses both the specialized UML metamodel of the *Observer* pattern and the UML metamodel of an Eiffel platform as source and target parameters respectively. The source metamodel describes a family of packages whose elements are only classes and associations. The postconditions establish correspondences among classes, their superclasses, parameters, operations, and associations. The transformation specification guarantees, for instance, that for each class *sourceClass* in the source exists a class *targetClass* in the target model, both of them with the same name, the same parent classes and same child classes and so on.

We describe a transformation from a model of the pattern Observer at PIM level to a PSM in the Eiffel platform. The definition uses PIM and PSM metamodels as source and target parameters.

Postconditions establish mappings between classes and interfaces in the source model and classes in the target one. The different relationships between the source and the target model are commented in the text of the transformation. .

FORMALIZATION OF MEGAMODEL INSTANCES

The formalization implies formalizing metamodels, refinements and links among them. We describe how to transform metamodels and metamodel-based refinements.

Constructing Metamodel Formalization

MOF-metamodels and NEREUS have similar constructs and structuring mechanisms. Then, every package in a metamodel is translated into a package in NEREUS. Also, every class or association in a metamodel is translated into a class or an association in NEREUS.

In this section we partially show the Package ObserverMetamodel that specifies in NEREUS the pattern Observer at PIM level. The names of the associations refer to the linked classes, for instance, *AssocEndConcreteObserver-ConcreteObserver* denotes an association between the classes *AssocEndConcreteObserver* and *ConcreteObserver*. Classes and association in the Package ObserverMetamodel are shown in lexical orden.

```
PACKAGE ObserverMetamodel
IMPORTS Kernel, Interfaces, Dependencies
-- Specification of Metaclasses
...
CLASS ClassObserver
IS-SUBTYPE-OF Class, Observer
ASSOCIATES
<<ClassObserver-Update>>
GENERATED_BY create
TYPES ClassObserver
OPERATIONS
create: * → ClassObserver
END-CLASS

CLASS ClassSubject
```

IS-SUBTYPE-OF Class, Subject
ASSOCIATES
<< Attach-ClassSubject>>
<<ClassSubject-Detach>>
<<ClassSubject-Notify>>
GENERATED_BY create
TYPES
ClassSubject
OPERATIONS
create: * → ClassSubject
END-CLASS

CLASS ConcreteObserver
IS-SUBTYPE-OF Class
ASSOCIATES
<<AssocEndConcreteObserver-ConcreteObserver>>
<<ConcreteObserver-GeneralizationObserver>>
<<ConcreteObserver-InterfaceRealizationObserver>>
TYPES ConcreteObserver
OPERATIONS
create: * → ConcreteObserver
AXIOMS obs: ConcreteObserver; CI: ConcreteObserver-InterfaceRealiza-
tionObserver
not isAbstract (obs)
notEmpty (get_interfaceRealizationObserver (CI, obs)) => oclIsKindOf
(obs, BehavioredClassifier)
END-CLASS

CLASS ConcreteSubject
IS-SUBTYPE-OF Class
ASSOCIATES
<<AssocEndConcreteSubject-ConcreteSubject>>
<<ConcreteSubject-SetState>>
<<ConcreteSubject-GeneralizationSubject>>
<<ConcreteSubject-GetState>>
<<ConcreteSubject-InterfaceRealizationSubject>>
<<ConcreteSubject-Property>>
TYPES
ConcreteSubject
OPERATIONS
create: * → ConcreteSubject
AXIOMS sub:ConcreteSubject; CP: ConcreteSubject-Property;
AP: Association-Property;
CI: ConcreteSubject-InterfaceRealizationSubject

```
not isAbstract (sub)
notEmpty (get_interfaceRealizationObserver (CI, sub)) =>
oclIsKindOf(sub, BehavioredClassifier)
forAll (p) (get_state (CP, sub), [isEmpty (get_association (AP, p)
])
```
END-CLASS

CLASS Observer
IS-SUBTYPE-OF Classifier
ASSOCIATES
<<AssocEndObserver-Observer>>
GENERATED_BY create
DEFFERREDTYPES
Observer
OPERATIONS
create: * → Observer
END-CLASS

CLASS ObserverSubject
IS-SUBTYPE-OF Association
ASSOCIATES
<<AssocEndConcreteSubject-ObserverSubject>>
<<AssocEndConcreteObserver-ObserverSubject>>
GENERATED_BY create
TYPES
ObserverSubject
OPERATIONS
create: * → ObserverSubject
AXIOMS a: ObserverSubject; AP: Association-Property
size (get_memeberEnd(AP, a)) = 2
END-CLASS

CLASS Subject
IS-SUBTYPE-OF Classifier
ASSOCIATES
<<AssocEndSubject-Subject>>
GENERATED_BY create
DEFFERREDTYPES Subject
OPERATIONS
create: * → Subject
END-CLASS

CLASS SubjectObserver
IS-SUBTYPE-OF Association

ASSOCIATES
<<AssocEndSubject-SubjectObserver>>
<<AssocEndObserver-SubjectObserver>>
GENERATED_BY create
TYPES
SubjectObserver
OPERATIONS
create: * → SubjectObserver
AXIOMS a: SubjectObserver ; AP: Association-Property
Size (get_memberEnd (AP, a)) = 2
END-CLASS
...
-- *Specification of associations***ASSOCIATION** AssocEndConcreteObserver-ConcreteObserver
IS Bidirectional-1 [AssocEndConcreteObserver: Class1; ConcreteObserver: Class2;
assocEndConcreteObserver: role1; participant: role2; 1:mult1;
1:mult2; +:visibility1; +:visibility2]
END

ASSOCIATION AssocEndConcreteObserver-ObserverSubject
IS Bidirectional-1 [AssocEndConcreteObserver: Class1; ObserverSubject: Class2;
assocEndConcreteObserver: role1; association: role2; 1:mult1;
1:mult2; +:visibility1; +:visibility2]
CONSTRAINED_BY
assocEndConcreteObserver: subsets memberEnd
association: redefines association
END

ASSOCIATION AssocEndConcreteSubject-ConcreteSubject
IS Bidirectional-1 [AssocEndConcreteSubject: Class1; ConcreteSubject: Class2;
assocEndConcreteSubject:role1; participant:role2; 1:mult1; 1:mult2;
+:visibility1; +:visibility2]
END

ASSOCIATION AssocEndConcreteSubject-ObserverSubject
IS Bidirectional-1 [AssocEndConcreteSubject: Class1; ObserverSubject: Class2;
assocEndConcreteSubject:role1; association:role2; 1:mult1; 1:mult2;
+:visibility1; +:visibility2]
CONSTRAINED_BY
assocEndConcreteSubject: subsets memberEnd

```
association: redefines association
```
END

...

END-PACKAGE

Formalizing Refinements

Instances of refinement classes are translated into NEREUS specifications by instantiating reusable schemes (see Figure 18).

Below, the specification of the refinement between a PIM-UML and a PSM-Eiffel is shown. The function *TranslateNEREUS (transformation.precondition)* that appears in the transformation scheme as a precondition of the operation addLink translates into NEREUS the OCL precondition. The function *TranslateNEREUS (transformation.postcondition)* that appears in the axioms translates into NEREUS axioms the OCL postconditions. An instantiation of the transformation scheme is the following:

```
[TransformationName:PIM-UML to PSM-EIFFEL;
sourceMetamodel: Observer-PIM -Metamodel;
```

Figure 18. A scheme for translating refinements: From UML/OCL to NEREUS

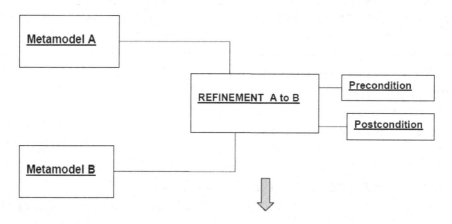

CLASS *transformationName* [source: <u>*Metamodel A;*</u> target: <u>*Metamodel B*</u>]
GENERATED-BY addLink
EFFECTIVE
TYPE
transformationName
OPERATIONS
addLink : source x target -> *transformationName*
pre : Translate _{NEREUS} (<u>*Transformation_AtoB. Precondition*</u>)
getSource : *transformationName* -> source
getTarget : *transformationName* -> target
AXIOMS m1 : source ; m2 : target ; l: *transformationName*
getSource (addLink(m1,m2)) = m1
getTarget (addLink (m1,m2)) = m2
Translate _{NEREUS} (<u>*Transformation.Postcondition*</u>)

END-CLASS

targetMetamodel: Observer-PSM-EIFFEL-Metamodel;
precondition: OCLexp1;
postcondition: OCLexp2]

CLASS PIM-UML_to_PSM-EIFFEL
GENERATED-BY addLink
EFFECTIVETYPES
PIM -UML_to_PSM-EIFFEL
OPERATIONS
addLink:
Observer-PIM-Metamodel x Observer-PSM-EIFFEL-Metamodel → PIM-UML_to_PSM-EIFFEL
get-source: PIM -UML_to_PSM-EIFFEL → Observer-PIM-Metamodel
get-target: PIM -UML_to_PSM-EIFFEL → Observer-PSM-EIFFEL-Metamodel
equal: PIM-UML_to_PSM-EIFFEL x PIM-UML_to_PSM-EIFFEL → Boolean
-- *local operations (private)*
classClassMatch:
Observer-PSM-EIFFEL-Metamodel::EiffelClass x Observer-PIM-Metamodel::Class → Boolean
classInterfaceMatch: Observer-PSM-EIFFEL-Metamodel::EiffelClass x
Observer-PIM-Metamodel::Interface → Boolean …
AXIOMS
m1: Observer-PIM-Metamodel, m2: Observer-PSM-EIFFEL-Metamodel;
t1, t2: PIM-UML_to_PSM-EIFFEL; PP: Package-PackageableElement;
e: Observer-PSM-EIFFEL-Metamodel::EiffelClass; c: Observer-PIM -Metamodel::Class; …
get-source (addLink (m1, m2)) = m1
get-target (addLink (m1, m2)) = m2
equal (t1, t2) = **IF** get-source (t1) = get-source (t2) and get-target (t1) = get-target (t2)
 THEN true **ELSE** false
-- *TranslateNEREUS (Transformation.postcondition)-- sourceModel and targetModel have the equal number of classifiers.*
size (select (elem) (get_ownedMember(PP,m2), [oclIsTypeOf (elem, EiffelClass)])) =
size (select (elem) (get_ownedMember (PP, m1), [oclIsTypeOf (elem, Class)])) +
size (select (elem) (get_ownedMember (PP, m1), [oclIsTypeOf (elem, Interface)])) and
-- *For each interface 'sourceInterface' in sourceModel exists a class 'targetClass'-- in targetModel so that:*
forAll (sourceInterface) (select (elem) (get_ownedMember (PP, m1), [oclIsTypeOf (elem, Interface)]),
[exists (targetClass) (select (elem) (get_ownedMember (PP,m2),

```
[oclIsTypeOf (elem, EiffelClass)]),
-- sourceInterface and targetClass match
[interfaceClassMatch (oclAsType (targetClass, EiffelClass),
oclAsType (sourceInterface, Interface)) ]) ]) and
-- for each class 'sourceClass' in sourceModel exists a class 'tar-
getClass' in targetModel so that:
forAll (sourceClass) (select (elem) (get_ownedMember (PP, m1),
[oclIsTypeOf (elem, Class)]),
[exists (targetClass) (select (elem) (get_ownedMember (PP, m2),
[oclIsTypeOf (elem, EiffelClass)]),
-- sourceClass and targetClass match
[classClassMatch (oclAsType (targetClass, EiffelClass),oclAsType
(sourceClass, Class)])])
-- local operations
classClassMatch (e, c) = equal (name (e), name (c)) and equal (isDe-
ferred (e),isAbstract (c)) and
...
```

END-CLASS

REFERENCES

Albin-Amiot, H., & Guéhéneuc, Y. (2008). Abstract Design Patterns: A Round-trip. *CiteSearX*. Retrieved on July 20, 2009 from http://www.st.informatik.tu-darmstadt.de:8080/phdws/PHDOOS.pdf

Alpert, S., Brown, K., & Woolf, B. (1998). *The design Patterns Smalltalk Companion*. Reading: Addison-Wesley.

Arnout, K. (2004). *From Patterns to Components*. Ph. D. Thesis, Swiss Institute of Technology (ETH Zurich). Retrieved on July 20, 2009 from http://se.ethz.ch/people/arnout/patterns/

Bettin, J. (2003). Practicalities of Implementing Component-Based Development and Model-Driven Architecture. In *Proceedings of the Workshop Process Engineering for Object-Oriented and Component-Based Development, OOSPLA 2003, USA*. Retrieved on July 20 from www.open.org.au/Conferences/oopsla2003/PE_Papers/Bettin.pdf

Bezivin, J., Jouault, F., & Valduriez, P. (2004). On the need for Megamodels. In J. Bettin, G. van Emde Boas, A. Agrawal, M. Volter, & J. Bezivin (Eds.), *Proceedings of Best Practices for Model-Driven Software Development (MDSD 2004). OOSPLA 2004 Workshop. Vancouver, Canada*. Retrieved on July 20, 2009 from www.softmetaware.com/oospla2004.

Budinsky, F., Finni, M., Vlissides, J., & Yu, P. (1996). Automatic code generation from design patterns. *IBM Systems Journal, 35*(2), 151–171.

CASE. (2009). *CASE Tools*. Retrieved on July 20, 2009 from www.objectsbydesign.com/tools/uml-tools_byCompany.html

D'Souza, D., & Cameron Wills, A. (1999). *On Components, and Framework with UML*. Reading: Addison-Wesley.

Favre, L. (2005). Foundations for MDA-based Forward Engineering. *Journal of Object Technology (JOT)*, *4*(1), 129-153). Retrieved on July 20, 2009 from www.jot.fm

Favre, L. (2006). A Rigorous Framework for Model Driven Development. In K. Siau (Ed.), *Advanced Topics in Database Research, Vol. 5* (pp. 1-27). Hershey, PA: Idea Group Publishing.

Favre, L., & Martinez, L. (2006). Formalizing MDA Components. In *Proceedings of 9th International Conference on Software Reuse* (LNCS 4039, pp. 326-339). Heidelberg: Springer-Verlag.

Florijn, G., Meijers, M., & van Winsen, P. (1997) Tool support for object-oriented patterns. In *Proceedings of ECOOP '97 (European Conference on Object Oriented Programming), Jyväskylä, Finland* (pp. 472-795).

France, R., Kim, D., Ghosh, S., & Song, E. (2004). A UML-Based Pattern Specification Technique. *IEEE Transactions on Software Engineering, 30*(3), 193–206. doi:10.1109/TSE.2004.1271174

Gamma, E., Helm, R., Johnson, R., & Vlissides, J. (1995). Design Patterns. Elements of Reusable Object-Oriented Software. Reading: Addison-Wesley.

Grand, M. (1998). Patterns in Java. *A Catalog of Reusable Design Patterns Illustrated with UML*. Wiley Computer Publishing.

Judson, S., Carver, D., & France, R. (2003). A metamodeling approach to model transformation. *OOPSLA Companion, 2003*, 326–327.

Kim, D., France, R., Ghosh, S., & Song, E. (2003b). A Role-Based Metamodeling Approach to Specifying Design Patterns. In *Proceedings of the 27th Annual International Computer Software and Applications Conference (COMPSAC'03)* (pp. 452-457). Los Alamitos: IEEE Computer Society.

Krueger, C. (1992). Software Reuse. *ACM Computing Surveys, 24*(2), 131–183. doi:10.1145/130844.130856

Meyer, B. (2003). The Grand Challenge of Trusted Components. In *Proceedings of the 25th International Conference on Software Engineering, Portland, Oregon* (pp. 660-667).

Szyperski, C., Gruntz, D., & Murer, S. (2002). *Component Software: Beyond Object-Oriented Programming* (2nd ed.). Reading: Addison-Wesley.

UML. (2009a). *Unified Modeling Language: Infrastructure*. Version 2.2. OMG Specification formal/2009-02-04. Retrieved on July 20, 2009 from www.omg.org.

UML. (2009b). *UML: Unified Modeling Language: Superstructure*. Version 2.2. OMG Specification: formal/2009-02-02. Retrieved on July 20, 2009 from www.omg.org

Chapter 9
Evolution of Models and MDA–Based Refactoring

INTRODUCTION

In MDA is crucial to define, manage, and maintain traces and relationships between different models, and automatically transform them and produce implementations.

Refactoring is a powerful technique when is repeatedly applied to a model to obtain another one with the same behavior but enhancing some non functionality quality factor such as simplicity, flexibility, understandability and performance (Fowler, 1999) (Mens, Van Eetvelde, Demeyer & Janssens, 2005). Refactorings are horizontal transformations for supporting perfective model evolution.

In MDA, a crucial part of the evolution from abstract models to executable components or applications (forward engineering) or, from code to abstract models (reverse engineering) is accomplished by means of refactoring. Although the most effective forms of refactorings are at the design levels (for example, PIMs or PSMs), MDA-based CASE tools provide limited facilities for refactoring only on source code through an explicit selection made by the designer (CASE, 2009).

MDA-based refactorings can be specified in OCL as contracts between meta-patterns (MOF meta-model), consisting of pre- and post-conditions that hold for the model before/after refactoring. Besides, we propose an alternative formalization based on the NEREUS language. We propose a uniform treatment of refactoring at platform independent, platform specific and implementation specific abstraction levels.

DOI: 10.4018/978-1-61520-649-0.ch009

Refactoring is an important technique in MDA processes such as forward engineering and reverse engineering. In this context, refactoring techniques should be raised to higher levels of abstraction in order to achieve software evolution.

We propose an MDA framework for refactoring that is structured at three different levels of abstraction linked to models, metamodels and formal specification. The model level includes different kind of models (PIM, PSM, ISM) related by refinement.

Considering there is a need for rigorous techniques that address refactoring in a more consistent and precise way, we propose a rigorous approach to identify refactorings by formal specification matching.

In the following sections we describe an MDA-based refactoring approach. First, we describe some related work.

RELATED WORK

This section shows the evolution of refactoring techniques and remarks the advantages of an MDA approach.

The first relevant publication on refactoring was carried out by Opdyke (1992), showing how functionalities and attributes can migrate among classes, how classes can be joined and separated using a class diagram notation (subset of current UML). Roberts (1999) completed this work describing techniques based on refactoring contracts. Fowler (1999) is the classical book on code refactoring. It informally analyzes refactoring techniques on Java source code, explaining the structural changes through examples with class diagrams.

Several approaches provide support to restructure UML models. In (Sunyé, Pollet, LeTraon, and Jézéquel, 2001) a set of refactorings is presented and how they may be designed to preserve the behavior of UML models is explained. Mens, Demeyer, DuBois, Stenten, and Van Gorp (2003) provide an overview of existing research in the field of refactoring. Porres (2003) defines and implements model refactorings as rule-based transformations. Van Gorp, Stenten, Mens, and Demeyer (2003) propose a set of minimal extensions to UML metamodel, which allows reasoning about refactoring for all common object-oriented languages.

There is a tendency to integrate refactoring tools into industrial software development environments. For example, Together ControlCenter (CASE, 2009) applies code refactoring on user requirements. Mens, Van Eetvelde, Demeyer, and Janssens (2005) explore the use of graph rewriting for specifying refactorings and prove that them preserve some properties. (France, Ghosh, Song, & Kim, 2003), (Laplante, & Neill, 2005) and Kerievsky (2004) describe methods for pattern-directed refactorings.

Long, Jifeng, and Liu (2005) formalizes Fowler´s refactorings (Fowler, 1999) as refinement laws in a relational calculus.

Batory (2007) explores the underlying connections among program refactoring, program synthesis and MDD from an architectural meta-programming perspective.

Folli and Mens (2008) analyze refactoring of UML models in the context of graph transformation approach. They use a specific graph transformation tool, AGG, and provide suggestions of how AGG may be improved to better support model refactoring.

(Demeyer, Ducasse, & Nierstrasz, 2002), (Mens, & Tourwe, 2004), (Thomas, 2005) and (France & Rumpe, 2007) describe the state-of-the-art of refactoring.

Figure 1. A framework for MDA refactoring

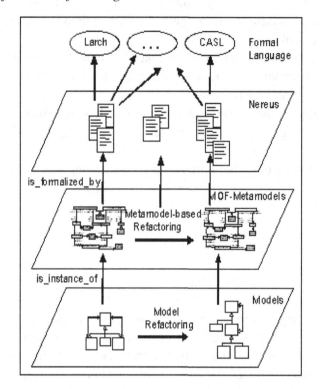

MDA-BASED REFACTORING

We propose an MDA framework for refactoring that is structured at three different levels of abstraction linked to models, metamodels and formal specification (Favre & Pereira, 2008) (Favre & Pereira, 2006). The model level includes different kind of models (PIM, PSM, ISM) related by refinement. At this level refactorings are based on a set of model refactoring rules. The metamodel level imposes relations between a source metamodel and a target metamodel, both represented as MOF-metamodels. Every PIM, PSM and ISM is an instance of a MOF-metamodel.

The level of formal specifications links MOF-metamodels and metamodel-based refactorings to formal specifications. We propose to formalize MOF-metamodels and metamodel-based transformations by using the NEREUS language. NEREUS can be used as a common specification language and is connected with different semiformal, formal and programming languages. Figure 1 depicts the levels of the framework.

In summary, in the level of models, the refactoring of instances of PIMs, PSMs and ISMs is based on classical pattern-directed refactoring techniques, MOF-metamodels "control" the consistency of these transformations and, NEREUS facilitates the connection of the metamodels with different formal languages. NEREUS can be used to reason and ensure consistency of refactoring and to take advantage of all existing theoretical background on formal methods, using different tools such as theorem provers, model checkers or rewrite engines.

SPECIFYING MDA REFACTORING

We define a catalog of semantics-preserving transformation rules. This catalog includes the classical refactorings (Fowler, 1999) (Kerievsky, 2004) and, a repertory of refactorings of UML class diagrams linked to PIMs and PSMs.

The next section describes the Extract-Composite Refactoring that will be used as a running example (Kerievsky, 2004, pp. 214).

The Extract Composite Refactoring

The Extract Composite refactoring was described in terms of JAVA code in (Kerievsky, 2004, p. 214). We propose to specify this rule at the PIM level. Figure 2 exemplifies the Extract Composite refactoring as a pattern-directed rule.

The source pattern in Figure 2 depicts subclasses in a hierarchy that implement the same composite. The rule application extracts a superclass that implements the composite removing duplicate behavior. The main steps in the proposed transformation are: create a composite; make each class that contains duplicate behavior a subclass of the composite and identify methods that are purely duplicated or partially duplicated across the subclasses of a composite. A purely duplicated method can be moved with all child containers to the composite. If the method is partially duplicated only the common behavior across all subclasses can be moved.

Within MDA, refactorings are a particular kind of model-to-model transformation. Metamodel transformations impose relations between a source metamodel and a target metamodel both represented as MOF- metamodels (MOF, 2006).

REFACTORING AT METAMODEL LEVEL

We propose to express refactorings as metamodel transformations between source and target meta-patterns. A meta-pattern defines a family of patterns, its instances. A meta-pattern transformation describes

Figure 2. The Extract Composite refactoring

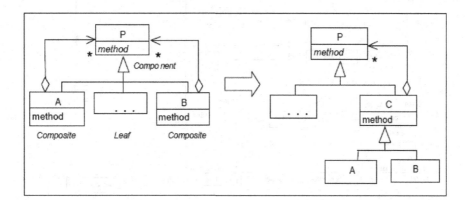

Figure 3. The Extract Composite Refactoring: Source metamodel

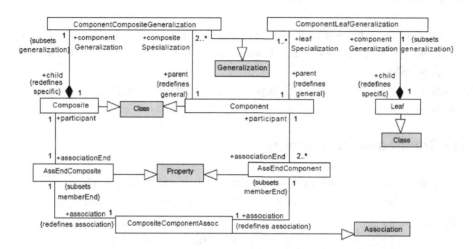

a mechanism to convert the elements of a pattern that are instances of a particular meta-pattern, into elements of another pattern.

Refactorings could be specified as contract imposing relations between a source metamodel and a target metamodel both represented as MOF- metamodel. Figure 3 and Figure 4 show the source and target metamodels for the Extract-Composite. The source metamodel defines the family of source models to which refactorings can be applied and the target metamodel characterizes models that are generated. The models to be transformed and the resulting models of the transformations will be instances of the corresponding metamodel.

The source and target metamodels include metaclasses linked to the essential participants in the patterns of Figure 2: Composite, Component and Leaf and, three relationships: Composite-Component-Assoc, Component-Leaf-Generalization and Component-Composite-Generalization. The metamodel also

Figure 4. The Extract Composite Refactoring: Target metamodel

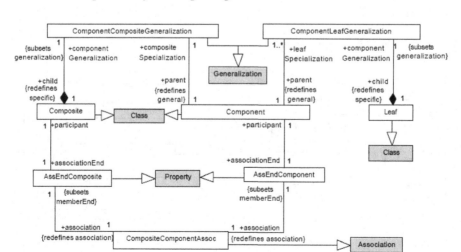

shows metaclasses linked to properties such as AssEndComposite and AssEndComponent and, shaded metaclasses that correspond to the UML metamodel.

We can remark the following differences between the source and target metamodel. On the one hand, in the source metamodel, an instance of Component has two or more instances of Component-Composite-Generalization (compositeSpecialization) and two or more association-ends (associationEnd).

On the other hand, in the target metamodel, an instance of Component has exactly one instance of Component-Composite-Generalization and one association-end.

Extract Composite Refactoring: Source Metamodel

Notation of the Design Pattern Metamodels

Metamodels are expressed as UML class diagrams following the UML 2.2 notation. Metaclasses of the UML metamodel are shown in dark gray; metaclasses of the specific platforms and programming languages are shown gray whereas the remaining metaclasses corresponds to the specialization of the UML metamodel. The description of metaclasses is organized in alphabetical order.

Abstract Syntax

Figure 3 shows the metaclasses linked to the essential participants in the source metamodel to which can be applied the refactoring *Extract Composite*:

- *Composite*, *Component* and *Leaf*, refer to one class of the model with special features,
- *CompositeComponentAssoc*, *ComponentLeafGeneralization* and*ComponentCompositeGeneralization*, refer particular relationships between the classes Composite, Component and Leaf,
- *AssEndComposite* and *AssEndComponent*, represent class properties,

The source metamodel specifies an instance of *Component* that has two or more instances of *ComponentCompositeGeneralization* (*compositeSpecialization*), i.e., two or more generalizations that have a subclass that is an instance of *Composite*.

On the other hand, an instance of *Component* has two or more association-ends (*associationEnd*), each of them is linked to an association whose type is *CompositeComponentAssoc* which in turn, has another association-end whose participant is an instance of *Composite*. An instance of *Component* has one or more instances of *ComponentLeafGeneralization*, i.e., one or more generalizations that has a subclass that is an instance of *Leaf*.

Description of the Metaclasses

AssEndComponent

Description
It describes the link between the association *CompositeComponentAssoc* and the class *Component*.

Generalizations

- Property (from *Kernel)*.

Attributes
No additional attributes.

Associations

- association: CompositeComponentAssoc [1] It denotes the association that links the classes *Component* and *Composite*. It redefines *Property::association*.
- participant: Component [1] It denotes the class that participates in the association in this association-end.

Constraints
No additional constraints

AssEndComposite

Description
It denotes the link between the association *CompositeComponentAssoc* and the class *Composite*.

Generalizations

- Property (from Kernel)

Attributes
No additional attributes.

Associations

- association: CompositeComponentAssoc [1] It refers to the association that links the classes *Component* and *Composite*. It redefines *Property::association*.
- participant: Composite [1] It denotes the class that participates in the association in this association-end.

Constraints

[1]   The association-end is an aggregation or a composition. self.aggregation = #shared or self.aggregation = #composite

Component

Description
It represents a class having the role of *Component* in an inheritance hierarchy.

Generalizations

• Class (from Kernel)

Attributes
No additional attributes.

Associations

• associationEnd: AssEndComponent [2..*] It denotes the set of association-ends, in which the class *Component* participates. These association-ends belong to associations that connect with the class *Composite*.
• compositeSpecialization: ComponentCompositeGeneralization [2..*] It specifies the set of generalizations in which *Component* is the superclass and a class *Composite* is a subclass.
• leafSpecialization: ComponentLeafGeneralization [1..*] It specifies the set of generalizations in which *Component* is the superclass and a class *Leaf* is the subclass.

Constraints

[1]   The associations between *Composite* and *Component* are equivalent.

AssEndComposite

Description
It denotes the connection between the association *CompositeComponentAssoc* and the class *Composite*.

Generalizations

• Property (from *Kernel*)

Attributes
No additional attributes.

Associations

• association: CompositeComponentAssoc [1] It refers to the association that connects instances of the classes *Component* and *Composite*. It redefines *Property::association*.

- participant: Composite [1] It refers to the class that participates in the association of this association-end.

Constraints

[1] The association-end is aggregation or composition. self.aggregation = #shared or self.aggregation = #composite

Component

Description
It represents a class having the role of *Component* in an inheritance hierarchy.

Generalizations

- Class (from Kernel)

Attributes
No additional attributes.

Associations

- associationEnd: AssEndComponent [2..*] It denotes the set of association-ends (in which the class *Component* participates) belonging to associations that are linked to the class *Composite*.
- compositeSpecialization: ComponentCompositeGeneralization [2..*] It specifies the set of generalizations in which *Component* is the superclasss and a class *Composite* is the subclass.
- leafSpecialization: ComponentLeafGeneralization [1..*] It specifies the set of generalizations in which *Component* is the superclass and a class *Leaf* is the subclass.

Constraints

[1] The associations between *Composite* and *Component* are equivalent. self.associationEnd → collect (assEnd | assEnd.association) → forAll (a1, a2 | a1 = a2 or a1.isEquivalentTo (a2))

[2] In each class *Composite*, that is subclass of *Component*, exists operations that have functionality equivalents to operations of other classes *Composite*. The operation *isEquivalentOperationTo()* verifies whether the operation passed as parameter is equivalent to the operation to which the operation is applied. This implies that they verify signature, plug-in and exact match. The operation *isEquivalentOperationTo()* is specified as additional operation in the UML metamodel (Appendix A).
-- for all class *Composite*, subclass of *Component* self.compositeSpecialization.child → forAll (class |
-- exists operations class.ownedOperation → exists (op | self.compositeSpecialization.child →
excluding (class) → forAll (c | c.ownedOperation → exists (o |
-- functionally equivalent to operations of another classes Composite op.isEquivalentOperationTo (o)))))

Local Operations

- CompositeComponentAssoc:
  isEquivalentTo (a: CompositeComponentAssoc): Boolean;
  -- It verifies whether or no the association passed as parameter is equivalent to the
  -- association to which the operation is applied, i.e., they are equivalent, except
  -- their names; the other features are preserved.
  isEquivalentTo (a) = (self.name = a.name or self.name $\diamond$ a.name) and
  self.isDerived = a.isDerived and self.visibility = a.visibility and
  self.memberEnd $\rightarrow$ forAll (a1End | a.memberEnd $\rightarrow$ exists (a2End |
  (a1End.name = a2End.name or a1End.name $\diamond$ a2End.name) and
  a1End.visibility = a2End.visibility and a1End.isLeaf = a2End.isLeaf and
  a1End.isStatic = a2End.isStatic and a1End.isDerived = a2End.isDerived and a1End.isReadOnly
  = a2End.isReadOnly and a1End.isDerivedUnion = a2End.isDerivedUnion and a1End.aggre-
  gation = a2End.aggregation and a1End.upper = a2End.upper and a1End.lower = a2End.lower
  and a1End.subsettedProperty = a2End.subsettedProperty and a1End.redefinedProperty = a2End.
  redefinedProperty))

ComponentCompositeGeneralization

Description
It represents a generalization that exists between classes *Component* and *Composite*.

Generalizations

- Generalization(from *Kernel*)

Attributes
No additional attributes

Associations

- parent: Component [1] It refers to a class that takes the role of parent in the generalization. It redefines *Generalization::general*.
- child: Composite [1] It refers to a class that takes the role of child in the generalization. It redefines *Generalization::specific*.

Constraints
No additional constraints.

Component LeafGeneralization

Description
It represents a generalization that exists between the classes *Component* and *Leaf*.

Generalizations

- Generalization (from *Kernel*)

Attributes

No additional attributes

Associations

- parent: Component [1] It refers to a class that takes the role of parent in the generalization. It redefines *Generalization::general*.
- child: Leaf [1] It refers to a class that takes the role of child in the generalization. It redefines *Generalization::specific*.

Constraints

No additional constraints.

Composite

Description

It represents a class having the role of *Composite* in an inheritance hierarchy.

Generalizations

- Class (from *Kernel*)

Attributes

No additional attributes

Associations

- associationEnd: AssEndComposite [1] It denotes the set of association-ends, in which the class *Composite* participates, belonging to associations that are linked to the class *Component*.
- componentGeneralization: ComponentCompositeGeneralization [1] It specifies the set of generalizations in which *Composite* is the subclass and a class *Component* is the superclass.
  It is a subset of *Classifier::generalization*.

Constraints

No additional constraints.

CompositeComponentAssoc

Description

It describes a binary association that relates the metaclasses *Composite* and *Component*.

Generalizations

- Association (from Kernel)

Attributes
No additional attributes

Associations

- assEndComposite: AssEndComposite [1] It refers to the association-end linked to the *Composite* of the association *CompositeComponentAssoc*. It is a subset of *Association::memberEnd*.
- assEndComponent: AssEndComponent [1] It refers to the association-end linked to a *Component* of the association *CompositeComponentAssoc*. It is a subset of *Association::memberEnd*.

Constraints

[1] *CompositeComponentAssoc* is a binary association; the only association-ends are *assEndComposite* and *assEndComponent*. self.memberEnd -> size () = 2

Leaf

Description
It represents a class that is a leaf in the inheritance hierarchy.

Generalizations

- Class (form *Kernel*).

Attributes
No additional attributes

Associations

- componentGeneralization: ComponentLeafGeneralization [1] It refers to a generalization where *Leaf* is subclass of the class *Component*. It is a subset of *Classifier::generalization*.

Constraints
No additional constraints.

Extract Composite Refactoring: Target Metamodel

Abstract Syntax

Figure 4 shows the metaclasses related to the essential participants in the generated models when the Extract Composite refactoring is applied. The transformation establishes:

- In the source model, an instance of *Component* has two or more instances of *ComponentCompositeGeneralization* (*compositeSpecialization*) and two or more association-ends (*associationEnd*);
- In the target model, an instance of *Component* has exactly one instance of *ComponentCompositeGeneralization* and an only association-end of type *AssEndComponent*.

Description of Metaclasses

AssEndComponent
It describes the connection of *CompositeComponentAssoc* with the class *Component*.

Generalizations

- Property (from *Kernel*)

Attributes
No additional attributes.

Associations

- association: CompositeComponentAssoc [1] It refers to the association that connects the classes *Component* and *Composite*. It redefines *Property::association*.
- participant: Component [1] It denotes the class that participates in the association in this association-end.

Constraints
No additional Constraints.

AssEndComposite
It denotes the connection of the association *CompositeComponentAssoc* with the class *Composite*.

Generalizations

- Property (from *Kernel*).

Attributes
There are no additional attributes.

Associations

- association: CompositeComponentAssoc [1] It refers the association that connects classes *Component* and *Composite*. It redefines *Property::association*.
- participant: Composite [1] It denotes the class that participates in the association in this association-end.

Constraints

[1] The association-end is aggregation or composition. self.aggregation = #shared or self.aggregation = #composite

Component
It represents a class having the role of *Component* in an inheritance hierarchy.

Generalizations

- Class (from *Kernel)*

Attributes
No additional attributes.

Associations

- associationEnd: AssEndComponent [1] It denotes the association-end, in which the class *Component* participates, belonging to the association that connects to the class *Composite*.
- compositeSpecialization: ComponentCompositeGeneralization [1] It specifies the generalization in which *Component* is the superclass and a class *Composite* is the subclass.
- leafSpecialization: ComponentLeafGeneralization [1..*] It specifies the set of generalizations in which *Component* is the superclass and a class *Leaf* is the subclass.

Constraints
No additional restrictions.

ComponentCompositeGeneralization
It represents the generalization that exists between the classes *Component* and *Composite*.

Generalizations

- Generalization (from *Kernel*)

Attributes
No additional attributes.

Associations

- parent: Component [1] It refers to the class that takes the role of parent in the relation of generalization. It redefines *Generalization::general*.
- child: Composite [1] It refers to the class that takes the role of child in the generalization. It redefines *Generalization::specific*.

Constraints

No additional constraints.

ComponentLeafGeneralization

It denotes the generalization that exists between the classes *Component* and *Leaf*.

Generalizations

- Generalization (from *Kernel*)

Attributes

No additional attributes.

Associations

- parent: Component [1] It refers to the class that takes the role of parent in the generalization. It redefines *Generalization::general*.
- child: Leaf [1] It refers to the class that takes the role of children in the generalization. It redefines *Generalization::specific*.

Constraint

No additional constraints.

Composite

It denotes a class having the role of *Composite* in an inheritance hierarchy.

Generalizations

- Class (from *Kernel*)

Attributes

No additional attributes.

Associations

- associationEnd: AssEndComposite [1] It denotes the set of association-ends (in which the class *Composite* participates), belonging to associations that connect them with the class *Component*.

- componentGeneralization: ComponentCompositeGeneralization [1] It specifies the set of generalization in which *Composite* is the subclass and a class *Component* is the superclass.
  It is a subset of *Classifier::generalization*.

Constraints

No additional constraints.

CompositeComponentAssoc

It denotes a binary association that relates the metaclasses *Composite* and *Component*.

Generalizations

- Association (from *Kernel*)

Attributes

No additional attributes.

Associations

- assEndComposite: AssEndComposite [1] It refers to the association-end linked to the *Composite* of the association *CompositeComponentAssoc*. It is a subset of *Association::memberEnd*.
- assEndComponent: AssEndComponent [1] It refers to the association-end linked to *Component* of the association *CompositeComponentAssoc*.
  It is a subset of *Association::memberEnd*.

Constraints

[1] *CompositeComponentAssoc* is a binary association, i.e. the only association-ends that are members of the association are *assEndComposite* and *assEndComponent*. self.memberEnd -> size () = 2

Leaf

It denotes a class having the role of Leaf in the inheritance hierarchy.

Generalizations

- Class (from *Kernel*).

Attributes

No additional attributes.

Associations

- componentGeneralization: ComponentLeafGeneralization [1] It refers to a generalization where *Leaf* is a subclass of a class *Component*. It is a subset of *Classifier::generalization*.

Constraints

No additional constraints.

Extract Composite Refactoring Rule

The models to be transformed and the resulting models of the transformations will be instances of the source and target metamodels.

The transformations between models are described relating each element of the source model to one or more elements of the target model at metamodel level. In other words, relating the metaclass of an element of the source model with the corresponding metaclass of the element in the target model.

Refactorings are expressed as OCL contracts that consist of a name, a set of parameters, a precondition and a postcondition. Each parameter is a metamodel element. The precondition, which deals with the state of the model before the transformation, states relations at the metamodel level between the elements of the source model. The postcondition, which deals with the state of the model after the transformation, states relations at metamodel level between the elements of the source model and a target model. Rules can also include local declarations that are used in preconditions and postconditions.

The pattern *Extract Composite* identifies an inheritance hierarchy with two or more subclasses (*Composite*) that store a collection of children. When the children being collected are classes in the same hierarchy, it is probable that duplicated operations can be removed by refactoring to Composite. The application of this rule creates a superclass (*Composite*) and moves attributes and equivalent operations of the subclasses to the superclass. The inheritance hierarchy is simplified by factorizing in a superclass the common behavior.

The following steps can be distinguished:

- Create an abstract class *Composite*.
- Reflect as subclass of the composite to each class of the original hierarchy that contains equivalent attributes and operations to manage their children (subclasses of the same hierarchy).
- Detect equivalent operations in classes of the original hierarchy and move them to the superclass *Composite*.
- Detect equivalent attributes and move them to the superclass *Composite*. Rename attributes (if it is necessary) and update each reference to them in the classes.
- Check the client classes of classes *Composite* in the original hierarchy to communicate them through the new interface.

Refactorings are specified as OCL contracts that are written by using the notation described in Chapter 3. Following, the Extract-Composite rule specifies the above steps as a transformation rule in OCL. Comments in the text explain the different OCL expressions.

```
Transformation Extract-Composite {parametersource: Source Metamodel
Extract Composite:: Package
target: Target Metamodel Extract Composite:: Package
local operationspostconditionspost
-- For each instance of class Component(SourceClass) in the source,
source.ownedMember -> select (oclIsTypeOf (Component)) -> forAll
```

```
(sourceClass |
   -- there is an instance of Component(targetClass) in the target
so that, target.ownedMember -> select (oclIsTypeOf (Component)) ->
exists (targetClass |
      -- targetClass has only a generalization
         -- its type is ComponentCompositeGeneralization,
            -- targetClass is the parent of a class whose type is
Composite, targetClass.oclAsType (Component).compositeSpecialization
-> size() =1 and
            -- targetClass has an only association-end relating with a
class
         -- whose type is Composite, targetClass.oclAsType (Compo-
nent).associationEnd -> size () =1 and
         -- the set of subclasses of targetClass whose type is Leaf,
is equal -- to the set of subclasses of sourceClass whose type is
Leaf
         targetClass.oclAsType (Component).leafSpecialization.child =
sourceClass. oclAsType (Component).leafSpecialization.child and
         -- inherited attributes of NamedElement targetClass.name =
sourceClass.name and targetClass.visibility = sourceClass.visibility
and
         -- targetClass has the following values for:
         -- inherited attribute of RedefinableElement targetClass.
oclAsType (Class).isLeaf = sourceClass.isLeaf and
         -- inherited attribute of Classifier targetClass.oclAsType
(Class).isAbstract = sourceClass.isAbstract and
         -- inherited associations of Class
         -- targetClass has the same set of nested classifiers as
         -- sourceClass
            targetClass.oclAsType(Class).nestedClassifier = source-
Class.oclAsType(Class).nestedClassifier and
         -- targetClass has the same subset of own operations as
         -- sourceClass
            targetClass.oclAsType(Class).ownedOperation = source-
Class.oclAsType(Class).ownedOperation and
         -- the set of own attributes of targetClass is the resulting
set of
         --excluding to the set of own attributes of sourceClass, the
         -- attributes that are the association-end that relates
sourceClass
         -- with the different classes whose type is Composite in the
source-- package.and including the association-end that links it
with the
         -- only class Composite in the target package,
```

```
            targetClass.oclAsType(Class).ownedAttribute =
            sourceClass.oclAsType(Class).ownedAttribute ->
            excluding (sourceClass.oclAsType (Component).
            associationEnd.association.assEndComposite) ->
            including (targetClass. oclAsType (Component).
            associationEnd.association.assEndComposite) and
        -- inherited associations of Classifier
        -- both classes have the same set of generalizations tar-
getClass.oclAsType (Class).generalization = sourceClass.oclAsType
(Class).generalization and
        -- both classes belong to the same package targetClass.
oclAsType (Class).package = sourceClass.oclAsType (Class).package
and
        -- both classes have the same set of redefined classifi-
ers targetClass.oclAsType (Class).redefinedClassifier = sourceClass.
oclAsType (Class).redefinedClassifier and
        -- inherited associations of Namespace
        -- both classes have the same restrictions targetClass.
oclAsType (Class).ownedRule = sourceClass.oclAsType (Class).owne-
dRule and
        -- both classes have the same set of imported ele-
ments targetClass.oclAsType (Class).elementImport = sourceClass.
oclAsType (Class).elementImport))
```

post
```
-- for each instance of Composite (sourceClass), in the source pack-
age, source.ownedMember -> select(oclIsTypeOf (Composite)) -> forAll
(sourceClass |
    -- exists an instance of Class (targetClass) in the target pack-
age, so that target.ownedMember -> select(oclIsTypeOf(Class)) ->
exists (targetClass |
    -- the class of the package target (targetClass) has as parent a
    -- class whose type is Composite, targetClass.oclAsType (Class).
superClass.oclIsTypeOf (Composite)) and
        -- targetClass has the following values for:
        -- inherited attribute of RedefinableElement targetClass.
oclAsType(Class).isLeaf = sourceClass.oclAsType (Composite).isLeaf
and
        -- inherited attributes of NamedElement targetClass.name =
sourceClass.name and targetClass.visibility = sourceClass.visibility
and
        -- inherited attribute of Classifier targetClass.oclAsType
(Class).isAbstract = sourceClass.oclAsType (Composite).isAbstract
and
        -- for each operation of sourceClass sourceClass.oclAsType
```

```
(Composite).ownedOperation -> forAll(op |
      -- that is equivalent to operations belonging to another
classes
      -- whose types is Composite in the source package (source.
ownedMember -> select(oclIsTypeOf(Composite)) ->
excluding(sourceClass)) -> collect (oclAsType(Composite).ownedOpera-
tion) -> forAll (o | if o.isEquivalentOperationTo (op)
            -- the operation isEquivalentOperationTo () is specified as
            --additional operation of the class Operation of the UML
            --metamodel (see Appendix A)
      then-- if the operations o and op are equivalents then,
            -- an equivalent operation exists in the class parent of
            -- targetClass in the package target targetClass.
oclAsType(Class).superClass.ownedOperation-> exists (targetOp | op.
isEquivalentOperationTo (targetOp)) and
            -- and that operation is excluded of targetClass target-
Class.oclAsType(Class).ownedOperation -> excludes(op) and
            -- operations which are referred directly or indirectly by
op
            -- and have an equivalent operation op (that is referred by
            -- o) are moved to the parent of targetClass op.referenced-
Operation -> forAll (refOp | o.referencedOperation -> forAll (refO |
            -- the operation referencedOperation is specified as
            -- additional operation of the class Operation of the
            -- metamodel UML (see Appendix A)
      if refOp.isEquivalentOperationTo(refO)
            then
            targetClass.oclAsType (Class).superClass. oclAsType (Class).
ownedOperation->
                  exists (targetOp |
                  refOp.isEquivalentOperationTo (targetOp)) and
            -- and that operation is excluded of targetClass target-
Class.oclAsType (Class).ownedOperation -> excludes (refOp)
            else
            -- if that operations are not equivalents then they
            -- are moved to the parent class targetClass as an
            -- abstract operation.
            targetClass.oclAsType(Class).superClass.
            ownedOperation -> exists (targetOp |
            refOp.isEquivalentOperationTo (targetOp) and targetOp.owned-
Member ->
            select (oclIsKindOf(Action)) -> size() = 0)))
      else
      -- if the operation of sourceClass (op) does not have
```

```
    -- equivalent operations in the remaining classes, then it is
-- an operation of targetClass in the package target targetClass.
oclAsType (Class).ownedOperation -> includes(op)
      endif))
    -- for each attribute of sourceClass sourceClass.
oclAsType(Composite).ownedAttribute -> forAll(sa |
    -- that is equivalent to the attributes of the remaining classes
    -- whose type is Composite in the package source (source.owned-
Member -> select(oclIsTypeOf(Composite)) -> excluding (source-
Class)).oclAsType (Composite). ownedAttribute -> forAll (a |
      if a.isEquivalentPropertyTo (sa)
      -- the operation isEquivalentPropertyTo() is specified as
      -- an additional operation of the class Property of the
      -- metamodel UML.
      then-- if attributes a and sa are equivalents then an
      -- equivalent attribute exists in the class parent of
      -- targetClass in the package target targetClass.oclAsType
(Class).superClass. ownedAttribute -> exists (targetAt |
          sa.isEquivalentPropertyTo (targetAt)) and
      -- and that attribute is excluded of targetClass
      targetClass.oclAsType(Class).ownedAttribute -> excludes(sa)
and
      -- in the implementations (if they exists) of the operations
      -- of sourceClass and their descendents, every reference
      -- to the property sa is changed by the property targetAt in
      -- the class parent of targetClass and their descendents.
      sourceClass.oclAsType(Composite).referencedProperty
          -> includes (sa) implies
      targetClass.oclAsType(Class).superClass.
          referencedProperty -> excludes(sa) and
      targetClass.oclAsType(Class).superClass.
          referencedProperty -> includes(targetAt) and
  -- in the expressions OCL related to the invariants,
  -- preconditions and postconditions and operation body of
  -- sourceClass or of a descendent class,
  -- every reference to a property sa is replaced by the property
  -- targetAt in the parent class of targetClass and in its
  -- descendents.
        sourceClass.oclAsType(Composite).
        referencedPropertyInOcl -> includes (sa)
          implies
          targetClass.oclAsType(Class).superClass.
          referencedPropertyInOcl -> excludes(sa) and
          targetClass.oclAsType(Class).superClass.
```

```
          referencedPropertyInOcl -> includes(targetAt)
      else-- if the attribute of sourceClass (sa) does not have
      -- equivalent attributes in the remaining classes, then it
      -- is an attribute of targetClass in the package target
      targetClass.oclAsType(Class).
      ownedAttribute -> includes(sa)
      endif)) and
    -- both classes belongs to the same package targetClass.
oclAsType(Class).package = sourceClass.oclAsType(Composite).package
and
    -- both classes have the same set of redefined classifi-
ers targetClass.oclAsType (Class).redefinedClassifier = sourceClass.
oclAsType (Composite).redefinedClassifier and
    -- both classes have the same set of imported elements target-
Class.oclAsType (Class).elementImport = sourceClass.oclAsType (Com-
posite).elementImport))
post
-- for each class sourceClass in the package source, source.owned-
Member -> select (oclIsTypeOf (Class)) -> forAll (sourceClass |
-- exists a class targetClass in the package target so that,
  target.ownedMember -> select(oclIsTypeOf(Class)) ->
  exists (targetClass |
    -- if sourceClass is client of same class whose type is Com-
positeif (sourceClass.oclAsType (Class).clientDependency ->
      exists (c | c.supplier.oclIsTypeOf(Composite)))
    then
    -- targetClass has the following values for:
    -- inherited attribute of RedefinableElement
    targetClass.oclAsType(Class).isLeaf =
      sourceClass.oclAsType(Class).isLeaf and
    -- inherited attributes of NamedElement
    targetClass.name = sourceClass.name and
    targetClass.visibility = sourceClass.visibility and
    -- inherited attribute of Classifier
    targetClass.oclAsType(Class).isAbstract =
      sourceClass.oclAsType(Class).isAbstract and
    -- inherited associations of Class
    -- targetClass has the same set of nested classifiers as
sourceClass
    targetClass.oclAsType(Class).nestedClassifier =
      sourceClass.oclAsType(Class).nestedClassifier and
    -- own operations of targetClass.
    -- for each own operation of sourceClass, in the package
source, sourceClass.oclAsType(Class).ownedOperation -> forAll (sOp /
```

```
      -- exists in targetClass or in its descending an operation
with the following
      -- properties
        targetClass.oclAsType (Class).allDescendant.ownedOperation
        -> exists (tOp /
          -- if the return type and/or the parameters of the opera-
tion sOp are
          -- of type Composite (from the source metamodel), they
are of the -- type Composite (from the target metamodel) in tOp,
i.e., for
          -- each parameter of the operation sOp of sourceClass
          sOp.ownedParameter -> forAll (sP /
          -- exists a parameter in the operation (tOp) of target-
Class so that
          tOp.ownedParameter -> exists (tP /
          -- if the type of the parameter is Composite (from the
source
          -- metamodel), in targetClass, it is the type Composite
(from the
          -- target metamodel)
            if (sP.type.oclIsTypeOf(Composite))
            then
              tP.type = Composite
            else
              tP.type = sP.type
            endif and
          -- the remaining properties of the parameters are pre-
served. tP.direction = sP.direction and
            tP.defaultValue = sP.defaultValue and
            tP.isOrdered = sP.isOrdered and
            tP.isUnique = sP.isUnique and
            tP.upperValue = sP.upperValue and
            tP.lowerValue = sP.lowerValue)) and
          -- the remaining properties of the operation are
          -- preserved
          tOp.name = sOp.name and
          tOp.class = sOp.class and
          tOp.isQuery = sOp.isQuery and
          tOp.precondition = sOp.precondition and
          tOp.postcondition = sOp.postcondition and
          tOp.bodyCondition = sOp.bodyCondition and
          tOp.raisedException = sOp. raisedException and
          tOp.redefinedOperation = sOp.redefinedOperation)) and
      -- own attributes of targetClass (attributes and association-
```

```
end).
        -- for each own attribute of sourceClass, sourceClass.oclAs-
Type (Class).ownedAttribute -> forAll (sAt /
        -- exists in targetClass or in its descending an attribute
with the
        -- following properties
        targetClass.oclAsType (Class).allDescendant.ownedAttribute
        -> exists (tAt /
        -- if the attribute of sourceClass is of type Composite
(from the
        -- source metamodel)
    if (sAt.type.oclIsTypeOf (Composite))
    then
        -- the type of the attribute of targetClass is Composite (from
        -- the target metamodel);
        tAt.type.oclIsTypeOf (Composite) and
        -- and the remaining properties of the attribute are
        -- preserved
        tAt.visibility = sAt.visibility and
        tAt.isLeaf = sAt.isLeaf and
        tAt.isStatic = sAt.isStatic and
        tAt.isDerived = sAt.isDerived and
        tAt.isReadOnly = sAt.isReadOnly and
        tAt.isDerivedUnion = sAt.isDerivedUnion and
        tAt.aggregation = sAt.aggregation and
        tAt.upper = sAt.upper and
        tAt.lower = sAt.lower and
        tAt.association = sAt.association and
        tAt.owningAssociation = sAt.owningAssociation and
        tAt.redefinedProperty = sAt.redefinedProperty and
        tAt.subsettedProperty = sAt.subsettedProperty
    else
        -- on the contrary, the attributes of targetClass are equal to
        -- whose of sourceClass
        tAt = sAt
    endif)) and
    -- inherited associations of Classifier
    -- both classes have the same set of generalizations targetClass.
oclAsType (Class).generalization = sourceClass.oclAsType (Class).
generalization and
    -- both classes belongs to the same package targetClass.oclAsType
(Class).package = sourceClass.oclAsType (Class).package and
    -- both classes have the same set of classifiers targetClass.
oclAsType (Class).redefinedClassifier = sourceClass.oclAsType
```

```
(Class).redefinedClassifier and
   -- both classes have the same set of imported elements target-
Class.oclAsType (Class).elementImport = sourceClass.oclAsType
(Class).elementImport and
else
-- on the contrary, targetClass is equal to sourceClass.
targetClass = sourceClass
endif))
}
```

REFACTORING AT MODEL LEVEL

The Extract-Composite rule describes a family of refactoring at model level. One of them is exemplified on the open source HyperText Markup Language (HTML) Parser. When the parser HTML analyzes code HTML, identifies and creates objects representing HTML tags and pieces of text. The following example is analyzed in (Kerievsky, 2004):

```
"<HTML>
  <BODY>
     Hello, and welcome to my Web page! I work for
     <A REF= "http://industriallogic.com">
< IMG SRC= "http://industriallogic.com/images/logo141x145.gif">
< /A>
< /BODY >
< /HTML> "
```

The parser creates the following kind of objects:

- *HTMLTag* (for the <BODY> tag)
- *HTMLStringNode* (for the string "Hello, and welcome...")
- *HTMLLinkTag* (for the <A HREF= "...."> tag)

The link tag (<A HREF= "....">) contains an image tag (<IMG SRC "...">) that the parser handles as a child of *HTMLLinkTag*. When the parser detects that the link tag contains an image tag, constructs an object *HTMLImageTag* as child of the object *HTMLLinkTag*. Another tag such as *HTMLFormTag* and *HTMLTitleTag* are also child containers.

Figure 5 and Figure 6 show an instance of the Extract Composite pattern of Figure 2. Figure 5 shows a simplified hierarchy of the HyperText Markup Language (HTML) tags, that is an instance of the source metamodel of Figure 2. The HTML tags can be form, link and image tag. The form and link tags are child containers; for example, a link tag can contain an image tag. HTML tags can be: form, link and image. The form and link tags are containers of children, that is to say, a link tag can contain an image tag.

Figure 5. The Extract Composite Refactoring: A source instance

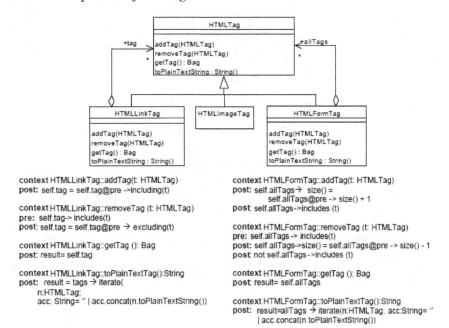

Figure 5 exemplifies the Extract Composite refactoring rule at the PIM level specified in OCL (Favre, & Pereira, 2007). (Kerievsky, 2004, pp. 214) describes this rule at the ISM-JAVA level.

The source pattern in Figure 2 depicts subclasses in a hierarchy that implement the same composite. The rule application extracts a superclass that implements the composite removing duplicate behavior. The main steps in the proposed transformation are: create a composite; make each class that contains duplicate behavior a subclass of the composite and identify methods that are purely duplicated or partially duplicated across the subclasses of a composite. A purely duplicated method can be moved with all child containers to the composite. If the method is partially duplicated only the common behavior across all subclasses can be moved.

The classes *HTMLLinkTag* and *HTMLFormTag* are instances of the metaclass *Composite* of the source metamodel of the Extract Composite refactoring, *HTMLTag* is an instance of the metaclass *Component* and *HTMLImageTag* is an instance of the metaclass *Leaf*.

In this example, the application of the Extract Composite refactoring includes the following steps:

- create a new class,
- rename the new class by *CompositeHTMLTag* (name given in the designer),
- make *CompositeHTMLTag* child of *HTMLTag* and parent of *HTMLFormTag* y *HTMLLinkTag*,
- move the equivalent operations from the classes *HTMLFormTag* and *HTMLLinkTag* to the new class,
- remove the aggregations that each class has with the class *HTMLTag* (*HTMLFormTag-HTMLTag* and *HTMLLinkTag-HTMLTag)* and replace them by an only aggregation between *CompositeHTMLTag* and *HTMLTag*.

Figure 6. The Extract Composite Refactoring: A target instance

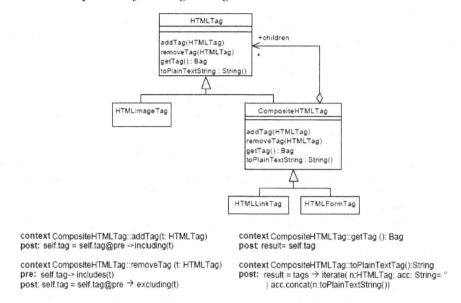

context CompositeHTMLTag::addTag(t: HTMLTag)
post: self.tag = self.tag@pre ->including(t)

context CompositeHTMLTag::getTag (): Bag
post: result= self.tag

context CompositeHTMLTag::removeTag (t: HTMLTag)
pre: self.tag-> includes(t)
post: self.tag = self.tag@pre → excluding(t)

context CompositeHTMLTag::toPlainTextTag():String
post: result = tags → iterate(n:HTMLTag; acc: String= "
| acc.concat(n.toPlainTextString())

To identify patterns we propose to adapt the ideas of specification matching described in (Zaremski & Wing, 1997). The HTMLLinkTag and HTMLFormTag classes are instances of the Composite metaclass of the Extract Composite Source Metamodel, HTMLTag is an instance of the Component metaclass and HTMLImageTag is an instance of the Leaf metaclass (Figure 2).

The refactoring rule needs to identify duplicate operations of the HTMLFormTag and HTMLLinkTag classes. Under signature matching, the addTag operation of HTMLLinkTag class is matched by both addTag and removeTag operations of the HTMLFormTag class.

Let the following match be:

- **Exact Pre/Post Match:** Two specifications, S and S', satisfy the exact pre/post match if their preconditions are equivalent and their postconditions are equivalent: match $_{E\text{-pre/post}}$ (S, S') = (S'$_{pre}$ <=> S$_{pre}$) and (S$_{post}$ <=> S'$_{post}$)
- **Plug-In Match:** Under this match, S' is matched by any specifications S whose precondition is weaker (to allow at least all of the conditions that S' allows) and whose postcondition is stronger (to provide a guarantee at least as strong as S'): match $_{plug\text{-}in}$ (S, S') = (S'$_{pre}$ => S$_{pre}$) and (S$_{post}$ => S'$_{post}$)

S is behaviorally equivalent to S', since we can replace S' with S and have the same observable behavior, but this is not a true equivalence because it is not symmetric.

Then, under Plug-In Match, addTag operation of HTMLLinkTag class is only matched by addTag operation of HTMLFormTag class. Let S be the specification of the addTag operation of the HTMLLinkTag class and let S' be the specification of the addTag operation of the HTMLFormTag class with allTag renamed to tag. The precondition requirement $(S'_{pre} => S_{pre})$ holds, since $S'_{pre} = S_{pre} = true$, so showing match plug-in (S, S') reduces to proving (S$_{post}$ => S'$_{post}$), in OCL:

Table 1. Specification Matching

Operation Specification S	Operation Specification S'	Specification Matching
HTMLLinkTag::removeTag	HTMLFormTag::removeTag	$Match_{plug-in}(S, S')$
HTMLLinkTag::getTag	HTMLFormTag::getTag	$match_{E-pre/post}(S, S')$
HTMLLinkTag::toPlainTextTag	HTMLFormTag::toPlainTextTag	$match_{E-pre/post}(S, S')$

```
(self.tag = self.tag@pre -> including (t)) implies
(self.tag→size() = self.tag@pre -> size()+1 and
self.tag -> includes (t))
```

So, S is behaviorally equivalent to S', since we can plug in S for S' and have the same observable behavior, but this is not a true equivalence because it is not symmetric. Therefore, addTag operation of the HTMLLinkTag class is moved to the new Composite class generated in the target model and addTag operation of the HTMLFormTag class is removed.

Table 1 shows the resulting match for the operations removeTag, getTag and toPlainTextTag. Figure 6 depicts a target instance, the refactoring of the source model (Figure 5).

REFACTORING AT FORMAL LANGUAGE LEVEL

Formal techniques are clearly needed in order to ensure that behavioral properties of the software are preserved by refactorings maintaining consistency between the refactored artifact and other software artifacts. Next, we show the specification of the Extract Composite source metamodel in NEREUS. This specification can be built by using the bases described in Chapter 4, that is to say, by using reusable schemes and the system of transformation rules described in Chapter

```
PACKAGE ExtractCompositeSourceMetamodel
IMPORTS Kernel

CLASS AssEndComposite
IS-SUBTYPE-OF Property
ASSOCIATES
<< AssEndComposite-Composite >>
<< AssEndComposite-CompositeComponentAssoc >>
TYPES
AssEndComposite
OPERATIONS
create: * → AssEndComposite
AXIOMS assEnd: AssEndComposite
get-aggregation(assEnd) = "shared" or get-aggregation(assEnd) =
"composite"
END-CLASS
```

CLASS AssEndComponent
IS-SUBTYPE-OF Property
ASSOCIATES
<< AssEndComponent-Component >>
<< AssEndComponent-CompositeComponentAssoc >>
TYPES
AssEndComposite
OPERATIONS
create: * → AssEndComponent
...
END-CLASS

CLASS CompositeComponentAssoc
IS-SUBTYPE-OF Association
ASSOCIATES
<< AssEndComposite-CompositeComponentAssoc >>
<< AssEndComponent-CompositeComponentAssoc >>
TYPES
CompositeComponentAssoc
OPERATIONS
create: * → CompositeComponentAssoc
isEquivalentTo: CompositeComponentAssoc x CompositeComponentAssoc
->boolean
AXIOMS c, cc: CompositeComponentAssoc; AP: Association-Property
size (get-memberEnd (AP, cc)) = 2
isEquivalentTo (c,cc) = (get-isDerived (c) = get-isDerived (cc) and
get-visibility (c) = get-visibility (cc) and
(get-name (c)=get-name (cc) or get-name (c) <> get-name (cc))and
forAll (end1) (get-memberEnd (AP, c), [exists (end2) (get-memberEnd
(AP, cc),
[(get-name (end1) = get-name (end2) or get-name (end1) <> get-name
(end2))and
get-visibility (end1) = get-visibility (end2) and get-isLeaf (end1)
= get-isLeaf (end2) and
get-isStatic (end1) = get-isStatic (end2) and
get-isDerived (end1) = get-isDerived (end2) and
get-isReadOnly (end1) = get-isReadOnly(end2) and
get-aggregationv(end1) = get-aggregation (end2) and
get-upper (end1) = get-upper(end2) and get-lower(end1) = get-
lower(end2) and
get-subsettedProperty (end1) = get-subsettedProperty (end2) and
get-redefinedProperty (end1) = get-redefinedProperty (end2)]]))
END-CLASS

```
CLASS Component
IS-SUBTYPE-OF M_Class
ASSOCIATES
<< Component-ComponentCompositeGeneralization >>
<< Component-ComponentLeafGeneralization >>
<< AssEndComponent-Component >>
TYPES
Component
OPERATIONS
create: * → Component
AXIOMS c: Component; Ap: AssEndComponent-Component;
Aa: AssEndComponent-CompositeComponentAssoc;
Cp: Component-ComponentCompositeGeneralization;
Oc: Class-Operation; Cc: ComponentCompositeGeneralization-Composite
forAll (a1,a2) (collect (assEnd) (get_associationEnd (Ap, c),
[get_association (Aa, assEnd)]), [a1 = a2 or isEquivalentTo(a1, a2)
])
forAll (cl) (collect (child) (get_compositeSpecialization (Cp, c),
[get_child (Cc, child) ]),
[exists (op) (get_ownedOperation (Oc, cl),
[forAll (c) (excluding (collect (child) (get_compositeSpecialization
(Cp, c),
[get_child (Cc, child)]), cl),
[exists (o) (get_ownedOperation (Oc, c)),
[isEquivalentTo (op, o)] ]]
END-CLASS


CLASS ComponentCompositeGeneralization
IS-SUBTYPE-OF Generalization
ASSOCIATES
<< ComponentCompositeGeneralization-Composite >>
<< Component-ComponentCompositeGeneralization >>
TYPES
ComponentCompositeGeneralization
OPERATIONS
create: * → ComponentCompositeGeneralization
...
END-CLASS


CLASS ComponentLeafGeneralization
IS-SUBTYPE-OF Generalization
ASSOCIATES
<< Component-ComponentLeafGeneralization >>
<< ComponentLeafGeneralization-Leaf >>
```

TYPES
ComponentLeafGeneralization
OPERATIONS
create: * → ComponentLeafGeneralization
...
END-CLASS

CLASS Leaf
IS-SUBTYPE-OF M_Class
ASSOCIATES
<< ComponentLeafGeneralization-Leaf >>
TYPES Leaf
OPERATIONS
create: * → Leaf
...
END-CLASS

CLASS Composite
IS-SUBTYPE-OF M_Class
ASSOCIATES
<< ComponentCompositeGeneralization-Composite >>
<< AssEndComposite-Composite >>
TYPESComposite
OPERATIONS
create: * → Composite
...
END-CLASS

ASSOCIATION AssEndComposite-Composite
IS Bidirectional-1 [Composite: class1; AssEndComposite: class2; participant: role1; associationEnd: role2; 1: mult1; 1: mult2; +: visibility1; +: visibility2]
END

ASSOCIATION AssEndComponent-Component
IS Bidirectional-5 [AssEndComponent: class1; Component: class2; associationEnd: role1; participant: role2; 2..*: mult1; 1: mult2; +: visibility1; +: visibility2]
END

ASSOCIATION AssEndComposite-CompositeComponentAssoc
IS Bidirectional-1 [AssEndComposite: class1; CompositeComponentAssoc: class2; assEndComposite: role1; association: role2; 1: mult1; 1: mult2; +: visibility1; +: visibility2]

END

ASSOCIATION AssEndComponent-CompositeComponentAssoc
IS Bidirectional-1 [AssEndComponent: class1; CompositeComponentAssoc: class2; assEndComponent: role1; association: role2; 1: mult1;
1: mult2; +: visibility1; +: visibility2]
END

ASSOCIATION Component-ComponentCompositeGeneralization
IS Bidirectional-5 [ComponentCompositeGeneralization: class1; Component: class2; compositeSpecialization: role1; parent: role2; 2..*:
mult1; 1: mult2; +: visibility1; +: visibility2]
CONSTRAINED-BY
parent: redefines general
END

ASSOCIATION Component-ComponentLeafGeneralization
IS Bidirectional-5 [ComponentLeafGeneralization: class1; Component:
class2; leafSpecialization: role1; parent: role2; 1..*: mult1; 1:
mult2; +: visibility1; +: visibility2]
CONSTRAINED-BY
parent: redefines general
END

ASSOCIATION ComponentCompositeGeneralization-Composite
IS Composition-1 [Composite: whole; ComponentCompositeGeneralization: part; child: role1; componentGeneralization: role2; 1: mult1;
1: mult2; +: visibility1; +: visibility2]
CONSTRAINED-BY
child: redefines specific
componentGeneralization: subsets generalization
END

ASSOCIATION ComponentLeafGeneralization-Leaf
IS Composition-1 [Leaf: whole; ComponentLeafGeneralization: part;
child: role1; componentGeneralization: role2; 1: mult1; 1: mult2; +:
visibility1; +: visibility2]
END

END-PACKAGE

Instances of refactorings are translated into NEREUS specifications by instantiating the reusable schemes shown in Figure 6.

Following we shows the specification of the refactoring ExtractCompositeRefactoring. The function *Translate*$_{NEREUS}$ *(transformation.precondition)* that appears in the transformation scheme as a precondition of the operation create translates into NEREUS precondition the OCL precondition. The function, *Translate$_{NEREUS}$ (transformation.postcondition)*, that appears in the axioms translates into NEREUS axioms the OCL postconditions. An instantiation of the transformation scheme is the following:

```
[name: ExtractComposite;
sourceMetamodel: ExtractCompositeSourceMetamodel;
targetMetamodel: ExtractCompositeTargetMetamodel;
OCLexp1: precondition;
OCLexp2: postcondition ]
```

CLASS ExtractCompositeRefactoring
[source: *ExtractCompositeSourceMetamodel;*
target*: ExtractCompositeTargetMetamodel*]
GENERATED-BY addLink
EFFECTIVETYPE
ExtractCompositeRefactoring
OPERATIONS
addLink: source x target → ExtractCompositeRefactoring
get_source: ExtractCompositeRefactoring → source
get_target: ExtractCompositeRefactoring → target
...
AXIOMS
r: ExtractCompositerefactoring;
m1: source;
m2: target;
PP: PackageableElement-Package
get_source (addLink (m1, m2)) = m1
get_target (addLink (m1, m2)) = m2
forAll (sourceClass) (select (sourceC) (get_ownedMember(PP, m1),
[oclIsTypeOf(sourceC, Component)],
[exists (targetClass)
(select (targetC) (get_ownedMember(PP, m2),
[oclIsTypeOf(targetC, Component)]),
name (targetClass) = name (sourceClass) and
visibility (targetClass) = visibility (sourceClass)
....
END-CLASS

EXAMPLE 9-1: STATE MACHINE DIAGRAM REFACTORING

Following, we specify a refactoring on state machine diagrams at PIM level. We describe in the context of our approach an example of refactoring analyzed in Folli and Mens (2008). The authors specify a

Figure 7. A scheme for translating transformations: From MOF to NEREUS

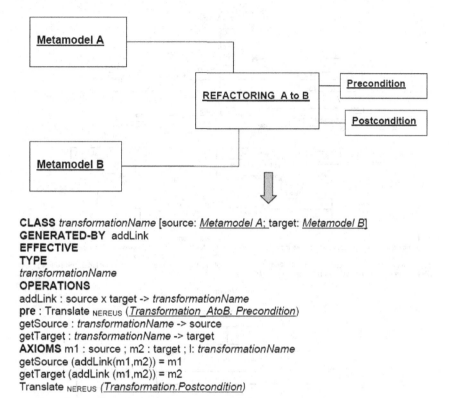

```
CLASS transformationName [source: Metamodel A; target: Metamodel B]
GENERATED-BY addLink
EFFECTIVE
TYPE
transformationName
OPERATIONS
addLink : source x target -> transformationName
pre : Translate NEREUS (Transformation_AtoB. Precondition)
getSource : transformationName -> source
getTarget : transformationName -> target
AXIOMS m1 : source ; m2 : target ; l: transformationName
getSource (addLink(m1,m2)) = m1
getTarget (addLink (m1,m2)) = m2
Translate NEREUS (Transformation.Postcondition)

END-CLASS
```

refactoring, called *"Introduce Initial Pseudostate"* by using a graph transformation-based technique. We highlight the advantages of our proposal contrasting it with graph transformation.

The *Introduce Initial Pseudostate refactoring* is used to improve the structure of a state machine diagram. When all the incoming transitions of a region have the same target state it is possible to simplify the diagram by adding an initial pseudostate to the region and by setting the region itself as target of the incoming transitions. In general, it is a good convention not to cross boundaries of a composite state. This refactoring does not modify other kinds of diagrams.

Figure 7 (a) shows a diagram containing a transition that crosses the boundaries of the ACTIVE composite state. The refactoring leads to Figure 7 (b):

- add an initial pseudostate to the ACTIVE composite state,
- change the target of the transition, which initially refers to the *Ready* state, to the region itself,
- define an automatic transition between the initial pseudostate and the *Ready* state and
- if the ACTIVE composite state contains an entry action, it is moved to the transition.

As a result, the *Ready* state will become the default initial state of the ACTIVE region, a transition whose target is the ACTIVE state will lead the state machine to the *Ready* state.

Figure 8. UML state machine diagram refactoring: Introducing initial pseudostate

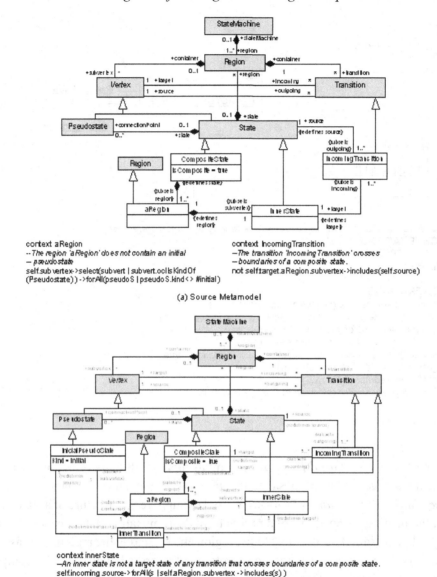

To specify this refactoring, source and target metamodels are specified as specialized UML meta-models. Figure 9 shows the UML simplified metamodel of state machines and Figure 10 metamodels for the "Introduce State Refactoring".

Source metamodel establishes that a source model has at least a composite state (instance of *CompositeState*), which contains one or more regions (instances of *aRegion*) without initial pseudostate. These regions have an inner state (instance of *InnerState*), which is the target of transitions (instances of *IncomingTransition*) that cross boundaries of its containing composite state (Figure 10a).

Target metamodel establishes that a target model has at least a composite state (instance of *CompositeState*), whose regions (instances of *aRegion*) contain an initial pseudostate (Figure 10b).

Figure 9. Simplified state diagram metamodel

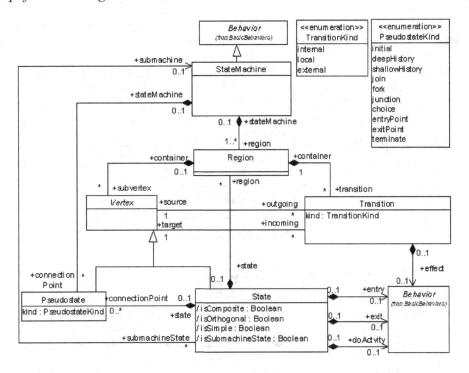

Model refactoring is specified relating each element of the source model to one or more elements of the target model at metamodel level. Following we partially shows the specification of the *Introduce Initial Pseudostate* refactoring as an OCL contract emphasizing the main changes in the diagrams. The refactoring specification is explained by comments.

```
Transformation Introduce Initial Pseudostate {

parameter
source: Source_Metamodel::StateMachine
target: Target_Metamodel::StateMachine

postcondition
-- A 'CompositeState' in source model matches a 'CompositeState' in
target model
-- (allVertex is an additional operation of the StateMachine meta-
class of the UML metamodel) source.allVertex -> select(oclIsTy
peOf(CompositeState)) -> forAll (sourceState | target.allVer-
tex -> select(oclIsTypeOf(CompositeState)) -> exists (target-
State | targetState.oclAsType(CompositeState).matches(sourceState.
oclAsType(CompositeState)))) and
-- A 'Pseudostate' in source model matches a 'Pseudostate' in target
model source.allVertex -> select(oclIsTypeOf(Pseudostate)) -> forAll
```

Figure 10. Introducing initial pseudostate refactoring: Source and target metamodels

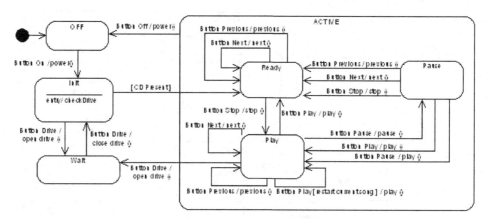

(a) Before Refactoring

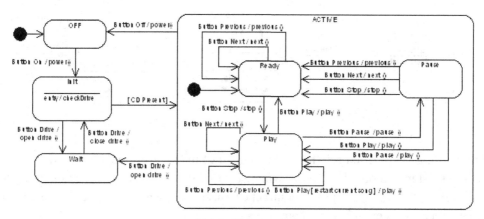

(b) After Refactoring

```
(sourcePState | ….

…

local operations

Target_Metamodel::CompositeState matches (aSourceState: Target_
Metamodel::CompositeState): Boolean

matches (aSourceState) =
-- 'aSourceState' and 'targetState' (self) have the same name self.
name = aSourceState.name
and
```

```
-- The cardinality of the 'targetState' entry transition set is
equal to the cardinality of the
-- 'aSourceState' entry transition set plus the cardinality of the
innerState incomingTransition set of -- the source model self.in-
coming -> size() = aSourceState.incoming -> size() + (aSourceState.
aRegion.innerState.incomingTransition) -> size()
```
and
```
-- for each transition that crosses the compositeState in the source
model, there is a transition in
--the target model, so that:
aSourceState.aRegion.innerState.incomingTransition ->
forAll(sourceTransition |
   self.incoming ->exist (targetTransition |
      --both transitions have the same name, guard and container
and targetTransition.name = sourceTransition.name and …
      --both transitions have the same source state targetTransi-
tion.source = sourceTransition.source and
      -- the target of the targetTransition is the CompositeState
(self) targetTransit.target = self))
```
and
```
   -- for each region of 'aSourceState', there is a region in 'tar-
getState' (self), so that:
   aSourceState.aRegion -> forAll(sourceRegion| self.aRegion ->
exist(targetRegion|
   -- the vertex set of 'targetRegion' is equal to the vertex set of
'sourceRegion' union an initialPseudoState
      targetRegion.subvertex = sourceRegion.subvertex -> union (tar-
getRegion.initialPseudoState)
      and
      -- for each innerState of 'sourceRegion' there is an inner-
State in 'targetRegion' so that:
      sourceRegion.innerState -> forAll (innerSourceState| targetRe-
gion.innerState -> exists (innerTargetState|
         -- both innerStates have the same name and
         innerTargetState.name = innerSourceState.name
      and
      -- the set of the 'innerTargetState' incoming transitions is
equal to the set of the
      --'innerSourceState' incoming transition minus the transition
that crosses the boundaries --of the composite state plus the tran-
sition from the initial pseudoState.
      innerTargetState.incoming = innerSourceState.incoming - (in-
nerSourceState.incomingTransition) -> union(innerTargetState.inner-
```

```
Transition)))
and …))
and … }
```

This example was previously analyzed in the context of graph transformation. Next, we discuss advantages of our approach regarding the use of graph transformation to specify model refactoring according to the results shown in (Mens, 2006) and (Folli and Mens, 2008). Graph transformation allows representing complex transformations in a compact visual way using a tool, however "current state-of-the-art in graph transformation does not suffice to easily define model refactorings, so their expressive power needs to be increased" (Folli and Mens, 2008, p. 11). Some limitations are:

- the *type graph*, which represent UML metamodel, does not allow representing concepts like *Aggregation* and *Composition*, which are represented by a more generic concept of association;
- the *type graph* cannot expresses all well-formedness constraints imposed on the UML metamodel. This problem can be resolved by adding additional *global graph constraints* but "Trying to formalize OCL constraints as graph constraints, however, is a far from trivial task." (Folli and Mens, 2008, pp. 11).

In our approach metamodeling-based refactorings are specified as OCL contracts between MOF metamodels which are defined as specializations of the UML metamodel itself. Aggregations and compositions can be specified and OCL constraints are included.

Considering there is a need for rigorous techniques that address refactoring in consistent and precise way, we propose, on the one hand, a rigorous approach to identify refactorings by specification matching, and on the other hand a formalization in the NEREUS language.

REFERENCES

Batory, D. (2007) Program Refactoring, Program Synthesis, and Model Driven Development (LNCS 4420, pp. 156-171) Heidelberg: Springer-Verlag.

CASE. (2009). *CASE Tools*. Retrieved on July 20, 2009 from www.objectsbydesign.com/tools/uml-tools_byCompany.html

Demeyer, S., Ducasse, S., & Nierstrasz, O. (2002). *Object-Oriented Reengineering Patterns*. Amsterdam: Morgan Kaufmann.

Favre, L., & Pereira, C. (2007). Improving MDA-based Process Quality through Refactoring Patterns. *1st International Workshop on Software Patterns and Quality (SPAQu'07) Nagoya, Japan, December 3, 2007- 14th Asia-Pacific Software Engineering Conference (APSEC'07) Information Processing Society of Japan* (pp. 17-22)

Favre, L., & Pereira, C. (2008). Formalizing MDA-based Refactorings. *19th Australian Software Engineering Conference (ASWEC 2008)* (pp. 377-386). Los Alamitos: IEEE Computer Society.

Folli, A., & Mens, T. (2008) Refactoring of UML models using AGG. *Electronic Communications of the EASST. Volume 8: ERCIM Symposium on Software Evolution 2007* (pp. 1-15).

Fowler, M. (1999). *Refactoring: Improving the Design of Existing Programs.* Reading: Addison-Wesley.

France, R., Ghosh, S., Song, E., & Kim, D. (2003). A metamodeling approach to pattern-based model refactoring. *Software IEEE, 20*(5), 52–58. doi:10.1109/MS.2003.1231152

France, R., & Rumpe, B. (2007). Model-driven Development of Complex software: A Research Roadmap. In *Proceedings of the Future of Software Engineering (FOSE 2007)* (pp. 37-54). Los Alamitos: IEEE Computer Society.

Kerievsky, J. (2004). *Refactoring to Patterns.* Reading: Addison-Wesley.

Laplante, P., & Neill, C. (2005). *Antipatterns: Identification, Refactoring and Management.* Auerbach Publications.

Long, Q., Jifeng, H., & Liu, Z. (2005). *Refactoring and Pattern-directed Refactoring: A Formal Perspective.* Technical Report 318, UNU-IIST, P.O. Box 3058, Macau.

Mens, T., & Tourwé, T. (2004). A Survey of Software Refactoring. *IEEE Transactions on Software Engineering, 30*(2), 126–139. doi:10.1109/TSE.2004.1265817

Mens, T., Van Eetvelde, N., Demeyer, S., & Janssens, D. (2005). Formalizing refactorings with graph transformations. *Journal of Software Maintenance, 17*(4), 247–276. doi:10.1002/smr.316

Mens, T., Van Gorp, P., Varró, D., & Karsai, G. (2006). Applying a Model Transformation Taxonomy to Graph Transformation Technology. *Electronic Notes in Theoretical Computer Science, 152*, 143–159. doi:10.1016/j.entcs.2005.10.022

Mens, T., Demeyer, S., Du Bois, B., Stenten, H., &. Van Gorp, P. (2003). Refactoring: Current Research and Future Trends. In *Proceedings of Third Workshop on Language Descriptions, Tools and Applications (LDTA 2003)* (pp. 120-130).

MOF. (2006). *MOF: Meta Object facility (MOF ™) 2.0.* OMG Specification formal/2006-01-01. Retrieved on July 20, 2009 from www.omg.org/mof

Opdyke, W. (1992). *Refactoring Object-Oriented Frameworks.* PhD thesis, University of Illinois, Urbana-Champaign.

Porres, I. (2003). Model Refactorings as Rule-Based Update Transformations (LNCS 2863, pp. 159-174. Heidelberg: Springer-Verlag.

Roberts, D. (1999). *Practical Analysis for Refactoring.* PhD thesis, University of Illinois.

Sunyé, G., Pollet, D., LeTraon, D., & Jézéquel, J. (2001). Refactoring UML Models (LNCS 2185, pp. 134-138). Heidelberg: Springer-Verlag.

Thomas, D. (2005). Refactoring as Meta Programming? *Journal of Object Technology, 4*(1), 7-11. Retrieved on July 20, 2009 from http://www.jot.fm/issues/issue_2005_01/column1

Zaremski, A., &. Wing, J. (1997). Specification Matching of Software Components. ACM Transactions on Software Engineering and methodology. Vol. 6, 4 (pp. 333 - 369).

Van Gorp, P., Stenten, H., Mens, T., & Demeyer, S. (2003). Towards automating source-consistent UML Refactorings (LNCS 2863, pp. 144-158). Heidelberg: Springer Verlag.

Chapter 10
MDA–Based Object–Oriented Reverse Engineering

INTRODUCTION

Reverse engineering is the process of analyzing software systems to extract software artifacts at a higher level of abstraction so that it is easier to understand them, e.g., for reengineering, modernizing, reuse, migration or documenting purposes.

This chapter describes an approach to reverse engineering object oriented code. A central idea in reverse engineering is exploiting the source code as the most reliable description both of the system behavior and of the organization and its business rules.

We propose an approach for MDA-based object oriented reverse engineering that integrates classical compiler techniques, metamodeling techniques and formal specification for recovering designs and architectures.

We analyze reverse engineering of PSMs and PIMs from object-oriented code. Models are expressed using UML and OCL. On the one hand, the subset of UML diagrams, that are useful for platform-dependent models, includes class diagram, object diagram, state diagram, interaction diagram (collaboration diagram and sequence diagram) and package diagram. On the other hand, a PIM can be expressed by means of use case diagrams, activity diagrams, interaction diagrams to model system processes and state diagrams to model lifecycle of the system entities.

DOI: 10.4018/978-1-61520-649-0.ch010

Reverse engineering involves processes with different degrees of automation, which can go from totally automatic static analysis to human intervention requiring processes to dynamically analyze the resultant models. Then, we analyze static and dynamic analysis techniques for recovering models at different abstraction levels.

We show how MOF-based metamodels can be used to drive model recovery processes. Besides, considering that validation, verification and consistency analysis are crucial activities in the modernization of systems, we propose an algebraic formalization of these MOF-defined reverse engineering processes.

Next, we describe related work and the features of existing reverse engineering tools.

RELATED WORK

Many works had contributed to reverse engineering object oriented code. (Muller, Jahnke, Smith, Storey, Tilley, & Wong, 2000) presents a roadmap for reverse engineering research for the first decade of the 2000s. (Angyal, Lengyel, & Charaf, 2006) is an overview of the state-of-the-art of reverse engineering techniques. A more recent survey of existing work in the area of reverse engineering is (Canfora & Di Penta, 2007). This article compares existing work, discusses success and provides a road map for possible future developments in the area.

Fanta and Rajlich (1998) describe the reengineering of a deteriorated object-oriented industrial program written in C++. In order to deal with this problem, they designed and implemented several restructuring tools and used them in specific reengineering scenarios.

Systa (2000) describes an experimental environment to reverse engineer JAVA software that integrates dynamic and static information.

Demeyer, Ducasse, & Nierstrasz (2002) distinguish a variety of techniques for object-oriented reengineering based on patterns.

Qiao, Yang, Chu and Xu (2003) present an approach to bridging legacy systems to MDA that includes an architecture description language and a reverse engineering process.

Koehler, Hauser, Kapoor, Wu, and Kumaran (2003) describe a method that implements model driven transformations between particular platform-independent (business views) and platform-specific (IT architectural) models. On the PIM level, they use business process models and on the PSM level, the IT architectural models are service-oriented and focus on specific platform using Web service and workflows.

Gueheneuc (2004) proposes a study of class diagram constituents with respect to their recovery from object oriented code.

Boronat, Carsi and Ramos (2005) describe MOMENT, a rigorous framework for automatic legacy system migration in MDA.

MacDonald, Russell, and Atchison (2005) report on a project that assessed the feasibility of applying MDD to the evolution of a legacy system.

Deissenboeck and Ratiu (2006) show the first steps towards the definition of a metamodel that unifies a conceptual view on programs with the classical structure-based reverse engineering metamodels.

Tonella and Potrich (2005) provide a relevant overview of techniques that have been recently investigated and applied in the field of reverse engineering of object oriented code. They describe the algorithms involved in the recovery of UML diagrams from code and some of the techniques that can be adopted for their visualization. The algorithms deal with the reverse engineering of the following diagrams: class diagram, object and interaction diagram, state diagram and package diagram. The underling principle in this approach is that information is derived statically by performing propagation of proper data in a data flow graph.

(Greevy, Ducasse & Girba, 2005) describes a novel approach to analyze the evolution of a system in terms of features reflecting how the functional roles of software artifacts change. They introduce visualizations to support reasoning about the evolution of a system from a feature perspective.

Reus, Geers and van Deursen (2006) describe a feasibility study in reengineering legacy systems based on grammars and metamodels.

The increased use of data warehouse and data mining techniques had motivated an interest in data reverse technologies. In general, reverse engineering of persistent data structure of software systems is more specifically referred to as database reverse engineering. Kagdi, Collard and Maletic (2007) provide a survey and taxonomy of approaches for mining software repositories in the context of software evolution. The term mining software repositories (MSR) describes a broad kind of research into the examination of software repositories including artifacts that are produced and stored during software evolution. The main contribution of this article is to present a layered taxonomy identifying four dimensions in order to objectively describe and compare the different existing approaches.

Novel approaches analyze the evolution of a system in terms of features. A feature in a program represents some functionality that is accessible by and visible to the developers, and usually captured by explicit requirements. The process of identifying the parts of code that correspond to specific functionality is called feature (or concept) location and it is part of the incremental change process. (Pohyvanyk, Gueheneuc, Marcus, Antoniol, & Rajlich, 2007) analyzes feature location using probabilistic ranking of methods based on execution scenarios and information retrieval and, proposes a new technique for feature location which combines an information retrieval technique with dynamic analysis.

Nowadays, software industry evolves to manage new platform technologies, design techniques and processes and there is a need for information integration and tool interoperation based on Model Driven Development (MDD). There is an increased demand of modernization systems that are still business-critical in order to extend their useful lifetime. The success of system modernization depends on the existence of technical frameworks for information integration and tool interoperation like the Model Driven Architecture (MDA). Reverse engineering techniques play a crucial role in modernizing systems in a way that fits with the Model Driven Architecture (MDA).

OMG is involved in the definition of standards to successfully modernize existing information systems. The OMG Architecture-Driven Modernization (ADM) Task Force is developing a set of modernization standards with the purpose of software improvement, modifications, interoperability, refactoring, restructuring, reuse, porting, migration and MDA migration.

In the following section we analyze different tools linked to reverse engineering.

CASE TOOLS

Twenty years ago, reverse engineering was focused mainly on recovering high-level architecture or diagrams from procedural code to face up to problems such as comprehending data structures or databases, or the Y2K problem. At that time, many different tools for extracting intermediate representations from the source code and storing it into databases were built. Many reverse engineering tools have been implemented to reverse engineering code written in procedural programming languages such as C

Table 1. UML CASE tools

Basic Drawing Tools	Visio
Main Stream Object Oriented Case Tools	Rational Rose, Argo/UML, Together, UModel, MagicDraw, MetaEdit+, Poseidon, Fujuba
Real Time/Embedded Tools	Rapsody, Rational Rose Real Time, RapidRMA
MDA-based tools	OptimalJ, AndroMDA, Ameos, Together Architect, Codagen, ArcStyler, MDE Studio, Objecteering

and Cobol (Antoniol, Fiutem, Lutteri, Tonella & Zanfei, 1997). Examples of tools include CIA (Chen, Nishimoto, & Ramamoorthy, 1990) and the Software Refinery that used an object database, called Refine, to store artifacts in the form of an attribute Abstract Syntax Tree (Markosian, Newcomb, Brand, Burson, & Kitzmiller, 1994).

A growing demand of reverse engineering systems appeared on the stage when object oriented languages emerged. The compiler techniques were adapted to perform a propagation of proper data in an essentially dynamic context. During this time, the focus of software analysis moved from static analysis to dynamic one. Many works has been aimed at identifying abstract data types in procedural code. This process cannot be fully automated and the output of reverse engineering was only the starting point for highly human-interaction reengineering.

Bellay and Gall (1998) evaluate the capabilities of reverse engineering tools by applying them to a real-world embedded software system which implements part of a train control system. The selected tools were Refine/C (Markosian, Newcomb, Brand, Burson, & Kitzmiller, 1994), Imagix4D (Imagix4D, 2000), SNiFF+ (SNiFF+, 1996) and Rigi (Muller & Klashinsky, 1988).

Amstrong and Trudeau (1998) examined tools focusing on the abstraction and visualization of system components and interactions. The five tools they examine were: Rigi (Muller & Klashinsky, 1988), the Dali workbench (Kazman, & Carriere, 1999), the Software Bookshelf (Finnigan, Holt, Kalas, Kerr, Kontogiannis et al, 1997), CIA (Chen, Nishimoto, & Ramamoorthy, 1990) and SNiFF+(SNiFF+, 1996).

When the Unified Modeling Language (UML) emerged, a new problem was how to extract higher level views of the system expressed by different kind of diagrams. (Dwyer, Hatcliff, Joehanes, Laubach, Pasareanu, Robby, Zheng, & Visser, 2001) describes an integrated collection of program analysis and transformation components, called Bandera, that enables the automatic extraction of safe, compact finite-state models from program source code.

The reverse engineering tool RevEng extracts UML diagrams from C++ code. Among the diagrams that RevEng extracts are class diagram, object diagram, state diagram, sequence and collaboration diagrams and package diagram (Potrich & Tonella, 2000).

To date, there are about 150 UML CASE tools that vary widely in functionality, usability, performance and platforms (CASE, 2009). Some of them can only help with the mechanics of drawing and exporting UML diagrams. The main stream object-oriented CASE tools support forward engineering and reverse engineering processes and can help with the analysis of consistency between diagrams. Only a few UML tools include extension for real time modeling. Table 1 exemplifies taxonomy of the UML CASE tools (CASE, 2009).

The current techniques available in the commercial tools do not allow generating complete and executable code and after generation, the code needs additions. A source of problems in the code generation processes is that, on the one hand, the UML models contain information that cannot be expressed in object- oriented languages while, on the other hand, the object-oriented languages express implementation characteristics that have no counterpart in the UML models.

Moreover, the existing CASE tools do not exploit all the information contained in the UML models. For instance, cardinality and constraints of associations and preconditions, postconditions, and class invariants in OCL are only translated as annotations. It is the designer's responsibility to make good use of this information either selecting an appropriate implementation from a limited repertoire or implementing the association by himself.

On the other hand, many CASE tools support reverse engineering, however, they only use more basic notational features with a direct code representation and produce very large diagrams. Reverse engineering processes are facilitated by inserting annotations in the generated code. These annotations are the link between the model elements and the language. As such, they should be kept intact and not be changed. It is the programmer's responsibility to know what he or she can modify and what he or she cannot modify.

UML CASE tools provide limited facilities for refactoring on source code through an explicit selection made for the designer. However it will be worth thinking about refactoring at the design level. The advantage of refactoring at UML level is that the transformations do not have to be tied to the syntax of a programming language. This is relevant since UML is designed to serve as a basis for code generation with the MDA paradigm (Sunye, Pollet, LeTraon, & Jezequel, 2001).

Techniques that currently exist in UML CASE tools provide little support for validating models in the design stages. Reasoning about models of systems is well supported by automated theorem provers and model checkers, however these tools are not integrated into CASE tools environments. Another problem is that as soon as the requirements specifications are handed down, the system architecture begins to deviate from specifications. Only research tools provide support for formal specification and deductive verification.

Nowadays, software and system engineering industry evolves to manage new platform technologies, design techniques and processes. A new architectural framework for information integration and tool interoperation such as MDD had created the need to develop new analysis tools and specific techniques. MDD refers to a range of development approaches that are based on the use of software models as first class entities, one of them is MDA.

The success of MDA depends on the existence of CASE tools that make a significant impact on software processes such as forward engineering and reverse engineering processes (CASE, 2009).

The tool market around MDA tools is still in flux and, only about 10% of UML Case tools provide some support for MDA (CASE, 2009). All of the MDA tools are partially compliant to MDA features. They provide good support for modeling and limited support for automated transformation. In general, they support MDD from the PIM level and use UML class diagrams for designing PIMs. Some of them provide only one level of transformation from PIM to code (Codagen, Ameos, Arcstyler) and, in general, there is no relation between QVT and the current existing MDA tools. As an example, OptimalJ from Compuware supports MDD from PIM level. It allows generating PSMs from a PIM and a partial code generation. It distinguishes three kinds of models: a domain model that correspond to a PIM model, an application model that includes PSMs linked to different platforms (Relational-PSM, EJB-PSM and web-PSM) and an implementation model. The transformation process is supported by transformation and functional patterns.

(Mansurov, & Campara, 2005) describes a tool-assisted way of introducing models in the migration towards MDA. They propose to automatically extract architecturally significant models (called Container models) and then refactoring them to achieve models in higher-level of abstraction.

Eclipse is an open source framework that can be extended by external plug-in and several transformation tools are implemented as Eclipse plug-in. Eclipse generative Modeling Tools (EclipseGMT) is a collection of tools for model driven development (Eclipse, 2009). Atlas Transformation Language (ATL) implements the MOF-metamodel *Query, View, Transformation* (QVT).

MetaEdit+ is an integrated environment for building and using solutions in a language that uses concepts and rules from the problem domain, a Domain-Specific Language (DSL). High-level models are expressed in a DSL and code can then be automatically generated from them using customized code generators (MetaEdit, 2009).

The Fujaba Tool Suite project is suited to provide an easy to extend UML, Story Driven Modeling and Graph Transformation platform with the ability to add plug-ins (FUJUBA, 2009). It combines UML static diagrams and UML behavior diagrams (Story Diagrams). Furthermore, it supports the generation of Java code. Fujaba is configured with plug-ins for Reverse Engineering and Design Pattern recognition.

The MDA-based tools use MOF to support OMG standards such as UML and XMI (XML Metadata Interchange). MOF has a central role in MDA as a common standard to integrate all different kinds of models and metadata and to exchange these models among tools; however, MOF does not allow capturing semantic properties in a platform independent way and there is no rigorous foundations for specifying transformations among different kinds of models.

A FRAMEWORK FOR REVERSE ENGINEERING

We propose to reverse engineering MDA models from object oriented code starting from the integration of compiler techniques, metamodeling and formal specification. With the emergence of MDA, the static analysis based on compiler techniques and dynamic analysis must be integrated with metamodeling techniques (Favre, 2008a) (Favre, 2008b) (Favre, Martinez, & Pereira, 2009).

Figure 1 shows a framework for reverse engineering that integrates static and dynamic analysis, metamodeling and formal specification. It distinguishes three different abstraction levels linked to models, metamodels and formal specifications.

The model level includes code, PIMs and PSMs. A PIM is a model with a high level of abstraction that is independent of an implementation technology (MDA, 2005). A PSM is a tailored model to specify a system in terms of specific platform such J2EE or .NET. PIMs and PSMs are expressed in UML and OCL (UML, 2009a) (UML, 2009b) (OCL, 2006). The subset of UML diagrams that are useful for PSMs includes class diagram, object diagram, state diagram, interaction diagram and package diagram. On the other hand, a PIM can be expressed by means of use case diagrams, activity diagrams, interactions diagrams to model system processes and state diagrams to model lifecycle of the system entities. An ISM is a specification of the system in source code.

At model level, transformations are based on classical compiler construction techniques. They involve processes with different degrees of automation, which can go from totally automatic static analysis to human intervention requiring processes to dynamically analyze the resultant models. All the algorithms that deal with the reverse engineering share an analysis framework. The basic idea is to describe source code or models by an abstract language and perform a propagation analysis in a data-flow graph called

Figure 1. MDA-based reverse engineering

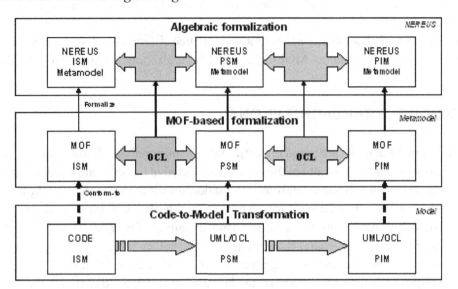

in this context object-data flow. This static analysis is complemented with dynamic analysis supported by tracer tools.

The metamodel level includes MOF metamodels that describe the transformations at model level (MOF, 2006). A metamodel is an explicit model of the constructs and rules needed to construct specific models. MOF metamodels use an object modeling framework that is essentially a subset of UML 2.2 core (UML, 2009a). The modeling concepts are classes which model MOF metaobjects, associations, which model binary relations between metaobjects, data types which model other data, and packages which modularize the models. At this level MOF metamodels describe families of ISMs, PSMs and PIMs. Every ISM, PSM and PIM conforms to a MOF metamodel. Metamodel transformations are specified as OCL contracts between a source metamodel and a target metamodel. MOF metamodels "control" the consistency of these transformations.

The level of formal specification includes specifications of MOF metamodels and metamodel transformations in the metamodeling language NEREUS that can be used to connect them with different formal and programming languages (Favre, 2006) (Favre, 2009).

To sum up, in the level of models, instances of ISMs, PSMs and PIMs are generated by applying static and dynamic analysis. Static analysis builds an abstract model of the state and determines how the program executes to this state. Dynamic analysis operates by executing a program and evaluating the execution trace of the program. Contracts based on MOF-metamodels "control" the consistency of these transformations and NEREUS facilitates the connection of the metamodels and transformations with different formal languages.

Our work could be considered as an MDA-based formalization of the process described by Tonella and Potrich (2005). Additionally, we propose algorithms for extracting UML diagrams that can differ on the ones proposed by the mentioned authors. For instance, a different algorithm for extracting State Diagrams is proposed. We also propose to include OCL specifications (preconditions, postconditions and invariants) in UML Diagrams. Other advantages are linked to the automation of the formalization process and interoperability of formal languages (Favre, 2007) (Favre, 2008a) (Favre, 2008b) (Favre, Martinez & Pereira, 2009).

The following sections describe reverse engineering at three different levels of abstraction corresponding to code-to-model transformation, MOF-metamodel formalization and algebraic formalization.

CODE-TO-MODEL TRANSFORMATIONS

At model level, transformations are based on static and dynamic analysis. Static analysis extracts static information that describes the structure of the software reflected in the software documentation (e.g., the text of the source code) while dynamic analysis information describes the structure of the run-behavioral. Static information can be extracted by using techniques and tools based on compiler techniques such as parsing and data flow algorithms. On the other hand, dynamic information can be extracted by using debuggers, event recorders and general tracer tools.

We suppose that the reverse engineering process starts from the ISM that reflects the migration of legacy code to object-oriented code. The next step in the migration towards MDA is the introduction of PSMs. Then, a PIM is abstracted from the PSMs omitting platform specific details.

Next, we describe the process for recovery PSMs from code. Figure 2 shows the different phases. The source code is parsed to obtain an abstract syntax tree (AST) associated with the source programming language grammar. Then, a metamodel extractor extracts a simplified, abstract version of language that ignores all instructions that do not affect the data flows, for instance all control flows such as conditional and loops.

Figure 2. Reverse engineering at model level: Static and dynamic analysis

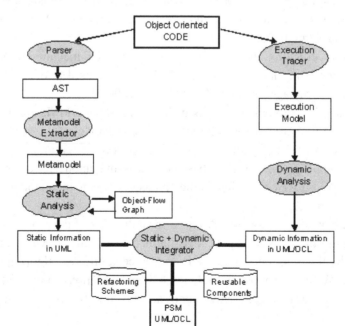

The information represented according to this metamodel allows building the data-flow graph for a given source code, as well as conducting all other analysis that do not depend on the graph. The idea is to derive statically information by performing a propagation of data. Different kinds of analysis propagate different kinds of information in the data-flow graph, extracting the different kinds of diagrams that are included in a PSM.

The static analysis is based on classical compiler techniques (Aho, Sethi & Ullman, 1985) and abstract interpretation (Jones & Nielson, 1995). On the one hand, data-flow graph and the generic flow propagation algorithms are specializations of classical flow analysis techniques (Aho, Sethi & Ullman, 1985). Because there are many possible executions, it is usually not reasonable to consider all state of the program. Thus static analysis is based on abstract models of the program state that are easier to manipulate, although lose some information. Abstract interpretation of program state allows obtaining automatically as much information as possible about program executions without having to run the program on all input data and then ensuring computability or tractability. These ideas were applied in compiler optimizations. They require information about program semantics and are semantics- preserving program transformations.

In our context, an abstract interpretation performs method invocation using abstract domains instead of concrete attribute values to deduce information about the object computation on its actual state from the resulting abstract descriptions of its attributes. This implies to abstract equivalence classes grouping attribute values corresponding to the different states in which the class can be.

The static analysis builds a partial PSM that must be refined by dynamic analysis. Ernst (2003) provides a comparison of static and dynamic analysis from the point of view of their synergy and duality. He argues that static analysis is conservative and sound. Conservatism means reporting weak properties that are guaranteed to be true, preserving soundness, but not be strong enough to be useful. Soundness guarantees that static analysis provides an accurate description of the behavior, no matter on what input or in what execution environment. Dynamic analysis is precise due to it examines the actual run-time behavior of the program. However the results of executions may not generalize to other executions.

Ernst (2003) argues that whereas the chief challenge of static analysis is choosing a good abstract interpretation, the chief challenge of performing good dynamic analysis is selecting a representative set of test cases. A test can help to detect properties of the program, but it can be difficult detect whether results of a test are true program properties or properties of a particular execution context.

Dynamic analysis is based on testing and profiling. Execution tracer tools generate execution model snapshots that allow us to deduce complementary information. Execution models, programs and UML models coexist in this process. An object-oriented execution model has the following components: a set of objects, a set of attributes for each object, a location for each object, each object refers to a value of an object type and, a set of messages that include a name selector and may include one or more arguments. Additionally, types are available for describing types of attributes and parameters of methods or constructors. On the other hand, an object-oriented program model has a set of classes, a set of attributes for each class, a set of operations for each class, and a generalization hierarchy over classes.

The static analysis is based on program models but dynamic analysis is based on execution models. For instance a basic algorithm for the recovery of class diagram can be obtained by a static analysis. From the source code, associations, generalization, realizations and dependencies may be inferred. But, to distinguish between aggregation and composition, or to include OCL specifications (e.g. preconditions and postconditions of operations, invariants and association constraints) we need to capture system states through dynamic analysis.

Dynamic analysis allows generating execution snapshot to collect life cycle traces of object instances and reason from tests and proofs. The combination of static and dynamic analysis can enrich reverse engineering process. There are different ways of combination, for instance performing first static analysis and then dynamic one or perhaps iterating static and dynamic analysis.

The ideas of transformations at model level are based on techniques described in (Tonella & Potrich, 2005). The underlying algorithms to these techniques deal with reverse engineering of UML diagram from object-oriented code, e.g., Java, Eiffel and C++. The following UML diagrams are considered: class diagram, interaction diagram (sequence and collaboration diagram), object diagram, state diagram and package diagram.

Classical compiler techniques such as parsing and data flow are integrated in a common analysis framework that is shared by all recovering processes. The basic idea is that information is derived statically by performing a propagation of data. Different kinds of analysis propagate different kind of information in a dataflow graph. This is built by parsing the source code described by a grammar.

The remaining parts of the chapter describe how to recover UML diagrams from source object-oriented code.

Static Analysis

The concepts and algorithms of data flow analysis described in (Aho, Sethi & Ullman, 1985) are adapted for reverse engineering object oriented code. The data flow analysis can be viewed as the transmission of useful relationships from all parts of the code to the places when the information can be used.

The basic representation of the static analysis is the Data Flow Graph (OFG) that allows tracing information of object interactions from the object creation, through object assignment to variables, the storage of objects in attributes or their use in messages (method invocations). OFG is defined as an oriented graph that represents all data flows linking objects.

The static analysis is data flow sensitive, but control flow insensitive. This means that programs with different control flows and the same data flows are associated with the same analysis results (Tonella & Potrich, 2005).

A consequence of the control flow insensitivity is that the construction of the OFG can be described with reference to a simplified, abstract version of the object-oriented languages in which instructions related to flow control are ignored. A generic algorithm of flow propagation working on the OFG processes object information. Then, the three essential components of the common analysis framework are the simplified abstract object-oriented language, the data flow graph and the flow propagation algorithm. Following, we describe them.

A Simplified Object-Oriented Language

All instructions that refer to data flows are represented in the abstract language, while all control flow instructions such as conditional and different iteration constructs are ignored. Moreover, to avoid name conflicts all identifiers are given fully scoped names including a list of enclosing packages, classes and methods.

Table 2 shows the abstract syntax of simplified language (Tonella & Potrich, 2005).

Table 2 shall employ some notational conventions summarized below:

Table 2. Simplified object-oriented language: Abstract syntax

(1)	P	::=	D*S*
(2)	D	::=	a
(3)		|	m $(p_1,p_2,\ldots,p_j)$
(4)		|	cons $(p_1,p_2,\ldots,p_j)$
(5)	S	::=	x = new c $(a_1,a_2,\ldots a_j)$
(6)		|	x = y
(7)		|	[x =] y.m $(a_1,a_2,\ldots,a_j)$

- non-terminals are denoted by upper case letters
- a: class attribute name
- m: method name
- $p_1, p_2, \ldots p_j$: formal parameters
- x, y: program locations
- $a_1,a_2,\ldots a_j$: actual parameters
- cons: class constructor
- c: class name

A program P consists of zero or more declarations (D*) concatenated with zero or more statements (S*). The order of declarations and instructions is irrelevant. The nesting structure of packages, classes and statements is flattened, i.e. statements belonging to different methods are merged and identified by their fully scope names. The process of transformation of an object oriented program into a simplified language can be easily automated.

Table 2 shows three types of declaration production: attribute declarations (2), method declarations (3) and constructor declaration (4). An attribute declaration is defined by the scope determined by the list of packages, classes, followed by the attribute identifier. A method declaration consists in its name followed by a list of formal parameter $(p_1, p_2, \ldots p_j)$. Constructors have a similar declaration.

Table 2 also shows three types of statement production: allocation statements (5), assignments (6) and method invocation (7). The left hand side and the right hand side of all statements is a program location. The target of a method invocation is also a program location. Program locations are either, local variables, class attributes or method parameters.

Data Flow Graph (OFG)

OFG is a pair (N, E) where N is a set of nodes and E is a set of edges. A node is added for each program location (i.e., attribute, formal parameter or attribute). Edges represent the data flows appearing in the program. They are added to the OFG according to the rules specified in (Tonella & Potrich, 2005, pp. 26). Table 3 shows the rules for constructing OFG from Java statements.

When a constructor or method is invoked, edges are built which connect each actual parameter a_i to the respective formal parameter p_i. In case of constructor invocation, the newly created object, referenced by *cons.this* is paired with the left hand side x of the related assignment. In case of method invocation, the target object y becomes *m.this* inside the called method, generating the edge *(y, m.this)*,

Table 3. Rules for constructing OFG from Java statements

(1)	P	::=	D*S*	{ }
(2)	D	::=	a	{ }
(3)		|	$m(p_1, p_2, ..., p_j)$	{ }
(4)		|	$cons(p_1, p_2, ..., p_j)$	{ }
(5)	S	::=	$x = new\ c\ (a_1, a_2, ... a_j)$	$\{(a_1, p_1) \in E, ..(a_j, p_j) \in E, (cons.this, x) \in E\}$
(6)		|	$x = y$	$\{(y, x) \in E\}$
(7)		|	$[x =]\ y.m\ (a_1, a_2, ..., a_j)$	$\{(y, m.this) \in E, (a_1, p_1) \in E, ..(a_j, p_j) \in E, (m.return, x) \in E\}$

and the value returned by method *m* (if any) flows to the left hand side *x* (pair *(m.return, x)*) (Tonella & Potrich, 2005, pp. 26).

Some edges in the OFG may be related to the usage of library classes. Each time a library class introduces a data flow from a variable *x* to a variable *y* an edge *(x,y)* must be included in the OFG. Containers are an example of library classes that introduce external data flows. For instance, any Java class implementing the interface Collection or the interface Map, or any Eiffel class reusing Container introduces external data flows.

Object containers provide two basic operations affecting the OFG: *insert* and *extract* for adding an object to a container and accessing an object in a container respectively. In the abstract program representation insertion and extraction methods are associated with container objects.

The OFG treats the two cases:

c.insert (y) and *y =c. extract ()* where *c* is a container and *x* is an object. These statements introduce the edges shown in Table 4 to the OFG.

Other cases require that data flows are modeled semi-automatically in a similar way as done for the class libraries, for instance dynamic loading and the access to code written in other programming languages.

Flow Propagation Algorithm

Next, we show a pseudo-code of generic flow propagation algorithm that is a specific instance of the algorithms applied to control flow graph described in (Aho, Sethi & Ullman, 1985). It was presented in (Tonella & Potrich, 2005, pp. 31).

```
Algorithm: Forward propagationfor each node n∈ N
in[n] = emptyset
out[n]= gen[n] ∪ (in[n] - kill[n])
end-forwhile any in[n] or out[n] changes
```

Table 4.

c.insert(x)	$(x,c) \in E$
x = c.extract ()	$(c,x) \in E$

```
for each node n∈ N
in[n] = ∪ ₚₑpred(n) out[p]
out[n] = gen[n] ∪ (in[n] - kill[n])
end-forend-while
```

Let *gen[n]* and *kill[n]* be two sets of each basic node n ∈ N. *gen[n]* is the set of flow information entities generated by *n*. *kill[n]* is the set of definition outside of *n* that define entities that also have definitions within n. There are two sets of equations, called data-flow equations that relate incoming and outgoing flow information inside the sets in[n] and out[n]:

```
in[n] = ∪ ₚₑpred(n) out[p]
out[n] = gen[n] ∪ (in[n] - kill[n])
```

Each node n stores the incoming and outgoing flow information inside the sets *in[n]* and *out[n]*, which are initially empty. Each node *n* generates the set of flow information entities included in *gen[s]* set, and prevents the elements of *kill[n]* set from being further propagated after node n. In forward propagation *in[n]* is obtained from the predecessors of node n as the union of the respective out sets.

In some cases, it may be appropriate to propagate information in reverse order by collecting the incoming information from the out sets of the successors. Next, we show the pseudo-code of backward propagation algorithm:

```
Algorithm: Backward propagationfor each node n∈ N
in[n] = emptyset
out[n]= gen[n] ∪ (in[n] - kill[n])
end-forwhile any in[n] or out[n] changes
   for each node n∈ N
   in[n] = ∪ ₚₑsucc(n) out[p]
   out[n] = gen[n] ∪ (in[n] - kill[n])
   end-forend-while
```

The algorithm can distinguish when entities are scoped at the class level (for instance, class attributes, method names, program location). That means that it is not possible to distinguish two entities (e.g. two attributes) when they belong to the same class but to different class instances (objects).

The OFG constructed in based on the previous rules is "object insensitive". An object sensitive OFG might improve the analysis results. It can be built by giving all non-static program names an object scope instead a class scope and object can be identified statically by their allocation points. Thus, in an object sensitive OFG, non-static class attributes and methods with their parameters and local variables, are replicated for every statically identified object.

A detailed description of the basis of static analysis may be found at (Systa, 2000) and (Tonella & Potrich, 2005) which presents static analysis with reference to a Java program.

The remaining parts of this chapter contain details on dynamic analysis and on how to adapt and extend the proposed techniques in the MDA context.

Dynamic Analysis

Integrating dynamic and static analysis seems to be beneficial. For instance, the static analysis is not enough to determine the actual method invocations due to polymorphism. This is only possible by analyzing the behavior. The static and dynamic information could be shown as separated views or merged in a single view. In general, the dynamic behavior could be visualized as a scenery diagram which describes interaction between objects. To extract specific information, it is necessary to define particular views of these sceneries. Although, the construction of these views can be automated, their analysis requires some manual processing in most cases. In order to describe an integration of static and dynamic analysis we define the syntax at levels of execution scenery models and object-oriented programs.

Object-Oriented Execution Scenery Model

An execution model has the following components:

- a set of objects
- a set of attributes for each object
- a location for each object
- each object refers to a value of an object type
- a set of messages

Additionally, types such as Integer, String, Real and Boolean are available for describing types of attributes and parameters of methods or constructors. For naming elements, we assume an alphabet A and a set of finite, non-empty of identifiers $N \subseteq A+$ over alphabet A. All identifiers are given fully scope name, being preceded by a dot separated list of enclosing elements.

Objects are associated with attribute values describing properties of the objects that define their state. All attributes have different names.

A message includes a name selector and may include one or more arguments. Normally, there exist a determined number of arguments. The acceptable values of arguments belong to a type, not necessarily basic.

Object-Oriented Program Model

Such a model has the following components:

- a set of classes
- a set of attributes for each class
- a set of operations for each class
- a generalization hierarchy over classes

Additionally, types such as Integer, String, Set (Real) are available for describing types of attributes and operation parameters.

We assume that there is a signature $\sum = (T, O)$ with T being a set of type names, and O being a set of operations over types in T.

Classes

The central concept of OO programs is the class. A class is a static concept that provides a common description for a set of objects sharing the same properties.

The set of classes is a finite set of names $CLASS \subseteq N$. Each class $c \subseteq CLASS$ induces an object type $tc \in T$ having the same name of the class.

Attributes

Attributes are part of a class declaration. An attribute has a name and a type specifying the domain of attribute values. Let $t \in T$ be a type. The attributes of a class have distinct names. Attributes with the same name may, however, appear in different classes that are not related by generalization. The set of attribute names and class names need not be disjoint.

Operations

Operations are part of a class definition. They are used to describe behavioral properties of objects. Operations of a class $c \in CLASS$ with $tc \in T$ are defined by a set OPc of signatures w: tc x t1 x... x tn -> t with operation symbols w being elements of N.

The name of an operation is determined by the symbol w. The first parameter tc denotes the type of the class instance to which the operation is applied. An operation may have any number of parameters but only a single return type.

Generalization

A generalization is a taxonomic relationship between two classes. This relationship is a specialization of a general class into a more specific class. Specialization and generalization are different views of the same concept. Generalization relationships form a hierarchy over a set of classes.

A child class implicitly inherits attributes and operation of its parent class. It contains all inherits attributes and operations of its parent classes. It contains all inherited attributes (and operations) and those that are defined directly in the class.

Dynamic analysis allows producing specifications in OCL or detecting specific relationships such as composition. Nimmer and Ernst (2002) investigate combining dynamic and static analysis for recovering formal specifications. They propose to generate specifications from program executions, then verify them, i.e., to dynamically detect and then statically verify program specifications. They suggest that dynamic analysis can capture all semantics information of interest in certain applications. Their experimental results demonstrate that a specific technique, dynamic invariant detection, is effective at generating consistent specifications that can be used by a static checker. Recovering specifications is useful in testing, debugging, verification, maintenance and optimizations. These ideas can be adapted for recovering OCL specifications in MDA models.

Now, we are in the situation to analyze reverse engineering of UML diagrams from object-oriented code. First, we analyze code to model transformations for two classical diagrams: Class Diagram and State Diagram.

CODE-TO-MODEL TRANSFORMATIONS: THE BASES FOR RECOVERING CLASS DIAGRAM

A class diagram is a representation of the static view that shows a collection of static model elements, such as classes, interfaces, methods, attributes, types as well as their properties (e.g., type and visibility). Besides, the class diagram shows the interrelationships holding among the classes (UML, 2009a; UML, 2009b).

Reverse engineering of class diagram from code is difficult task that cannot be automated. Certain elements in the class diagram carry behavioral information that cannot be inferred just from the analysis of the code.

The static analysis is based on program models but dynamic analysis is based on execution models. For instance a basic algorithm for the recovery of class diagram can be obtained by a static analysis. By analyzing the syntax of the source code, internal class features such as attributes and methods and their properties (e.g. the parameters of the methods and visibility) can be recovered. From the source code, associations, generalization, realizations and dependencies may be inferred too. However, to distinguish between aggregation and composition, or to include OCL specifications (e.g. preconditions and postconditions of operations, invariants and association constraints) we need to capture system states through dynamic analysis.

Figure 3 shows relationships that can be detected statically between a Java program and a UML class diagram.

The association between A and B could be an aggregation or a composition. An aggregation models the situation where an object is made up of several parts. The whole shows at least an emergent property, i.e. "the whole is more than the sum of its parts". Other properties that characterize the aggregation are the following:

- type-anti-symmetry: the aggregation from a type A (as whole) to a type B (as part), prevents the existence of another aggregation from B (as a whole) to A (as part)
- instance-reflexivity
- instance anti-symmetry

Dynamic analysis allows generating execution snapshot to collect life cycle traces of object instances and reason from tests and proofs. Execution tracer tools generate execution model snapshots that allow us to deduce complementary information.

Execution models, programs and UML models coexist in this process. An object-oriented execution model has the following components: a set of objects, a set of attributes for each object, a location for each object, each object refers to a value of an object type and, a set of messages that include a name selector and may include one or more arguments. Additionally, types are available for describing types of attributes and parameters of methods or constructors. On the other hand, an object-oriented program model has a set of classes, a set of attributes for each class, a set of operations for each class, and a generalization hierarchy over classes.

A composition is a particular aggregation in which the lifetime of the part is controlled by the whole (directly or transitively). Then, we can detect a composition by generating tests and scanning dependency configurations between the birth and the death of a part object according to those of the whole.

Figure 3. Java constructs versus class diagram constructs

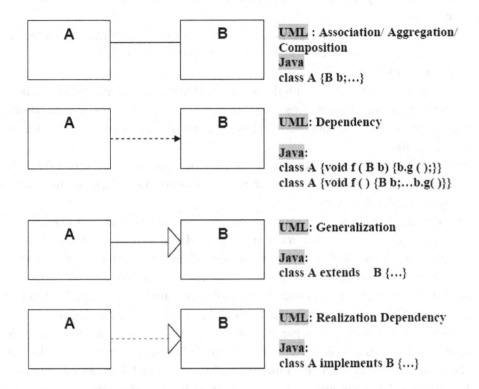

In the same way, the execution traces of different instances of the same class or method, could guide the construction of invariants or pre- and post-conditions respectively.

CODE-TO-MODEL TRANSFORMATION: THE BASES FOR RECOVERING STATE DIAGRAM

Below, we describe how to reverse engineering state diagrams from code by integrating static and dynamic analysis.

A state transition diagram describes the life cycle of objects that are instances of a class from the time they are created until they are destroyed. Object state is determined by the value of its attributes and possibly by the variables involved in attribute computations. The basic elements of a state diagram are states, identified as equivalence classes of attribute values and, transitions triggered by method invocation.

Our approach to recover state diagrams has similar goals to abstract interpretation that allows obtaining automatically as much information as possible about program executions without having to run it on all input data and then ensuring computability or tractability (Jones, & Nielsen, 1995). These ideas were applied to optimizing compilers, often under the name data-flow analysis (Aho, Sethi, & Ullman (1985). In our context, an abstract interpretation performs method invocation using abstract domains instead of concrete attribute values to deduce information about the object computation on its actual state from the resulting abstract descriptions of its attributes. This implies to abstract equivalence classes that group attribute values corresponding to the different states in which the class can be and the transitions among state equivalence classes.

Then, the first step is to define an appropriate abstract interpretation for attributes (which give the state of the object) and transformer class method (which give the transitions from state to state to be represented in the state diagram).

A taxonomy of finite-state automata minimization can be found at (Watson, 1995) and (Daciuk, 1998). The main characteristic of these algorithms is that they are incremental. The minimization algorithm should compare incrementally the equivalence between pairs of states to determine whether they can be merged in an only state.

The recovery algorithm iterates over the following activities: the construction of a finite automata by executing abstract interpretations of class methods and the minimization of the automata for recovering approximate state equivalence classes.

To ensure tractability, our algorithm proposes an incremental minimization every time a state is candidate to be added to the automaton. When it is detected that two states are equivalents, they are merged in an only state. This could lead to modification of the parts of the automaton that had been previously minimized. To optimize the comparison of pairs of states, these are classified according to their emerging transitions. Let m be a bound of the number of transformer methods of a class, the idea is to generate subsets of the set of transformer methods. The subset of emerging transitions of a new state belongs, in a particular snapshot, to one of them. Two states are candidates to be equivalent if they belong to the same subset. Then, it is sufficient to compare all the pairs composed by the state and one element of the subset. Considerable human interaction to select which abstract interpretations should be executed is required. Then, our approach is so significantly less automatic than traditional abstract interpretation (Nielsen & Jones, 1995).

As an example, Figure 4.a shows a diagram including states (s_1, s_2,.., s_8) and transitions (m_1,m_2,... ,m_6). Figure 4.b shows a simplified snapshot of the automaton when a transition to s_5 is added. Then, the shaded states could belong to the same equivalence state class. s_8 belongs to the same subset of s_4 and an equivalence analysis is carried out concluding that s_8 and s_4 can be merged (Figure 4.c, Figure

Figure 4. Recovering minimum State Diagram

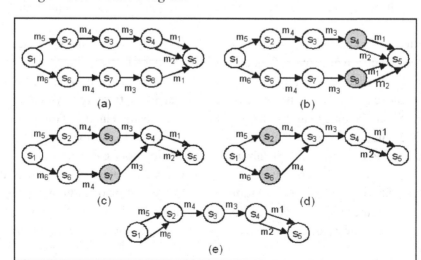

4.d) . Figure 4.e shows the successive transformations. Next, we show the pseudo code of the recovery algorithm.

Algorithm for recovering State Diagrams

```
-- initialization of different sets
   set-of-states initialStates = {}; -- states defined by class con-
structors
   set-of-states pendingStates ={};-- set of states pending of anal-
ysis
   set-of-states allStates = {};-- set of all states
--definition of initial states for the objects of the class
   for each class construtor c
   {-- executing an abstract interpretation of each class construc-
tor
      state s = abstractInterpretationState (c, {});
      initialStates = initialStates ∪ {s};
      pendingStatesPending = pendingStates ∪ {s};
      allStates = allStates ∪{s};
   }
-- initialization of transition set
set-of-transitions transitionSet = {};
-- generation of subsets of transformer methods
set-of-bins b = classifiedStates (allStates);
while |pendingStates| > 0
   { state r = extract (pendingStates);
      pendingState = pendingStates - {r};
         for each transformer class method m
            {-- generating transitions of the state r
               s = abstractInterpretationState (m, r);
               if s ∉ allStates
                  {pendingStates = pendingStates ∪ {s};
                   allStates = allStates ∪ {s};}
                  transitionSet = transitionSet ∪ abstractInterpreta-
tionTransition (m,r,s);}
         -- updating subsets of transformer methods
         b = modifyBins (r, transitionSet, allStates);
         for each e ∈ b
            if s ∈ b
         {-- defining equivalence of states and merging equivalent
states
            for each q ∈ bin and s< > q
```

Figure 5. Java ISM metamodel

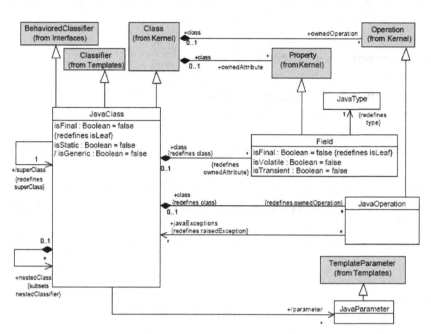

```
        if equivalents (s, q) mergeStates (transitionSet, all-
States, s, q);}
     }
  }
```

MOF-BASED FORMALIZATION: REVERSE ENGINEERING UML CLASS DIAGRAM

We specify reverse engineering processes as MOF-based transformations. A refinement is the process of building a more detailed specification that conforms to another that is more abstract. On the other hand, we call anti-refinement the process of extracting from a more detailed specification (or code) another one, more abstract, that is confirmed by the more detailed specification. Then, we describe how to specify anti-refinements within the proposed framework.

Figures 5 and 6 partially depict an ISM metamodel for Java. A metamodel is an explicit model of the constructs and rules needed to build specific models (its instances). The ISM includes metaclasses linked to the constructs needed to build specific Java programs. Figure 7 depicts a PSM Java metamodel.

Figure 5 shows partially an ISM-Java metamodel that includes constructs for representing classes, field and operations. It also shows different kind of relationships such as composition and generalization. For example, an instance of JavaClass could be related to another instance of JavaClass that takes the role of superclass or, it could be composed by other instances of JavaClass that take the role of *nestedClass*. Figure 6 shows the metamodel for operations. An operation is a subtype of the metaclass Operation of the UML kernel. There is a generalization between operation and constructor and method and so on.

Figure 6. Java ISM metamodel: Operations

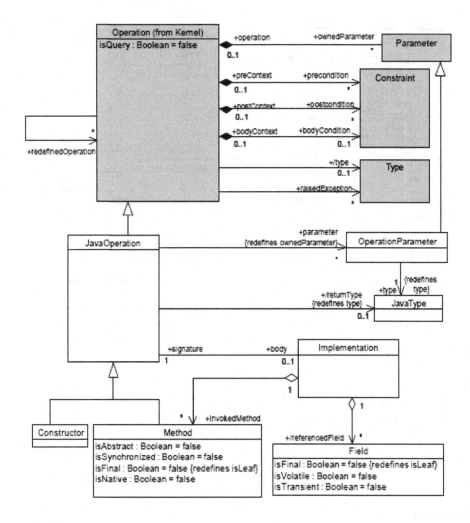

Figure 7 shows partially a PSM-Java metamodel that includes constructs for representing classes, field, operations and association-end. It also shows different kind of relationships such as composition and generalization. For example, an instance of JavaClass could be related to another instance of JavaClass that takes the role of superclass or, it could be composed by other instances of JavaClass that takes the role of nestedClass. The main difference between a Java-ISM and a Java-PSM is that the latter includes constructs for associations.

Metamodel transformations impose relations between a source metamodel and a target metamodel, both represented as MOF-metamodels. The transformations between models are described starting from the metaclass of the elements of the source model and the metaclass of the elements of the target model. The models to be transformed and the target models will be instances of the corresponding metamodel.

The transformation specification is an OCL contract that consists of a name, a set of parameters, a precondition and postconditions. The precondition states relations between the metaclasses of the source metamodel. The postconditions deal with the state of the models after the transformation. Next, an anti-refinement between an ISM-Java (Figure 5) and a PSM-Java (Figure 7) is partially specified.

Figure 7. Java PSM metamodel

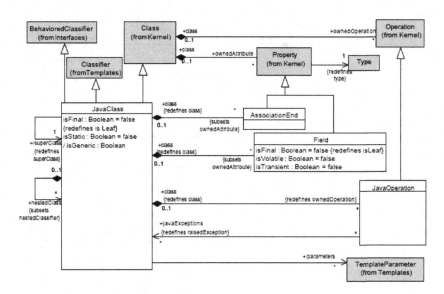

Transformation ISM-Java to PSM-Java

parameters
source: ISM-JavaMetamodel::JavaPackage
target: PSM-JavaMetamodel::Java Package

preconditions
-- True

postconditionslet
SetClassSource: Set[ISM-JavaMetamodel::JavaPackage::JavaClass] =
source.ownedMember ->
select (oclIsKindOf (JavaPackage).javaClasses
in-- for each Java class in the ISM exists a PSM class with the same
name
SetClassSource ->
forAll (sClass| target.ownedMember ->
select (oclIsKindOf (JavaClass)) ->
exists (tClass|sClass.name = tClass.name)
and

-- for each associationEnd of a class in the PSM exists a private
attribute of the same name in
-- the ISM
sClass.fields->forAll (sField| SetClassSource->

```
exists (tc1| tc1.type = sField.type implies
tc1.associationEnd -> includes (sField.type)
and

--for each extends relation in Java exists a generalization in the
PSM
(source.ownedMember ->
select(oclIsKindOf (JavaClass).extendingClass ->
   includes(sClass)) implies SetClassSource ->
      exists (t1 | t1.superclass.name = sClass.name)…
```

MOF-BASED FORMALIZATION: REVERSE ENGINEERING UML STATE DIAGRAM

The State Diagram metamodel (Figure 8) defines a set of concepts than can be used for modeling discrete behavior through finite state transition systems such as state machines, state and transitions. OCL can be used to attach consistency rules to metamodel components. The following rules are attached to the State-Diagram metamodel:

Context Statemachine
--The connection points of a state machine are pseudostates of kind entry point or exit point. conectionPoint -> forAll (c | c.kind = #entryPoint or c.kind = #exitPoint)

Figure 8. State diagram metamodel

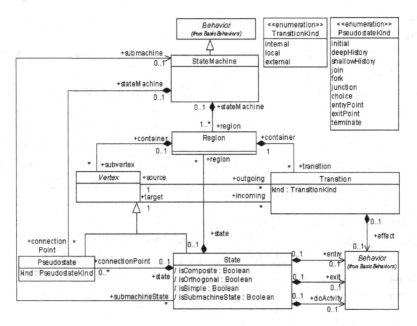

```
Context PseudoState
--An initial vertex can have at most one ongoing transition (self.
kind = #initial) implies (self.outgoing -> size <= 1)
```

```
Context Region
--A region can have at most one initial vertex. self.subvertex ->
select (v |v.oclIsKindOf (Pseudostate)) -> select (p:Pseudostate
|p.kind = #initial) -> size () <=1
```

With respect to reverse engineering processes, two types of consistency can be distinguished, vertical consistency between different levels of refinements and horizontal consistency or inter-consistency between models at the same abstraction level. For instance, a vertical consistency analysis detects when a state model is associated to a class that does not exist in the ISM. A horizontal consistency analysis could detect that the sequence of interactions shown in the sequence diagram does not exist as a trace of the state diagram linked to the respective class. We propose to specify consistency relationships as OCL contracts based on MOF- metamodels.

Next, we partially exemplify a transformation from an ISM-Java (Figures 5 & 6) to a PSM-Java (Figure 7). This transformation uses both the specialized UML metamodel of Java code and the UML metamodel of a Java platform as source and target parameters respectively. The postconditions state relations at metamodel level between the elements of the source and target model. The transformation specification guarantees that for each class in Java code there is a class in the PSM-Java, both of them with the same name, the same parent class, equivalent operations and so on. Besides, the PSM-Java has a 'stateMachine' for each class having a significant dynamic behavior.

```
Transformation ISM-JAVA to PSM-JAVA {parameter
sourceModel: ISM-JAVA-Metamodel:: JavaPackage
targetModel: PSM-JAVA-Metamodel:: JavaPackage
postconditions
-- For each class 'sourceClass' in the sourceModel
sourceModel.ownedMember -> select (oclIsTypeOf (JavaClass)) ->
forAll (sourceClass |
--there is a class 'targetClass' in the targetModel so that both
classes have the same
--name,
targetModel.ownedMember -> select (oclIsTypeOf (JavaClass)) ->
exists (targetClass | targetClass.name = sourceClass.name and
-- if 'sourceClass' has an extends relation, targetModel has a su-
perclass so that
-- both superclasses are equivalent.
sourceClass.extends -> size () = 1 implies (targetClass.superClass
-> size () = 1 and targetClass.superClass.classMatch(sourceClass.
extends)) and
--For each operation of 'sourceClass' there is an operation in tar-
getClass so that
```

```
--both operations are equivalent.
sourceClass.javaOperation -> forAll (sourceOp |
targetClass.javaOp -> exists (targetOp | targetOp.operationMatch
(sourceOp))) and
```
--*For each field in 'sourceClass' whose type is a primitive type
there is a field in*
--*'targetClass' so that:*
```
sourceClass.field -> select (f | f.javaType.oclIsTypeOf (Primitive))
->
forAll (sourceField | targetClass.field -> exists (targetField |
```
-- *'targetField' and 'sourceField' have the same name, type,...*
```
targetField.name = sourceField.name and targetField.type = source-
Field.javaType...)) and
```
-- *For each field in 'sourceClass' whose type is a user defined type
there is an*
--*association end in ' targetClass' so that:*
```
   sourceClass.field -> select (f | f.javaType.oclIsTypeOf (UserJa-
vaClass)) ->
forAll (sourceField | targetClass.associationEnd -> exists (tar-
getAssocEnd |
```
-- *'targetAssocEnd' and 'sourceField' have the same name, type,...*
```
   targetAssocEnd.name = sourceField.name and
   targetAssocEnd.opposite.type = sourceField.javaType and ...))
and...
```
--If 'sourceClass' has some significant dynamic behavior, target-
Model has
-- a 'stateMachine' so that:
```
   sourceClass.hasSignificantDynamicBehavior() implies
   targetModel.ownedMember -> select(oclIsTypeOf(JavaStateMachin
e))->
   exists (targetMachine |
```
   -- 'targetMachine' and 'sourceClass' have the same name and
```
   targetMachine.name = sourceClass.name and
```
   -- For each modifier operation in the 'sourceClass' there is a
transition in 'targetClass'
```
   sourceClass.javaOperation -> select (op | op.isModifier ()) ->
   forAll (op | targetMachine.region.transition -> exists(t |
t.isCreatedFrom(op)))
   )) and
... }
```

SPECIFYING ANTI-REFINEMENTS IN NEREUS

The formalization of the metamodel level implies to formalize metamodels and links among them. The specification in NEREUS of the State Diagram Metamodel shown in Figure 8 is as follows:

```
PACKAGE StateDiagramMetamodel
IMPORTS TransitionKind, PseudoStateKind


CLASS StateMachine
IS-SUBTYPE-OF UML::CommonBehaviors::BasicBehaviors::Behavior
ASSOCIATES
<< StateMachine-State>>
<< StateMachine-PseudoState >> …
AXIOMS a: StateMachine-PseudoState; sm:StateMachine
forAll (c) (get_connectionPoint (a, sm),
[kind (c) = #entryPoint or kind (c) = #exitPoint]) …
END-CLASS


CLASS Region
IS-SUBTYPE-OFUML::Classes::Kernel::Namespace
ASSOCIATES
<< State-Region>>
<< StateMachine-Region>>
<< Region-Vertex >>…
AXIOMS a: Region-Vertex; r: Region
size (select (p) (select(v) (get_subvertex (a, r), oclIsKinfOf (v,
PseudoState) ]),
[kind (p) = #initial ])) <= 1
END-CLASS


CLASS PseudoState
IS-SUBTYPE-OF Vertex,…
ASSOCIATES
<<Vertex-Transition-1>>
<<Vertex-Transition-2>>
<< StateMachine-PseudoState>>…
ATTRIBUTE
kind: PseudoState -> PseudoStateKind
AXIOMS ps: PseudoState; a: Vertex-Transition-1
kind (ps) = #initial implies size (get_outgoing (a, ps)) <=1…
END-CLASS


ASSOCIATION stateMachine-PseudoState
IS Composition-2 [StateMachine: class1; PseudoState:
```

```
class2;stateMachine: role1; conectionPoint: role2; 0..1: mult1; *:
mult2; +: visibility1;+: visibility2]
```
CONSTRAINED-BY StateMachine: subsets namespace;
PseudoState: subsets ownedMember
ENDASSOCIATION Region-Vertex
IS Composition-2 [Region: class1; Vertex:class2; container: role1;
subvertex: role2; 0..1: mult1; *: mult2; +: visibility1; +: visibil-
ity2]
CONSTRAINED-BY Vertex: subsets ownedMember
END

...

END-PACKAGE

Anti-refinements are specified as links between metamodels, where *OCLexp1* and *OCLexp2* are the precondition and postconditions in a transformation respectively. Instances of metamodel-based transformations are automatically translated into NEREUS specifications by instantiating the following reusable scheme:

CLASS*transformationName* [source: *Metamodel A;* target: *Metamodel B*]
GENERATED-BY addLink
EFFECTIVE
TYPE*transformationName*
OPERATIONS
addLink: source x target -> metaLink
pre: Translate $_{NEREUS}$ (*Transformation AtoB. Precondition*)
getSource: metamodelLink -> source
getTarget: metaLink -> target

AXIOMS m1: source ; m2: target ; l: *transformationName*
getSource (addLink(m1,m2)) = m1
getTarget (addLink (m1,m2)) = m2
Translate $_{NEREUS}$ (*Transformation.Postcondition*)
END-CLASS

The function *Translate$_{NEREUS}$ (transformation.precondition)* that appears in the transformation scheme as a precondition of the operation *addLink* translates into NEREUS precondition the OCL precondition. The function *Translate$_{NEREUS}$ (transformation.postcondition)* that appears in the axioms translates into NEREUS axioms the OCL postconditions. An instantiation of the transformation scheme is the following:

```
[TransformationName: ISMJava to PSMJava;
sourceMetamodel: ISM -JAVA-Metamodel:: JavaPackage;
targetMetamodel: PSM -JAVA-Metamodel:: JavaPackage ;
precondition: OCLexp1;
postcondition: OCLexp2 ]
```

REFERENCES

Aho, A., Sethi, R., & Ullman, J. (1985). *Compilers: Principles, Techniques, and Tools* (2nd ed.). Reading: Addison-Wesley.

Amstrong, M., & Trudeau, C. (1998) Evaluating architecture extractors. In *Proceedings of the 5th Working Conference on Reverse Engineering (WCRE 98). Honolulu, Hawaii, USA* (pp. 30-39).

Angyal, L., Lengyel, L., & Charaf, H. (2006). An Overview of the State-of-the-Art Reverse Engineering Techniques. In *Proceedings of the 7th International Symposium of Hungarian Researchers on Computational Intelligence* (pp. 507 - 516).

Antoniol, G., Fiutem, R., Lutteri, G., Tonella, P., & Zanfei, S. (1997) Program understanding and mintenance with the CANTO environment. In *Proceedings of the International Conference on Software Maintenance. Bari, Italy* (pp. 72-81)

Bellay, B., & Gall, H. (1998). An evaluation of reverse engineering tool capabilities. *Journal of Software Maintenance: Research and Practice, 10*, 305–331. doi:10.1002/(SICI)1096-908X(199809/10)10:5<305::AID-SMR175>3.0.CO;2-7

Boronat, A., Carsi, J., & Ramos, I. (2005). Automatic reengineering in MDA using rewriting logic a transformation engine. In *Proceedings of the Ninth European Conference on Software Maintenance and Reengineering (CSMR'05)* (pp. 228-231). Los Alamitos: IEEE Computer Society.

Canfora, G., & Di Penta, M. (2007). New Frontiers of reverse Engineering. Future of Software engineering. In *Proceedings of Future of Software Engineering (FOSE 2007)* (pp. 326-341). Los Alamitos: IEEE Press.

CASE. (2009). *CASE Tools*. Retrieved on July 20, 2009 from www.objectsbydesign.com/tools/uml-tools_byCompany.html

Chen, Y., Nishimoto, M., & Ramamoorthy, C. (1990). The C information abstraction system. *IEEE Transactions on Software Engineering, 16*(3), 325–334. doi:10.1109/32.48940

Daciuk, J. (1998). *Incremental Construction of Finite-State Automata and Transducers, and their use in the Natural Language Processing*. Ph. D. Thesis. Technical University of Gdansk.

Deissenboeck, F., & Ratiu, D. (2006). A Unified Meta Model for Concept-Based Reverse Engineering. In *Proceedings of 3rd International Workshop on Metamodels, Schemes, Grammars, and Ontologies for Reverse Engineering*. Retrieved on July 20, 2009 from http://planet-mde.org/atem2006/atem06Proceedings.pdf

Demeyer, S., Ducasse, S., & Nierstrasz, O. (2002). *Object-Oriented Reengineering Patterns*. Amsterdam: Morgan Kaufmann.

Dwyer, M., Hatcliff, J., Joehanes, R., Laubach, S., & Pasareanu, C. Robby, Zheng, H., & Visser, W. (2001). Tool-supported program abstraction for finite-state verification. In *Proceedings of the International Conference on Software Engineering* (pp. 177-187).

Eclipse (2009). *The eclipse modeling framework*. Retrieved from July 20, 2009 from http://www.eclipse.org/emf/

Ernst, M. (2003) Static and Dynamic Analysis: Synergy and duality. In *Proceedings of ICSE Workshop on Dynamic Analysis (WODA 2003)* (pp. 24-27).

Fanta, R., & Rajlich, V. (1998). Reengineering object-oriented code. In *Proceedings of International Conference on Software Maintenance* (pp. 238-246). Los Alamitos: IEEE Computer Society.

Favre, L. (2006). A Rigorous Framework for Model Driven Development. In K. Siau (Ed.), *Advanced Topics in Database Research, Vol. 5* (pp. 1-27). Hershey, PA: Idea Group Publishing.

Favre, L. (2008a). Formalizing MDA-based Reverse Engineering Processes. In *Proceedings of the 6th ACIS International Conference on Software Engineering Research, Management and Applications, SERA 2008* (pp. 153-160). Los Alamitos: IEEE Computer Society.

Favre, L. (2008b). Modernizing Software & System Engineering Processes. In *Proceedings of the 19th International conference on System Engineering* (pp. 442-447). Los Alamitos: IEEE Computer Society.

Favre, L., Martinez, L., & Pereira, C. (2009). MDA-based Reverse Engineering of Object-Oriented Code. *Lecture Notes in Business Information Processing, 29* (pp. 251-263). Heidelberg: Springer-Verlag.

Favre, L., Pereira, C., & Martinez, L. (2009). Foundations for MDA CASE Tools. In M. Khosrow-Pour (Ed.) Encyclopedia of Information Science and Technology, Second Edition. (pp. 159 – 166). Hershey, PA: IGI Global.

Finnigan, P., Holt, R., Kalas, I., Kerr, S., Kontogiannnis, K., & Muller, H. (1997). The software bookshelf. *IBM Systems Journal, 36*(4), 564–593.

Greevy, O., Ducasse, S., & Girba, T. (2005). Journal of Software Maintenance and Evolution . *Research and Practice, 18*(6), 425–456.

Gueheneuc, Y. (2004) A Systematic Study of UML Class Diagram Constituents for their Abstract and Precise Recovery. In *Proceedings of 11th Asia-Pacific Software Engineering Conference (APSEC 2004)* (pp. 265-274). Los Alamitos: IEEE Computer Society.

IMAGIX4D (2000) *Imagix Corp*. Retrieved from http://www.imagix.com

Jones, N., & Nielson, F. (1995). Abstract interpretation: A semantic based tool for program analysis. In D. Gabbay, S. Abramsky, & T. Maibaum (Eds), *Handbook of Logic in Computer Science* (Vol. 4, pp. 527-636). Oxford: Clarendon Press.

Kagdi, H., Collard, M. L., & Maletic, J. (2007). A survey and taxonomy of approaches for mining software repositories in the context of software evolution. *Journal of Software Maintenance and Evolution: Research and Practice, 19*, 77–131. doi:10.1002/smr.344

Kazman, R., & Carriere, S. (1999). Playing detective: reconstructing software architecture from available evidence. *Journal of Automated Software Engineering, 6*(2), 107–138. doi:10.1023/A:1008781513258

Koehler, J., Hauser, R., Kapoor, S., Wu, F., & Kumaran, S. (2003). A model-driven transformation method. In . *Proceedings of Seven IEEE Enterprise Distributed Object Computing Conference, EDOC, 2003*, 186–197. doi:10.1109/EDOC.2003.1233848

MacDonald, A., Russell, D., & Atchison, B. (2005). Model driven Development within a Legacy System: An industry experience report. In *Proceedings of the 2005 Australian Software Engineering Conference (ASWEC 05)* (pp. 14-22). Los Alamitos: IEEE Press.

Mansurov, N., & Campara, D. (2005). Managed architecture of existing code as a practical transition towards MDA (LNCS 3297, pp. 219-233). Heidelberg: Springer-Verlag.

Markosian, L., Newcomb, P., Brand, R., Burson, S., & Kitzmiller, T. (1994). Using an enabling technology to reengineer legacy systems. *Communications of the ACM, 37*(5), 58–70. doi:10.1145/175290.175297

MDA. (2005). *The Model Driven Architecture*. Retrieved on July 20, 2009 from www.omg.org/mda.

MetaEdit. (2009) *MetaEdit++*. Retrieved on July 20, 2009 from http://www.metacase.com/MetaEdit.html

MOF. (2006). *MOF: Meta Object facility (MOF ™) 2.0*. OMG Specification formal/2006-01-01. Retrieved on July 20, 2009 from www.omg.org/mof

Muller, H., & Klashinsky (1988). Rigi- A System for programming in the large. In *Proceedings of the 10th International Conference on Software Engineering (ICSE)* (pp. 80-86). Los Alamitos: IEEE Computer Society Press.

Muller, H., Jahnke, J., Smith, D., Storey, M., Tilley, S., & Wong, K. (2000). Reverse Engineering: A Roadmap. In *Proceedings of the 22nd International Conference on Software Engineering (ICSE 2000), Limerick, Ireland*. ACM Press. Retrieved on July 20, 2009 from http://www.cs.ucl.ac.uk/staff/A.Finkelstein/fose/finalmuller.pdf

Nimmer, J., & Ernst, M. (2002) Automatic generation of program specifications. In *Proceedings of the 2002 International Symposium on Software Testing and Analysis* (pp. 232-242). Rome, Italy.

OCL. (2006). *OCL: Object Constraint Language. Version 2.0*. OMG: formal/06-05-01.Retrieved on July 20, 2009 from www.omg.org

Pohyvanyk, D., Gueheneuc, Y.-G., Marcus, A., Antoniol, G., & Rajlich, V. (2007). Feature Location Using Probabilistic ranking of Methods Based on Execution Scenarios and Information Retrieval. *IEEE Transactions on Software Engineering, 23*(6), 420–432. doi:10.1109/TSE.2007.1016

Qiao, B., Yang, H., Chu, W., & Xu, B. (2003). Bridging legacy systems to model driven architecture. In *Proceedings of 27th Annual International Computer Aided Software and Applications Conference* (pp. 304-309). Los Alamitos: IEEE Press.

Reus, T., Geers, H., & van Deursen, A. (2006). Harvesting Software System for MDA-based Reengineering (LNCS 4066, pp. 220-236). Heidelberg: Springer-Verlag.

SNiFF+ (1996) SNiFF+. *User Guide and Reference, Take-Five Software*. Retrieved on July 20, 2009 from www.takefive.com

Sunyé, G., Pollet, D., LeTraon, D., & Jézéquel, J. (2001). Refactoring UML Models (LNCS 2185, pp. 134-138). Heidelberg: Springer-Verlag.

Systa, T. (2000). *Static and Dynamic Reverse Engineering Techniques for Java Software Systems*. Ph.D Thesis, University of Tampere, Report A-2000-4.

Tonella, P., & Potrich, A. (2005). Reverse Engineering of Object Oriented Code. *Monographs in Computer Science*. Heidelberg: Springer-Verlag.

UML. (2009a). *Unified Modeling Language: Infrastructure*. Version 2.2. OMG Specification formal/2009-02-04. Retrieved on July 20, 2009 from www.omg.org.

UML. (2009b). *UML: Unified Modeling Language: Superstructure*. Version 2.2. OMG Specification: formal/2009-02-02. Retrieved on July 20, 2009 from www.omg.org

Watson, B. (1995). *Taxonomies and Toolkits of Regular Language Algorithms*. PhD thesis. Eindhoven University of Technology, The Netherlands.

Section 4
Conclusions

Chapter 11
Summing Up the Parts

REVERSE ENGINEERING: A DIFFERENT POINT OF VIEW

This chapter summarizes the main results described in this book and challenges and strategic directions in MDA reverse engineering.

Reverse engineering is the process of analyzing software systems to extract software artifacts at a higher level of abstraction.

Nowadays, software and system engineering industry evolves to manage new platform technologies, design techniques and processes. Architectural framework for information integration and tool interoperation, such as MDA, had created the need to develop new analysis tools and specific techniques.

MDA is not itself a technology specification but it represents an evolving plan to achieve cohesive model-driven technology specifications. The original inspiration around the definition of MDA had to do with the middleware integration problem in internet. Beyond interoperability reasons, there are other good benefits to use MDA such as to improve the productivity, process quality and maintenance costs.

The outstanding ideas behind MDA are separating the specification of the system functionality from its implementation on specific platforms, managing the software evolution from abstract models to implementations increasing the degree of automation and achieving interoperability with multiple platforms, programming languages and formal languages.

DOI: 10.4018/978-1-61520-649-0.ch011

MDA distinguishes at least three main models: Computation Independent Model (CIM), Platform Independent Model (PIM), Platform Specific Model (PSM) and Implementation Specific Model (ISM).

The initial diffusion of MDA was focused on its relation with UML as modeling language. However, there are UML users who do not use MDA, and MDA users who use other modeling languages such as DSLs. The essence of MDA is MOF that allows different kinds of artifacts from multiple vendors to be used together in a same project.

MOF-metamodels are expressed as a combination of UML, OCL and natural language. MOF has no built-in semantics apart from the well-formedness rules in OCL and what can deduced from them. This form of specification does not make possible validating that specific metamodels, like UML metamodel, conform MOF. A combination of MOF metamodeling and formal specification can help us to address MDA reverse engineering process.

With the emergence of MDA, new approaches should be developed in order to reverse engineering, both platform independent and platform specific models, from object oriented code.

This book describes MDA reverse engineering processes based on the integration of traditional reverse engineering techniques, advanced metamodeling techniques and formal specification. A framework to reverse engineering MDA models from object oriented code that distinguishes three different levels of abstraction linked to models, metamodel and formal specification was proposed.

The model level includes code, PIMs and PSMs. A PIM is a model with a high level of abstraction that is independent of an implementation technology. A PSM is a tailored model to specify a system in terms of specific platform such J2EE or .NET. PIMs and PSMs are expressed in UML and OCL. The subset of UML diagrams that are useful for PSMs includes class diagram, object diagram, state diagram, interaction diagram and package diagram. On the other hand, a PIM can be expressed by means of use case diagrams, activity diagrams, interactions diagrams to model system processes and state diagrams to model lifecycle of the system entities. An ISM is a specification of the system in source code.

At model level, transformations are based on classical compiler construction techniques. They involve processes with different degrees of automation, which can go from totally automatic static analysis to human intervention requiring processes to dynamically analyze the resultant models. All the algorithms that deal with the reverse engineering share an analysis framework. The basic idea is to describe source code or models by an abstract language and perform a propagation analysis in a data-flow graph called, in this context, object-data flow. This static analysis is complemented with dynamic analysis supported by tracer tools.

The metamodel level includes MOF metamodels that describe the transformations at model level. MOF metamodels describe families of ISMs, PSMs and PIMs. Every ISM, PSM and PIM conforms to a MOF metamodel. Metamodel transformations are specified as OCL contracts between a source metamodel and a target metamodel. These contracts "control" the transformation consistency.

This book describes a formalization of MDA processes in terms of MOF-based metamodels and QVT-based transformations. Both, MOF and QVT, depends on UML metamodel, which in turn depends on OCL. That is to say, the formalization of MDA processes depends on various OMG standards. Some of them, such as OCL and QVT, involve imperative constructions that are hard to formalize. To avoid this inconvenient, we analyzed the graph of package dependencies to select a minimal set of packages that allows us to precisely define the semantics of MDA process in a way independent of imperative constructions. . The formalization is based on a subset of OMG standard metamodels that we called MDA Infrastructure, including elements of UML Infrastructure, EssentialOCL, EMOF and the QVT-Core.

The level of formal specification includes specifications of MOF metamodels and metamodel transformations in the metamodeling language NEREUS that can be used to connect them with different formal and programming languages. NEREUS, like MDA, was designed for improving interoperability and reusability through separation of concerns. It is suited for specifying metamodels based on the concepts of entity, associations and systems. Formal specification can be automatically generated by using reusable schemes and a system of transformation rules for translating OCL specification into NEREUS.

We analyze how to define reusable components in a way that fits with MDA and propose a megamodel for defining MDA components. Considering the relevant role that design patterns take in software evolution we exemplify MDA components for them. We propose a megamodel to define families of design pattern components by means of PIM-, PSM- and ISM-metamodels and their interrelations. Instances of the "megamodel" are reusable components that describe specific design patterns at different levels of abstraction (PIMs, PSMs and ISMs). They can be viewed as "megacomponents" that allow defining in a concise way as many components as different pattern solutions can appear.

In MDA is crucial to define, manage, and maintain traces and relationships between different models, and automatically transform them and produce implementations. Refactoring is a powerful technique when is repeatedly applied to a model to obtain another one with the same behavior but enhancing some non functionality quality factor such as simplicity, flexibility, understandability and performance. Refactorings are horizontal transformations for supporting perfective model evolution. We propose an MDA framework for refactoring that is structured at three different levels of abstraction linked to models, metamodels and formal specification. The model level includes different kind of models (PIM, PSM, ISM) related by refinement.

Our approach to MDA processes has two main advantages linked to automation and interoperability. On the one hand, our approach shows how to generate automatically formal specifications from MOF metamodels. On the other hand, our approach focuses on interoperability of formal languages. Considering that there exist many formal algebraic languages, NEREUS allows any number of source languages such as different DSLs and target languages (different formal language) could be connected without having to define explicit metamodel transformations for each language pair. Such as MOF is a DSL to define semi-formal metamodels, NEREUS can be viewed as a DSL for defining formal metamodels.

Another advantage of our approach is linked to pragmatic aspects. NEREUS is a formal notation closed to MOF metamodels that allows meta-designers who must manipulate metamodels to understand their formal specification.

Our approach could be considered as an MDA-based formalization of traditional reverse engineering processes. The underlying ideas contribute to a more general goal, the definition of rigorous MDA processes such as forward engineering, reverse engineering and in general round trip engineering.

This book intends to shorten the path to this goal providing an overview of several techniques that can be adopted in the field of MDA-based processes. It presents principles of reverse engineering within system evolution and shows how to recover designs and architectures. Different techniques for helping in reverse engineering about how to define MDA-based reusable component and transformations are covered. The underlying concepts were giving with special emphasis on consistency, traceability, testing and verification combining semiformal metamodeling techniques and formal specification.

Although, this book uses some specific notation, the underlying ideas of our approach are independent of NEREUS and the proposed rule transformational system. The following are the bases of our approach:

- The integration of compiler techniques, metamodeling and formal specification.
- The formalization of an MDA Infrastructure.
- The definition of a formal Domain Specific Language (DSL) for defining metamodels and transformations.
- The automation of bridges between MOF metamodels and the DSL.
- The definition of MDA-based reuse and refactoring techniques.

CHALLENGES ON MDA-BASED REVERSE ENGINEERING

Reverse engineering techniques are used as a mean to design software systems by evolving existing ones based on new requirements or technologies. In particular, reverse engineering is an integral part of the modernization of legacy systems whose aging can or will have a negative impact on the economy, finance and society.

To date, software industry evolves to tackle new approaches that are aligned with internet, object orientation and distributed components. However, the majority of the large information systems running today in many organizations were developed many years ago with technology that is now obsolete. Many large systems remain in use after more than 20 years; they may be written for mainframe hardware which is expensive to maintain and which may not be aligned with current organizational politics. There is a high risk in replacing legacy systems that are still business-critical. That is the reason for the increased demand of reengineering techniques of legacy system to extend their useful lifetime.

The success of legacy system modernization depends on the existence of technical frameworks like MDA to cope with the diversity of languages and technologies used to develop a single software system. Besides, the existing CASE tools must incorporate new functionality that make a significant impact on the automation of reverse engineering processes.

In legacy system modernization, reverse engineering is an integral part of the software development cycle. Although this book was born with the problem of legacy systems in mind, reverse engineering has the power to address general problems related to program comprehension and modification.

Commercial MDA tools have recently begun to emerge, in general, UML preexisting tools are been extended to support MDA. The current techniques available in these tools provide forward engineering and limited facilities for reverse engineering. They only use more basic notational features with a direct code representation and produce very large diagrams.

Most CASE tools can reverse engineering static diagrams, but there is a lack of tool support for what regards the extraction of dynamic diagrams and also OCL pre- and post-conditions. One of the major challenges of reverse engineering is to deal with the high dynamicity. For example, object-oriented languages introduce the concept of reflection. This affects the static analysis then, future tasks in reverse engineering should promote a high integration of human feedbacks into automatic reverse engineering processes.

Refactoring is an important step for evolving models in reverse engineering processes however CASE tools provide limited facilities for refactoring only on source code through an explicit selection made for the designer but do not provide support for model refactorings. Formal techniques are needed in order to ensure behavioral properties of the software involved in the refactoring.

Another research trend of reverse engineering is design pattern identification to understand the design considerations promoting reuse and quality of different software artifacts. Pattern identification allows measuring quality of software reverse engineering, because pattern and anti-pattern can help to discover weakness of code or models.

MDA approach is useless without tools automating the model transformation. The existing MDA-based tools do not provide sophisticated transformation from PIM to PSM and from PSM to code. To date, they might be able to support forward engineering and partial round trip engineering between PIM and code. Little support for reverse engineering business models from code is provided for the existing CASE tools.

The MDA Case tools must evolve towards a new generation of tools that insure consistency of variety of artifacts representing different dimensions. MDA is an architectural framework for specifying software artifacts and their interrelations. It allows working with existing tools by abstracting information from the external representation used by them. This abstraction provides independence from the used tools and should be aligned to OMG standards such as XMI and in general, artifacts represented by MOF metamodels.

The existing tools should also handle dynamic information. The idea is determine, on the one hand what information need to be collected at run time, and then checking that the contracts are satisfied when the program run or, on the other hand inferring constraints that may be added to the artifact specification. Besides, there is a need to develop tools for new software architecture that have characteristics of being extremely dynamic, highly distributed, self-configurable and heterogeneous.

To date most MDD research focuses on "Software Language Engineering". Perhaps, in the coming years the focus will be on "Software Process Engineering". In the light of the advances, a new type of tools, that do a more intelligent job, might emerge. Probably, the next generation of tools might be able to describe the behavior of software systems in terms of business models and translate it into executable programs on distributed environment and to automate round-trip engineering processes. It will probably take several years before a full round trip engineering based on standards occurs (many authors are skeptical about this).

Chapter 12
Towards MDA Software Evolution

INTRODUCTION

This chapter discusses software evolution, challenges and strategic directions in the context of MDA.

Various authors agreed that it is difficult to define completely software and then, software evolution. Software is certainly more that bits stored in a file, it is an abstract idea that encompasses the concepts, algorithms embodied in the implementation as well as all its associated artifacts and processes. Research seems to confirm that computer software and process software have much in common. Osterweil (2003) assures that software processes are software too. In other paper (Osterweil, 2007), he suggests analyzing the nature of software and proposes to define taxonomies for exploring characteristics and approaches to the development, verification of qualities and software evolution. The exploration of these questions is an important current of software engineering research.

On the other hand, evolution is defined as a process of gradual change and development from fewer and simpler forms to higher, more complex, or better ones. In biology, evolution is related to develop over time often many generations, into forms that are better adapted to survive changes in their environment. Thus, evolution captures the notion of something improving and changes occur in species in successive generations, i.e. individuals get old and species evolve. Jazayeri (2005) analyzes the definition of software evolution. The concept of "specie" in software may be associated to meta-levels describing families (species) of software systems. These meta-levels or architectures are created as improvements to previous existing ones and describe evolved families of software systems.

Evolution must focus on "species" of software rather than individual software applications. Then, "Software, like people, get old" (Parnas, 1994) and meta-levels or architectures, like species, evolve.

DOI: 10.4018/978-1-61520-649-0.ch012

Starting from our understanding of software applications, their specification in terms of models (and metamodels) evolves to new generation of tools that have an improved structure and are based on new technologies.

Software evolution is multidimensional and is composed of different types of entities/concepts or artifacts that come from specifications, designs and architectures to source code, test cases and documentation. Each of them depends on other artifacts embodied in the implementation such as user interfaces, components, patterns and so on. The different ways and rates that these artifacts change, lead to unreliable software and cause many problems associated with software maintenance.

Software artifacts evolve at different rhythm and in different ways, for instance, an initial design is not updated to reflect the changes that are introduced in the code. Software evolution needs a software development framework that supports the consistency evolution of the different dimensions of the software.

In this light, an MDA-based approach can help to support consistently software evolution due to MDA can be viewed as an integration architectural framework that maintains consistency as the software evolves, i.e., the concept of multidimensional evolution is in the essence of MDA.

MDA can help to develop and support a common application framework for software evolution that raises issues such as common exchange formats, tool integration and interoperability. When the system evolves, MDA maintains the interrelation between software entities accommodating the evolution of higher level artifacts together with the code in a consistent way.

Next, we describe challenges in software evolution and the role of MDA to overcome or avoid the negative effect of software aging.

CHALLENGES ON MDA-BASED SOFTWARE EVOLUTION

(Mens, Wermelinger, Ducasse, Demeyer, Hirschfeld and Jazayeri, 2005) list 18 essential challenges in the software evolution that need to be addressed in the future. We include the main challenges that our MDA-based reverse engineering and software evolution could overcome:

- "To provide tools and techniques which preserve or even improve the quality characteristics of a software system, whatever its size and complexity".
- "To develop and support a common application framework for doing joint software evolution research".
- "Software evolution techniques should be raised to a higher level of abstraction, in order to accommodate not only evolution of programs, but also evolution of higher-level artifacts".
- "To achieve co-evolution between different types of software artifacts or different representation of them".
- "In order to become accepted as practical tools for software developers, formal methods need to embrace change and evolution as an essential fact of life".
- "Software evolution must provide more and better support for multi-language systems."
  (Mens, Wermelinger, Ducasse, Démeyer, Hirschfeld and Jazayeri, 2005)

A challenge on software evolution is the necessity to achieve co-evolution between different types of software artifacts or different representations of them. MDA allows us to develop and relate all different artifacts in a way that ensures their inter-consistency. MDA raises the level of reasoning to a more abstract level and therefore even more appropriate. It places change and evolution in the center of software development process. To give a few examples, in the context of MDA co-evolution is needed between:

- source code and models at levels of PSMs and PIMs
- structural and behavioral models at levels of PSMs
- structural and behavioral models at levels of PIMs
- code and CIMs

Among others, an interesting research direction would be treat the notion of change in programming and modeling languages as a first-class entity and provide support for multi language systems.

Existing formal methods provide a poor support for evolving specifications and incremental verification approaches. In particular, with the existing verification tools, simple changes in a system require to verify its complete specification again making the cost of the verification proportional to its size. To use formal methods that place change and evolution in the center of the software development process is another challenge (Canfora & Di Penta, 2007)

Component-based software offers interesting challenges in software evolution. New tools and techniques to analyze the evolution of systems and their components both in a way independent from each other and as interrelated artifacts must emerge. Perhaps, an interesting challenge would be an MDA adaptation of existing results for analyzing software evolution through feature views (Pohyvanyk, Gueheneuc, Marcus, Antoniol and Rajlich, 2007) (Greevy, Ducasse & Girba, 2005). Buckley, Mens and Zenger (2005) propose taxonomy of software change based on characterizing the mechanisms of change and the factors that influence these mechanisms. The goal is to relate concrete tools, formalisms and methods within the domain of software evolution.

The integration of business models with PIM, PSMs and code is crucial to achieve software evolution. Some works are producing advances in this direction. Hess (2005) describes an approach for mapping business requirements to application software, for using patterns to help translate business requirements to software requirements, and for using patterns to translate software requirements into potential solution designs. Besides, the integration between ontologies (that are essentially CIMs) and MDA is occupying a central place in software development (Djuric, Gasevic and Devedzic, 2005) (Kherraf, Lefrebe, & Suryn, 2008).

OMG is involved in the definition of standards to successfully modernize existing information systems. The OMG Architecture-Driven Modernization (ADM) Task Force is developing a set of modernization standards for the purpose of software improvement, modifications, interoperability, refactoring, restructuring, reuse, porting, migration and MDA migration. Current work involves building a Knowledge Discovery Meta-model (KDM) to facilitate the exchange of existing systems meta-data for various modernization tools. Subsequent standards will address analysis, visualization, refactoring and transformation related standards. A detailed description may be found at ADM (2007).

In summary, a lot remains to be done to provide support for MDA-based software evolution:

- Research on formalisms and theories to increase understanding of software evolution processes,
- Development of methods, techniques and heuristics to provide support for software changes,

- New verification tools that embrace change and evolution as central in software development processes
- Development of new sophisticated tools to develop industrial size software systems
- Definition of standards to evaluate the quality of evolved artifacts/systems.

Besides, the adoption of software evolution should be favored by educating future generations of software engineers, i.e., integrating background on software evolution into the computer science curriculum.

REFERENCES

Buckley, J., Mens, T., & Zenger, M. (2005). Towards a taxonomy of software change. *Journal of Software Maintenance and Evolution: Research and Practice*, 1-26.

Canfora, G., & Di Penta, M. (2007). New Frontiers of reverse Engineering. Future of Software engineering. In *Proceedings of Future of Software Engineering (FOSE 2007)* (pp. 326-341). Los Alamitos: IEEE Press.

Djuric, D., Gasevic, D., & Devedzic, V. (2006). *Model Driven Architecture and Ontology Development*. Heidelberg: Springer-Verlag.

Greevy, O., Ducasse, S., & Girba, T. (2005). Journal of Software Maintenance and Evolution . *Research and Practice*, *18*(6), 425–456.

Hess, H. (2005). Aligning technology and business: Applying patterns for legacy transformation. *IBM Systems Journal*, *44*(1), 25–45.

Jazayeri, M. (2005) Species evolve, individuals age. In *Proceedings of the 2005 Eight International Workshop on Principles of Software Evolution (IWPSE'05)* (pp. 3-9). Los Alamitos: IEEE Computer Society.

Kherraf, S., Lefebre, E., & Suryn, W. (2008). Transformation From CIM to PIM Using Patterns and Archetypes. In *Proceedings of the 19th Australian Conference on Software Engineering* (pp. 338-346). Los Alamitos: IEEE Computer Society.

Mens, T., Wermelinger, M., Ducasse, S., Demeyer, S., Hirschfeld, R., & Jazayeri, M. (2005). Challenges in Software Evolution. In *Proceedings of Eighth International Workshop on Principles of Software Evolution* (pp. 13-22). Los Alamitos: IEEE Computer Society.

Osterweil, L. (2003). Software Processes Are Software Too, Revisited [Los Alamitos: IEEE Computer Press.]. *An Invited Talk on the Most Influential Paper of ICSE, 1997*, 540–548.

Osterweil, L. (2007) A Future for Software Engineering? In *Proceedings of Future of Software Engineering (FOSE 2007)* (pp. 1-11). Los Alamitos, IEEE Computer Society

Parnas, D. (1994) Software aging. In *Proceedings of the International Conference on Software Engineering* (pp. 279-287). Los Alamitos: IEEE Computer Press.

Pohyvanyk, D., Gueheneuc, Y.-G., Marcus, A., Antoniol, G., & Rajlich, V. (2007). Feature Location Using Probabilistic ranking of Methods Based on Execution Scenarios and Information Retrieval. *IEEE Transactions on Software Engineering, 23*(6), 420–432. doi:10.1109/TSE.2007.1016

Section 5
Selected Readings

Chapter 13
Foundations for MDA Case Tools

Liliana Favre
Universidad Nacional del Centro de la Pcia. de Buenos Aires, Argentina

Claudia Teresa Pereira
Universidad Nacional del Centro de la Pcia. de Buenos Aires, Argentina

Liliana Inés Martinez
Universidad Nacional del Centro de la Pcia. de Buenos Aires, Argentina

INTRODUCTION

The model driven architecture (MDA) is an initiative proposed by the object management group (OMG), which is emerging as a technical framework to improve productivity, portability, interoperability, and maintenance (MDA, 2003).

MDA promotes the use of models and model-to-model transformations for developing software systems. All artifacts, such as requirement specifications, architecture descriptions, design descriptions, and code are regarded as models. MDA distinguishes four main kinds of models: computation independent model (CIM), platform independent model (PIM), platform specific models (PSM), and implementation specific model (ISM).

A CIM describes a system from the computation independent viewpoint that focuses on the environment of and the requirements for the system. In general, it is called domain model. A PIM is a model that contains no reference to the platforms that are used to realize it. A PSM describes a system with full knowledge of the final implementation platform. In this context, a platform is "a set of subsystems and technologies that provide a coherent set of functionality which any application supported by that platform can use without concern for the details of how the functionality is implemented" (MDA, 2003, p. 2-3). PIMs and PSMs are expressed using the unified modeling language (UML) combined with the object constraint language (OCL) (Favre, 2003; OCL, 2004; UML, 2004).

The idea behind MDA is to manage the evolution from CIMs to PIMs and PSMs that can be used to generate executable components and applications. In MDA is crucial to define, manage, and maintain traces and relationships between different models and automatically transform them and produce code that is complete and executable.

Metamodeling has become an essential technique in model-centric software development. The metamodeling framework for the UML itself is based on architecture with four layers: meta-metamodel, metamodel, model, and user objects. A metamodel is an explicit model of the constructs and rules needed to build specific models, its instances. A meta-metamodel defines a language to write metamodels. OCL can be used to attach consistency rules to models and metamodels. Related OMG standard metamodels and meta-metamodels such as meta object facility (MOF), software process engineering metamodel (SPEM) and common warehouse model (CWM) share a common design philosophy (CWM, 2001; MOF, 2005; SPEM, 2005).

MOF defines a common way for capturing all the diversity of modeling standards and interchange constructs. MOF uses an object modeling framework that is essentially a subset of the UML core. The four main modeling concepts are "classes, which model MOF metaobjects; associations, which model binary relationships between metaobjects; data types, which model other data; and packages, which modularize the models" (MOF, 2005, p. 2-6). The query, view, transformation (QVT) standard depends on MOF and OCL for specifying queries, views, and transformations. A query selects specific elements of a model, a view is a model derived from other model, and a model transformation is a specification of a mechanism to convert the elements of a model, into elements of another model, which can be instances of the same or different metamodels (QVT, 2003).

The success of MDA depends on the existence of CASE (computer-aided software engineering) tools that make a significant impact on software processes such as forward engineering and reverse engineering processes (CASE, 2006). This article explains the most important challenges to automate the processes that should be supported by MDA tools. We propose an integration of knowledge developed by the community of formal methods with MDA. We describe a rigorous framework that comprises the metamodeling notation NEREUS and bridges between MOF-metamodels and NEREUS, and between NEREUS and formal languages. NEREUS can be viewed as an intermediate notation open to many other formal specifications. We analyze metamodeling techniques for expressing model transformations such as refinements and refactorings. Our approach focuses on interoperability of formal languages in model driven development (MDD).

This article is organized as follow. We first analyze the limitations of the existing MDA-based CASE tools. Then, we describe the bases of rigorous MDA-based processes. Next, we show how the formalization of MOF metamodels and metamodel-based model transformations allows us automatic software generation. Finally, we highlight the key directions in which MDA is moving forward.

BACKGROUND

To date, there are about 120 UML CASE tools that vary widely in functionality, usability, performance, and platforms (CASE, 2006). Some of them can only help with the mechanics of drawing and exporting UML diagrams. The mainstream object-oriented CASE tools support forward engineering and reverse engineering processes and can help with the analysis of consistency between diagrams. Only a few UML tools include extension for real time modeling. The tool market around MDA tools is still in flux and only about 10% of them provide some support for MDA. Table 1 exemplifies a taxonomy of the UML CASE tools (CASE, 2006).

The current techniques available in the commercial tools do not allow generating complete

Table 1. UML CASE tools

Basic drawing tools	Visio
Main stream object oriented case tools	Rational Rose, Argo/UML, Together, UModel, MagicDraw, MetaEdit+, Poseidon
Real time/embedded tools	Rapsody, Rational Rose Real Time, RapidRMA
MDA-based tools	OptimalJ, AndroMDA, Ameos, Together Architect, Codagen, ArcStyler, MDE Studio, Objecteering

and executable code and after generation, the code needs additions. A source of problems in the code generation processes is that, on the one hand, the UML models contain information that cannot be expressed in object-oriented languages while, on the other hand, the object-oriented languages express implementation characteristics that have no counterpart in the UML models.

Moreover, the existing CASE tools do not exploit all the information contained in the UML models. For instance, cardinality and constraints of associations and preconditions, postconditions, and class invariants in OCL are only translated as annotations. It is the designer's responsibility to make good use of this information either selecting an appropriate implementation from a limited repertoire or implementing the association by himself.

On the other hand, many CASE tools support reverse engineering, however, they only use more basic notational features with a direct code representation and produce very large diagrams. Reverse engineering processes are facilitated by inserting annotations in the generated code. These annotations are the link between the model elements and the language. As such, they should be kept intact and not be changed. It is the programmer's responsibility to know what he or she can modify and what he or she cannot modify.

UML CASE tools provide limited facilities for refactoring on source code through an explicit selection made for the designer. However, it will be worth thinking about refactoring at the design level. The advantage of refactoring at UML level is that the transformations do not have to be tied to the syntax of a programming language. This is relevant since UML is designed to serve as a basis for code generation with MDA (Sunye et al., 2001).

Techniques that currently exist in UML CASE tools provide little support for validating models in the design stages. Reasoning about models of systems is well supported by automated theorem provers and model checkers, however, these tools are not integrated into CASE tools environments. Another problem is that as soon as the requirements specifications are handed down, the system architecture begins to deviate from specifications (Kollmann & Gogolla, 2002). Only research tools provide support for formal specification and deductive verification.

All of the MDA CASE tools are partially compliant to MDA features. They provide good support for modeling and limited support for automated transformation. In general, they support MDD from the PIM level and use UML class diagrams for designing PIMs. Some of them provide only one level of transformation from PIM to code (Codagen, Ameos, Arcstyler) and, in general, there is no relation between QVT and the current existing MDA tools. As an example, OptimalJ from Compuware supports MDD from PIM level. It allows generating PSMs from a PIM and a partial code generation. It distinguishes three kinds of models: a domain model that correspond to a PIM model, an application model that includes PSMs linked to different platforms (Relational-PSM, EJB-PSM and Web-PSM), and an implementation model. The transformation process is supported by transformation and functional patterns.

The MDA-based tools use MOF to support OMG standards such as UML and XMI (XML metadata interchange). MOF has a central role in MDA as a common standard to integrate all different kinds of models and metadata and to exchange these models among tools; however, MOF does not allow capturing semantic properties in a platform independent way and there is no rigorous foundations for specifying transformations among different kinds of models.

A lot of research work has been carried out dealing with the advanced metamodeling techniques and formalization of different kinds of transformations. For instance, the main task of USE tool (Gogolla, Bohling, & Ritchers, 2005) is to validate and verify specifications consisting of UML/OCL class diagrams. Key (Ahrendt et al., 2002) is a tool based on together (CASE, 2006) enhanced with functionality for formal specification and deductive verification.

Akehurst and Kent (2002) propose an approach that uses metamodeling patterns that capture the essence of mathematical relations. The proposed technique is to adopt a pattern that models a transformation relationship as a relation or collections of relations, and encode this as an object model. Hausmann (2003) defined an extension of a metamodeling language to specify mappings between metamodels based on concepts presented in Akehurst et al. (2002). Kuster, Sendall, and Wahler (2004) compare and contrast two approaches to model transformations: one is graph transformation and the other is a relational approach. Czarnecki and Helsen (2003) describe a taxonomy with a feature model to compare several existing and proposed model-to-model transformation approaches.

RIGOROUS MODEL-DRIVEN DEVELOPMENT

Developing or reengineering a system in an MDA perspective should be done through automated transformation with the help of tools. Figure 1 illustrates the different processes and artifacts beyond this idea. Forward engineering and reverse engineering processes should be supported in MDA tools. Forward engineering is the process of transforming higher-level or abstract models into concrete ones. Reverse engineering reconstructs higher-level models from low ones. Reengineering is the process that transforms one concrete representation to another, while reconstituting the higher-level models along the way. We describe a rigorous framework compliant to MDA forward engineering processes. A model-driven development is carried out as a sequence of model transformations that includes, at least, the following steps: construct a CIM, transform the CIM into a PIM that provides a computing architecture independent of specific platforms, transform the PIM into one or more PSMs, each one suited for specific platforms, and derive code directly from the PSMs.

A model transformation is the process of converting one model into another model preserving some kind of equivalence relation between them. We can distinguish two types of transformations to support model evolution from CIMs to ISMs: refinements and refactorings. A refinement is the process of building a more detailed specification that conforms to another that is more abstract. On the other hand, a refactoring means changing a model leaving its behavior unchanged, but enhancing some non-functionality quality factors such as simplicity, flexibility, understandability, and performance.

Metamodeling is a powerful technique to specify families of models and model transformations. Figure 1 shows the different correspondences that may be held between several models and metamodels and their interrelations. A CIM is related to one or more PIM-metamodels. A PIM-metamodel is related to more than one PSM-metamodels, each one suited for different platforms (e.g., .NET, J2EE, or relational). The PSM-metamodels correspond to ISM-metamodels. A metamodel is a

Figure 1. Rigorous model-driven development

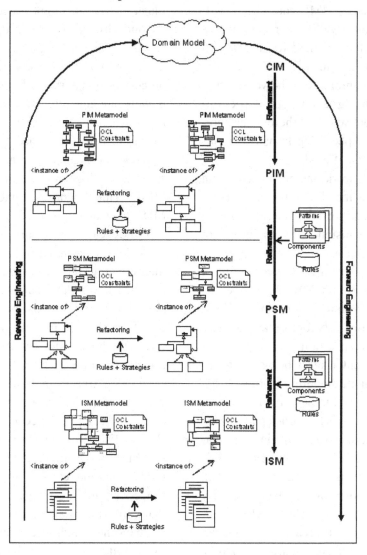

description of all the concepts that can be used in the respective level. For instance, a metamodel linked to a relational platform refers to concepts of table, foreign key and column. An ISM-metamodel includes concepts of programming languages such as constructor and method.

The following types of model transformations can be distinguished:

- **CIM to PIM refinement:** It describes how a CIM that is an instance of a MOF-metamodel is transformed into a PIM that is an instance of a specialized metamodel for a specific computation dependent model.

- **PIM to PSM refinement:** It describes how a PIM that is an instance of a MOF-Metamodel is transformed into a PSM that is an instance of a specialized MOF-metamodel for a specific platform.

- **PSM to ISM refinement:** It describes how a PSM is transformed into code (which is an instance of MOF-metamodel for a platform and specific language technologies).

- **Refactoring:** It specifies how a model in a given level is transformed into a new restructured model in the same level (for instance, PIM to PIM, PSM to PSM, ISM to ISM). The source and target models are instances of the same MOF-metamodel.

Metamodel transformations are a specific type of model transformations that impose relations between pairs of metamodels. A metamodel-based transformation is a specification of a mechanism to convert the elements of a model, that are instances of a particular metamodel, into elements of another model, which can be instances of the same or different metamodels. We specify metamodel-based model transformations as OCL contracts that are described by means of a transformation name, parameters, preconditions, postconditions, and additional operations.

The MDA-based processes are based on the adaptation of reusable components and systems of transformations rules. We analyzed basic techniques for MDA-based processes such as refactoring (Kerievsky, 2004; Long, Jifeng & Liu, 2005; Mens, Demeyer, Du Bois, Stenten, & Van Gorp, 2004) and design pattern (France, Kim, Ghosh, & Song, 2004; Gamma, Helm, Johnson, & Vlissides, 1995).

Pereira and Favre (2006) propose a metamodeling technique to define refactorings at different abstraction levels (e.g., PIM, PSM, and ISM). A transformational system based on behaviour-preserving model-to-model transformations was defined. To reason about correctness and robustness we propose to specify refactorings as OCL contracts that are based on metamodels capturing common properties to a family of refactorings.

Martinez and Favre (2006) describe a metamodeling technique to define design pattern components from an MDA perspective. In this context, we propose a "megamodel" for defining reusable components that integrates different kinds of models with their respective metamodels. We analyze metamodel-based model transforma-tions among levels of PIMs, PSMs and ISMs. We illustrate the approach to define reusable design pattern components using the popular Gamma patterns (Gamma et al., 1995).

FORMALIZATION OF MDA-BASED PROCESSES

UML and OCL are too imprecise and ambiguous when it comes to simulation, verification, validation, and forecasting of system properties and even when it comes to generating models/implementations through transformations. Although OCL is a textual language, OCL expressions rely on UML class diagrams (i.e., the syntax context is determined graphically). OCL does also not have the solid background of a classical formal language. In the context of MDA, model transformations should preserve correctness. To achieve this, the different modeling and programming languages involved in an MDD must be defined in a consistent and precise way. Then, the combination of UML/OCL specifications and formal languages offers the best of both worlds to software developer. In this direction, we define NEREUS to take advantage of all the existing theoretical background on formal methods, using different tools such as theorem provers, model checkers, or rewrite engines in different stages of MDD.

Favre (2006) proposes a rigorous framework to model driven developments. The bases of this approach are the metamodeling notation NEREUS and, bridges between UML/OCL and NEREUS and between NEREUS and algebraic languages.

NEREUS can be viewed as an intermediate notation open to many other formal specifications, such as algebraic, functional or logic ones. NEREUS is suited for specifying MOF. Most of the MOF concepts for metamodels (entity, associations, and packages) can be mapped to NEREUS in a straightforward manner. This language is relation-centric which means that it expresses different kinds of UML relations (dependency, association, aggregation, and composition) as primitives to develop specifications. In Favre (2006), we show how to integrate NEREUS with algebraic languages using the common algebraic specification language (CASL) (Bidoit & Mosses, 2004).

The formalization of MDA-based processes implies to specify metamodels and metamodel-based transformations.

On the one hand, we define a bridge between MOF-metamodels and NEREUS that is based on a system of transformation rules to convert automatically UML/OCL into NEREUS specifications. Starting from UML class diagrams, an incomplete algebraic specification can be built by instantiating reusable schemes and components, which already exist in the NEREUS predefined library. Analyzing OCL specifications, it is possible to derive axioms that will be included in the NEREUS specification. Preconditions written in OCL are used to generate preconditions in NEREUS. Postconditions and invariants allow us to generate axioms in NEREUS. Thus, an incomplete specification can be built semi-automatically (Favre, 2005; Favre, Martinez, & Pereira, 2003).

On the other hand, we formalize transformations (refinements and refactorings) as OCL contracts that are translated into NEREUS specifications by instantiating reusable schemes.

We have applied the approach to transform UML/OCL class diagrams into NEREUS specifications, which in turn, are used to generate object-oriented code (Favre, 2005; Favre et al.,

2005). The process is based on the adaptation of MDA-based reusable components. NEREUS allows us to keep a trace of the structure of UML models in the specification structure that will make easier to maintain consistency between the various levels when the system evolves. All the UML model information (classes, associations, and OCL specifications) is overturned into specifications having implementation implications. The transformation of different kinds of UML associations into object-oriented code was analyzed, as well as, the construction of assertions and code from algebraic specifications. The proposed transformations preserve the integrity between specification and code. The transformation process is based on reusable components.

In Favre and Martinez (2006) we describe how formalize MOF- metamodels and metamodel-based transformations exemplifying with MDA design pattern components.

In contrast to other works, our approach is the only one focusing on interoperability of formal languages in model-driven software development. There are UML formalizations based on different languages that do not use an intermediate language such as NEREUS. However, this extra step provides some advantages. NEREUS would eliminate the need to define formalizations and specific transformations for each different formal language. The metamodel specifications and transformations can be reused at many levels in MDA. Languages that are defined in terms of NEREUS metamodels can be related to each other because they are defined in the same way through a textual syntax.

Figure 2. Interoperability of formal languages

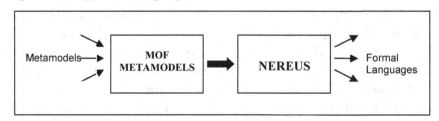

Any number of source languages (modeling language) and target languages (formal language) could be connected without having to define explicit model/metamodel transformations for each language pair. NEREUS embraces changes at different levels of abstraction (Figure 2).

FUTURE TRENDS

Nowadays, there exists an increased demand of reengineering of legacy systems towards new technologies. Advanced MDA tools should reverse existing code to abstract models to facilitate platform migration. It will probably take several years before a full round trip engineering based on standards occurs (many authors are skeptical about this). The existing MDA-based tools do not provide sophisticated transformation from PIM to PSM and from PSM to code.

To solve problems basic research on formalisms and theories will have to be carried out dealing with software evolution in MDA. If MDA becomes a commonplace, adapting it to formal development will become crucial. Formal and semi-formal techniques can play complementary roles in software development processes. This integration is beneficial for both graphical and formal specification techniques. On the one hand, semi-formal techniques have the ability to visualize language constructs allowing a great difference in the productivity of the specification process, especially when the graphical view is supported by means of good tools. On the other hand, formal specifications allow us to produce a precise and analyzable software specification before implementation and to define semi-automatic forward engineering processes.

The integration between ontology (that are essentially CIMs) and MDA will occupy a central place in MDD (Djuric, Gasevic, & Devedzic, 2006). The use of formal specification will make it possible to perform automated reasoning about ontology. A new type of MDA tools that do a more intelligent job might emerge. Probably, the next generation of tools might be able to describe the behavior of software systems in terms of domain models and translate it into executable programs on distributed environment.

CONCLUSION

There is a great number of UML CASE tools in existence that facilitates code generation and limited support for reverse engineering. Unfortunately, the current techniques available in these tools provide little automation for MDD. The formalization of metamodels and metamodel-based model transformations can help to overcome these problems. We propose to integrate knowledge developed by the community of formal methods with MDA. A rigorous framework for MDD was defined. It is comprised of a metamodeling notation NEREUS, a "megamodel" for defining MDA components and the definition of metamodeling/model transformations based on MOF and NEREUS. We define basic techniques for forward engineering and reverse engineering.

We define systems of transformation rules that allow translating MOF-metamodels to formal specifications and implementations. A bridge between NEREUS and algebraic languages was defined by using CASL. Our approach focuses on interoperability of formal languages.

We want to define foundations for MDA tools that permit designers to directly manipulate the visual models they have created. However, meta-designers need to understand metamodels and metamodel transformations.

This research is still evolving and additional issues will have to be tackled in order to fit advances in MDD.

ACKNOWLEDGMENT

This work is partially supported by the Comisión de Investigaciones Científicas de la Provincia de Buenos Aires (CIC).

REFERENCES

Ahrendt, W., Baar, T., Beckert, B., Giese, M., Hähnle, R., Menzel, W., Mostowski, W., & Schmitt, P. (2002). The Key system: Integrating object-oriented design and formal methods. In R. Kutsche, & H. Weber (Eds.), *Lecture notes in computer science 2306* (pp. 327-330). Berlin: Springer-Verlag.

Akehurst, D., & Kent, S. (2002). A relational approach to defining transformations in a meta-model. In J. M. Jezequel, H. Hussmann, & S. Cook (Eds.), *Lecture notes in computer science 2460* (pp. 243-258). Berlin: Springer-Verlag.

Bidoit, M., & Mosses, P. (2004). CASL User manual--Introduction to using the common algebraic specification language. *Lecture Notes in Computer Science 2900*. Berlin: Springer-Verlag,

CASE. (2006). *CASE TOOLS*. Retrieved December 2006, from www.objectsbydesign.com

CWM. (2001). *Common warehouse metamodel (CWM) Specification, Version 1.1*. Retrieved December 2006, from www.omg.org/cgi-bin/doc?ad/2001-02-01

Czarnecki, K., & Helsen, S. (2003). Classification of model transformation approaches. In J. Bettin, G. Van Emde, A. Agrawal, E. Willink, & J. Bezivin (Eds.), *Proceedings of OOPSLA'03 Workshop on Generative Techniques in the Context of Model-Driven Architecture*. Retrieved December 2006, from www.oopsla.org/oopsla2003

Djuric, D., Gasevic, D., & Devedzic, V. (2006). *Model driven architecture and ontology development*. Berlin: Springer.

Favre, L. (2003). *UML and the unified process*. USA: IRM Press.

Favre, L. (2006). A rigorous framework for model driven development. In K. Siau (Ed.), *Advanced topics in database research* (Vol. 5, Chapter I, pp. 1-27). Hershey, PA: Idea Group Publishing.

Favre, L. (2005). Foundations for MDA-based forward engineering. *Journal of Object Technology (JOT), 4*(1), 129-153.

Favre, L., & Martinez, L. (2006). Formalizing MDA components. In M. Morisio (Ed.), *Proceedings of the 9th International Conference on Software Reuse. Lecture Notes in Computer Science 4039* (pp. 326-339). Berlin: Springer-Verlag.

Favre, L., Martinez, L., & Pereira, C. (2005). Forward engineering of UML static models. In M. Khosrow-Pour (Ed.), *Encyclopedia of Information Science and Technology* (pp. 1212-1217). Hershey, PA: Idea Group Publishing.

France, R., Kim, D., Ghosh, S., & Song, E. (2004). A UML-based pattern specification technique. *IEEE Transactions on Software Engineering, 30*(3), 193-206.

Gamma, E., Helm, R., Johnson, R., & Vlissides, J. (1995). *Design patterns. Elements of reusable object-oriented software*. USA: Addison-Wesley.

Gogolla, M., Bohling, J., & Richters, M. (2005). Validating UML and OCL models in USE by automatic snapshot generation. *Journal on Software and System Modeling*. Retrieved December 2006, from http://db.informatik.uni-bremen.de/publications

Hausmann, J. (2003). Relations-relating metamodels. In A. Evans, P. Sammut, & J. Williams (Eds.), *Proceedings of Metamodeling for MDA. The 1st International Workshop*. Retrieved December 2006, from http://wwwcs.uni-paderborn.de/cs/ag-engels/Papers/2004/MM4MDAhausmann.pdf

Kerievsky, J. (2004). *Refactoring to patterns*. USA: Addison-Wesley.

Kim, S., & Carrington, D. (2002). A formal model of the UML metamodel: The UML state machine and its integrity constraints. *Lecture Notes in Computer Science 2272* (pp. 477-496). Berlin: Springer-Verlag.

Kuster, J., Sendall S., & Wahler M. (2004). Comparing two model transformation approaches. In J. Bezivin et al. (Eds.), *Proceedings of OCL and Model Driven Engineering Workshop*. Lisboa, Portugal. Retrieved December 2006, from http://www.cs.kent.ac.uk/projects/ocl/oclmdewsuml04

Kollmann, R., & Gogolla, M. (2002). Metric-Based Selective Representation of UML Diagrams. In T. Gyimóthy & F. Brito e Abreu (Eds.), *Proceedings of 6th European Conf. Software Maintenance and Reengineering (CSMR'02)*. Los Alamitos: IEEE.

Long, Q., Jifeng, H., & Liu, Z. (2005). *Refactoring and pattern-directed refactoring: A formal perspective*. Technical Report 318, UNU-IIST, P.O. Box 3058, Macau. Retrieved December 2006, from www.iist.unu.edu/home/Unuiist/newrh/I/3/14/docs/report_14.html

Martinez, L., & Favre, L. (2006). MDA-based design pattern components. In M. Khosrow-Pour (Ed.), *Proceedings of the 17th IRMA International Conference. Emerging Trends and Challenges in Information Technology Management* (pp. 259-263). Hershey, PA: Idea Group Publishing.

MDA. (2003). *MDA Guide V1.0.1*. Retrieved December 2006, from omg/03-06-01 http://www.omg.org/cgi-bin/doc?omg/03-06-01

Mens, T., Demeyer, S., Du Bois, B., Stenten, H., & Van Gorp, P. (2003). Refactoring: Current research and future trends. *Electronic Notes in Computer Science, 82*(3).

MOF. (2005). *Meta object facility (MOF ™) 1.4*. Document formal/2002-04-03. Retrieved December 2006, from www.omg-org/mof

OCL. (2006). *OCL specification. Version 2.0*. Document: formal/2006-05-01. Retrieved December 2006, www.omg.org

Pereira, C., & Favre, L. (2006). Specifying refactorings as metamodel-based transformation. In Mehdi Khosrow-Pour (Ed.), *Proceedings of the 17th IRMA International Conference. Emerging Trends and Challenges in Information Technology Management* (pp. 264-268). Hershey, PA: Idea Group Publishing.

QVT. (2003). *Revised submission for MOF 2.0 Query/Views/Transformations RFP. Version 1.1*. OMG Adopted Specification. ptc/05-11-01. Retrieved December 2006, from www.omg.org

SPEM. (2005). *Software process engineering metamodel, version 1.1*. Retrieved December 2006, from www.omg.org/cgi-bin/doc?formal/2005-01-06

Sunyé, G., Pollet, D., Y. Le Traon, Y., & Jezequel, J.M. (2001). Refactoring UML Models. In M. Gogolla, & C. Kobryn (Eds.) *Lecture Notes in Computer Science 2185* (pp. 134-148). Berlin: Springer-Verlag.

Szyperski, C., Gruntz, D., & Murer, S. (2002). *Component software. Beyond object-oriented programming* (2nd ed.). USA: Addison-Wesley.

Thomas, D. (2005). Refactoring as meta programming? *Journal of Object Technology, 4*(1), 7-11. Retrieved December 2006, from www.jot.fm/issues/issue_2005_01/column1

UML. (2005). *UML 2.0 Superstructure Specification*. Document formal/2005-07-04. Retrieved December 2006, from www.omg.org/cgi-bin/doc?formal/05-07-04

KEY TERMS

CASE Tool: Computer aided software engineering (CASE); a tool to aid in the analysis and design of software systems.

Forward Engineering: The process of transforming a model into code through a mapping to a specific implementation language.

MDA (Model Driven Architecture): A framework based on UML and other industry standards for visualizing, storing, and exchanging software design and models. It separates the specification of functionality from the specification of the implementation of that functionality on a specific technology platform.

Metamodel: A model that defines the language for expressing a model.

Meta-Metamodel: A model that defines the language for expressing a metamodel.

Model Transformation: The process of converting one model into another model preserving some kind of equivalence relation between them.

OCL (Object Constraint Language): A notational language for analysis and design of software systems that allows software developers to write constraints and queries over object models such as UML models.

Refactoring: A change to a system that leaves its behavior unchanged but enhances some nonfunctional quality factors such as simplicity, flexibility, understanding and performance.

Reverse Engineering: The process of transforming code into a model through a mapping from a specific implementation language.

UML (Unified Modeling Language): An OMG standard language for visualizing, specifying, constructing, and documenting the artifacts of a software-intensive system.

Chapter 14
A Rigorous Framework for Model–Driven Development

Liliana Favre

Universidad Nacional del Centro de la Provincia de Buenos Aires, Argentina

ABSTRACT

The model-driven architecture (MDA) is an approach to model-centric software development. The concepts of models, metamodels, and model transformations are at the core of MDA. Model-driven development (MDD) distinguishes different kinds of models: the computation-independent model (CIM), the platform-independent model (PIM), and the platform-specific model (PSM). Model transformation is the process of converting one model into another model of the same system, preserving some kind of equivalence relation between them. One of the key concepts behind MDD is that models generated during software developments are represented using common metamodeling techniques. In this chapter, we analyze an integration of MDA metamodeling techniques with knowledge developed by the community of formal methods. We describe a rigorous framework that comprises the NEREUS metamodeling notation (open to many other formal languages), a system of transformation rules to bridge the gap between UML/OCL and NEREUS, the definition of MDA-based reusable components, and model/metamodeling transformations. In particular, we show how to integrate NEREUS with algebraic languages using the Common Algebraic Specification Language (CASL). NEREUS focuses on interoperability of formal languages in MDD.

INTRODUCTION

The model-driven architecture (MDA) is an initiative of the Object Management Group (OMG, www.omg.org), which is facing a paradigm shift from object-oriented software development to model-centric development. It is emerging as

a technical framework to improve portability, interoperability, and reusability (MDA, www. omg.org/docs/omg/03-06-01.pdf). MDA promotes the use of models and model-to-model transformations for developing software systems. All artifacts, such as requirement specifications, architecture descriptions, design descriptions, and code, are regarded as models and are represented using common modeling languages. MDA distinguishes different kinds of models: the computation-independent model (CIM), the platform-independent model (PIM), and the platform-specific model (PSM). Unified Modeling Language (UML, www.uml.org) combined with Object Constraint Language (OCL, www.omg.org/cgi-bin/doc?ptc/2003-10-14) is the most widely used way to specify PIMs and PSMs.

A model-driven development (MDD) is carried out as a sequence of model transformations. Model transformation is the process of converting one model into another model of the same system, preserving some kind of equivalence relation between them. The high-level models that are developed independently of a particular platform are gradually transformed into models and code for specific platforms.

One of the key concepts behind MDA is that all artifacts generated during software developments are represented using common metamodeling techniques. Metamodels in the context of MDA are expressed using meta object facility (MOF) (www.omg.org/mof). The integration of UML 2.0 with the OMG MOF standards provides support for MDA tool interoperability (www.uml.org). However, the existing MDA-based tools do not provide sophisticated transformations because many of the MDA standards are recent or still in development (CASE, www.omg.org/cgi-bin/doc?ad/2001-02-01). For instance, OMG is working on the definition of a query, view, transformations (QVT) metamodel, and to date there is no way to define transformations between MOF models (http://www.sce.carleton.ca/courses/sysc-4805/w06/courseinfo/OMdocs/MOF-QVT-ptc-05-11-01.pdf). There is currently no precise foundation for specifying model-to-model transformations.

MDDs can be improved by means of other metamodeling techniques. In particular, in this chapter, we analyze the integration of MDA with knowledge developed by the formal method

community. If MDA becomes a commonplace, adapting it to formal development will become crucial. MDA can take advantage of the different formal languages and the diversity of tools developed for prototyping, model validations, and model simulations. Currently, there is no way to integrate semantically formal languages and their related tools with MDA. In this direction, we define a framework that focuses on interoperability of formal languages in MDD. The framework comprises:

- The metamodeling notation NEREUS;
- A "megamodel" for defining MDA-based reusable components;
- A bridge between UML/OCL and NEREUS; and
- Bridges between NEREUS and formal languages.

Considering that different modeling/programming languages could be used to specify different kinds of models (PIMs, PSMs, and code models) and different tools could be used to validate or verify them, we propose to use the NEREUS language, which is a formal notation suited for specifying UML-based metamodels. NEREUS can be viewed as an intermediate notation open to many other formal specifications, such as algebraic, functional, or logic ones.

The "megamodel" defines reusable components that fit with the MDA approach. A "megamodel" is a set of elements that represent and/or refer to models and metamodel (Bezivin, Jouault, & Valduriez, 2004). Metamodels that describe instances of PIMs, PSMs, and code models are defined at different abstraction levels and structured by different relationships. The "megamodel" has two views, one of them in UML/OCL and the other in NEREUS.

We define a bridge between UML/OCL and NEREUS consisting of a system of transformation rules to convert automatically UML/OCL metamodels into NEREUS specifications. We also formalize model/metamodel transformations among levels of PIMs, PSMs, and implementations.

A bridge between NEREUS and algebraic languages was defined by using the common algebraic specification language (CASL) (Bidoit & Mosses, 2004), that has been designed as a general-purpose algebraic specification language and subsumes many existing formal languages.

Rather than requiring developers to manipulate formal specifications, we want to provide rigorous foundations for MDD in order to develop tools that, on one hand, take advantage of the power of formal languages and, on the other hand, allow developers to directly manipulate the UML/OCL models that they have created.

This chapter is structured as follows. We first provide some background information and related work. The second section describes how to formalize UML-based metamodels in the intermediate notation NEREUS. Next, we introduce a "megamodel" to define reusable components in a way that fits MDA. Then, we show how to bridge the gap between UML/OCL and NEREUS. An integration of NEREUS with CASL is then described. Next, we compare our approach with other existing ones, and then discuss future trends in the context of MDA. Finally, conclusions are presented.

BACKGROUND

The Model-Driven Architecture

MDA distinguishes different kinds of models: the computation-independent model (CIM), the platform-independent model (PIM), the platform-specific model (PSM), and code models. A CIM describes a system from the computation-independent viewpoint that focuses on the environment of and the requirements for the system. In general, it is called a domain model and may be expressed using business models. A PIM is a model that contains no reference to the platforms that are used to realize it. A PSM describes a system in the terms of the final implementation platform, for example, .NET or J2EE. UML combined with OCL is the most widely used way of writing either PIMs or PSMs.

The transformation for one PIM to several PSMs is at the core of MDA. A model-driven development is carried out as a sequence of model transformations that includes, at least, the following steps: construct a CIM; transform the CIM into a PIM that provides a computing architecture independent of specific platforms; transform the PIM into one or more PSMs, and derive code directly from the PSMs (Kleppe, Warmer, & Bast, 2003).

Metamodeling has become an essential technique in model-centric software development. The UML itself is defined using a metamodeling approach. The metamodeling framework for the UML is based on an architecture with four layers: meta-metamodel, metamodel, model, and user objects. A model is expressed in the language of one specific metamodel. A metamodel is an explicit model of the constructs and rules needed to construct specific models. A meta-metamodel defines a language to write metamodels. The meta-metamodel is usually self-defined using a reflexive definition and is based on at least three concepts (entity, association, and package) and a set of primitive types. Languages for expressing UML-based metamodels are based on UML class diagrams and OCL constraints to rule out illegal models.

Related OMG standard metamodels and meta-metamodels such as Meta Object Facility (MOF) (www.omg.org/mof), software process engineering metamodel (SPEM, www.omg.org/technology/documents/formal/spem.htm), and common warehouse metamodel (CWM) (www.omg.org/cgi-bin/doc?ad/2001-02-01) share a common design philosophy. Metamodels in the context of MDA are expressed using MOF. It defines a common way for capturing all the diversity of modeling standards and interchange constructs that are used in MDA. Its goal is to define languages in a same way and then integrate them semantically. MOF and the core of the UML metamodel are closely aligned with their modeling concepts. The UML metamodel can be viewed as an "instance of" the MOF metamodel. OMG is working on the definition of a query, view, transformations (QVT) metamodel for expressing transformations as an extension of MOF.

Figure 1 depicts a "toy" metamodel that includes the core modeling concepts of the UML class diagrams, including classes, interfaces, associations, association-ends, and packages. As an example, Figure 1 shows some OCL constraints that also complement the class diagram.

MDA-Based Tools

There are at least 100 UML CASE tools that differ widely in functionality, usability, performance, and platforms. Currently, about 10% of them provide some support for MDA. Examples of these tools include OptimalJ, ArcStyler, AndroMDA, Ameos, and Codagen, among others. The tool market around MDA is still in flux. References to MDA-based tools can be found at www.objects-bydesign.com/tools. As an example, OptimalJ is an MDA-based environment to generate J2EE applications. OptimalJ distinguishes three kinds of models: a domain model that correspond to a PIM model, an application model that includes PSMs linked to different platforms (Relational-PSM, EJB-PSM and web-PSM), and an implementation model. The transformation process is supported by transformation and functional patterns. OptimalJ allows the generation of PSMs from a PIM and a partial code generation.

UML CASE tools provide limited facilities for refactoring on source code through an explicit selection made for the designer. However, it will be worth thinking about refactoring at the design

Figure 1. A simplified UML metamodel

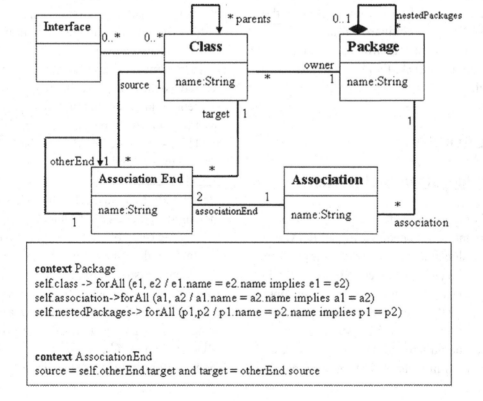

level. The advantage of refactoring at the UML level is that the transformations do not have to be tied to the syntax of a programming language. This is relevant since UML is designed to serve as a basis for code generation with the MDA approach (Sunyé, Pollet, Le Traon, & Jezequel, 2001).

Many UML CASE tools support reverse engineering; however, they only use more basic notational features with a direct code representation and produce very large diagrams. Reverse engineering processes are not integrated with MDDs either.

Techniques that currently exist in UML CASE tools provide little support for validating models in the design stages. Reasoning about models of systems is well supported by automated theorem provers and model checkers; however, these tools are not integrated into CASE tools environments.

A discussion of limitations of the forward engineering processes supported by the existing UML CASE tools may be found in Favre, Martinez, and Pereira (2003, 2005).

The MDA-based tools use MOF to support OMG standards such as UML and XML metadata interchange (XMI). MOF has a central role in MDA as a common standard to integrate all different kinds of models and metadata and to exchange these models among tools. However, MOF does not allow the capture of semantic properties in a platform-independent way, and there are no rigorous foundations for specifying transformations among different kinds of models.

MDA and Semi-Formal/Formal Modeling Techniques

Various research analyzed the integration of semiformal techniques and object-oriented designs with formal techniques. It is difficult to compare the existing results and to see how to integrate them in order to define standard semantics since they specify different UML subsets and are based on different formalisms. Next, we mention only

some of numerous existing works. U2B transforms UML models to B (Snook & Butler, 2002). Kim and Carrington (2002) formalize UML by using OBJECT-Z. Reggio, Cerioli, and Astesiano (2001) present a general framework of the semantics of UML, where the different kinds of diagrams within a UML model are given individual semantics and then such semantics are composed to get the semantics on the overall model. McUmber and Cheng (2001) propose a general framework for formalizing UML diagrams in terms of different formal languages using a mapping from UML metamodels and formal languages. Kuske, Gogolla, Kollmann, and Kreowski (2002) describe an integrated semantics for UML class, object, and state diagrams based on graph transformation.

UML CASE tools could be enhanced with functionality for formal specification and deductive verification; however, only research tools provide support for advanced analysis. For example, the main task of USE tool (Gogolla, Bohling, & Ritchers, 2005) is to validate and verify specifications consisting of UML/OCL class diagrams. Key (Ahrendt et al., 2005) is a tool based on Together (CASE, www.omg.org/cgi-bin/doc?ad/2001-02-01) enhanced with functionality for formal specification and deductive verification.

To date, model-driven approaches have been discussed at several workshops (Abmann, 2004; Evans, Sammut, & Willans, 2003; Gogolla, Sammut, & Whittle, 2004). Several metamodeling approaches and model transformations have been proposed to MDD (Atkinson & Kuhne, 2002; Bezivin, Farcet, Jezequel, Langlois, & Pollet, 2003; Buttner & Gogolla, 2004; Caplat & Sourrouille, 2002; Cariou, Marvie, Seinturier and Duchien, 2004; Favre, 2004; Gogolla, Lindow, Richters, & Ziemann, 2002; Kim & Carrington, 2002).

Akehurst and Kent (2002) propose an approach that uses metamodeling patterns that capture the essence of mathematical relations. The proposed technique is to adopt a pattern that models a transformation relationship as a relation or col-

Figure 2. Class syntax in NEREUS

CLASS className [<parameterList>] **IMPORTS** <importsList> **INHERITS** <inheritsList> **IS-SUBTYPE-OF** <subtypeList> **GENERATED-BY** <basicConstructors> **ASSOCIATES**<associatesList> **DEFERRED** **TYPES** <typesList>	**FUNCTIONS** <functionList> **EFFECTIVE** **TYPES** <typesList> **FUNCTIONS** <functionList> **AXIOMS** <varList> <axiomList> **END-CLASS**

lections of relations, and encode this as an object model. Hausmann (2003) defined an extension of a metamodeling language to specify mappings between metamodels based on concepts presented in Akehurst and Kent (2002). Kuster, Sendall, and Wahler (2004) compare and contrast two approaches to model transformations: one is graph transformation and the other is a relational approach. Czarnecki and Helsen (2003) describe a taxonomy with a feature model to compare several existing and proposed model-to-model transformation approaches. To date, there is no way to integrate semantically formal languages and their related tools with Model-Driven Development.

FORMALIZING METAMODELS: THE NEREUS LANGUAGE

A combination of formal specifications and metamodeling techniques can help us to address MDA. A formal specification clarifies the intended meaning of metamodel/models, helps to validate model transformations, and provides reference for implementation. In this light, we propose the intermediate notation NEREUS that focuses on interoperability of formal languages. It is suited for specifying metamodels based on the concepts of entity, associations, and systems. Most of the UML concepts for the metamodels can be mapped to NEREUS in a straightforward manner. NEREUS is relation-centric; that is, it expresses different kinds of relations (dependency,

association, aggregation, composition) as primitives to develop specifications.

Defining Classes in NEREUS

In NEREUS the basic unit of specification is the class. Classes may declare types, operations, and axioms that are formulas of first-order logic. They are structured by three different kinds of relations: importing, inheritance, and subtyping. Figure 2 shows its syntax.

NEREUS distinguishes variable parts in a specification by means of explicit parameterization. The elements of <parameterList> are pairs C1:C2 where C1 is the formal generic parameter constrained by an existing class C2 (only subclasses of C2 will be actual parameters). The IMPORTS clause expresses clientship relations. The specification of the new class is based on the imported specifications declared in <importList> and their public operations may be used in the new specification.

NEREUS distinguishes inheritance from subtyping. Subtyping is like inheritance of behavior, while inheritance relies on the module viewpoint of classes. Inheritance is expressed in the INHERITS clause; the specification of the class is built from the union of the specifications of the classes appearing in the <inheritsList>. Subtypings are declared in the IS-SUBTYPE-OF clause. A notion closely related with subtyping is polymorphism, which satisfies the property that each object of a subclass is at the same time an object of its superclasses.

Figure 3. The collection class

```
CLASS Collection [Elem:ANY]              AXIOMS  c : Collection; e : Elem; f : Elem -> Boolean;
IMPORTS Boolean, Nat                     g : Elem x Acc -> Acc; base : -> Acc
GENERATED-BY create, add                 isEmpty ( c ) = (size (c ) = 0 )
DEFERRED                                 iterate (create, g, base ) = base
TYPE Collection                          iterate (add (c, e), g, base) = g (e, iterate (c, g, base))
FUNCTIONS create : -> Collection         count (c,e) =
add : Collection x Elem -> Collection       LET
count : Collection x Elem -> Nat            FUNCTIONS
iterate :                                       f1: Elem x Nat ->Nat
Collection x ( Elem x Acc: ANY ) x ( -> Acc ) -> Acc    AXIOMS e1:Elem; i:Nat
EFFECTIVE                                        f1(e1, i) = if e = e1 then i+1 else i
FUNCTIONS isEmpty: Collection ->Boolean      IN  iterate (c, f1, 0)
size: Collection -> Nat                   END-LET
includes: Collection x Elem ->Boolean    includes (create , e ) = False
includesAll: Collection x Collection -> Boolean    includes (add (c, e), e1) = if e = e1   then True
excludes: Collection x Elem -> Boolean                                     else includes (c, e1)
forAll : Collection x ( Elem -> Boolean) -> Boolean    forAll (create , f ) = True
exists : Collection x ( Elem -> Boolean) -> Boolean    forAll (add(c,e), f) =  f (e) and forAll (c, f)
select: Collectionx ( Elem -> Boolean) -> Collection    exists (create, f ) = False
                                         exists (add (c, e)) =  f (e) or  exists (c, f )
                                         select (create, f) = create
                                         select (add (c,e), f) = if f(e) then  add (select(c,f ),e)
                                                                  else  select (c, f)...

                                         END-CLASS
```

NEREUS allows us to define local instances of a class in the IMPORTS and INHERITS clauses by the following syntax ClassName [<bindingList>] where the elements of <bindingList> can be pairs of class names C1: C2 being C2 a component of ClassName; pairs of sorts s1: s2, and/or pairs of operations o1: o2 with o2 and s2 belonging to the own part of ClassName.

NEREUS distinguishes deferred and effective parts. The DEFERRED clause declares new types or operations that are incompletely defined. The EFFECTIVE clause either declares new types or operations that are completely defined or completes the definition of some inherited type or operation.

Operations are declared in the FUNCTIONS clause that introduces the operation signatures, the list of their arguments, and result types. They can be declared as total or partial. Partial functions must specify its domain by means of the PRE clause that indicates what conditions the function's arguments must satisfy to belong to the function's domain. NEREUS allows us to specify operation signatures in an incomplete way. NEREUS supports higher order operations (a function f is higher order if functional sorts appear in a parameter sort or the result sort of f). In the context of OCL Collection formalization, second-order operations are required. In NEREUS, it is possible to specify any of the three levels of visibility for operations: public, protected, and private. NEREUS provides the construction LET... IN to limit the scope of the declarations of auxiliary symbols by using local definitions.

Several useful predefined types are offered in NEREUS, for example, Collection, Set, Sequence, Bag, Boolean, String, Nat, and enumerated types. Figure 3 shows the predefined type OCL-Collection.

Defining Associations

NEREUS provides a taxonomy of constructor types that classifies binary associations according to kind (aggregation, composition, association, association class, qualified association), degree

Figure 4. The binary association hierarchy

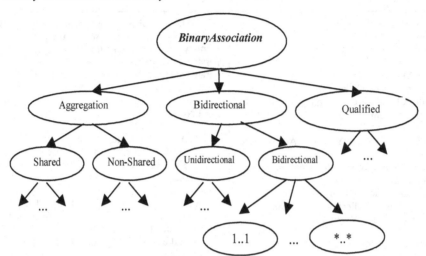

Figure 5. Association syntax in NEREUS

ASSOCIATION <relationName>
IS <constructorTypeName> [...: Class1; ...: Class2; ...: Role1; ...: Role2;   ...: mult1; ...:
mult2; ...: visibility1; ...: visibility2]
CONSTRAINED-BY <constraintList>
END

(unary, binary), navigability (unidirectional, bidirectional), and connectivity (one-to-one, one-to-many, many-to-many). Figure 4 partially depicts the hierarchy of Binary Associations.

Generic relations can be used in the definition of concrete relations by instantiation. New associations can be defined by means of the syntax shown in Figure 5.

The IS paragraph expresses the instantiation of <constructorTypeName> with classes, roles, visibility, and multiplicity. The CONSTRAINED-BY clause allows the specification of static constraints in first-order logic. Relations are defined in a class by means of the ASSOCIATES clause.

Defining Packages

The package is the mechanism provided by NEREUS for grouping classes and associations

Figure 6. Package syntax

PACKAGE packageName
IMPORTS <importsList>
INHERITS <inheritsList>
<elements>
END-PACKAGE

and controlling its visibility. Figure 6 shows the syntax of a package.

<importsList> lists the imported packages; <inheristList> lists the inherited packages and <elements> are classes, associations, and packages. Figure 7 partially shows the NEREUS specification of Figure 1.

Figure 7. A simplified UML metamodel in NEREUS

```
PACKAGE Core                              CLASS TheInterface
CLASS TheClass                            ASSOCIATES <<ClassInterface>>,...
ASSOCIATES<<ClassPackage>>,               END-CLASS
<< ClassClass >>,                         ASSOCIATION PackagePackage
<< SourceAssociationEnd >>,               IS Composition-2 [ThePackage: class1;
<<TargetAssociationEnd>>,                 ThePackage: class2; thePackage : role1;
<<ClassInterface>>,...                    nestedPackages: role2; 0..1: mult1;
TYPES TheClass                             *: mult2; +: visibility1; +: visibility2]
FUNCTIONS                                 END
name: TheClass -> String                  ASSOCIATION ClassPackage
                                          IS Bidirectional-2 [TheClass: class1;
...                                       ThePackage: class2; theClass: role1;
END-CLASS                                 owner: role2; *: mult1; 1: mult2;
CLASS ThePackage                          +: visibility1; +: visibility2]
ASSOCIATES <<PackagePackage>>,            END
<<ClassPackage>>,                         ASSOCIATION ClassClass
<< PackageAssociation >>...               IS Unidirectional-3 [TheClass: class1;
TYPE ThePackage                           TheClass: class2; theClass: role1;
FUNCTIONS                                 parents: role2; 1: mult1; *: mult2;
name: ThePackage -> String                +: visibility1; +: visibility2]
                                          END
...                                       ASSOCIATION ClassInterface
END-CLASS                                 IS Bidirectional-4 [ TheClass: class1;
CLASS TheAssociation                      TheInterface: class2; theClass: role1;
ASSOCIATES <<PackageAssociation>>,        implementedInt: role2; 0..*: mult1;
<<AssociationAssociationEnd>>             0..*: mult2; +: visibility1; +: visibility2]
TYPES TheAssociation                      END
FUNCTIONS                                 ASSOCIATION SourceAssociationEnd
name: TheAssociation -> String            ...
                                          ASSOCIATION TargetAssociationEnd
...                                       ...
END-CLASS                                 ASSOCIATION PackageAssociation
CLASS TheAssociationEnd                   ...
ASSOCIATES                                ASSOCIATION
<<AssociationAssociationEnd>>,            AssociationendAssociationend
<<AssociationEndAssociationEnd>>,         ...
<<SourceAssociationEnd>>,
<<TargetAssociationEnd>>,
...
END-CLASS                                 END-PACKAGE
```

DEFINING REUSABLE COMPONENTS: A "MEGAMODEL"

Developing reusable components requires a high focus on software quality. The traditional techniques for verification and validation are still essential to achieve software quality. The formal specifications are of particular importance for supporting testing of applications, for reasoning about correctness and robustness of models, for checking the validity of a transformation and for generating code "automatically" from abstract models. MDA can take advantages of formal languages and the tools developed around them. In this direction, we propose a "megamodel" to define MDA reusable components. A "megamodel" is a set of elements that represent and/or refer to models and metamodels at different levels of abstraction and structured by different relationships (Bezivin, Jouault, & Valduriez, 2004). It relates PIMs, PSMs, and code with their respective metamodels specified both in UML/OCL and NEREUS. NEREUS represents the transient stage in the process of conversion of UML/OCL specifications to different formal specifications.

We define MDA components at three different levels of abstraction: platform- independent component model (PICM), platform-specific component model (PSCM), and implementation component model (ICM). The PICM includes a UML/OCL metamodel that describes a family of all those PIMs that are instances of the metamodel. A PIM is a model that contains no information of the platform that is used to realize it. A platform is defined as "a set of subsystems and technologies that provide a coherent set of functionality, which any application supported by that platform can use without concern for the details of how the functionality is implemented" (www.omg.org/docs/omg/03-06-01.pdf, p.2.3).

A PICM-metamodel is related to more than one PSCM-metamodel, each one suited for different platforms. The PSCM metamodels are specializations of the PICM-metamodel. The PSCM includes UML/OCL metamodels that are linked to specific platforms and a family of PSMs that are instances of the respective PSCM-metamodel. Every one of them describes a family of PSM instances. PSCM-metamodels correspond to ICM-metamodels. Figure 8 shows the different correspondences that may be held between several models and metamodels. A "megamodel" is based on two views, one of them in UML/OCL and the other in NEREUS. A metamodel is a description of all the concepts that can be used in the respective level (PICM, PSCM, and ICM). The concepts of attribute, operations, classes, associations, and packages are included in the PIM-metamodel. PSM-metamodels constrain a PIM-metamodel to fit a specific platform, for instance, a metamodel linked to a relational platform refers to the concepts of table, foreign key, and column. The ICM-metamodel includes concepts of programming languages such as constructor and method.

A model transformation is a specification of a mechanism to convert the elements of a model that are instances of a particular metamodel into elements of another model, which can be instances of the same or different metamodel. A metamodel transformation is a specific type of model transformations that impose relations between pairs of metamodels. We define a bridge between UML/OCL and NEREUS. For a subsequent translation into formal languages, NEREUS may serve as a source language. In the following sections, we describe how to bridge the gap between NEREUS and formal languages. In particular, we analyze how to translate NEREUS into CASL.

A BRIDGE BETWEEN UML AND NEREUS

We define a bridge between UML/OCL static models and NEREUS. A detailed analysis may be found in Favre (2005a). The text of the NEREUS specification is completed gradually. First, the signature and some axioms of classes are obtained by instantiating the reusable schemes BOX_ and ASSOCIATION_. Next, OCL specifications are transformed using a set of transformation rules. Then, a specification that reflects all the information of UML models is constructed. Figure 9 depicts the main steps of this translation process.

Figure 10 shows the reusable schemes BOX_ and ASSOCIATION_. In BOX_, the attribute mapping requires two operations: an access operation and a modifier. The access operation takes no arguments and returns the object to which the receiver is mapped. The modifier takes one argument and changes the mapping of the receiver to that argument. In NEREUS, no standard convention exists, but frequently we use names such as get_ and set_ for them. Association specification is constructed by instantiating the scheme ASSOCIATION_.

Figure 11 shows a simple class diagram P&M in UML. P&M introduces two classes (Person and Meeting) and a bidirectional association between them. This example was analyzed by Hussmann, Cerioli, Reggio, and Tort (1999), Padawitz (2000), and Favre (2005a). We have meetings in which persons may participate. The NEREUS specifi-

Figure 8. A "megamodel" for MDA

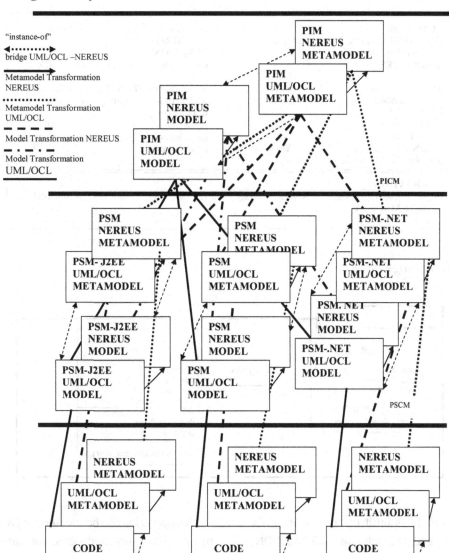

Figure 9. From UML/OCL to NEREUS

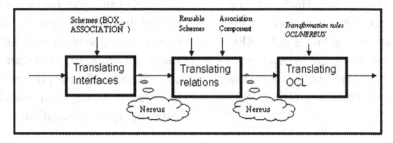

*Figure 10. The reusable schemes BOX_ and ASSOCIATION_*

CLASS *BOX_*
IMPORTS $TP_1,..., TP_m, T\text{-}attr_1, T\text{-}attr_2,..., Tattr_n$
INHERITS $B1, B2,..., Bm$
ASSOCIATES
$<<Aggregation\text{-}E_1>>,...,<<Aggregation\text{-}E_m>>,$
$<<Composition\text{-}C_1>>,...,<<CompositionC_k>>,$
$<<Association\text{-}D_1>>,...,<<Association\text{-}D_k>>$
EFFECTIVE
TYPE *Name*
FUNCTIONS
createName : $T\text{-}attr_1$ x ... x $T\text{-}attr_n$ -> *Name*
set_i : *Name* x $T\text{-}attr_i$ -> *Name*

get_i: *Name* -> $T\text{-}attr_i$ $1<=i<=n$
DEFERRED
FUNCTIONS
$meth_1$: *Name* x TPi_1 x TPi_2 x TPi_n -> TPi_j
...
$meth_r$: *Name* x TPr_1 x TPr_2 ... x TPi_n -> TPi_j
AXIOMS t_1, t_1': **T-attr$_1$**; t_2, t_2': **T-attr$_2$**;...;
t_n, t_n': **T-attr$_n$**
$get_i(create(t_1,t_2,...,t_n)) = t_i$ $1 \le i \le n$
$set_i (create (t_1,t_2,...,t_n), t_i') = create (t_1,t_2,...t_i',...,t_n)$
END-CLASS

ASSOCIATION ___
IS ___ [__: Class1; __:Class2; __: Role1;__:Role2;__:Mult1; __:Mult2; __:Visibility1; __:Visibility2]
CONSTRAINED BY __
END

Figure 11. The package P&M

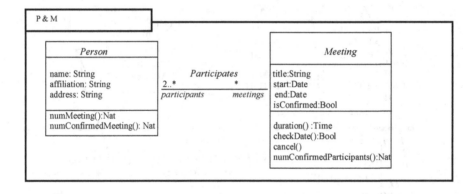

cation of Figure 12 is built by instantiating the scheme BOX_ and the scheme ASSOCIATION_ (see Figure 10).

The transformation process of OCL specifications to NEREUS is supported by a system of transformation rules. Figure 13 shows how to translate some OCL expressions into NEREUS.

By analyzing OCL specifications, we can derive axioms that will be included in the NEREUS specifications. Preconditions written in OCL are used to generate preconditions in NEREUS. Postconditions and invariants allow us to generate axioms in NEREUS. Figure 14 shows how to map OCL specifications of P&M onto NEREUS.

An operation can be specified in OCL by means of pre- and post-conditions. self can be used in the expression to refer to the object on which the operation was called, and the name result is the name of the returned object, if there is any. The names of the parameter (parameter1,...) can also be used in the expression. In a postcondition, the expression can refer to two sets of values for each property of an object: the value of a property at the start of the operation and the value of a property upon completion of the operation. To refer to the value of a property at the start of the operation, one has to postfix the property name with "@", followed by the keyword "pre". For example, the following OCL spcification:

Figure 12. The package P&M: Translating interfaces and relations into NEREUS

```
PACKAGE P&M                                    ASSOCIATES <<Participates>>
CLASS Person                                   EFFECTIVE
IMPORTS String, Nat                            TYPE Meeting
üüüüüü            Participates>>                GENERATED-BY createMeeting
EFFECTIVE                                      FUNCTIONS
TYPE  Person                                   createMeeting:
GENERATED-BY Create_Person                     String x Date x Date x Boolean  -> Meeting
FUNCTIONS                                       title: Meeting -> String
createPerson: String x String x String -> Person   start : Meeting -> Date
name: Person -> String                         end : Meeting -> Date
affiliation: Person -> String                  isConfirmed : Meeting -> Boolean
address: Person -> String                      set-tittle: Meeting x String -> Meeting
set-name: Person x String -> Person            set-start : Meeting x Date -> Meeting
set-affiliation : Person x String -> Person    set-end: Meeting x Date -> Meeting
set-address: Person x String -> Person         set-isConfirmed: Meeting x Boolean -> Boolean
AXIOMS p:Person; m: Meeting; s,  s1, s2, s3:   AXIOMS s: String; d, d1,: Date; b:
String; pa: Participates                       Boolean;…
name(createPerson(s1,s2, s3)) = s1            title( createMeeting (s, d, d1, b) ) =  s
affiliation (createPerson (s1, s2, s3) ) = s2  start ( createMeeting (s, d, d1, b)) = d
address (createPerson (s1, s2, s3)) = s3       end ( createMeeting (s, d, d1, b)) = d1
set-name ( createPerson (s1, s2, s3), s) =     isConfirmed ( createMeeting (s, d, d1, b)) = b
createPerson (s,s2,s3))                         …
set-affiliation (createPerson( s1,s2, s3), s) =   END-CLASS
createPerson (s1, s, s3))                       ASSOCIATION Participates
                                               IS Bidirectional-Set [Person: Class1; Meeting:
…                                              Class2; participants: Role1; meetings: Role2; *:
END-CLASS                                       Mult1; * : Mult2; + : Visibility1; +: Visibility2]
CLASS Meeting                                   END
IMPORTS String, Date, Boolean, Time            END_PACKAGE
```

Figure 13. Transforming OCL into NEREUS: A system of transformation rules

OCL	NEREUS
v (variable)	v (variable)
Type-> operationName (parameter1: Type1,...): Rtype	operationName : TypexType1x...-> Rtype
v. operation (v')	operation (v, v')
v->operation (v')	operation (v, v')
v.attribute	attribute (v)
context A object.rolename	get_ rolename (A, object)
e.op	op (Translate $_{NEREUS}$ (e)) *Let Translate$_{NEREUS}$ be functions that translate logical expressions of OCL into first-order formulae in NEREUS.*
collection-> op (v:Elem |boolean-expr-with-v) op ::=select| forAll| reject| exists	**LET** **FUNCTIONS** f: Elem -> Boolean **AXIOMS v : Elem** f (v)= Translate $_{NEREUS}$ (boolean-expr-with-v) **IN** op (collection, f) **END-LET** -------------------------------- op$_v$ (collection, [f(v)]) *Equivalent concise notation*

Figure 14. The package P&M: Transforming OCL contracts into NEREUS

context Meeting:: checkDate():Bool **post:** result = self.participants->collect(meetings) ->forAll(m | m<> self and m.isConfirmed implies (after(self.end,m.start) or after(m.end,self.start)))	***OCL***

context Meeting::isConfirmed () **post:** result= self.checkdate() and self.numConfirmedParticipants >= 2

context Person:: numMeeting ( ): Nat **post:** result = self.meetings -> size

context Person :: numConfirmedMeeting ( ) : Nat **post:** result= self.meetings -> select (isConfirmed) -> size

Rule 1 $T \to Op$ (<parameterList>) : ReturnType **post:** expr	**AXIOMS** t : T, ... *Translate*$_{NEREUS}$ (exp)
Rule 2 T-> forAll op (v:Type |bool-exprwith-v) op ::= exists |select | reject	forAll$_v$ op (*Translate*$_{NEREUS}$ (T), *Translate*$_{NEREUS}$ (bool-exprwith-v)
Rule 3 T -> collect (v :type |v.property)	collect$_v$ (*Translate* $_{NEREUS}$ (T), *Translate* $_{NEREUS}$ (v.property))

CLASS Person... **AXIOMS p:Person; s,s': String; Pa: Participates**   ***NEREUS*** numConfirmedMeetings (p) = size(select$_m$ (getMeetings(Pa,p), [isConfirmed (m)]) **Rule 1, 2** numMeetings (p) = size (getMeetings (Pa, p))   **Reglas 1** **END-CLASS**
CLASS Meeting... **AXIOMS m,m1:Meeting; s,s':String; d,d',d1,d1':Date; b,b':Boolean;** **Pa:Participates** isConfirmed (cancel(m)) = False isConfirmed (m)=checkDate(m) and NumConfirmedParticipants (m) >= 2 **Rule 1** checkDate(m) =   **Rules 1, 2, 3** forAll$_{me}$ (collect$_p$ (getParticipants(Pa,m), [getMeetings (Pa, p)]), [consistent (m,m$_e$)]) consistent(m,m1)= not (isConfirmed(m1)) or (end(m) < start(m1) or end(m1) < start(m)) NumConfirmedParticipants (m) = size (getParticipants(Pa,m)) **END-CLASS**

AddPerson (p:Person) **pre:** not meetings -> includes(p) **post:** meetings = meetings@pre -> including(p)	AddPerson: Participates (a) x Person (p) -> Participates **pre:** not includes(getMeetings(a), p) **AXIOMS** a: Participates; p:Person;.... getMeetings(AddPerson(a,p)) =including(getMeetings(a), p)

is translated into:

Figure 15. Translating parameters

NEREUS	CLASS CartesProd [E: ANY; E1 : ANY]
CASL	spec CARTESPROD [sort E] [sort E1]
NEREUS	CLASS HASH [T: ANY; V: HASHABLE]
CASL	spec HASH [sort T] [HASHABLE]

INTEGRATING NEREUS WITH ALGEBRAIC LANGUAGES: FROM NEREUS TO CASL

In this section, we examine the relation between NEREUS and algebraic languages using Common Algebraic Specification Language (CASL) as a common algebraic language (Bidoit & Mosses, 2004).

CASL is an expressive and simple language based on a critical selection of known constructs, such as subsorts, partial functions, first-order logic, and structured and architectural specifications. A basic specification declares sorts, subsorts, operations, and predicates, and gives axioms and constraints. Specifications are structured by means of specification-building operators for renaming, extension, and combining. Architectural specifications impose structure on implementations, whereas structured specifications only structure the text of specifications. It allows loose, free, and generated specifications.

CASL is at the center of a family of specification languages. It has restrictions to various sublanguages and extensions to higher order, state-based, concurrent, and other languages. CASL is supported by tools and facilitates interoperability of prototyping and verification tools.

Algebraic languages do not follow similar structuring mechanisms to UML or NEREUS. The graph structure of a class diagram involves cycles such as those created by bidirectional associations. However, the algebraic specifications are structured hierarchically and cyclic import structures between two specifications are avoided.

In the following, we describe how to translate basic specification in NEREUS to CASL, and then analyze how to translate associations (Favre, 2005b).

Translating Basic Specifications

In NEREUS, the elements of <parameterList> are pairs C1:C2 where C1 is the formal generic parameter constrained by an existing class C2 or C1: ANY (see Figure 2). In CASL, the first syntax is translated into [C2] and the second in [sort C1]. Figure 15 shows some examples.

NEREUS and CASL have a similar syntax for declaring types. The sorts in the IS-SUBTYPE paragraph are linked to subsorts in CASL.

The signatures of the NEREUS operations are translated into operations or predicates in CASL. Datatype declarations may be used to abbreviate declarations of types and constructors.

Any NEREUS function that includes partial functions must specify the domain of each of them. This is the role of the PRE clause that indicates what conditions the function's arguments must satisfy to belong to the function's domain. To indicate that a CASL function may be partial, the notation uses -›?; the normal arrow will be reserved for total functions. The translation includes an axiom for restricting the domain. Figure 16 exemplifies the translation of a partial function remove (see Figure 2).

In NEREUS, it is possible to specify three different levels of visibility for operations: public, protected, and private. In CASL, a private visibility requires hiding the operation by means of

Figure 16. Translating partial functions

NEREUS
remove: Bidirectional (b) x Class1(c1) x Class2 (c2)-> Bidirectional
      pre: isRelated (b,c1,c2)

CASL
remove: Bidirectional (b) x Class1 x Class2 ->? Bidirectional
...
forall b:Bidirectional, c1:Class1; c2: Class2
def remove(b,c1,c2) <=> isRelated (b,c1,c2)

Figure 17. Translating importing relations

spec SN [SP_1] [SP_2]... [SP_n] **given** SP_1', SP_2',..., SP_m'=
    SP_1" **and** SP_2" **and** ...
then
SP
end

Figure 18. Translating inheritance relations

NEREUS	**CLASS** A **INHERITS** B, C
CASL	**spec** A = B **and** C **end**

the operator Hide. On the other hand, a protected operation in a class is included in all the subclasses of that class, and it is hidden by means of the operator Hide or the use of local definitions.

The IMPORTS paragraph declares imported specifications. In CASL, the specifications are declared in the header specification after the keyword given or like unions of specifications. A generic specification definition SN with some parameters and some imports is depicted in Figure 17.

SN refers to the specification that has parameter specifications SP1, SP2, ... SPn, (if any). Parameters should be distinguished from references to fixed specifications that are not intended to be instantiated such as SP1', SP2', .., SPm'(if any). SP1", SP2", ... are references to import that can be instantiated. Unions also allow us to express inheritance relations in CASL. Figure 18 exemplifies the transla-

tion of inheritance relations. References to generic specifications always instantiate the parameters. In NEREUS, the instantiation of parameters [C : B]—where C is a class already existing in the environment and B is a component of A, and C is a subclass of B—constructs an instance of A in which the component B is substituted by C. In CASL, the intended fitting of the parameter symbols to the argument symbols may have to be specified explicitly by means of a fit C|-> B.

NEREUS and CASL have the similar syntax for defining local functions. Then, this transformation is reduced to a simple translation.

NEREUS distinguishes incomplete and complete specifications. In CASL, the incomplete specifications are translated to loose specifications and complete ones to free specifications. If the specification has basic constructors, it will be

Figure 19. Translating higher order functions

```
spec Operation [ sort X] =              for all c,c1:Collection; e:Elem
  Z1 and Z2 and ... Zr                  isEmpty (create)
  then                                  includes(add (c,e),e1) =
  pred                                  if e=e1 then true else includes(c,e1)
  f1_j : X          | 1≤ j ≤ m          select_i (create) = create
  f2_j : X          | 1≤ j ≤ n          select_i (add (c,e)) =
  f3_j : X          | 1≤ j ≤ k          if f1_i(e) then add ( select_i(c),e) else select_i(c)
  f4_j : X          | 1≤ j ≤ l          |1≤i ≤ m
  ops                                   includesAll (c,add (c1,e)) =
  base_j : -> Z_j       | 1 ≤j ≤ r      includes (c,e) and includesAll (c,c1)
  g_j: Z_j x X -> Z_j   | 1≤j ≤r        reject_i (create) = create
  end                                   reject_i (add(c,e))=
  spec Collection [sort Elem]           if not f2_i(e) then add (reject_i(c), e) else reject_i(c)
    given NAT=OPERATION [Elem]          |1≤i ≤ n
    then                                forAll_i(add(c,e))= f3_i(e) and for-all_i(c)
    generated type Collection ::=       |1≤i ≤ k
    create | add (Collection ; Elem)    exists_i (add (c,e))= f4_i(e) or  exists_i(c)
    pred                                |1≤i ≤ l
    isEmpty : Collection                iterate_j(create) = base_j
    includes: Collection x Elem         iterate_j(add (c,e) ) = g_j(e, iterate_j(c) )
    includesAll: Collection x Collection | 1≤i≤r
    forAll_i: Collection       |1≤ ≤ k  local ops f2: Elem x Nat ->Nat
    exists_i: Collection       |1≤ ≤ l  for all e: Elem; i: Nat
    iterate_i: Collection→ Z_j | 1≤i≤r       f2(e,i) = i+1
    ops                                 within size(c) =  iterate (c, f2, 0)
    size: Collection  -> Nat            end-local
    select_i: Collection -> Collection  end
    reject_i: Collection -> Collection
    |1≤i ≤m
```

translated into generated specifications. However, if it is incomplete, it will be translated into loose generated specifications. Both NEREUS and CASL allow loose extensions of free specifications.

The classes that include higher order operations are translated inside parameterized first-order specifications. The main difference between higher order specifications and parameterized ones is that, in the first approach, several function-calls can be done with the same specification and parameterized specifications require the construction of several instantiations. Figure 19 shows the translation of the Collection specification (see Figure 3) to CASL. Take into account that there are as many functions f1, f2, f3, and f4 as functions select, reject, forAll and exists. There are also as many functions base and g as functions iterate.

Translating Associations

NEREUS and UML follow similar structuring mechanisms of data abstraction and data encapsulation. The algebraic languages do not follow these structuring mechanisms in an UML style. In UML, an association can be viewed as a local part of an object. This interpretation cannot be mapped to classical algebraic specifications, which do not admit cyclic import relations.

We propose an algebraic specification that considers associations belonging to the environment in which an actual instance of the class is embedded. Let Assoc be a bi-directional association between two classes called A and B; the following steps can be distinguished in the translation process. We exemplify these steps with the transformation of P&M (see Figure 11).

Figure 20. Translating Participates association. Step 1.

LOCAL TO...	OPERATIONS/ATTRIBUTES
PERSON	NAME
MEETING	TITTLE, START, END, DURATION
PERSON, MEETING, PARTICIPATES	CANCEL, ISCONFIRMED, NUMCONFIRMEDMEETINGS, CHECKDATE, NUMMEETINGS

Step 1:

> Regroup the operations of classes A and B distinguishing operations local to A, local to B and, local to A and B and Assoc (Figure 20).

Step 2:

> Construct the specifications A' and B' from A and B where A' and B' include local operations to A and B respectively (Figure 21).

Step 3:

> Construct specifications Collection[A'] and Collection[B'] by instantiating reusable schemes (Figure 22).

Step 4:

> Construct a specification Assoc (with A' and B') by instantiating reusable schemes in the component Association (Figure 23).

Step 5:

> Construct the specification AssocA+B by extending Assoc with A', B' and the operations local to A', B' and Assoc (Figure 24).

Figure 25 depicts the relationships among the specifications built in the different steps.

BENEFITS OF THE RIGOROUS FRAMEWORK FOR MDA

Formal and semiformal techniques can play complementary roles in MDA-based software development processes. We consider it beneficial for both semiformal and formal specification techniques. On one hand, semiformal techniques lack precise semantics; however, they have the ability to visualize language constructions, allowing a great difference in the productivity of the specification process, especially when the graphical view is supported by good tools. On the other hand, formal specifications allow us to produce a precise and analyzable software specification and automate model-to-model transformations; however, they require familiarity with formal notations that most designers and implementers do not currently have, and the learning curve for the application of these techniques requires considerable time.

UML and OCL are too imprecise and ambiguous when it comes to simulation, verification, validation, and forecasting of system properties and even when it comes to generating models/implementations through transformations. Although OCL is a textual language, OCL expressions rely on UML class diagrams, that is, the syntax context is determined graphically. OCL does also not have the solid background of a classical formal language. In the context of MDA, model transformations should preserve correctness. To achieve this, the different modeling and programming languages involved in a MDD must be defined in a consistent and precise way. Then, the combination of UML/OCL specifications and formal languages offers the best of both worlds to the software developer. In this direction, we define NEREUS to take advantage of all the existing theoretical background on formal methods, using different tools such as theorem provers, model checkers, or rewrite engines in different stages of MDD.

In contrast to other works, our approach is the only one focusing on the interoperability of formal languages in model-driven software development.

Figure 21. Translating Participates association. Step 2.

```
spec PERSON given  STRING, NAT =
then
generated type Person ::= create-Person (String)
ops
name: Person -> String
setName :Person x String -> Name
end


spec MEETING given  STRING, DATE =
then generated type Meeting ::=  create-Meeting ( String; Date; Date)
ops
tittle: Meeting -> String
set-title: Meeting x String -> Meeting
start : Meeting -> Date
set-start: Meeting x Date -> Meeting
isEnd: Meeting -> Date
set-end: Meeting x Date -> Meeting
end
```

Figure 22. Translating Participates association. Step 3.

```
spec SET-PERSON  given NAT= PERSON and BAG[PERSON] and ...
then
generated type Set[Person] :: = create | including (Set[Person]; Person)
ops
union : Set[Person] x Set[Person] -> Set [Person]
intersection : Set[Person] x Set[Person] -> Set [Person]
count: Set[Person] x Person -> Nat
...

spec SET-MEETING given  NAT =  MEETING and BAG[MEETING] and ...
then
generated type Set [Meeting] :: = create | including (Set[Meeting]; Meeting)
...
```

There are UML formalizations based on different languages that do not use an intermediate language. However, this extra step provides some advantages. NEREUS would eliminate the need to define formalizations and specific transformations for each different formal language. The metamodel specifications and transformations can be reused at many levels in MDA. Languages that are defined in terms of NEREUS metamodels can be related to each other because they are defined in the same way through a textual syntax.

We define only one bridge between UML/OCL and NEREUS by means of a transformational system consisting of a small set of transformation rules that can be automated. Our approach avoids defining transformation systems and the formal languages being used. Also, intermediate specifications may be needed for refactoring and for forward and reverse engineering purposes based on formal specifications.

We have applied the approach to transform UML/OCL class diagrams into NEREUS speci-

Figure 23. Translating Participates association. Step 4.

```
spec PARTICIPATES = SET-PERSON and SET-MEETING and
BINARY-ASSOCIATION [PERSON][MEETING]
with BinaryAssociation |-> Participates
pred
isRightLinked: Participates x Person
isLeftLinked: Participates x Meeting
isRelated: Participates x Person x Meeting
ops
addLink: Participates x Person x Meeting -> Participates
getParticipants: Participates x Meeting -> Set [Person]
getMeetings: Participates x Person -> Set[Meeting]
remove: Participates x Person x Meeting -> Participates
∀ a : Participates; p,p1: Person; m,m1: Meeting
def addLink (a,p,m) ⇔ not isRelated (a,p,m)
def getParticipants (a, m) ⇔ isLeftLinked (a,m)
def getMeetings (a, m) ⇔ isRightLinked ( a, m)
def remove (a,p,m) ⇔ isRelated (a, p, m)
endspec
```

Figure 24. Translating Participates association. Step 5.

```
spec PERSON&MEETING = PARTICIPATES
then ops
numMeeting : Participates x Person -> Nat
numConfirmedMeeting : Participates x Person -> Nat
isConfirmed : Participates x Meeting -> Boolean
numConfirmedParticipants: Participates x Meeting -> Nat
checkDate: Participates x Meeting -> Participates
select : Participates x Set[Meeting]  -> Set[Meeting]
collect: Participates x Set[Person]  -> Bag[Meeting]
pred    forall: Participates x Set[Meeting] x Meeting
∀s : Set[Meeting]; m:Meeting; pa:Participates; p:Person; m:Meeting; sp:Set[Person];
bm: Bag[Meeting]
forall (pa, including(s,m),m1) = isConsistent(pa, m,m1) and forall(pa, s, m1)
select( pa, create-Meeting) = create-Meeting
select ( pa, including (s, m)) = including(select(pa,s), m) when isConfirmed (pa, m)
                                    else select (pa,s)
collect (pa, create-Person,s) = asBag (create-Person)
collect (pa, including (sp, p) ) = asBag (including (collect (pa,sp), p))
numMeeting( pa, p) = size (getMeetings(pa, p))
isConfirmed (pa, m) = checkDate (pa,m) and NumConfirmedParticipants (pa,m) >= 2
numConfirmedMeeting (pa, p) = size (select (getMeetings (pa,p)))
checkDate (pa, m) = forall (pa, collect (pa, getParticipants(pa,m), m)
isConsistent (pa, m, m1) =
not (isConfirmed (pa,m1)) or (end(m) < start (m1) or  end (m1) < start(m))
numParticipantsConfirmed (pa, m) = size( getParticipants (pa, m))
end
```

fications, which, in turn, are used to generate object-oriented code. The process is based on the adaptation of MDA-based reusable components. NEREUS allows us to keep a trace of the structure of UML models in the specification structure that will make it easier to maintain consistency between the various levels when the system evolves. All the UML model information (classes, associations, and OCL specifications) is overturned into specifications having implementa-

Figure 25. Translating Participates association into CASL

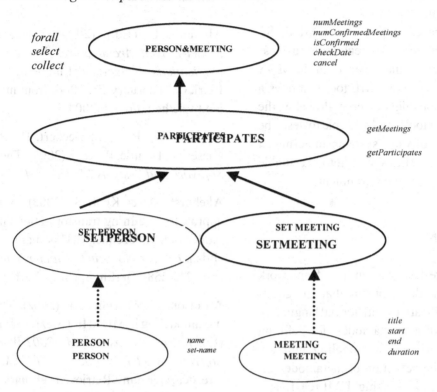

tion implications. The transformation of different kinds of UML associations into object-oriented code was analyzed, as was the construction of assertions and code from algebraic specifications. The proposed transformations preserve the integrity between specification and code. The transformation of algebraic specifications to object-oriented code was prototyped (Favre, 2005a). The OCL/NEREUS transformation rules were prototyped (Favre et al., 2003).

FUTURE TRENDS

Currently, OMG is promoting a transition from code-oriented to MDA-based software development techniques. The existing MDA-based tools do not provide sophisticated transformation from PIM to PSM and from PSM to code. To date, they might be able to support forward engineering and partial round-trip engineering between PIM

and code. However, it will probably take several years before a full round-trip engineering based on standards occurs (many authors are skeptical about this).

To solve these problems, a lot of work will have to be carried out dealing with the semantics for UML, advanced metamodeling techniques, and rigorous transformation processes. If MDA becomes commonplace, adapting it to formal development will become crucial. In this light, we will investigate the NEREUS language for integrating formal tools. NEREUS would allow different formal tools to be used in the same development environment to translate models expressed in different modeling languages into the intermediate language, and back, by using NEREUS as an internal representation that is shared among different formal languages/tools. Any number of source languages (modeling language) and target languages (formal language) could be connected without having to define explicit model/metamodel transformations for each language pair.

Techniques that currently exist in UML CASE tools provide little support for generating business models. In the light of the advances of the MDA paradigm, a new type of UML tool that does a more intelligent job might emerge. Probably, the next generation of tools might be able to describe the behavior of software systems in terms of business models and translate it into executable programs on distributed environment.

CONCLUSION

In this chapter, we describe a uniform framework for model-driven development that integrates UML/OCL specifications with formal languages. It is comprised of a "megamodel" for defining MDA components, a metamodeling notation NEREUS, and the definition of metamodeling/model transformations using UML/OCL and NEREUS.

A "megamodel" integrates PIMs, PSMs and code models with their respective metamodels. We formalize UML-based metamodels in NEREUS, which is an intermediate notation particularly suited for metamodeling. We define a system of transformation rules to bridge the gap between UML/OCL models and NEREUS. We propose to specify metamodel transformations independently of any technology. We investigate the way to define them using UML/OCL and NEREUS.

We want to define foundations for MDA tools that permit designers to directly manipulate the UML/OCL models they have created. However, meta-designers need to understand metamodels and metamodel transformations.

We are validating the "megamodel" through forward engineering, reverse engineering, model refactoring, and pattern applications.

We foresee the integration of our results in the existing UML CASE tools, experimenting with different platforms such as .NET and J2EE.

REFERENCES

Abmann, U. (Ed.). (2004). *Proceedings of Model-Driven Architecture: Foundations and applications.* Switzerland: Linkoping University. Retrieved February 28, 2006, from http://www.ida.liv.se/henla/mdafa2004

Ahrendt, W., Baar, T., Beckert, B., Bubel, R., Giese, M., Hähnle, R., et al. (2005). The key tool. *Software and Systems Modeling, 4,* 32-54.

Akehurst, D., & Kent, S. (2002). A relational approach to defining transformations in a metamodel. In J. M. Jezequel, H. Hussmann, & S. Cook (Eds.), *Lecture Notes in Computer Science 2460* (pp. 243-258). Berlin: Springer-Verlag.

Atkinson, C., & Kuhne, T. (2002). The role of metamodeling in MDA. In J. Bezivin & R. France (Eds.). *Proceedings of UML 2002 Workshop in Software Model Engineering (WiSME 2002),* Dresden, Germany. Retrieved February 28, 2006, from http://www.metamodel.com/wisme-2002

Bézivin, J., Farcet, N., Jézéquel, J., Langlois, B., & Pollet, D. (2003). Reflective model driven engineering. In P. Stevens, J. Whittle, & G. Booch (Eds.), *Lecture Notes in Computer Science 2863* (pp.175-189). Berlin: Springer-Verlag.

Bézivin, J., Jouault, F., & Valduriez, P. (2004). On the need for megamodels. In J. Bettin, G. van Emde Boas, A. Agrawal, M. Volter, & J. Bezivin (Eds.), *Proceedings of Best Practices for Model-Driven Software Development (MDSD 2004), OOSPLA 2004 Workshop,* Vancouver, Canada. Retrieved February 28, 2006, from http://www.softmetaware.com/oospla2004

Bidoit, M., & Mosses, P. (2004). CASL user manual- Introduction to using the Common Algebraic Specification Language. In *Lecture Notes in Computer Science 2900* (p. 240). Berlin: Springer Verlag.

Büttner, F., & Gogolla, M. (2004). Realizing UML metamodel transformations with AGG. In R. Heckel (Ed.), *Proceedings of ETAPS Workshop Graph Transformation and Visual Modeling Techniques (GT-VMT 2004)*. Retrieved February 28, 2006, from http://www.cs.uni-paderborn.de/cs/ag-engels/GT-VMT04

Caplat, G., & Sourrouille, J. (2002). Model mapping in MDA. In J. Bezivin & R. France (Eds.), *Proceedings of UML 2002 Workshop in Software Model Engineering (WiSME 2002)*. Retrieved February 28, 2006, from http://www.metamodel.com/wisme-2002

Cariou, E., Marvie, R., Seinturier, L., & Duchien, L. (2004). OCL for the specification of model transformation contracts. In J. Bezivin (Ed.), *Proceedings of OCL&MDE'2004, OCL and Model Driven Engineering Workshop*, Lisbon, Portugal. Retrieved February 28, 2006, from http://www.cs.kent.ac.uk/projects/ocl/oclmdewsuml04

Czarnecki, K., & Helsen, S. (2003). Classification of model transformation approaches. In J. Bettin et al. (Eds.). *Proceedings of OOSPLA'03 Workshop on Generative Techniques in the Context of Model-Driven Architecture*. Retrieved February 28, 2006, from http://www.softmetaware.com/oopsla.2003/mda-workshop.html

Evans, A., Sammut, P., & Willans, S. (Eds.). (2003). *Proceedings of Metamodeling for MDA Workshop*, York, UK. Retrieved February 28, 2006, from http://www.cs.york.uk/metamodel4mda/onlineProceedingsFinal.pdf

Favre, J. (2004). Towards a basic theory to model driven engineering. In M. Gogolla, P. Sammut, & J. Whittle (Eds.), *Proceedings of WISME 2004, 3rd Workshop on Software Model Engineering*. Retrieved February 28, 2006, from http://www.metamodel.com/wisme-2004

Favre, L. (2005a). Foundations for MDA-based forward engineering. *Journal of Object Technology (JOT), 4*(1),129-154.

Favre, L. (2005b). A rigorous framework for model-driven development. In T. Halpin, J. Krogstie, & K. Siau (Eds.), *Proceedings of CAISE'05 Workshops. EMMSAD '05 Tenth International Workshop on Exploring Modeling Method in System Analysis and Design* (pp. 505-516). Porto, Portugal: FEUP Editions.

Favre, L., Martinez, L., & Pereira, C. (2003). Forward engineering and UML: From UML static models to Eiffel code. In L. Favre (Ed.), *UML and the unified process* (pp. 199-217). Hershey, PA: IRM Press.

Favre, L., Martinez, L. & Pereira, C. (2005). Forward engineering of UML static models. In M. Khosrow-Pour (Ed.), *Encyclopedia of information science and technology* (pp. 1212-1217). Hershey, PA: Idea Group Reference.

Gogolla, M., Bohling, J., & Richters, M. (2005). Validating UML and OCL models in USE by automatic snapshot generation. *Journal on Software and System Modeling*. Retrieved from http://db.informatik.uni-bremen.de/publications

Gogolla, M., Lindow, A., Richters, M., & Ziemann, P. (2002). Metamodel transformation of data models. In J. Bézivin & R. France (Eds.), *Proceedings of UML 2002 Workshop in Software Model Engineering (WiSME 2002)*. Retrieved February 28, 2006, from http://www.metamodel.com/wisme-2002

Gogolla, M., Sammut, P., & Whittle, J. (Eds.). (2004). *Proceedings of WISME 2004, 3rd Workshop on Software Model Engineering*. Retrieved February 28, 2006, from http://www.metamodel.com/wisme-2004

Haussmann, J. (2003). Relations-relating metamodels. In A. Evans, P. Sammut, & J. Williams (Eds.), *Proceedings of Metamodeling for MDA. First International Workshop*. Retrieved February 28, 2006, from http://www.cs.uni-paderborn.de/cs/ag-engels/Papers/2004/MM4MDAhausmann.pdf

Hussmann, H., Cerioli, M., Reggio, G., & Tort, F. (1999). *Abstract data types and UML models* (Tech. Rep. No. DISI-TR-99-15). University of Genova, Italy.

Kim, S., & Carrington, D. (2002). A formal model of the UML metamodel: The UML state machine and its integrity constraints. In *Lecture Notes in Computer Science 2272* (pp. 477-496). Berlin: Springer-Verlag.

Kleppe, A., Warner, J., & Bast, W. (2003). *MDA explained. The model driven architecture: Practice and promise.* Boston: Addison Wesley Professional.

Kuske, S., Gogolla, M., Kollmann, R., & Kreowski, H. (2002, May). An integrated semantics for UML class, object and state diagrams based on graph transformation. In *Proceedings of the 3rd International Conference on Integrated Formal Methods (IFM'02)*,Turku, Finland. Berlin: Springer-Verlag.

Kuster, J., Sendall, S., & Wahler, M. (2004). Comparing two model transformation approaches. In J. Bézivin et al. (Eds.), *Proceedings of OCL&MDE'2004, OCL and Model Driven Engineering Workshop*, Lisbon, Portugal. Retrieved February 28, 2006, from http://www.cs.kent.ac.uk/projects/ocl/oclmdewsuml04

McUmber, W., & Cheng, B. (2001). A general framework for formalizing UML with formal languages. In *Proceedings of the IEEE International Conference on Software Engineering (ICSE01)*, Canada (pp. 433-442). IEEE Computer Society.

Padawitz, P. (2000). Swinging UML: How to make class diagrams and state machines amenable to constraint solving and proving. In A. Evans & S. Kent (Eds.), *Lecture Notes in Computer Science 1939* (pp. 265-277). Berlin: Springer-Verlag.

Reggio, G., Cerioli, M., & Astesiano, E. (2001). Towards a rigorous semantics of UML supporting its multiview approach. In *Proceedings of Fundamental Approaches to Software Engineering (FASE 2001)* (LNCS 2029, pp. 171-186). Berlin: Springer-Verlag.

Snook, C., & Butler, M. (2002). *Tool-supported use of UML for constructing B specifications.* Technical report, Department of Electronics and Computer Science, University of Southampton, UK.

Sunyé, G., Pollet, D., LeTraon, Y., & Jezequel, J-M. (2001). Refactoring UML models. In M. Gogolla & C. Kobryn (Eds.), *Lecture Notes in Computer Science 2185* (pp. 134-148). Berlin: Springer-Verlag.

ENDNOTE

[1] This work is partially supported by the Comisión de Investigaciones Científicas (CIC) de la Provincia de Buenos Aires in Argentina.

This work was previously published in Advanced Topics in Database Research, Volume 5, edited by K. Siau, pp. 1-27, copyright 2006 by IGI Publishing (an imprint of IGI Global).

Section 6
Appendices

Appendix A:
Platform Specific Metamodels and Language Metamodels

The following metamodels are partially described:

A.1: PSM-Eiffel Metamodel
A.2: PSM-Java Metamodel
A.3: ISM-Eiffel Metamodel
A.4: ISM-Java Metamodel
A.5: ISM-C++ Metamodel

Metamodels are specified by using the UML notation:

- **Abstract syntax:** It consists of one or more UML class diagrams that show the metaclasses defining constructs and relationships. The shaded metaclasses belong to the UML metamodel.
- **Metaclasses description:** Natural language is used to describe metaclasses, generalizations and associations. Constraints are specified in OCL. Metaclasses are listed in alphabetic order.

A.1 PSM METAMODEL: EIFFEL PLATFORM

Description of Metaclasses

AssociationEnd

Description
It represents the own association-ends of the class.

DOI: 10.4018/978-1-61520-649-0.ch015

Figure 1. PSM-Eiffel metamodel: Diagram of classes

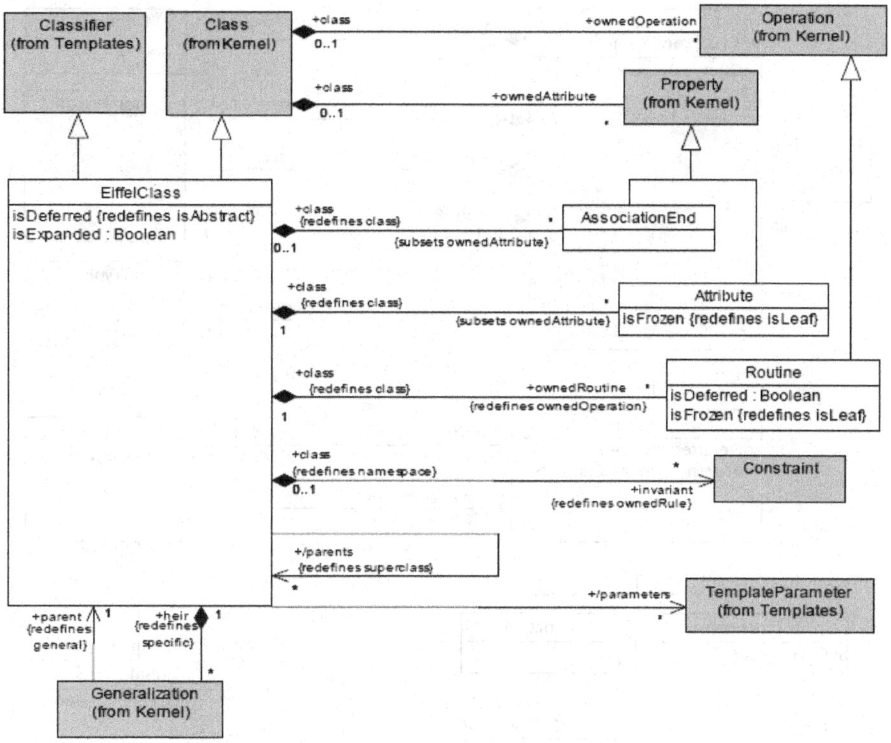

Generalization

- Property (from Kernel)

Attributes
No additional attributes

Associations

- class: EiffelClass [0..1] It refers to the class of which this association-end is part

Attribute

Description
It represents the attributes declared in a class Eiffel.

Generalization

- Property (from Kernel)

Figure 2. PSM-Eiffel metamodel: Diagram of operations

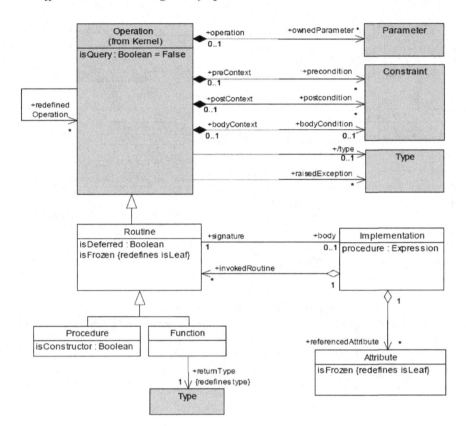

Attributes

- isFrozen: Boolean [1] It specifies whether an attribute is frozen, i.e., constant. In this case, it must have an initial value. It redefines RedefinableElement::isLeaf.

Associations

- class: EiffelClass [1] It refers to the class declaring this attribute. It redefines Property::class.

Constraints

[1]   An attribute is a property which is part of a class and but not member of any association. self.class -> size () = 1 and self.association-> isEmpty () and self.opposite-> isEmpty ()

EiffelClass

Description
An Eiffel class describes a set of objects which share the same specifications of features, restrictions and semantics.

Figure 3. PSM-Eiffel metamodel: Diagram of types (UML, OCL and Eiffel)

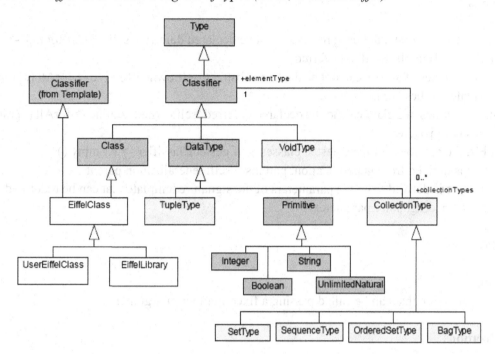

Generalizations

- Class (from Kernel), Classifier (from Templates).

Attributes

- isDeferred Boolean [1] It specifies whether a class is deferred, i.e., one or more features, that are specified but not implemented, are included in the class. It redefines Classifier::isAbstract.
- isExpanded: Boolean [1] It specifies whether the class is flattened, i.e., its instances are objects but no references to objects.

Associations

- associationEnd: AssociationEnd [*] It refers to the own association-ends of the class Eiffel. It is a subset of Class::ownedAttribute.
- attribute: Attribute [*] It refers to the own variables of the Eiffel class. It is a subset of Class::ownedAttribute.
- generalization: Generalization [*] It specifies generalizations.
- invariant: Constraint [*] It refers to class invariants. It redefines NameSpace::ownedRule.
- /parameters: TemplateParameter [*] It refers to the set of parameters of the class. It is derived.
- /parents: EiffelClass [*] It refers to supeclasses of an Eiffel class. It redefines Class::superclass. It is derived.
- routine: Routine [*] It refers the own operations of the class. It redefines Class::ownedOperation.

Constraints

[1]   A class, with at least a deferred routine, must be declared deferred. self.ownedRoutine -> exists (r | r.isDeferred) implies self. isDeferred

[2]   Private routines of a class can not be declared abstract. self.ownedRoutine -> forAll (r | r.visibility = #private implies not r.isAbstract)

[3]   Frozen routines of a class can not be declared deferred. self.ownedRoutine -> forAll (r | r.isFrozen implies not r.isDeferred)

[4]   An Eiffel class does not have nested classes. self.nestedClassifier -> isEmpty ()

[5]   parents is derived from generalization. parents = self.generalization.parent

[6]   parameters is derived from the parameters of the signature template that can be redefined. parameters = ownedSignature.parameter

Function

Description
It declares a function that can be called passing a fixed number of arguments.

Generalizations

•   Routine

Attributes
No additional attributes.

Associations

•   returnType: Type [1] It refers to the return type of the function. It redefines Operation::type.

Constraints

[1]   A function must have a return type and therefore, its set of arguments includes one argument whose type is return. self.ownedParameter -> select (p | p.direction = #return) -> size = 1

Implementation

Description
It specifies a procedure that realizes a routine.

Generalization

•   Element (from Kernel)

Attributes

- procedure: Expression [0..1] It refers to the procedure of the routine.

Associations

- invokedRoutine: Routine [*] It refers to the routines invoked in this implementation.
- referencedAttribute: Field [*] It specifies the variables referred in this implementation.
- signature: Routine [1] It refers to routine linked to this implementation.

Constraints

[1]   A routine can not call a constructor. self.invokedRoutine -> select (r | r.oclIsTypeOf (Procedure))
      -> forAll (p | not p.oclAsType (Procedure).isConstructor)

Procedure

Description
It declares a procedure that can be invoked by passing a fixed number of arguments.

Generalizations

- Routine

Attributes

- isConstructor: Boolean [1] It determines whether the procedure is constructor.

Associations
No additional associations.

Constraints

[1]   A procedure does not have a return type. self.ownedParameter -> select(p | p.direction = #return)
      -> isEmpty ()
[2]   The constructor of a class can not be abstract. self.isConstructor implies not self.isDeferred

Routine

Description
It specifies the characteristics of an Eiffel routine.

Generalizations

- Operation (from Kernel)

Attributes

- isDeferred: Boolean [1] It specifies whether a routine is deferred, i.e., without implementation.
- isFrozen: Boolean [1] It specifies whether a routine is final, i.e., it can not be redefined in a descendent class. It redefines RedefinableElement::isLeaf.

Associations

- body: Implementation [0..1] It refers to the routine implementation.
- class: EiffelClass [1] It refers to the class declaring this routine. It redefines Operation::class.

Constraints

[1] A deferred routine does not have implementations. self.isDeferred implies self.body -> isEmpty ()

A.2 PSM METAMODEL: JAVA PLATFORM

Description of Metaclasses

Next, we describe the main metaclasses of the PSM-Java

Figure 4. PSM-Java metamodel: Diagram of classes

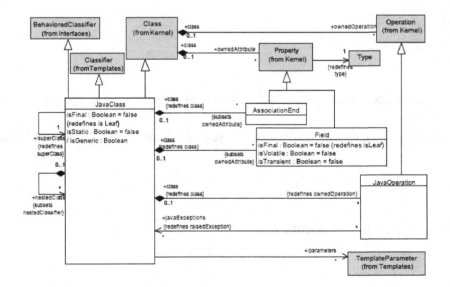

Figure 5. PSM-Java metamodel: Diagram of interfaces

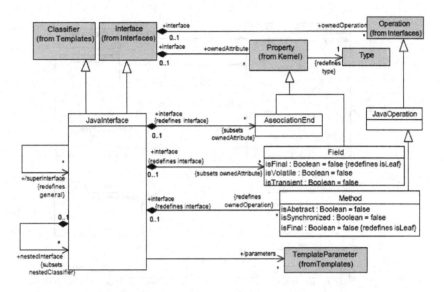

AssociationEnd

Description
It specifies the characteristics of an Eiffel routine.

Generalization

• Property (from Kernel)

Figure 6. PSM-Java metamodel: Diagram of classes and interfaces

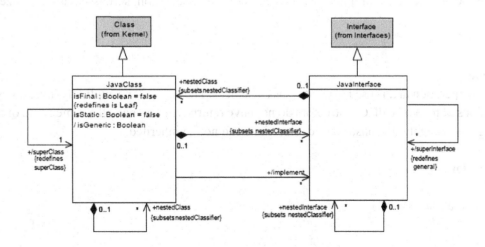

Figure 7. PSM-Java metamodel: Diagram of operations

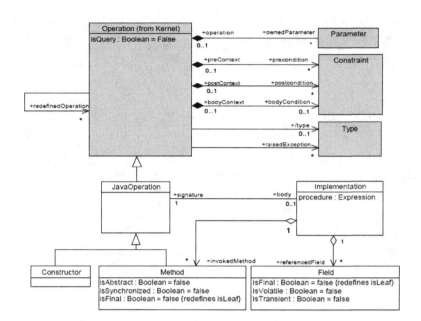

Attributes
No additional attributes.

Associations

- class: JavaClass [0..1] It refers to the class of which this association-end is part. It redefines Property::class.

Constraints

[1] An association-end is a property that is member of an association. self.association -> size () = 1

Constructor

Description
It designs an operation that is used to create class instances. They can not be explicitly invoked by means of expressions of method call. Constructors do not have return type and have the same name of the class containing the declaration. Constructor declarations can not be inherited.

Generalization

- JavaOperation

Figure 8. PSM-Java metamodel: Diagram of types (UML, OCL and Java)

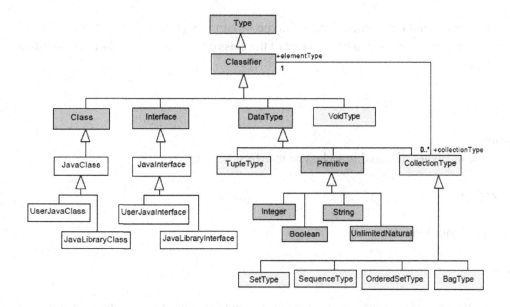

Attributes
No additional attributes.

Associations
No additional associations.

Figure 9. PSM-Java metamodel: Diagram of packages

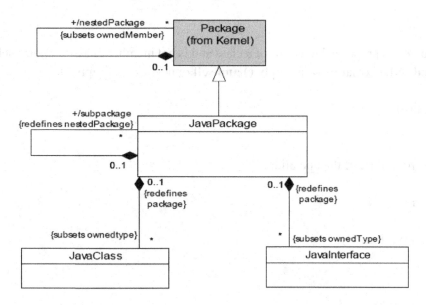

Constraints

[1]   Constructors do not have return type. self.type -> isEmpty ()

[2]   The constructor name is equal to the name of the class containing the declaration. self.name = self.class.name

Field

Description
It specifies the attributes declared in a class or interface.

Generalization

•   Property (from Kernel)

Attributes

•   isFinal: Boolean [1] It specifies whether an attribute is final, i.e., constant. In this case, it must have an initial value. It redefines *RedefinableElement::isLeaf.*

•   isTransient: Boolean [1] It specifies whether an attribute is part of the persistent state of the object.

•   isVolatile: Boolean [1] It specifies whether an attribute is volatile, i.e., it is accessed asynchronously.

Associations

•   class: JavaClass [0..1] It refers to the class declaring this attribute. It redefines Property::class.

Constraints

[1]   An attribute is a property that is part of a class and is not member of associations. self.class -> size () = 1 **and** self.association -> isEmpty () **and** self.opposite -> isEmpty ()

Implementation

Description
It specifies the procedure of the operation.

Generalization

•   Element (from Kernel)

Attributes

- Procedure: Expression [0..1] It refers to the procedure of the operation.

Associations

- invokedMethod: Method [*] It refers to the methods invoked in the body of an operation.
- referencedField: Field [*] It refers to the variables referred in the body of an operation.
- signature: JavaOperation [1] It specifies the operation that implements.

Constraints
No additional constraints.

JavaClass

Description
A Java class describes a set of objects sharing the same specifications of features, constraints and semantics.

Generalizations

- Class (from Kernel), Classifier (from Templates), BehavioredClassifier (from Interfaces)

Attributes

- isFinal: Boolean It specifies whether the class can have subclasses. It redefines *RedefinableElement::isLeaf.*
- /isGeneric: Boolean It specifies whether the class is generic. It is a derived attribute.
- isStatic: Boolean It specifies whether the class is static.

Associations

- associationEnd: AssociationEnd [*] It refers to the own association-end of the Java class. It is subset of *Class::ownedAttribute*
- field: Field [*] It refers to own variables of the Java class. It is a subset of *Class::ownedAttribute*
- /implement: JavaInterface [*] It refers to the Java interfaces implemented by this class. It is derived.
- javaOperation: JavaOperation [*] It refers the own operations of the class. It redefines *Class::ownedOperation*
- javaPackage: JavaPackage [0..1] It refers to the package in which it is declared. It redefines *Type::package.*
- nestedClass: JavaClass [*] It refers to the Java classes declared within of the body of a JavaClass (nested classes).

- nestedInterface: JavaInterface [*] It refers to the Java interfaces declared within the body of a JavaClass (nested interfaces). It is a subset of *Class::nestedClassifier.*
- /parameters: TemplateParameter [*] It refers the set of parameters of the class. It is derived.
- /superClass: JavaClass [1] It refers to the superclass of a Java class. It redefines *Class::superclass.* It is derived.

Constraints

[1] Nested classifiers of a class or interface can only be of the type JavaClass or JavaInterface. self. nestedClassifier -> forAll (c | c.oclIsTypeOf (JavaClass) **or** c.oclIsTypeOf (JavaInterface))

[2] The implemented interfaces are those referred through the interface realization. implement = self. interfaceRealization.contract

[3] A class having at least an abstract method must be declared abstract. self.javaOperation -> select (op | op.oclIsTypeOf (Method)) -> exists (m | m.oclAsType(Method).isAbstract) **implies** self. isAbstract

[4] A class that is declared abstract does not have a constructor explicitly defined. self.isAbstract **implies** self.javaOperation -> select (op | op.oclIsTypeOf (Constructor)) -> isEmpty ()

[5] A class that is declared final does not have subclasses, i.e., it is not superclass of any class. self. isFinal **implies** self.javaPackage.ownedMember -> select (m | m.oclIsTypeOf (JavaClass)) -> forAll (c | c.oclAsType (JavaClass).superClass <> self)

[6] The access level protected, private and static can be only applied to nested classes, i.e., declared within the declaration of another class. (self.visibility = #protected **or** self.visibility = #private **or** self.isStatic) **implies** self.javaPackage.ownedMember -> select (m | m.oclIsTypeOf (JavaClass)) -> exists (c | c.oclAsType (JavaClass).nestedClass -> includes (self))

[7] Private methods of a class can not be declared abstract. self.javaOperation -> select (op | op.oclIsTypeOf(Method)) -> forAll (m | m.visibility = #private **implies not** m.oclAsType (Method). isAbstract)

[8] Static methods of a class can not be declared abstract. self.javaOperation -> select (op | op.oclIsTypeOf (Method)) -> forAll (m | m.isStatic **implies not** m.oclAsType (Method).isAbstract)

[9] A method that isFinal can not be declared abstract. self.javaOperation -> select (op | op.oclIsTypeOf (Method)) -> forAll (m | m.oclAsType(Method).isFinal **implies not** m.oclAsType (Method). isAbstract)

[10] A class is generic if has a template signature. isGeneric = (self.ownedTemplateSignature -> size () =1)

[11] *parameters* is derived starting from of the parameters of the template signature. /parameters = self. ownedTemplateSignature.parameter

JavaInterface

Description

It describes the characteristics of the interfaces in the Java platform.

Generalizations

• Interface (from Interfaces), Classifier (from Templates)

Attributes
No additional attributes.

Associations

• associationEnd: AssociationEnd [*] It refers the own association-ends of a JavaInterface. It is a subset of *Interface::ownedAttribute.*
• field: Field [*] It refers to the own fields of a JavaInterface. It is a subset of *Interface::ownedAttribute.*
• javaPackage: JavaPackage [0..1] It refers to the package in which it is declared. It redefines *Type::package.*
• method: Method [*] It refers to the own methods of a JavaInterface. It redefines *Interface::ownedOperation.*
• nestedClass: It refers to the classes that are declared within the body of a JavaInterface (nested classes). It is a subset of *Interface::nestedClassifer.*
• nestedInterface: JavaInterface [*] It refers to the interfaces that are declared within the body of a JavaInterface (nested interfaces). It is a subset of *Interface::nestedClassifer.*
• /superInterface: JavaInterface [*] It refers to the super-interfaces of a JavaInterface. It is derived. It redefines *Classifier::general.*

Constraints

[1] The Java interfaces are implicitly abstract. self.isAbstract
[2] The own member of an interface are implicitly public. self.ownerMember -> forAll (m | m.visibility = #public)
[3] Nested classifiers of an interface can only be of the type JavaClass or JavaInterface. self.nestedClassifier -> forAll (c | c.oclIsTypeOf (JavaClass) **or** c.oclIsTypeOf (JavaInterface))
[4] An interface can only be declared private or protected if it is directly nested in the class declaration. (self.visibility = #protected **or** self.visibility = #private) **implies** self.package.ownedMember -> select (m | m.oclIsTypeOf (JavaClass)) -> exists (c | c.oclAsType (JavaClass).nestedInterface -> includes (self))
[5] An interface can only be declared static if it is directly nested in the class or interface declaration. self.isStatic **implies** self.package.ownedMember -> select (m | m.oclIsTypeOf (JavaClass)) -> exists (c | c.oclAsType (JavaClass).nestedInterface -> includes (self)) **or** self.package.ownedMember -> select (m | m.oclIsTypeOf (JavaInterface)) -> exists (i | i.oclAsType (JavaInterface).nestedInterface -> includes (self))
[6] Methods that are declared in an interface are abstract and hence do not have implementations. self.method ->forAll (m| m.isAbstract **and** m.body -> isEmpty ())
[7] Methods of an interface can not be declared static. self.method -> forAll (m| **not** m.isStatic)

[8] Methods of an interface can not be synchronized. self.method -> forAll (m| **not** m.isSynchronized)

[9] Fields of an interface are implicitly public, static or final. self.field ->forAll (f| f.visibility = #public **and** f.isStatic **and** f.isFinal)

[10] superInterface is derived of the generalization. /superInterface = self.generalization.general

[11] *Parameters* are derived from the parameters of the template signature. /parameters = self.ownedTemplateSignature.parameter

JavaOperation

Description

It describes the characteristics of the interfaces in the Java platform.

Generalization

- Operation (from Kernel, from Interfaces)

Attributes

No additional attributes.

Associations

- class: JavaClass [0..1] It refers to the class declaring the operation. It redefines *Operation::class*.
- body: Implementation [0..1] It refers to the implementation of the operation.
- javaException: JavaClass [*] It refers to the types that represent the exceptions that can appear during an invocation of this operation.

Constraints

[1] An abstract operation does not have implementation. self.isAbstract **implies** self.body -> isEmpty ()

JavaPackage

Description

It is used for grouping elements. Its members can be classes, interfaces or sub-packages.

Generalization

- Package (from Kernel)

Attributes

No additional attributes.

Associations

- javaClass: JavaClass [*] It refers to classes that are members of this package. It is a subset of *Package::ownedType*.
- javaInterface: JavaInterface [*] It refers to all interfaces that are members of this package. It is a subset of *Package::ownedType*.
- /subpackage: Package [*] It refers to the packages that are members of this package. It is derived.

Constraints

No additional constraints.

Method

Description

It declares an operation that can be invoked by passing a fixed number of the arguments.

Generalizations

- JavaOperation

Attributes

- isAbstract: Boolean [1] It specifies whether a method is abstract, i.e., it does not have implementation.
- isFinal: Bolean It specifies whether a method is final. In this case, it can not be overwritten in a derived class. It redefines *RedefinableElement::isLeaf*.
- isSyncronized: Boolean [1] It specifies whether a method is synchronized. It is true if acquires a lock before execution.

Associations

- interface: JavaInterface [0..1] It declares the interface that declares this method. It redefines *Operation::interface*.

Constraints

No additional restrictions.

A.3 ISM METAMODEL: EIFFEL LANGUAGE

Description of Metaclasses

Attribute

Description
It represents the attributes that are declared in a class, according to the specification of the Eiffel language.

Generalization

• Property (from Kernel).

Attributes

• isConstant: Boolean [1] It specifies whether an attribute is constant. In this case it must have a compulsory initial value.

Associations

• class: EiffelClass [1] It refers to the class that declares this attribute. It redefines *Property::class.*
• type: EiffelClass [1] It refers to the type of this attribute. It redefines *TypedElement::type*.

Constraints

[1] An attribute is a property that is part of a class and is not member of associations. self.class -> size () = 1 **and** self.association -> isEmpty () **and** self.opposite -> isEmpty ()

Assertion

Description
It describes assertions, according to the specification of the Eiffel language.

Generalization

• Constraint (from Kernel)

Attributes

• Tag_Mark: Identifier [0..1] It refers to the identifier of the assertion. It redefines *NamedElement::name*.

Figure 10. ISM-Eiffel metamodel: Diagram of classes

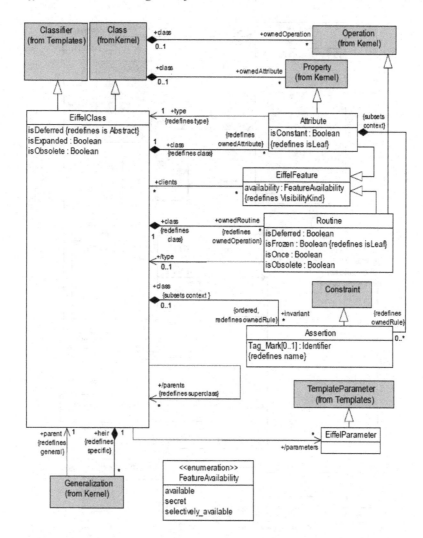

Associations

- class [0..1]: EiffelClass It refers to the class that is the context in which this restriction is evaluated. It is a subset of *Constraint::context*.
- routine [0..1]: Routine It refers to the routine that is the context in which this restriction is evaluated. It is a subset of *Constraint::context*.

Constraints

No additional restrictions.

Figure 11. ISM-Eiffel metamodel: Diagram of operations

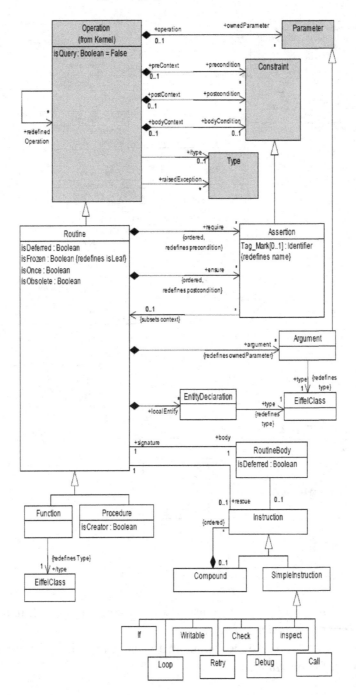

Argument

Description
It describes the arguments of a routine.

Figure 12. ISM-Eiffel metamodel: Diagram of types

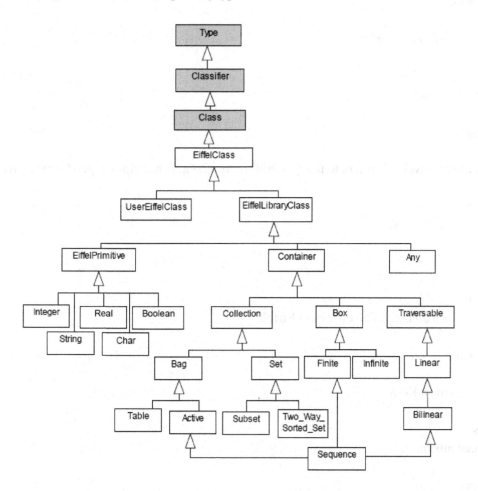

Figure 13. ISM-Eiffel metamodel: Diagram of clusters

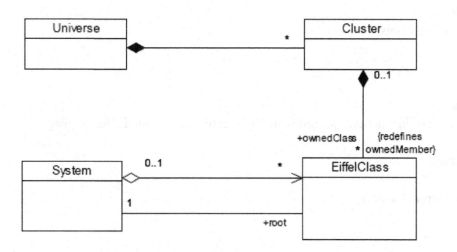

Generalization

- Parameter (from Kernel)

Attributes
No additional attributes.

Associations

- type: EiffelClass [1] It refers to the type of this argument. It redefines *TypedElement::type*.

Constraints
No additional constraints.

Cluster

Description
It is used to group and organize classes in Eiffel.

Generalization

- Package (from Kernel)

Attributes
No additional attributes.

Associations

- ownedClass: EiffelClass [*] It refers to Eiffel classes that are members of this cluster. It redefines *Package::ownedType*.

Constraints
No additional constraints.

Compound

Description
It describes a set of instructions, according to the specification of the Eiffel language.

Generalization

- Element (from Kernel)

Attributes

No additional attributes.

Associations

- instruction: Instruction [*] It specifies the set of instructions that forms the compound. It is ordered.

Constraints

No additional constraints.

EntityDeclaration

Description

It describes a local entity of a routine, according to the specification of the Eiffel language.

Generalization

- TypedElement (from Kernel)

Attributes

No additional attributes.

Associations

- type [1]: EiffelClass It specifies the type of the entity. It redefines *TypedElement::type*.

Constraints

No additional constraints.

EiffelClass

Description

An Eiffel class describes a set of objects sharing the same feature specifications, restrictions and semantics.

Generalizations

- Class (from Kernel), Classifier (from Templates)

Attributes

- isDeferred: Boolean [1] It specifies whether a class is deferred, i.e., it includes one or more features that are specified but no implemented. It redefines *Classifier::isAbstract*.

- isExpanded: Boolean [1] It specifies whether the class is flattened, i.e. its instances are objects but no references to objects.
- isObsolete: Boolean [1] It specifies whether the class is obsolete.

Associations

- attribute: Attribute [*] It refers to the own attributes of the Eiffel class. It redefines *Class::ownedAttribute*.
- eiffelFeatures: EiffelFeature [*] It refers the features of which this class is client.
- generalization: Generalization [*] It specifies the generalization for this class.
- invariant: Assertion [*] It refers to invariants of the class. It redefines *NameSpace::ownedRule*.
- ownedRoutine: Routine [*] It refers to the own routines of the class. It redefines *Class::ownedOperation*.
- /parameters: EiffelParameter [*] It refers to the set of parameters of the class. It is derived.
- /parent: EiffelClass [*] It refers to the parent class of an Eiffel class. It redefines *Class::superClass*. It is derived.

Constraints

[1] A class having a deferred routine must be declared deferred. self.ownedRoutine -> exists (r | r.isDeferred) **implies** self. isDeferred

[2] Secret routines can not be declared deferred. self.ownedRoutine -> forAll (r | r.availability = #secret **implies not** r.isDeferred)

[3] Frozen routines of a class can not be declared deferred. self.ownedRoutine -> forAll (r | r.isFrozen **implies not** r.isDeferred)

[4] An Eiffel class has not nested classes. self.nestedClassifier -> isEmpty ()

[5] *ancestors* is derived of the generalization. ancestors = self.generalization.parent

[6] *parameters* is derived from the parameters of the template signature that can be redefined. parameters = ownedSignature.parameter

[7] Parameters of a class are of the type Eiffel class. self.parameters.parameteredElement -> forAll (p | p.oclIsTypeOf (EiffelClass))

[8] A deferred class has not creation procedure. self.class.isDeferred **implies** self.ownedRoutine -> select (p | p.oclIsTypOf (Procedure) **and** p.isCreator) -> isEmpty ()

[9] A flattened class has only a creation procedure without arguments. self.class.isExpanded **implies** self. ownedRoutine -> select (p | p.oclIsTypeOf (Procedure) **and** p.isCreator) -> size () = 1 and self. ownedRoutine -> select (p | p.isCreator and p.argument -> isEmpty ()) -> size () = 1

[10] A flattened class does not have parameters. self.class.isExpanded **implies** self.parameter -> isEmpty ()

EiffelParameter

Description
It specifies the parameters of a class, according to the specification of the Eiffel language.

Generalizations

•   TemplateParameter (from Templates)

Attributes
No additional attributes.

Associations
No additional associations.

Constraints

[1]   The type of the parameters of a class is EiffelClass. self.parameteredElement -> forAll (p |
       p.oclIsTypeOf (EiffelClass))

EiffelFeature

Description
It declares a feature, according to the specification of the Eiffel language.

Generalizations

•   NamedElement

Attributes

•   availability: FeatureAvailability [1] It refers to the availability of the feature. It redefines
     NamedElement::visibility.

Associations

•   clients: EiffelClass[*] It refers to the classes for which this feature is available.

Constraints

[1]   If the feature is selectively available, then it must be associated to a list of clients, else the list of
       clients is empty. **if** self.availability = #selectively_available **then** self.client -> size () > 0 else self.
       client -> isEmpty() endif

FeatureAvailability

Description
FeatureAvailability is an enumeration of the following values:

- available
- secret
- selectively available

which determine whether a feature is available in all classes, some classes or no classes.

Generalizations

- None

Function

Description
It declares a function, according the specification of the Eiffel language.

Generalizations

- Routine

Attributes
No additional attributes.

Associations

- /type: EiffelClass[1] It refers to the return type of the function. It redefines *TypedElement::type*.

Constraints
No additional restrictions.

Instruction

Description
It describes an instruction, according to the specification of the Eiffel language.

Generalizations

- NamedElement (from Kernel)

Attributes
No additional attributes.

Associations

- routineBody: RoutineBody It refers to the body of the routine of which this instruction forms a part.

- routine: Routine It refers to the routine that declares the clause rescue of which this instruction is a part.

Constraints

No additional constraints.

Routinebody

Description

It specifies the body of the routine, according to the specification of the Eiffel language.

Generalization

- Element (from Kernel)

Attributes

- is Deferred: Boolean It specifies whether the body is deferred, i.e., it is not implemented.

Associations

- signature: Routine [1] It refers to the routine to which corresponds this implementation.
- instruction: Instruction [0..1] It refers to the instruction that composes the body of the routine.

Constraints

[1]   If the body if the routine is deferred, then the routine declaring it is also deferred. self.isDeferred **implies** self.signature.isDeferred

Procedure

Description

It declares a procedure, according the specification of the Eiffel language.

Generalizations

- Routine

Attributes

- isCreator: Boolean [1] It determines whether the procedure is the creation.

Associations

No additional associations.

Constraints

[1]   A procedure does not have a return type. self.ownedParameter -> select (p | p.direction = #return) -> isEmpty ()

[2]   If a procedure is a creation procedure then it can not be deferred. self.isCreator **implies not** self.isDeferred

Routine

Description

It specifies the features of a routine Eiffel.

Generalizations

* Operation (from Kernel), Feature

Attributes

* isDeferred: Boolean [1] It specifies whether a routine is deferred, i.e., it does not have implementation.
* isFrozen: Boolean [1] It specifies whether a routine is final, i.e., it can not be redefined in a descendent class. It redefines *RedefinableElement::isLeaf*
* isOnce: Boolean [1] It specifies whether the routine is executed only a time.
* isObsolete: Boolean [1] It specifies whether the routine is obsolete.

Associations

* argument: Argument [*] It refers to the formal arguments of the routine. It redefines *Operation::OwnedParameter*.
* body: RoutineBody [1] It refers to the implementation of the routine.
* class: EiffelClass [1] It refers to a class that declares this routine. It redefines *Operation::class*.
* ensure: Assertion [*] It specifies the postconditions of the routine. It redefines *Operation::postcondition*.
* localEntity: EntityDeclaration [*] It specifies the local entities of the routine.
* require: Assertion [*] It specifies the preconditions of the routine. It redefines *Operation::precondition*.
* rescue: Instruction [0..1] It specifies that the answer to an exception occurs during the execution of the routine.

Constraints

[1]   If a routine is deferred then it does not have implementation. self.isDeferred **implies** self.body->isEmpty ()

[2]   If a routine is frozen, then it can not be deferred. self.isFrozen **implies** self.isDeferred

Simple Instruction

Description

It describes a simple instruction, according to the specification of the Eiffel language.

Generalizations

* NamedElement (from Kernel)

Attributes

No additional attributes.

Associations

No additional associations.

Constraint

No additional restrictions.

A.4 ISM METAMODEL: JAVA LANGUAGE

Description of Metaclasses

Block

Description

It specifies the code block implementing an operation, according to the specification of the Java language.

Generalizations

* Action (from Action)

Attributes

No additional attributes

Associations

* blockStatement: blockStatement [0..1] It refers to the statements of which this block is part.
* implementation: Implementation [1] It refers to the implementation of which this block is part.

Figure 14. ISM-Java metamodel: Diagram of classes

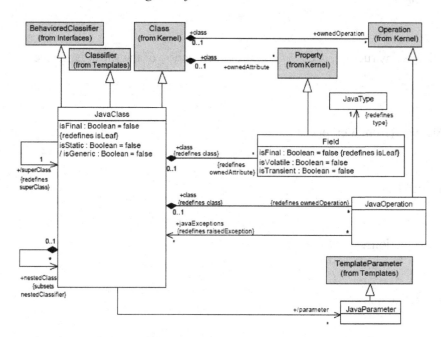

Figure 15. ISM-Java metamodel: Diagram of interfaces

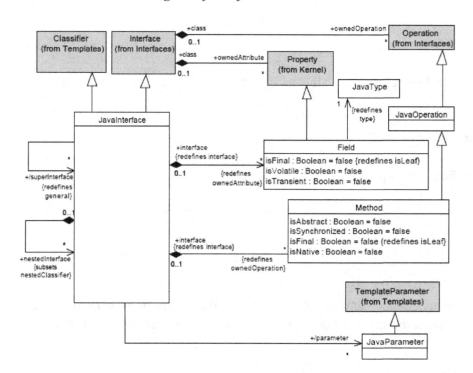

Figure 16. ISM-Java metamodel: Diagram of classes and interfaces

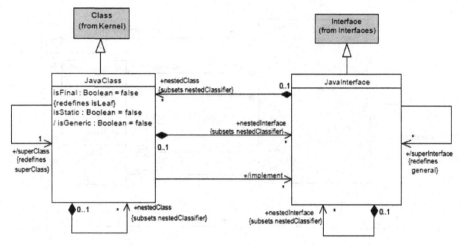

Constraints
No additional constraints.

Constructor

Description
It is a constructor, according to the definition in the Java language.

Generalization

•   JavaOperation

Attributes
No additional attributes.

Associations
No additional associations.

Constraints

[1]   A constructor does not have a return type. self.returnType -> isEmpty ()
[2]   The constructor name is equal to the class name including the declaration. self.name = self.class.
      name

Field

Description
It represents an attribute, as is defined in the Java language.

Figure 17. ISM-Java metamodel: Diagram of operations

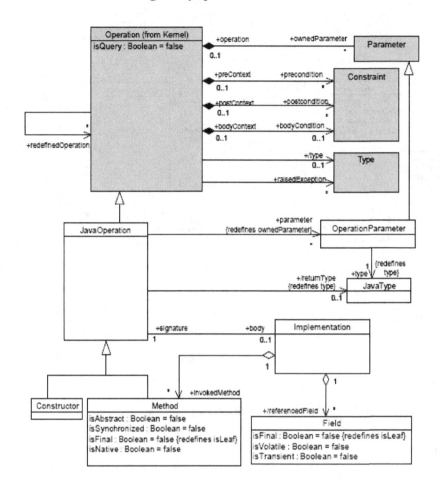

Generalization

- Property (from Kernel)

Attributes

- isFinal: Boolean [1] It specifies whether an attribute is final, i.e., constant. If an attribute is final, then it must have an initial value.
- isTransient: Boolean [1] It specifies whether an attribute is part of the persistent state of the object.
- isVolatile: Boolean [1] It specifies whether an attribute is volatile, i.e., it is accessed non-synchronically.

Figure 18. ISM-Java metamodel: Diagram of implementations

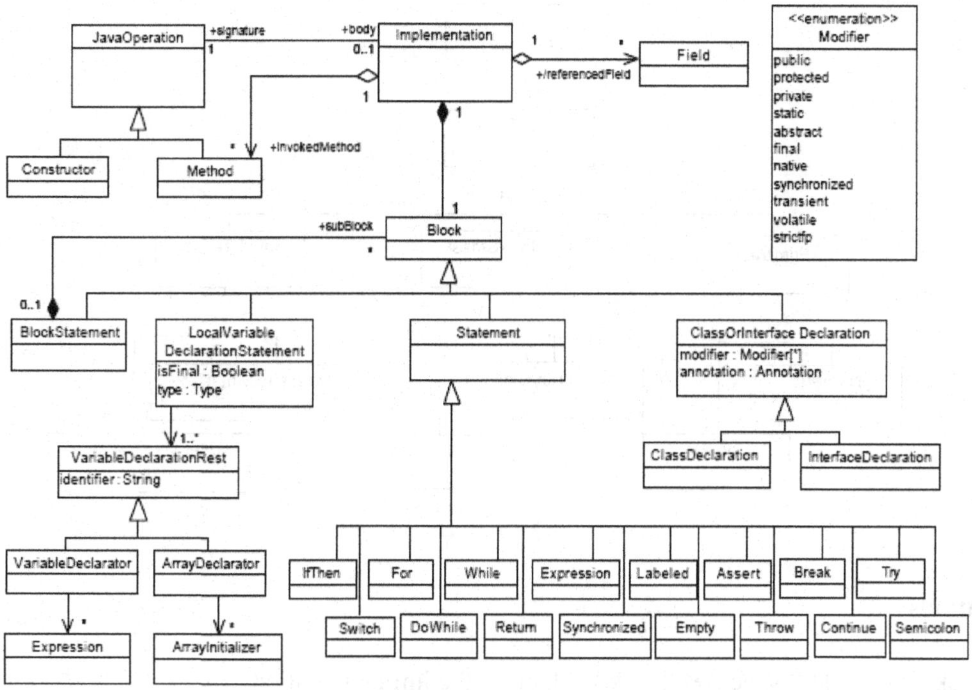

Associations

- class: JavaClass [0..1] It refers to the class declaring this attribute. It redefines *Property::class*.
- javaType: JavaType [1] It refers to the attribute type. It redefines *TypedElement::type*.

Constraints

[1]   An attribute is a property that is a part of a class and is not member of associations. self.class -> size () = 1 **and** self.association -> isEmpty () **and** self.opposite -> isEmpty ()

Implementation

Description
It specifies a procedure that obtains the result of the operation.

Generalization

- Element (from Kernel)

Attributes
No additional attributes.

Figure 19. ISM-Java metamodel: Diagram of types

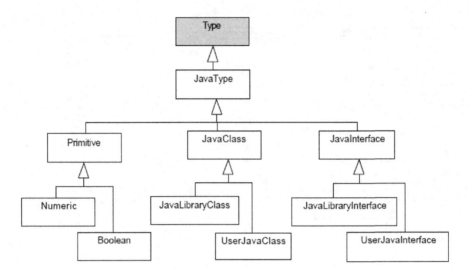

Associations

- block: Block [1] It specifies the code block of the implementation.
- invokedMethod: Method [*] It refers to the methods invoked in the body of an operation.
- referencedField: Field [*] It refers to the variables referred in the body of an operation.
- signature: JavaOperation [1] It specifies the operation signature

Constraints
No additional constraints.

JavaClass

Description
A Java class as is defined in the Java language.

Generalizations

- Class (from Kernel), Classifier (from Templates), BehavioredClassifier (from Interfaces)

Attributes

- isFinal: Boolean It specifies whether the class can have subclasses. It redefines *RedefinableElement::isLeaf.*
- /isGeneric: Boolean It specifies whether the class is generic. It is a derived attribute.
- isStatic: Boolean It specifies whether the class is static.

Figure 20. ISM - Java Metamodel: Diagram of packages

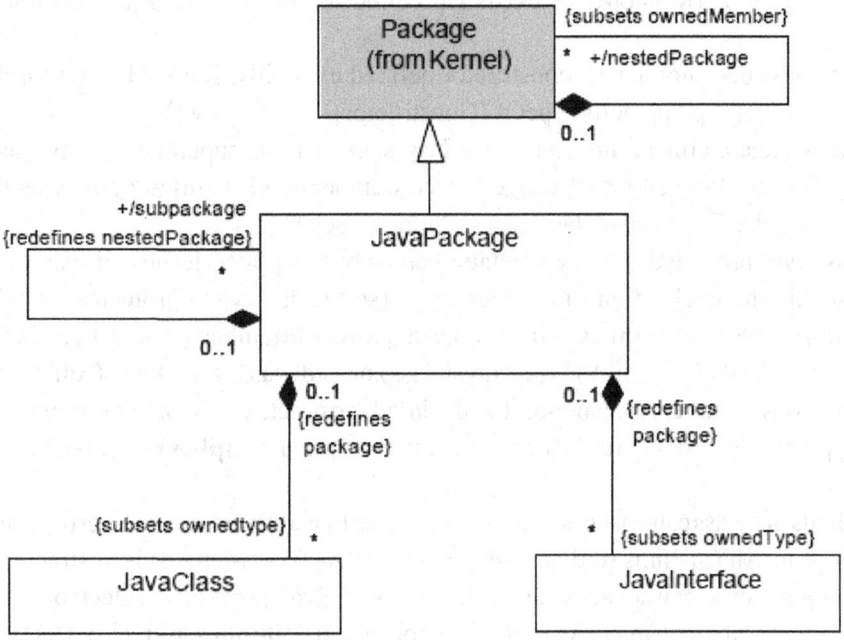

Associations

- field: Field [*] It refers to the own variables of the Java class. It redefines *Class::ownedAttribute*.
- /implement: It refers to the Java interfaces that are implemented by this class. It is derived.
- javaOperation: JavaOperation [*] It refers the own operations of the class. It redefines *Class::ownedOperation*.
- javaPackage: JavaPackage [0..1] It refers to the package in which is declared. It redefines *Type::package*.
- nestedClass: JavaClass [*] It refers to the Java classes that are declared within the body of a Java class (nested classes). It is a subset of *Class::nestedClassifier*.
- nestedInterface: JavaInterface [*] It refers to the Java interfaces that are declared within the body of a JavaClass (nested interfaces). It is a subset of *Class::nestedClassifier*.
- /parameters: JavaParametes [*] It refers to the set of parameters of a class. It is derived.
- /superClass: JavaClass [1] It refers to a superclass of a Java class. It redefines *Class::superClass*. It is derived.

Constraints

[1]   Nested classifiers belonging to a class or interface can only be of type JavaClass or JavaInterface. self. nestedClassifier -> forAll (c | c.oclIsTypeOf (JavaClass) **or** c.oclIsTypeOf (JavaInterface))

[2]   The implemented interfaces are those referred through the interface realization. implement = self. interfaceRealization.contract

[3] A class that has at least one abstract method must be declared abstract. self.javaOperation -> select (op | op.oclIsTypeOf (Method)) -> exists (m | m.oclAsType (Method).isAbstract) **implies** self. isAbstract)

[4] An abstract class does not have a constructor defined explicitly. self.isAbstract **implies** self.java-Operation -> select (op | op.oclIsTypeOf (Constructor)) -> isEmpty ()

[5] A class that is declared final cannot have subclasses, i.e., it is not superclass of any class in the package. self.isFinal **implies** self.javaPackage.ownedMember -> select (m | m.oclIsTypeOf(JavaClass)) -> forAll (c| c.oclAsType (JavaClass).superClass < > self)

[6] The access level protected, private or static can only be applied to nested classes, i.e., that are declared within the declaration of another class. (self.visibility = #protected **or** self.visibility = #private **or** self.isStatic) **implies** self.javaPackage.ownedMember -> select (m | m.oclIsTypeOf (JavaClass)) -> exists (c | c.oclAsType (JavaClass).nestedClass -> includes(self))

[7] Private methods of a class can not be declared abstract. self.javaOperation -> select (op | op.oclIsTypeOf(Method)) -> forAll (m | m.visibility = #private **implies not** m.oclAsType (Method). isAbstract)

[8] Static methods of a class can not be declared abstract. self.javaOperation -> select (op | op.oclIsTypeOf (Method)) -> forAll (m | m.isStatic **implies not** m.oclAsType(Method).isAbstract)

[9] Final methods of a class can not be declared abstract. self.javaOperation -> select (op | op.oclIsTypeOf (Method)) -> forAll (m | m.oclAsType (Method).isFinal **implies not** m.oclAsType (Method). isAbstract)

[10] A class is generic if it has a signature template. isGeneric = (self.ownedTemplateSignature -> size () =1)

[11] *Parameters* are derived through the parameters of the signature template. /parameters= self. ownedTemplateSignature.parameter

[12] A class is concrete, if its methods have associated an implementation. **not** self.isAbstract **implies** self.allMethod () -> forAll (m | self.allBody () -> exist (b | b.signature = m))

[13] Elements, that can be actual parameters of a formal parameter, are of type Java types. self.parameters.parameteredElement -> forAll (p | p.oclIsTypeOf (JavaType))

Additional Operations

[1] allMethod is the set of all methods, i.e., the methods that are own, inherited and the methods of the interfaces implemented. allMethod (): Set(Method) allMethod () = self.allClassMethod() -> union(self.implement.allInterfaceMethod()) allClassMethod(): Set(Method) allClassMethod () = self.javaOperation -> select (o | o.oclIsType(Method)) -> union (self.superClass.allClassMethod ()) allInterfaceMethod (): Set (Method) allInterfaceMethod () = self.method -> union(self.superInterface.allInterfaceMethod())

[2] *allBody* is the set of all method implementations of a class, i.e., both own and inherited. allBody (): Set (Implementation) allBody = self.allMethod ().body

JavaInterface

Description
It describes the characteristics of an interface according to the Java language.

Generalizations

• Interface (from Interfaces), Classifier (from Templates).

Attributes

No additional attributes.

Associations

• field: Field [*] It refers to the own fields of a JavaInterface. It redefines *Interface::ownedAttribute*.

• javaPackage: JavaPackage [0..1] It refers to the package in which is declared. It is subset of *Type::package*.

• method: Method [*] It refers to the own methods of a JavaInterface. It redefines *Interface::ownedOperation*.

• nestedClass: JavaClass [*] It refers to the classes that are declared within the body of a JavaInterface (nested classes). It is a subset of *Interface::nestedClassifer*.

• nestedInterface: JavaInterface [*] It refers all interfaces that are declared within the body of a JavaInterface (nested interfaces). It is a subset of *Interface::nestedClassifer*.

• /parameter: JavaParameter [1] It refers to the set of parameters of an interface. It is derived.

• /superInterface: JavaInterface [*] It refers to the superinterfaces of a JavaInterface. It is derived. It redefines *Classifier::general*

Constraints

[1] Interfaces are implicitly abstract. self.isAbstract

[2] The own members of an interface are implicitly public. self.ownerMember -> forAll (m | m.visibility = #public)

[3] Nested classifiers of an interface can only be of the type JavaClass or JavaInterface. self.nested-Classifier -> forAll (c | c.oclIsTypeOf (JavaClass) **or** c.oclIsTypeOf (JavaInterface))

[4] An interface that is directly nested in the class declaration can only be declared private or protected. (self.visibility = #protected **or** self.visibility = #private) **implies** self.package.ownedMember -> select (m | m.oclIsTypeOf (JavaClass)) -> exists (c | c.oclAsType(JavaClass).nestedInterface -> includes (self))

[5] An interface that in the class or interface declaration is nested can only be declared static. self. isStatic **implies** self.package.ownedMember -> select (m | m.oclIsTypeOf (JavaClass)) -> exists (c | c.oclAsType(JavaClass).nestedInterface -> includes (self)) **or** self.package.ownedMember -> select (m | m.oclIsTypeOf (JavaInterface)) -> exists (I | i.oclAsType (JavaInterface).nestedInterface -> includes (self))

[6] Methods that are declared in an interface are abstract and hence do not have implementation. self.method -> forAll (m| m.isAbstract **and** m.body -> isEmpty ())

[7] Methods of an interface can not be declared static. self.method -> forAll (m| **not** m.isStatic)

[8] Methods of an interface can not be synchronized. self.method -> forAll (m| **not** m.isSynchronized)

[9] Fields of an interface are implicitly public, static or final. self.field -> forAll (f| f.visibility = #public **and** f.isStatic **and** f.siFinal)

[10] superInterface is derived of the generalization. /superInterface = self.generalization.general

[11] *parameters* are derived through the parameters of the signature template. /parameters = self. ownedTemplateSignature.parameter

[12] Elements that can be actual parameters of a formal parameter are types of Java. self.parameters. parameteredElement -> forAll (p | p.oclIsTypeOf (JavaType))

JavaOperation

Description

It describes a method according to the specification of the Java language.

Generalizations

• Operation (from Kernel)

Associations

• body: Implementation [0..1] It refers to the implementation of the operation.
• class: JavaClass [0..1] It refers to the class that implements this operation. It redefines *Operation::class*.
• javaExceptions: JavaClass [*] It refers to the types representing the exceptions that can occur during an invocation of this operation. It redefines *Operation::raisedException*.
• parameter: OperationParameter [*] It specifies the parameter of the operation. It redefines *Operation::ownedParameter*
• /returnType: JavaType [0..1] It specifies the return type of the operation. It redefines *Operation::type*. It is derived.

Constraints

[1] An abstract operation does not have implementation. self.isAbstract **implies** self.body -> isEmpty ()

JavaPackage

Description

It is a package as is defined in the Java language.

Generalizations

• Package (from Kernel)

Attributes

No additional attributes.

Associations

- javaClass: JavaClas s [*] It refers to the classes that are members of this package. It is a subset of *Package::ownedType.*
- javaInterface: JavaInterface [*] It refers to the interfaces that are members of this package. It is a subset of *Package::ownedType.*
- /subpackage: JavaPackage [*] It refers to the packages that are members of this package. It redefines *Package::nestedPackage*. It is derived.

Constraints

[1]   Members of a package can only be classes, interfaces or sub-packages. self.ownedMember -> forAll (m | m.oclIsTypeOf (JavaInterface) **or** m.oclIsTypeOf (JavaClass) **or** m.oclIsTypeOf (JavaPackage))

Method

Description

It describes a method according to its definition in Java language.

Generalizations

- JavaOperation

Attributes

- isAbstract: Boolean [1] It specifies whether a method is abstract, i.e., without implementation.
- isFinal: Boolean [1] It specifies whether a method is final. In this case, it can not be overwritten in a derived class. It redefines *RedefinableElement::isLeaf.*
- isNative: Boolean [1] It specifies whether a method is native.
- isSyncronized: Boolean [1] It specifies whether a method is synchronized. It is true if acquires a lock before execution.

Associations

- interface: JavaInterface [0..1] It declares the interface declaring this method. It redefines *Operation::interface*.

Constraints

[1]   A native method can not be abstract. self.isNative **implies not** self.isAbstract

[2] If a method has a return type then it must have a return statement. self.type -> size () = 1 **implies** self. body.block.oclIsTypeOf(Return) **or** self.body.block.oclIsKindOf(BlockStatement) **and** self.body. block.allStatement() -> exists (sent | sent.oclIsTypeOf(Return))

Additional operations

[1] allStatement is the set of all statements that conforms the body of the method. allStatement(): Set(Statement) allStatement() = self.subBlock -> union (self.subBlock.allStatement ())

OperationParameter

Description
It specifies the parameters of an operation according to the specification of the Java language.

Generalization

- Parameter (from Kernel)

Attributes
No additional attributes.

Associations

- type: JavaType [1] It refers to the type of the parameter. It redefines *TypedElement::type*.

Constraints
No additional constraints.

A.5 ISM METAMODEL: C++ LANGUAGE

Descriptions of Metaclasses

C++ Class

Description
A C++ class describes a set of objects that share the same specifications of features, restrictions and semantics.

Generalizations

- Class (from Kernel), Classifier (from Templates)

Attributes

Figure 21. ISM–C++ metamodel: Diagram of classes

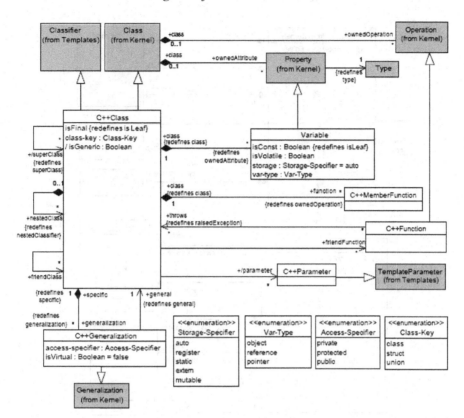

- class-key: Class-Key [1] It specifies the type of the class, i.e., if it is a class, structure or union.
- isFinal: Boolean [1] It specifies if the class has subclasses. It redefines *RedefinableElement::isLeaf*.
- /isGeneric: Boolean It specifies if the class is generic. It is a derived attribute.

Associations

- variable: Variable [*] It refers to the own variables of the C++ class. It redefines *Class::ownedAttribute*.
- nestedClass: C++Class [*] It refers to the C++ classes that are declared within the body of a C++ class (nested classes). It is a subset of *Class::nestedClassifier*.
- /superClass: C++Class [*] It refers to the superclasses of a C++ class. It redefines *Class::superClass*. It is derived.
- function: C++MemberFunction [*] It refers to the own functions of the class. It redefines *Class::ownedOperation*.
- generalization: C++Generalization [*] It refers to the generalizations of the class. It redefines *Class::Generalization*.
- friendClass: C++Class [*] It refers to the friend classes of the class.

Figure 22. ISM–C++ metamodel: Diagram of functions

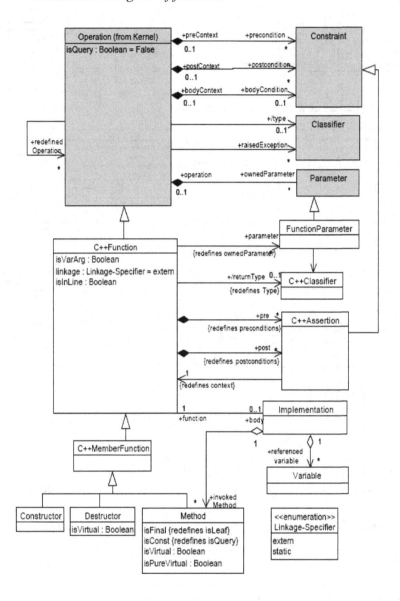

- friendFunction: C++Function [*] It refers to the friend functions of the class.
- /parameters: C++Parameter [*] It refers to the set of parameters of the class. It is derived.

Constraints

[1] A class that has pure virtual functions must be declared abstract. self.function -> select (oclIsTypeOf (Method)) -> exists (m | m.oclAsType (Method).isPureVirtual) implies self.isAbstract

[2] A class declared final does not have subclasses, i. e., it is not superclass of any class belonging to the package. self.isFinal implies self.package.ownedMember -> select (oclIsTypeOf (C++Class)) -> forAll (c | c.oclAsType (C++Class).superClass < > self)

Figure 23. ISM–C++ metamodel: Diagram of implementations

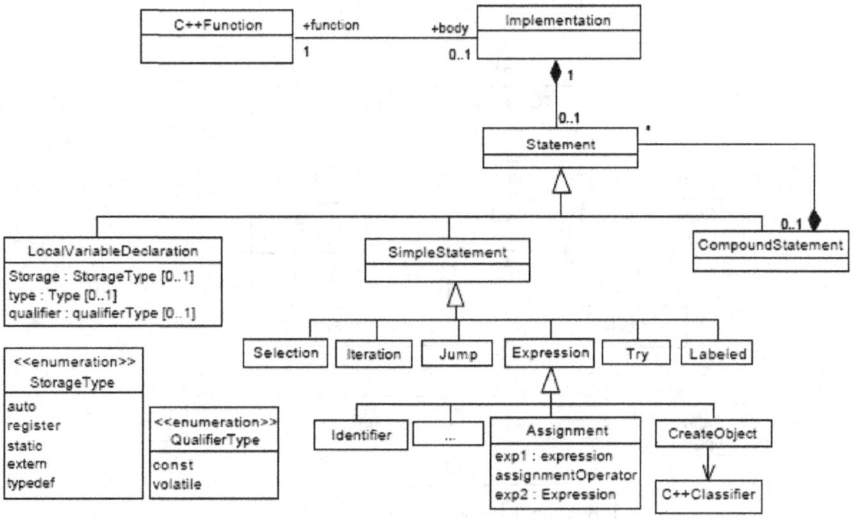

[3]   Private functions of a class can not be declared abstract. self.function -> select (oclIsTypeOf (Method)) -> forAll (m | m.visibility = #private implies not m.oclAsType (Method).isPureVirtual)

[4]   Final methods of a class can not be declared abstracts. self.function -> select (oclIsTypeOf (Method)) -> forAll (m | m.oclAsType (Method).isFinal implies not m.oclAsType (Method).isVirtual)

[5]   A class is generic if it has a signature template. isGeneric = (self.ownedTemplateSignature -> size () =1)

[6]   Parameters are derived from parameters of the signature template that is redefinable. /parameters = self.ownedTemplateSignature.parameter

[7]   Friend functions are C++ functions but no member functions of a class. self.friendFunction -> forAll (f | f.isTypeOf (C++Function))

[8]   A class only has a destructor. self.function -> select (oclIsTypeOf (Destructor)) ->size() <=1

C++File

Description

It represents a C++ file.

Generalizations

•   Namespace (from Kernel)

Attributes

•   extension: FileExtension [1] It specifies the extension of the file, i.e., if the file is header then "h", else, if it is an implementation "c" or "cpp".

Figure 24. ISM–C++ metamodel: Diagram of classifiers

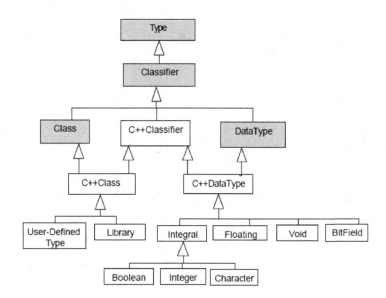

Associations

- c++Project: C++Project [1] It refers to the project of which the file is part.
- /includedFile: C++File [*] It refers to the set of files that are included. It is derived.
- globalVariableandConstantDeclaration:GlobalVariableandConstantDeclaration[*] It refers to the set of global variables and constants that are declared.
- precompilerDirectives: PrecompilerDirectives [*] It refers to the set of precompiler directives.
- classifierDeclaration: ClassifierDeclaration [*] It refers to the set of classifier declarations.
- classifierDefinition: ClassifierDefinition [*] It refers to the set of classifier definitions.
- functionDeclaration: FunctionDeclaration [*] It refers to the set of function declarations.
- functionDefinition: FunctionDefinition [*] It refers to the set of function definitions.

Constraints

[1]   The included files are derived through the files that are included by the directive *#include*. /includedFile = self.precompilerDirective -> collect (oclIsTypeOf (Include).headerFile)

C++Function

Description
It is a C++ function.

Generalizations

- Operation (from Kernel)

Figure 25. ISM–C++ metamodel: Diagram of projects

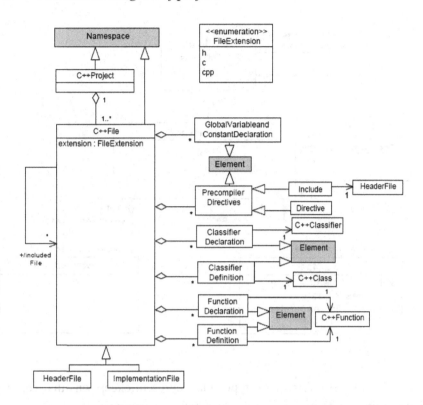

Attributes

- isVarArg: Boolean It specifies whether the function can have variable arguments.
- linkage: Linkage-Specifier It specifies whether the function is *extern*, indicating to compiler that the definition of the function is in another file, or is static, i.e., its name is invisible on the outside of the file declaring it.
- isInLine: Boolean True means that the compiler will replace the function call by the function code.

Associations

- parameter: FunctionParameter [*] It specifies the function parameters. It redefines *Operation::ownedParameter*.
- pre: C++Assertion [*] It refers to the preconditions of the function. It redefines *Operation::precondition*.
- post: C++Assertion [*] It refers to the postconditions of the function. It redefines *Operation::postcondition*.
- /returnType: C++Classifier [0..1] It specifies the return type of the function. It redefines *Operation::type*. It is derived.

Figure 26.

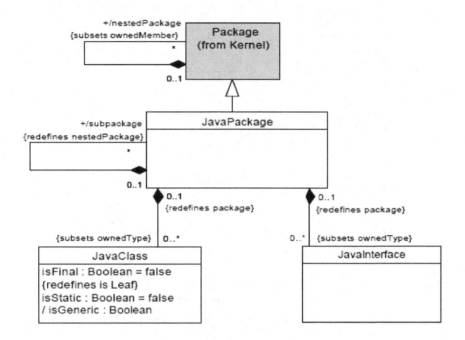

- throws: C++Class [*] It refers to the types that represent exceptions that can appear during an invocation of this operation. It redefines *Operation::raisedException*.
- body: Implementation [0..1] It refers to the implementation of the function.

Constraints

[1] A pure virtual function does not have implementation. self.isPureVirtual implies self.body -> isEmpty()

C++ Generalization

Description
It represents a generalization in C++.

Generalizations

- Generalization (from Kernel)

Attributes

- access-specifier: Access-Specifier It specifies what the access type of the members of the base class.
- isVirtual: Boolean It specifies whether the inheritance is virtual.

Associations

- general: C++Class [1] It refers to the more general class in the generalization. It redefines *Generalization::general*.
- specific: C++Class [1] It refers to the more specific class in the generalization. It redefines *Generalization::specific*.

Constraints
No additional constraints.

C++MemberFunction

It is a function that is member of a C++ class.

Generalizations

- C++Function

Attributes
No additional attributes.

Associations

- class: C++Class [1] It refers to the class to which the function belongs. It redefines *Operation::class*.

Constraints

[1]   A function that is member of a class can not be declared extern. self.linkage <> "extern"

C++Project

Description
It represents a C++ project.

Generalizations

- Namespace (from Kernel)

Attributes
No additional attributes.

Associations

- c++File: C++File [1.. *] It refers to the set of C++ files that belong to the project.

Constraints

No additional constraints.

ClassifierDeclaration

Description

It represents classifier declarations.

Generalizations

- Element (from Kernel)

Attributes

No additional attributes.

Associations

- C++Classifier: C++Classifier [1] It refers to the declared classifier.

Constraints

No additional constraints.

ClassifierDefinition

Description

It denotes classifier definitions.

Generalizations

- Element (from Kernel)

Attributes

No additional attributes.

Associations

- c++Class: C++Class [1] It refers to the class that is defined.

Constraints

No additional constraints.

Constructor

Description

It designs a function that is used to create class instances. It cannot be called explicitly by means of invocation expression. It does not have return type. Its name is the same of the class including it. Its declaration is no inherited.

Generalizations

• C++MemberFunction

Attributes

No additional attributes.

Associations

No additional associations.

Constraints

[1] Constructors do not have return type. self.type -> isEmpty()

[2] The name of the constructor is the same as the class name including its declaration. self.name = self.class.name

Destructor

Description

A destructor is a function member with the same name as the class prefixed by a "~". Classes have only a function destructor that does not have arguments nor return type. Destructors are usually used to de-allocate memory and do other cleanup for a class object and its class members when the object is destroyed.

Generalizations

• C++MemberFunction

Attributes

• isVirtual: Boolean [1] It specifies whether the destructor is virtual, i.e., if it can be redefined in the subclasses.

Associations

No additional associations.

Constraints

[1]   A destructor does not have arguments nor return type. self.ownedParameter -> isEmpty () and self. type -> isEmpty ()

[2]   The destructor name is the same as the name of the class containing it prefixed by a ~. self.name = "~".concat (self.class.name)

FunctionDeclaration

Description
It denotes function declarations.

Generalizations

•   Element (from Kernel)

Attributes
No additional attributes.

Associations

•   c++Function: C++Function [1] It denotes the function that declares.

Constraints
No additional restrictions.

FunctionDefinition

Description
It represents function definitions.

Generalizations

•   Element (from Kernel)

Attributes
No additional attributes.

Associations

•   c++Function: C++Function [1] It denotes the function that defines.

Constraints
No additional constraints.

GlobalVariableandConstantDeclaration

Description
It denotes global variables and constants that are declared in a C++ file.

Generalizations

- Element (from Kernel)

Attributes
No additional attributes.

Associations
No additional associations.

Constraints
No additional constraints.

HeaderFile

Description
It represents a C++ header file.

Generalizations

- C++File

Attributes
No additional attributes.

Associations
No additional associations.

Constraints
No additional constraints.

Implementation

Description
It specifies a procedure that carries out the function result.

Generalization

- Element (de Kernel)

Attributes

- Procedure: Expression [0..1] It refers to the procedure of the function.

Associations

- function: C++Function [1] It refers to the functions to which it belongs.
- invokedMethod: Method [*] It refers to the methods called in the body of a function.
- referencedVariable: Variable [*] It refers to the variables referred in the body of a function.
- statement: Statement [0..1] It refers to the statement block of the body of the function.

Constraints
No additional constraints.

ImplementationFile

Description
It denotes a C++ implementation file.

Generalizations

- C++File

Attributes
No additional attributes.

Associations
No additional associations.

Constraints
No additional constraints.

Include

Description
It denotes precompiler directives of type *#include*.

Generalizations

- PrecompilerDirective

Attributes
No additional attributes.

Associations

- headerFile: HeaderFile [1] It denotes the header file that is included through a directive.

Constraints
No additional constraints.

Method

Description
It declares a member function of a class that can be called by passing a fixed number of arguments.

Generalizations

- C++MemberFunction

Attributes

- isConst: Boolean [1] It specifies whether a method is constant. It redefines *Operation::isQuery*.
- isFinal: Boolean [1] It specifies whether a method is final, i.e., if it can not be redefined in the subclasses. It redefines *RedefinableElement::isLeaf*.
- isVirtual: Boolean [1] It specifies whther a method is virtual, i.e., if it can be redefined in the subclasses.
- isPureVirtual: Boolean [1] It specifies whether a method is pure, i.e., if it does not have implementation.

Associations
No additional associations.

Constraints
No additional restrictions.

PrecompilerDirective

Description
It denotes precompiler directives.

Generalizations

- Element (from Kernel)

Attributes
No additional attributes.

Associations

No additional associations.

Restrictions

No additional restrictions.

Statement

Description

It denotes the code block that implements a function.

Generalizations

- Action (from Action)

Attributes

No additional attributes.

Associations

- implementation: Implementation [1] It refers to the implementation of which the implementation is part.
- compoundStatement: CompoundStatement [0..1] It refers to the statement block of which this is part.

Constraints

No additional constraints.

Variable

Description

It denotes the variable that is declared in the class.

Generalizations

- Property (de Kernel)

Attributes

- isConst: Boolean [1] It specifies whether a variable is constant. If it is final, must have an initial value compulsory. It redefines *RedefinableElement::isLeaf*.

- isVolatile: Boolean [1] It specifies whether a variable is volatile, i.e., if it is not accessed synchronically.
- storage: Storage-Specifier [1] It specifies the type of the variable allocation.
- var-type: Var-Type [1] It specifies the type of the variable, i.e., if the variable is object, reference or pointer.

Associations

- class: C++Class [1] It refers to a class declaring this variable. It redefines *Property::class*.

Constraints

[1]   A variable is a property that is part of a class and is not member of associations. self.class -> size () = 1 and self.association -> isEmpty () and self.opposite -> isEmpty ()

Appendix B:
OCL and NEREUS: Type System

This Appendix includes the specification of the type system of OCL. It includes the OCL signature and the algebraic specification.

B.1: PRIMITIVE TYPES

1. 1. Boolean

1. 1. 1. OCL Signature

or (b: Boolean): Boolean
True if either self or b is true.

xor (b: Boolean): Boolean
True if either self or b is true, but not both.
   post: (self or b) and not (self = b)

and (b: Boolean): Boolean
True if both self and b are true.

DOI: 10.4018/978-1-61520-649-0.ch016

not: Boolean
True if self is false.
    post: if self then result = false else result = true endif

implies (b: Boolean): Boolean
True if self is false, or if self is true and b is true.
    post: (not self) or (self and b)

1. 1. 2. NEREUS Signature

TYPE Boolean

OPERATIONS

```
True: →Boolean
False: →Boolean
not_: Boolean → Boolean
_and_: Boolean x Boolean → Boolean
_=_: Boolean x Boolean → Boolean
_or_: Boolean x Boolean →Boolean
_xor_: Boolean x Boolean → Boolean
_⇒_: Boolean x Boolean → Boolean
_⇔:_ Boolean x Boolean → Boolean
if_then_else: Boolean x Boolean x Boolean → Boolean
```

1. 2. Real

1. 2. 1. OCL Signature

Integer is a subclass of Real

+ (r: Real): Real
The value of the addition of self and r.

- (r: Real): Real
The value of the subtraction of r from self.

* (r: Real): Real
The value of the multiplication of self and r.

-: Real
The negative value of self.

/ (r: Real): Real
The value of self divided by r. Evaluates to OclInvalid if r is equal to zero.

abs (): Real
The absolute value of self. **post**: if self < 0 then result = - self else result = self endif

floor (): Integer
The largest integer that is less than or equal to self. **post**: (result <= self) and (result + 1 > self)

round (): Integer
The integer that is closest to self. When there are two such integers, the largest one. **post**: ((self - result).abs() < 0.5) or ((self - result).abs() = 0.5 and (result > self))

max (r: Real): Real
The maximum of self and r. **post**: if self >= r then result = self else result = r endif

min (r: Real): Real
The minimum of self and r. **post**: if self <= r then result = self else result = r endif

< (r: Real): Boolean
True if self is less than r.

> (r: Real): Boolean
True if self is greater than r. **post**: result = not (self <= r)

<= (r: Real): Boolean
True if self is less than or equal to r. **post**: result = ((self = r) or (self < r))

>= (r: Real): Boolean
True if self is greater than or equal to r. **post**: result = ((self = r) or (self > r))

1. 2. 2. NEREUS Signature

TYPE Real

OPERATIONS

```
_=_: Real x Real → Boolean
_< >_: Real x Real → Boolean
-_: Real -> Real
_+_: Real x Real → Real
_-_: Real x Real → Real
_*_: Real x Real → Real
```

```
_/_: Real x Real → Real
abs: Real → Real
floor: Real → Integer
round: Real → Integer
max: Real x Real → Real
min: Real x Real → Real
_<_: Real x Real → Boolean
_>_: Real x Real → Boolean
_<=_: Real x Real → Boolean
_>=_: Real x Real → Boolean
```

1. 3. Integer

1. 3. 1. OCL Signature

-: Integer
The negative value of self.

+ (i: Integer): Integer
The value of the addition of self and i.

- (i: Integer): Integer
The value of the subtraction of i from self.

* (i: Integer): Integer

/ (i: Integer): Real
The value of self divided by i.Evaluates to OclInvalid if r is equal to zero.

abs (): Integer
The absolute value of self. **post**: if self < 0 then result = - self else result = self endif

div (i: Integer): Integer
The number of times that is completely within self. **pre**: i <> 0 **post**: if self / i >= 0 then result = (self / i).floor () else result = -((-self/i).floor ()) endif

mod (i: Integer): Integer
The result is self modulo i. **post**: result = self - (self.div (i) * i)

max (i: Integer): Integer
The maximum of self an i. **post**: if self >= i then result = self else result = i endif

min (i: Integer): Integer
The minimum of self an i. **post**: if self <= i then result = self else result = i endif

1. 3. 2 NEREUS Signature

TYPE Integer

OPERATIONS

```
_=_ : Integer x Integer → Boolean
_< >_: Integer x Integer → Boolean
-_: Integer → Integer
_+_: Integer x Integer → Integer
_-_: Integer x Integer → Integer
_*_: Integer x Integer → Integer
_/_: Integer x Integer → Integer
abs: Integer → Integer
floor: Integer → Integer
round: Integer → Integer
max: Integer x Integer → Integer
min: Integer x Integer → Integer
_<_: Integer x Integer → Boolean
_>_: Integer x Integer → Boolean
_<=_: Integer x Integer → Boolean
_>=_: Integer x Integer → Boolean
```

1. 4. String

1. 4. 1. OCL Signature

size (): Integer
The number of characters in self.

Concat (s: String): String
The concatenation of self and s. **post**: result.size () = self.size () + string.size () **post**: result.substring (1, self.size ()) = self **post**: result.substring (self.size () + 1, result.size ()) = s

substring(lower: Integer, upper: Integer): String
The sub-string of self starting at character number lower, up to and including character number upper. Character numbers run from 1 to self.size (). **pre**: 1 <= lower **pre**: lower <= upper **pre**: upper <= self. size ()

toInteger (): Integer
Converts self to an Integer value.

toReal (): Real
Converts self to a Real value.

1. 4. 2. NEREUS Signature

TYPE String

OPERATIONS

```
concat: String x String → String
size: String → Integer
subString: String x Integer x Integer → String
toInteger: String → Integer
toReal: String -> Real
```

1. 5. Tuple

```
CLASS Tuple
IMPORTS T1, T2
EFFECTIVETYPE
Tuple
OPERATIONS
createTuple: T1 x T2 → Tuple
modifFirst: Tuple x T1→ Tuple
modifSecond: Tuple x T2 → Tuple
selectFirst: Tuple → T1
selectSecond: Tuple → T2
AXIOMS t: Tuple; f1, f2: T1; s1, s2: T2
modifFirst (createTuple (f1, s1), f2) = createTuple (f2, s1)
modifSecond (createTuple (f1, s1), s2) = createTuple (f1, s2)
selectFirst (createTuple(f1,s1)) = f1
selectSecond (createTuple(f1,s1)) = s1
END-CLASS
```

B.2: COLLECTION TYPES

2. 1. Collection

2. 1. 1 OCL Signature

size (): Integer
The number of elements in the collection self. **post**: result = self -> iterate (elem; acc: Integer = 0 | acc + 1)

includes (object: T): Boolean
True if object is an element of self, false otherwise. **post**: result = (self -> count (object) > 0)

excludes (object: T): Boolean
True if object is not an element of self, false otherwise. **post**: result = (self -> count (object) = 0)

count (object: T): Integer
The number of times that object occurs in the collection self. **post**: result = self -> iterate (elem; acc: Integer = 0 | if elem = object then acc + 1 else acc endif)

includesAll (c2: Collection(T)): Boolean
Does self contain all the elements of c2 ? **post**: result = c2 -> forAll (elem | self -> includes (elem))

excludesAll (c2: Collection(T)): Boolean
Does self contain none of the elements of c2 ? **post**: result = c2 -> forAll (elem | self -> excludes (elem))

isEmpty (): Boolean
Is self the empty collection? **post**: result = (self -> size () = 0)

notEmpty (): Boolean
Is self not the empty collection? **post**: result = (self -> size () <> 0)

sum (): T
The addition of all elements in self. Elements must be of a type supporting the + operation. The + operation must take one parameter of type T and be both associative: (a + b) + c = a + (b + c), and commutative: a + b = b + a. Integer and Real fulfill this condition. **post**: result = self -> iterate (elem; acc: T = 0 | acc + elem)

product (c2: Collection (T2)): Set (Tuple (first: T, second: T2))
The cartesian product operation of self and c2.
  post: result = self -> iterate (e1; acc: Set (Tuple (first: T, second: T2)) = Set {} | c2 -> iterate (e2; acc2: Set (Tuple (first: T, second: T2)) = acc | acc2 -> including (Tuple {first = e1, second = e2})))

2. 1. 2. NEREUS Specification

CLASS Collection [Elem: ANY]
IMPORTS Boolean, Nat
GENERATED-BY create, add **DEFERREDTYPES**
Collection
OPERATIONS
create: → Collection
add: Collection x Elem → Collection
count: Collection x Elem → Nat
collect: Collection x (Elem → Elem1: ANY) → Collection
EFFECTIVEOPERATIONS isEmpty: Collection → Boolean
size: Collection → Nat
includes: Collection x Elem → Boolean
excludes: Collection x Elem → Boolean
includesAll: Collection x Collection → Boolean
forAll: Collection x (Elem → Boolean) → Boolean
exists: Collection x (Elem → Boolean) → Boolean
select: Collection x (Elem → Boolean) → Collection
reject: Collection x (Elem → Boolean) → Collection
iterate: Collection x (Elem x Acc: ANY) x (→ Acc) → Acc
AXIOMS c, c1: Collection; e: Elem; f: Elem → Boolean; g: Elem x Acc
→ Acc;
base: → Acc
isEmpty (c) = (size (c) = 0)
iterate (create, g, base) = base
iterate (add (c, e), g, base)= g (e, iterate (c, g, base))
count (c, e) = iterate (c, f1, 0)
  WHERE OPERATIONS f1: Elem x Nat→Nat
  AXIOMS e1: Elem; i: Nat
    f1 (e1, i) = if e = e1 then i + 1 else i
  END-WHERE
size (create) = 0
size (add (c, e)) = 1] + size (c)
    includes (create, e) = False
includes (add (c, e), e1) = if e = e1 then True else includes (c,
e1)
excludes (create, e) = True
excludes (add (c, e), e1) = if e = e1 then False else excludes (c,
e1)
includesAll (create, c) = True
includesAll (add (c, e), c1) = includesAll (c, c1) and includes (e,
c1)
excludesAll (create, c) = True

```
excludesAll (add (c, e), c1) = excludesAll (c, c1) and excludes (e,
c1)
forAll (create, f) = True
forAll (add (c, e), f) = f (e) and forAll (c, f)
exists (create, f) = False
exists (add (c, e), f) = f (e) or exists (c, f)
select (create, f) = create
select (add (c, e), f) = if f (e) then add (select (c, f), e) else
select (c, f)
reject (create, f) = create
reject (add (c, e), f) = if not f (e) then add (reject (c, f),e)
   else reject (c, f)
```
END-CLASS

Collection-with-suma

CLASS Collection-with-suma [Elem: Real]
INHERITS Collection [Elem]
EFFECTIVEOPERATIONS
suma: Collection-with-suma → Real
AXIOMS c: Collection-with-suma
suma (c) = iterate (c, f, 0)
  WHERE OPERATIONS
    f: Real x Real → Real
  AXIOMS r1, r2: Real
    f (r1, r2) = r1 + r2
  END-WHEREEND-CLASS

Collection-with-cartesian-product

CLASS Collection-with-cartesianProduct [Elem1, Elem2]IS-SUBTYPE-OF
Collection [Elem1] [Collection: Collection-with-cartesianProduct]
IMPORTS Collection [Elem2], Tuple [Elem1, Elem2], Set [Tuple] [set:
setTuple]
EFFECTIVEOPERATIONS
product: Collection-with-cartesianProduct x Collection → SetTuple
AXIOMS c: Collection-with-cartesianProduct; c2: Collection; t: tu-
ple; s: SetTuple
product (c, c2) = iterate (c, g, base)
  WHERE OPERATIONS
    g: Element x setTuple → setTuple
    base: → setTupla
  AXIOMS e: Element; acc: setTuple
    g (e, acc) =

```
    iterate (v) (c2, [including (acc2, createTuple (e, v)], [acc2 =
acc])
    base = emptyset
```
END-WHEREEND-CLASS

Collection-with-cartesian-product

CLASS Collection-with-cartesianProduct [Elem1, Elem2]
IS-SUBTYPE-OF
Collection [Elem1] [Collection: Collection-with-cartesianProduct]
IMPORTS Collection [Elem2], Tuple [Elem1, Elem2], Set [Tuple] [set: setTuple]
EFFECTIVEOPERATIONS
product: Collection-with-cartesianProduct x Collection → SetTuple
AXIOMS c: Collection-with-cartesianProduct; c2: Collection; t: tuple;
s: SetTuple
product (c, c2) = iterate (c, g, base)
  WHERE OPERATIONS
     g: Element x setTuple → setTuple
     base: → setTuple
  AXIOMS e: Element; acc: setTuple
    g (e, acc) = iterate (c2, g1, base1)
  WHERE OPERATIONS
       g1: Element x setTuple → setTuple
       base1: → setTuple
  AXIOMS v: Element; acc2: setTuple
       g1 (v, acc2) = including (acc2, createTuple (e, v))
      base1 = acc
END-WHERE END-WHEREEND-CLASS

2. 2. Set

2. 2. 1. OCL Signature

union (s: Set (T)): Set (T)
The union of self and s. **post:** result -> forAll (elem | self -> includes (elem) or s -> includes (elem)) **post:** self -> forAll (elem | result -> includes (elem)) **post:** s -> forAll (elem | result -> includes (elem))

union(bag: Bag(T)): Bag(T)
The union of self and bag.
   post: result -> forAll (elem | result -> count (elem) = self -> count (elem) + bag -> count (elem)) **post:** self -> forAll (elem | result -> includes (elem)) **post:** bag -> forAll (elem | result -> includes (elem))

= (s: Set(T)): Boolean

Evaluates to true if self and s contain the same elements. **post**: result = (self -> forAll (elem | s -> includes(elem)) and s -> forAll(elem | self -> includes(elem)))

intersection (s: Set (T)): Set (T)

The intersection of self and s (i.e., the set of all elements that are in both self and s). **post**: result -> forAll (elem | self -> includes (elem) and s -> includes (elem)) **post**: self->forAll (elem | s -> includes (elem) = result -> includes (elem)) **post**: s -> forAll (elem | self -> includes (elem) = result -> includes (elem))

intersection (bag: Bag (T)): Set (T)

The intersection of self and bag. **post**: result = self -> intersection (bag -> asSet)

ñ (s: Set (T)): Set (T)

The elements of self, which are not in s. **post**: result -> forAll (elem | self -> includes (elem) and s -> excludes (elem)) **post**: self ->forAll (elem | result -> includes (elem) = s -> excludes (elem))

including (object: T): Set (T)

The set containing all elements of self plus object. **post**: result -> forAll (elem | self -> includes (elem) or (elem = object)) **post**: self -> forAll (elem | result -> includes (elem)) **post**: result -> includes (object)

excluding (object: T): Set (T)

The set containing all elements of self without object. **post**: result -> forAll (elem | self -> includes (elem) and (elem < > object)) **post**: self -> forAll (elem | result -> includes (elem) = (object < > elem)) **post**: result -> excludes (object)

symmetricDifference (s: Set (T)): Set (T)

The sets containing all the elements that are in self or s, but not in both. **post**: result -> forAll (elem | self -> includes (elem) xor s -> includes (elem)) **post**: self -> forAll (elem | result -> includes (elem) = s -> excludes (elem)) **post**: s -> forAll (elem | result -> includes (elem) = self -> excludes (elem))

count (object: T): Integer

The number of occurrences of object in self. **post**: result <= 1

flatten (): Set (T2)

If the element type is not a collection type, this results in the same self. If the element type is a collection type, the result is the set containing all the elements of all the elements of self. **post**: result = if self.type. elementType.oclIsKindOf (CollectionType) then self -> iterate (c; acc: Set () = Set { } | acc -> union (c -> asSet ())) else self endif

asSet (): Set (T)

A Set identical to self. This operation exists for convenience reasons. **post**: result = self

asOrderedSet (): OrderedSet (T)

An OrderedSet that contains all the elements from self, in undefined order. **post**: result -> forAll (elem | self -> includes (elem))

asSequence (): Sequence (T)

A Sequence that contains all the elements from self, in undefined order. **post**: result -> forAll (elem | self -> includes (elem)) **post:** self -> forAll (elem | result -> count (elem) = 1)

asBag (): Bag (T)

The Bag that contains all the elements from self. **post**: result -> forAll (elem | self -> includes (elem)) **post:** self -> forAll (elem | result -> count (elem) = 1)

2. 2. 2. Nereus Specification

```
CLASS Set [T: ANY]
IS-SUBTYPE-OF Collection [T] [create: createSet; add: including]
IMPORTS Sequence, Bag [create: createBag; including: includingBag],
OrderedSet
GENERATED-BY createSet, including EFFECTIVETYPES
Set
OPERATIONS createSet, including, count
equal: Set x Set → Boolean
union: Set x Set → Set
union: Set x Bag → Bag
intersection: Set x Set → Set
intersection: Set x Bag → Set
ñ: Set x Set → Set
excluding: Set x T → Set
symmetricDifference: Set x Set → Set
collect: Set x (T → T1: ANY) → Bag [T1]
flatten: Set → Set [T1: ANY]
asSet: Set → Set
asOrderedSet: Set → OrderedSet
asSequence: Set → Sequence
asBag: Set → Bag
AXIOMS s, s2: Set; b: Bag; b1: Bag [T1] ; e, e1: T; g: T1 → Boolean
collect (createSet, g) = createBag
collect (including (s, e), g) = includingBag (collect (excluding (s,
e),g (e))
count (s, e) <= 1
forAll (v) (union (s, s2), [includes (s, v) or includes (s2, v)])
forAll (v) (s, [ includes (union (s, s2), v) ])
forAll (v) (s2, [ includes (union (s, s2), v) ])
forAll (v) (s, [ includes (union (s, b), v) ])
```

```
forAll (v) (b, [ includes (union (s, b), v) ])
forAll (v) (union (s, b),[ count (union (s, b), v) = count(s, v) +
count (b, v) ])
equal (s, s2) =
forAll (v) (s, [includes (s2, v)) and forAll (v1) (s2, [includes (s,
v1)]) ])
forAll (v) (intersection (s, s2), [includes (s,v) and includes
(s2,v)]
forAll (v) (s, [includes (s2, v)) = includes (intersection (s, s2),
v)])
forAll (v) (s2, [includes (s, v)) = includes (intersection (s, s2),
v)])
intersection (s, b) = intersection (s, asSet (b))
forAll (v) (s - s2, [includes (s, v) and excludes (s2, v) ])
forAll (v) (s, [includes (s - s2, v) = excludes (s2,v) ])
forAll (v) (including (s, e), [includes (s, v) or equal (v,e)]
forAll (v) (s, [includes (including (s, e), v) ])
includes (including (s, e), e)
forAll (v) (excluding (s, e), [includes (s, v) and not equal (v, e)
])
forAll (v) (s, [includes (excluding (s, e), v) = not equal (e, v) ])
excludes (excluding (s, e), e)
forAll (v) (symmetricDifference (s, s2), [includes (s, v) xor in-
cludes (s2, v) ])
forAll (v) (s, [includes (symmetricDifference (s, s2), v) = excludes
(s2, v) ])
forAll (v) [includes (symmetricDifference (s, s2), v) = excludes (s,
v) ])
flatten (s)= if oclIsKindOf (elementType (type (s)), Collection-
Type) then iterate (v) (s, [union (acc, asset (v)) ], [acc = create-
Set]) else s
asSet (s) = s
forAll (v) (asOrderedSet (s), [includes(asOrderedSet (s), v) ])
forAll (v) (asSequence (s), includes (s, v))
forAll (v) (s, count (asSequence (s), v) = 1)
forAll (v) (asBag (s), [includes (s, v)])
forAll (v) (s, [count (asBag (s), v) = 1])
forAll (v) (asOrderedSet (b), [includes (b, v) ])
forAll (v) (b, [includes (asOrdered(b), v))
forAll (v) (b, [count (asOrderedSet (b), v) = 1])
```
END-CLASS

344

2. 3. BAG

2. 3. 1. OCL Signature

= (bag: Bag (T)): Boolean
True if self and bag contain the same elements, the same number of times. **post**: result = (self -> forAll (elem | self -> count (elem) = bag -> count (elem)) and bag -> forAll (elem | bag -> count(elem) = self -> count(elem)))

union (bag: Bag (T)): Bag (T)
The union of self and bag. **post**: result -> forAll (elem | result -> count (elem) = self -> count (elem) + bag -> count (elem)) **post**: self -> forAll (elem | result -> count (elem) = self -> count (elem) + bag -> count (elem)) **post**: bag -> forAll (elem | result -> count (elem) = self -> count (elem) + bag -> count (elem))

union (set: Set (T)): Bag (T)
The union of self and set. **post**: result -> forAll (elem | result -> count (elem) = self -> count (elem) + set -> count (elem)) **post**: self -> forAll (elem | result -> count (elem) = self -> count (elem) + set -> count (elem)) **post**: set -> forAll(elem | result -> count (elem) = self -> count (elem) + set -> count (elem))

intersection (bag: Bag (T)): Bag (T)
The intersection of self and bag. **post**: result -> forAll (elem | result -> count (elem) = self -> count (elem).min (bag -> count (elem))) **post**: self -> forAll (elem | result -> count (elem) = self -> count (elem).min (bag -> count (elem))) **post**: bag -> forAll(elem | result -> count (elem) = self -> count (elem).min (bag -> count (elem)))

intersection (set: Set (T)): Set (T)
The intersection of self and set. **post**: result -> forAll (elem | result -> count (elem) = self -> count (elem).min (set -> count (elem))) **post**: self -> forAll (elem | result -> count (elem) = self -> count (elem).min (set -> count (elem))) **post**: set -> forAll (elem | result -> count (elem) = self -> count (elem).min (set -> count (elem)))

including (object: T): Bag (T)
The bag containing all elements of self plus object.
> **post**: result -> forAll (elem |
> if elem = object then result -> count(elem) = self -> count(elem) + 1
> else result -> count(elem) = self -> count(elem)
> endif)
> **post**: self -> forAll (elem |
> if elem = object then result -> count (elem) = self -> count (elem) + 1
> else result -> count(elem) = self -> count(elem)
> endif)

excluding (object: T): Bag (T)
The bag containing all elements of self apart from all occurrences of object.
> **post**: result -> forAll (elem |
> if elem = object then result -> count (elem) = 0
> else result -> count (elem) = self -> count (elem)
> endif)
> **post**: self -> forAll (elem |
> if elem = object then result -> count (elem) = 0
> else result -> count (elem) = self -> count (elem)
> endif)

count (object: T): Integer
The number of occurrences of object in self.

Flatten (): Bag (T2)
If the element type is not a collection type, this results in the same bag. If the element type is a collection type, the result is the bag containing all the elements of all the elements of self. **post**: result = if self.type.elementType.oclIsKindOf (CollectionType) then self -> iterate (c; acc: Bag () = Bag { } | acc -> union (c->asBag ())) else self endif

asBag (): Bag (T)
A bag identical to self. This operation exists for convenience reasons. **post:** result = self

asSequence (): Sequence (T)
A Sequence that contains all the elements from self, in undefined order. **post**: result -> forAll (elem | self -> count (elem) = result -> count (elem)) **post**: self -> forAll (elem | self -> count (elem) = result -> count (elem))

asset (): Set (T)
The Set containing all the elements from self, with duplicates removed. **post**: result -> forAll (elem | self -> includes (elem)) **post**: self -> forAll (elem | result -> includes (elem))

asOrderedSet (): OrderedSet (T)
An OrderedSet that contains all the elements from self, in undefined order, with duplicates removed. **post**: result -> forAll (elem | self -> includes (elem)) **post**: self -> forAll (elem | result -> includes (elem)) **post**: self -> forAll (elem | result -> count (elem) = 1)

2. 3. 2. NEREUS Specification

```
CLASS Bag [T]
IS-SUBTYPE-OF Collection [T] [create: createBag; add: including]
IMPORTS Sequence [T], Set [T]
GENERATED-BY createBag, including
EFFECTIVETYPES Bag
```

OPERATIONS
```
emptyBag, including, count
equal: Bag x Bag → Boolean
union: Bag x Bag → Bag
union: Bag x Set → Bag
intersection: Bag x Bag → Bag
intersection: Bag x Set → Set
excluding: Bag x T → Bag
collect: Bag x (T → T1) → Bag [T1]
asBag: Bag -> Bag
flatten: Bag -> Bag [T1:ANY]
asSequence: Bag → Sequence
asSet: Bag → Set
asOrderedSet: Bag → OrderedSet
```
AXIOMS b, b1: Bag; s: Set; e, e1: T; g: T → T1; f: T → Boolean
```
count (including (b, e), e1) = if e = e1 then 1 + count (b, e1) else
count (b, e1)
equal (b, b1) = forAll (v) (b, [count (b, v) = count (b1, v) and
   forAll (v1) (b1, count (b1, v) = count (b, v) ])
forAll (v) (union (b, b1), [count (union (b, b1), v) = count (b, v)
+ count (b1, v) ])
forAll (v) (b, [count (union (b, b1), v) = count (b, v) + count (b1,
v) ])
forAll (v) (b1, [count (union (b, b1), v) = count (b, v) + count
(b1, v) ])
forAll (v) (union(b, s), [count (union(b, s), v) = count (b, v) +
count (s, v) ])
forAll (v) (b, [count (union (b, s), v) = count (b, v) + count (s,
v) ])
forAll (v) (s, [count (union (b, s), v) = count (b, v) + count (s,
v) ])
forAll (v) (intersection (b, b1),
   [count (intersection (b, b1), v) = min (count (b, v), count (b1,
v) ])
forAll (v) (b, [count (intersection (b, b1), v) = min (count(b, v),
count (b1, v) ])
forAll (v) (b1, [count (intersection (b, b1), v) = min (count (b,
v), count (b1, v) ])
forAll (v) (intersection (b, s), [count(intersection(b,s),v) =
min(count(b,v), count(s,v)])
forAll (v) (b, [count (intersection (b, s), v) = min (count (b, v),
count (s, v) ])
forAll (v) (s, [count (intersection (b, s), v) = min (count (b, v),
count (s, v) ])
```

```
forAll (v) (asSequence (b), [count (b, v) = count (asSequence (b),
v) ])
forAll (v) (b, [count (b, v) = count (asSequence (b), v) ])
forAll (v) (asset (b), [includes(b, v) ])
forAll (v) (b, [includes (asSet (b), v) ])
asBag (b) = b
flatten (b) = if oclIsKindOf (elementType (type (b)), Collection-
Type)
   then iterate (v) (b, [union (acc, asBag (v)) ], [acc = createBag
])
   else b
forAll (v) (including (b, e),
   [if equal(v, e) then count (including (b, e) = count (b, v) + 1
   else count (including (b, e), v) = count (b, v) ])
forAll (v) (b, [if equal (v, e) then count (including (b, e)) =
count (b, v) + 1
   else count (including (b, e), v) = count (b, v) ])
collect (create, g) = createBag
collect (including (s, e), g) = including (collect (excluding (s,
e),g (e))
forAll (v) (excluding (b, e), [if equal (v, e)
   then count (excluding (b, e), v) = 0
   else count (excluding (b, e), v) = count (b, v) ])
forAll (v) (b, [ if equal (v, e)
   then count (excluding (b, e), v) = 0
   else count (excluding (b, e), v) = count (b, v) ])
```
END-CLASS

2. 4. Sequence

2. 4. 1 OCL Specification

count (object: T): Integer
The number of occurrences of object in self.

= (s: Sequence (T)): Boolean
True if self contains the same elements as s in the same order. **post**: result = Sequence {1..self -> size ()
} -> forAll (index: Integer | self -> at (index) = s -> at (index)) and self -> size () = s -> size ()

union (s: Sequence (T)): Sequence (T)
The sequence consisting of all elements in self, followed by all elements in s. **post**: result -> size () = self
-> size () + s -> size () **post**: Sequence {1..self -> size () } -> forAll (index: Integer | self -> at (index) =
result -> at (index)) **post**: Sequence {1..s -> size () } -> forAll (index: Integer | s -> at (index) = result
-> at (index + self -> size ())))

flatten (): Sequence (T2)

If the element type is not a collection type, this results in the same self. If the element type is a collection type, the result is the sequence containing all the elements of all the elements of self. The order of the elements is partial. **post**: result = if self.type.elementType.oclIsKindOf (CollectionType) then self -> iterate (c; acc: Sequence () = Sequence { } | acc -> union (c -> asSequence ()))

    else self

    endif

append (object: T): Sequence (T)

The sequence of elements, consisting of all elements of self, followed by object. **post**: result -> size () = self -> size () + 1 **post**: result -> at (result -> size ()) = object **post**: Sequence {1..self -> size () } -> forAll (index: Integer | result -> at (index) = self -> at (index))

prepend (object: T): Sequence (T)

The sequence consisting of object, followed by all elements in self. **post**: result -> size = self -> size () + 1 **post**: result -> at (1) = object **post**: Sequence {1..self -> size () } -> forAll(index: Integer | self -> at (index) = result -> at (index + 1))

insertAt (index: Integer, object: T): Sequence (T)

The sequence consisting of self with object inserted at position index. **post**: result -> size = self -> size () + 1 **post**: result -> at (index) = object **post**: Sequence {1..(index - 1)} -> forAll (i: Integer | self -> at (i) = result -> at (i)) **post**: Sequence { (index + 1)..self -> size () } -> forAll (i: Integer | self -> at (i) = result -> at (i + 1))

subsequence (lower: Integer, upper: Integer): Sequence (T)

The sub-sequence of self starting at number lower, up to and including element number upper. **pre**: 1 <= lower **pre**: lower <= upper **pre**: upper <= self -> size () **post**: result -> size () = upper - lower + 1 **post**: Sequence {lower..upper} -> forAll (index | result -> at (index - lower + 1) = self -> at (index))

at (i: Integer): T

The i-th element of sequence. **pre**: i >= 1 and i <= self -> size ()

indexOf (obj: T): Integer

The index of object obj in the sequence. **pre**: self -> includes(obj) **post**: self -> at (i) = obj

first (): T

The first element in self. **post**: result = self -> at (1)

last (): T

The last element in self. **post**: result = self -> at (self -> size ())

including (object: T): Sequence (T)

The sequence containing all elements of self plus object added as the last element. **post**: result = self. append (object)

excluding (object: T): Sequence (T)

The sequence containing all elements of self apart from all occurrences of object. The order of the remaining elements is not changed. **post**:result -> includes (object) = false **post**: result -> size () = self -> size () - self -> count (object) **post**: result = self -> iterate (elem; acc: Sequence (T) = Sequence {} | if elem = object then acc else acc -> append (elem) endif)

asBag (): Bag (T)

The Bag containing all the elements from self, including duplicates. **post**: result -> forAll (elem | self -> count (elem) = result -> count (elem)) **post**: self -> forAll (elem | self -> count (elem) = result -> count (elem))

asSequence (): Sequence(T)

The Sequence identical to the object itself. This operation exists for convenience reasons. **post**: result = self

asSet (): Set (T)

The Set containing all the elements from self, with duplicates removed. **post**: result -> forAll (elem | self -> includes (elem)) **post**: self -> forAll (elem | result -> includes (elem))

asOrderedSet (): OrderedSet (T)

An OrderedSet that contains all the elements from self, in the same order, with duplicates removed. **post**: result -> forAll (elem | self -> includes (elem)) **post**: self -> forAll (elem | result -> includes (elem)) **post**: self -> forAll (elem | result -> count (elem) = 1) **post**: self -> forAll (elem1, elem2 | self -> indexOf (elem1) < self -> indexOf (elem2) implies result -> indexOf (elem1) < result -> indexOf (elem2)

2. 4. 2. NEREUS Specification

```
CLASS Sequence [T]
IMPORTS Bag [T], Set [T], Integer
IS-SUBTYPE-OF Collection [create: createSeq; add: append]
GENERATED-BY createSeq, append
EFFECTIVE TYPES Sequence
OPERATIONS
createSeq, append, count
equal: Sequence x Sequence
prepend: Sequence x T → Sequence
union: Sequence x Sequence → Sequence
flatten: Sequence → Sequence [T1: ANY]
insertAt: Sequence x Integer x T → Sequence
subSequence:
```

```
Sequence(s) x Integer (lower) x Integer (upper) → Sequence
pre: 1<= lower and lower<= upper and upper<= size(s)
at: Sequence(s) x Integer(i) → T
pre: i >=1 and i<=size(s)
indexOf: Sequence(s) x T(e) → Integer
pre: includes(s,e)
first: Sequence → T
last: Sequence → T
including: Sequence x T → Sequence
excluding: Sequence x T → Sequence
collect: Sequence x (T->T1) → Sequence
asBag: Sequence → Bag
asSequence:Sequence → Sequence
asOrderedSet: Sequence → OrderedSet
asSet: Sequence → Set
AXIOMS s, s1: Sequence; e, e1: T; f: T → Boolean; i, index, lower,
upper: Integer;
g: T -> T1
count (append (s, e), e1) = if e = e1 then 1+ count (s, e1) else
count (s, e1)
equal (s, s1) = ((1<= index <= size (s)) implies
   at (s, index) = at (s1, index)) and size (s) = size (s1)
size (union (s, s1)) = size(s) + size (s1)
(1 <= index <= size (s)) implies at (s, index) = at (union (s, s1),
index)
(1 <= index <= size (s1)) implies
at (s1, index) = at (union (s, s1), index + size (s))
flatten (s) = if oclIsKindOf (elementType (type (s)), Collection-
Type)
   then iterate (v) (s, [union (acc, asSequence (v)) ], [acc = crea-
teSeq])
   else b
size (append (s, e)) = size (s) + 1
at (append (s, e), size (append (s, e)) = e
(1<= index <= size (s)) implies at (append (s, e), index) = at (s,
index)
size (prepend (s, e)) = size (s) + 1
at (prepend (s, e), 1) = e
(1<= index <= size (s)) implies at (s, index) = at (prepend(s, e),
index + 1)
size (insertAt (s, index, e) = size (s) + 1
at (insertAt (s, index, e), index) = e
(1<= i<= index - 1) implies at (s, i) = at (insertAt (s, index, e),
i)
```

```
(index + 1 <= i <= size (s)) implies at (s, i) = at (insertAt(s, in-
dex, e), i + 1)
size (subSequence (s, lower, upper)) = upper - lower + 1
(lower <= index <= upper) implies
at (subsequence (s, lower, upper), index - lower +1) = at (sequence,
index)
at (s, indexOf (s, e)) = e
first (s) = at (s,1)
last (s) = at (s, size (s))
including(s, e) = append(s, e)
not includes (excluding (s, e), e)
size (excluding (s, e)) = size (s) - count (s, e)
iterate (v) (s, [if e = v then acc else append (acc, v) ], [acc =
createSeq])
excluding (create, e) = create
excluding (append (s, e), e1) = if e = e1 then excluding (s, e)
   else append (excluding (s, e), e1)
forAll (v) (asBag (s), [count (s, v)) = count (asBag (s), e) ])
forAll (v) (s, [count (s, v) = count (asBag (s), v) ])
asSequence (s) = s
forAll (v) (asSet (s), [includes (s, v)])
forAll (v) (asset (s), [includes (asset (s), v) ])
forAll (v) (asOrderedSet (s), [includes (s, v) ])
forAll (v) (s, [includes (asOrderedSet (s), v) ])
forAll (v) (s, [count (isOrderdSet (s), e) = 1)
forAll (v1, v2) (s, [(indexOf (s, v1) < indexOf (s, v2)) implies
(indexOf (isOrderedSet (s), v1) < indexOf (isOrderedSet (s), v2) ])
collect (createSeq, g) = createSeq
collect (append (s, e), g) = including (collect (excluding (s, e),
g(e))
END-CLASS
```

2. 5. Ordered Set

2. 5. 1. OCL Specification

append (object: T): OrderedSet (T)
The set of elements, consisting of all elements of self, followed by object. **post**: result -> size () = self
-> size () + 1 **post**: result -> at (result -> size ()) = object **post**: Sequence {1..self -> size() } -> forAll
(index: Integer | result -> at (index) = self -> at (index))

prepend (object: T): OrderedSet (T)

The sequence consisting of object, followed by all elements in self. **post**: result -> size = self -> size () + 1 **post**: result -> at (1) = object **post**: Sequence {1..self -> size ()} -> forAll (index: Integer | self -> at (index) = result -> at (index + 1))

insertAt (index: Integer, object: T): OrderedSet (T)

The set consisting of self with object inserted at position index. **post**: result -> size = self -> size () + 1 **post**: result -> at (index) = object **post**: Sequence {1..(index - 1) } -> forAll (i: Integer | self -> at (i) = result -> at (i)) **post**: Sequence { (index + 1).. self -> size () } -> forAll (i: Integer | self -> at (i) = result -> at (i + 1))

subOrderedSet (lower: Integer, upper: Integer): OrderedSet (T)

The sub-set of self starting at number lower, up to and including element number upper. **pre**: 1 <= lower **pre**: lower <= upper **pre**: upper <= self -> size () **post**: result -> size () = upper - lower + 1 **post**: Sequence {lower..upper} -> forAll (index | result -> at (index - lower + 1) = self -> at (index))

at (i: Integer): T

The i-th element of self. **pre**: i >= 1 and i <= self -> size ()

indexOf (obj: T): Integer

The index of object obj in the sequence. **pre**: self -> includes (obj) **post**: self -> at (i) = obj

first (): T

The first element in self. **post**: result = self -> at (1)

last (): T

The last element in self. **post**: result = self -> at (self -> size ())

2. 5. 2. NEREUS Specification

```
CLASS OrderedSet [T: ANY]
IMPORTS Integer, Bag
IS-SUBTYPE-OF Collection [create: createOrderedSet; add: append]
GENERATED-BY createOrderedSet, including
EFFECTIVE TYPES OrderedSet
OPERATIONS
createOrderedSet, append, count
prepend: OrderedSet x T → OrderedSet
insertAt: OrderedSet x Integer x T → OrderedSet
subOrderedSet:
OrderedSet (s) x Integer (lower) x Integer (upper) → OrderedSet
pre: 1<= lower and lower <= upper and upper <= size (s)
at: OrderedSet (s) x Integer (i) → T
pre: i >=1 and I <= size (s)
```

```
indexOf: OrderedSet (s) x T (e) → Integer
```
pre: includes (s, e)
```
first: OrderedSet → T
last: OrderedSet → T
collect: OrderedSet x (T → T1: ANY) → Bag [T1]
excluding: OrderedSet x T → OrderedSet
```
AXIOMS s, s1: OrderedSet; e, e1:T; f:T -> Boolean; i, index, lower,
upper: Integer;
```
g: T->T1
count (s, e) <= 1
size (append (s, e)) = size (s) + 1
at (append (s, e), size (append (s, e)) = e
```
(1<= index <= size (s)) **implies** at (append (s, e), index) = at (s,
index)
```
size (prepend (s, e)) = size (s) + 1
at (prepend (s, e),1) = e
```
(1<= index <= size (s)) **implies** at (s, index) = at (prepend (s, e),
index + 1)
```
size (insertAt (s, index, e) = size (s) + 1
at (insertAt (s, index, e), index) = e
```
(1 <= I <= index - 1) **implies** at (s, i) = at (insertAt (s, index,
e), i)
(index + 1 <= I <= size (s)) **implies** at (s, i) = at (insertAt (s,
index, e), i + 1)
```
size (subOrderedSet (s, lower, upper)) = upper - lower + 1
```
(lower <= index <= upper) **implies**
```
at (subOrderedSet (s, lower, upper), index - lower + 1) = at (se-
quence, index)
at (s, indexOf (s, e)) = e
first (s) = at (s,1)
last (s) = at (s, size (s))
excluding (createOrderedSet, e) = createOrderedSet
excluding (append (s, e), e1) =
if e = e1 then excluding (s, e) else append (excluding (s, e), e1)
collect (createOrderedSet, g) = createBag
collect (including (s, e), g) = includingBag (collect (excluding (s,
e), g (e))
```
END-CLASS

B.3: ENUMERATION SIGNATURE

3. 1. OCL Signature

An enumerated type is defined by the following syntax

```
ENUM Name (#val₁, #val₂,..., #valₙ)
where valᵢ are the posible values associated to the respective type.
TYPE
Enumeration
OPERATIONS
_=_: Enumeration x Enumeration → Boolean
_ < > _: Enumeration x Enumeration → Boolean
```

3. 2. NEREUS Specification

```
CLASS EnumType
IMPORTS String, OrderedSet [String], Nat
GENERATED-BY createEnumType
EFFECTIVETYPES
EnumType
OPERATIONS
createEnumType: OrderedSet → EnumType
cardinality: EnumType → Nat
value: EnumType (t) x Nat (i) → String
pre: 1<= i <= cardinality (t)
AXIOMS t: EnumType; s: OrderedSet; i: Nat
cardinality (createEnumType (s)) = size (s)
value (s, i) = at (s, i)
END-CLASS
```

B.4: TYPE CONSTRUCTORS

4. 1. Cartesian Product

```
CLASS CartesProd
IMPORTS T₁, T₂,..., TₙTYPE
CartesProd
EFFECTIVEOPERATIONS
create: T₁ x T₂ x ...x Tₙ→ CartesProd
modif-i: CartesProd x Tᵢ → CartesProd
```

```
....  1≤i≤ n
select-i: Cartes-Prod → Ti
```
AXIOMS cp: CartesProd; $t_1:T_1$; t_2, $t_2,.:T_2$... $t_n:T_n$
modif-i (Create(t_1, $t_2,.t_i,..$, t_n)) = t_i
...
select-i (create(t_1, t_2, .., $t_i,..$ t_n), $t_i.$) = create(t_1, $t_2,..,$ $t_i,..$ t_n) 1≤i≤ n
END-CLASS

4. 2. The Constructor Type Association

4. 2. 1. Binary-Association

Relation scheme BinaryAssociation [*Class1: ANY, Class2: ANY*]
--Binary Association
IMPORTS Boolean, Multiplicity, Visibility, String, Typename
DEFERREDTYPES BinaryAssociation
OPERATIONS
```
name: BinaryAssociation → TypeName
frozen: BinaryAssociation → Boolean
changeable: BinaryAssociation → Boolean
addOnly: BinaryAssociation → Boolean
get_role1: BinaryAssociation → String
get_role2: BinaryAssociation → String
getMult1: BinaryAssociation → Multiplicity
getMult2: BinaryAssociation → Multiplicity
getVisibility1: BinaryAssociation → Visibility
getVisibility2: BinaryAssociation → Visibility
```
END-RELATION

4. 2. 2. Unidirectional- Effective/ 1 to 1

RELATION SCHEME Unidirectional-1
--Unidirectional/ 1 to 1
IS-SUBTYPE-OF BinaryAssociation
GENERATED-BY create, addLink
EFFECTIVETYPES Unidirectional-1
OPERATIONS
```
name, frozen, changeable, addOnly, get_role1, get_role2, getMult1,
getMult2, getVisibility1, getVisibility2
create: TypeName → Unidirectional-1
```
addLink: Unidirectional-1 (u) x *Class1* (c1) x *Class2* (c2) → Unidi-
rectional-1

pre: not frozen (u) and not isRelated (u, c1, c2) and rightCardinality (u, c1) < 1 and leftCardinality (u, c2) < 1
removeLink: Unidirectional-1 (u) x *Class1* (c1) x *Class2* (c2) → Undi-
rectional-1
pre: isRelated (u, c1, c2) and not addOnly (u) and not frozen (u)
get_*Class2*: Unidirectional-1(u) x Class1 (c1) → *Class2***pre**: isRight-
Linked (u, c1)
isRelated: Unidirectional-1 x *Class1* x *Class2* → Boolean
isRightLinked: Unidirectional-1 x *Class1* → Boolean
isLeftLinked: Unidirectional-1 x *Class2* → Boolean
isEmpty: Unidirectional-1→ Boolean
rightCardinality: Unidirectional-1 x *Class1* → Nat
leftCardinality: Unidirectional-1x *Class2*→ Nat
AXIOMS t: TypeName; u: Unidirectional-1; c1, cc1: *Class1*; c2, cc2:
Class2
get-role1 (u) = <*role name*>
get_role2 (u) = <*role name*>
getVisibility1 (u) = <*visibility*>
getVisibility2 (u) = <*visibility*>
frozen (u) = <*True or False*>
changeable (u) =<*True or False*>
addOnly (u) =<*True or False*>
getMult1(u) = 1
getMult2 (u) = 1
isRelated (create (t), c1, c2) = False
isRelated (addLink (u, c1, c2), cc1, cc2) =
(cc1 = c1 and cc2 = c2) or isRelated (u, cc1, cc2)
get_*Class2* (addLink (u, c1, c2), cc1) =
if c1 = cc1 then c2 else get_*Class2* (u, cc1)
removeLink (addLink (u, c1, c2), cc1, cc2) =
if c1 = cc1 and c2 = cc2 then u else addLink(removeLink (u, cc1,
cc2), c1, c2)
name (create (t)) = t
name (addLink (u, c1, c2))= name (u)
isEmpty (create (t)) = True
isEmpty (addLink (u, c1, c2)) = False
isRightLinked (create (t), c1) = False
isRightLinked(addLink (u, c1, c2), cc1) = (c1 = cc1) or isRight-
Linked (u, cc1)
isLeftLinked (create (t), c2) = False
isLeftLinked (addLink (u, c1, c2), cc2) = (c2 = cc2) or isLeftLinked
(u, cc2)
$0 \leq$ rightCardinality (u, c1) ≤ 1
$0 \leq$ leftCardinality (u, c2) ≤ 1

```
rightCardinality (create(t), c1) = 0
leftCardinality (create (t), c2) = 0
rightCardinality (addLink (u, c1, c2), cc1) =
if c1 = cc1 then 1 else rightCardinality (u, cc1)
leftCardinality (addLink (u, c1, c2), cc2) =
if c2 = cc2 then 1 else leftCardinality (u, cc2)
```
END-RELATION

4. 2. 3. Unidirectional/ Effective/ 1 to M

RELATION SCHEME Unidirectional-2
--Unidirectional/ 1to M
IMPORTS Collection-C2: *Collection* [*Class2*] [create-c2: create]
IS-SUBTYPE-OF BinaryAssociation
GENERATED-BY create, addLink
EFFECTIVETYPES Unidirectional-2
OPERATIONS
name, frozen, changeable, addOnly, get_role1, get_role2, getMult1,
getMult2, getVisibility1, getVisibility2
create: TypeName → Unidirectional-2
addLink: Unidirectional-2 (u) x *Class1* (c1) x *Class2 (c2)* → Unidi-
rectional-2
pre: not frozen (u) and not isRelated (u, c1, c2) and leftCardinality (u, c2) < 1
and rightCardinality (u, c1) < *<M>*
removeLink: Unidirectional-2 (u) x *Class1* (c1) x *Class2* (c2) → Undi-
rectional-2
pre: isRelated (u, c1, c2) and not addOnly (u) and not frozen (u)
get_*Class2*: Unidirectional-2 x *Class1* → Collection-C2
isRelated: Unidirectional-2 x *Class1* x *Class2* → Boolean
isRightLinked: Unidirectional-2 x *Class1* → Boolean
isLeftLinked: Unidirectional-2 x *Class2* → Boolean
isEmpty: Unidirectional-2 → Boolean
rightCardinality: Unidirectional-2 x *Class1* → Nat
leftCardinality: Unidirectional-2 x *Class2* → Nat
AXIOMS t: TypeName; u: Unidirectional-2; c1, cc1: *Class1*; c2, cc2:
Class2
get_role1 (u) = *<role name>*
get_role2 (u) = *<role name>*
getVisibility1 (u) = *<visibility>*
getVisibility2 (u) = *<visibility>*
frozen (u) = False
changeable (u) **=***<True or False>*
addOnly (u) **=***<True or False>*

```
getMult1 (u) = 1
getMult2 (u) = <multiplicity>
isRelated (create (t), c1, c2) = False
isRelated (addLink (u, c1, c2), cc1, cc2) =
(cc1 = c1 and cc2 = c2) or isRelated (u, cc1, cc2)
get_Class2 (create (t), c1) = create-c2
get_Class2 (addLink (u, c1, c2), cc1) =
if c1 = cc1 then add (get_Class2 (u, cc1), c2) else get_Class2 (u,
cc1)
removeLink (addLink (u, c1, c2), cc1, cc2) =
if c1 = cc1 and c2 = cc2 then u else addLink (removeLink (u, cc1,
cc2), c1, c2)
name (create (t)) = t
name (addLink (u, c1, c2)) = name (u)
isEmpty (create (t)) = True
isEmpty (addLink (u, c1, c2)) = False
isRightLinked (create (t), c1) = False
isRightLinked (addLink (u, c1, c2), cc1) = (c1 = cc1) or isRight-
Linked (u, cc1)
isLeftLinked (create (t), c2) = False
isLeftLinked (addLink (u, c1, c2), cc2) = (c2 = cc2) or isLeftLinked
(u, cc2)
rightCardinality (create (t), c1) =0
leftCardinality (create (t), c2) = 0
rightCardinality (addLink (u, c1, c2), cc1) =
if c1 = cc1 then 1 + rightCardinality (u, cc1) else rightCardinality
(u, cc1)
leftCardinality (addLink (u, c1, c2), cc2) =
if c2 = cc2 then 1 else leftCardinality (u,cc2)
```
END-RELATION

4. 2. 4. Unidirectional/Frozen/ n1..m1 to n2..m2

RELATION SCHEME Unidirectional-3
--*unidirectional/n1..n2 to m1..m2 / frozen***IMPORTS** PAIR: Cartes-Product [*Class1, Class2*] [create-pair: create]
Collection-Pair: Bounded-Collection [PAIR] [create-c2: create; re-latedC: isRelated]
IS-SUBTYPE-OF BinaryAssociation
GENERATED-BY create
EFFECTIVETYPES Unidirectional-3
OPERATIONS
name, frozen, changeable, addOnly, get_role1, get_role2, getMult1,
getMult2, getVisibility1, getVisibility2

```
create: TypeName x Collection-Pair (c2) → Unidirectional-3
pre: is-Bounded1 (c2, <n1>, <m1>) and is-Bounded2 (c2, <n2>, <m2>)
get_Class2: Unidirectional-3 x Class1 → Collection-Pair
isEmpty: Unidirectional-3→ Boolean
rightCardinality: Unidirectional-3 x Class1 → Nat
leftCardinality: Unidirectional-3 x Class2→ Nat
isRightLinked: Unidirectional-3 x Class1→ Boolean
isLeftLinked: Unidirectional-3 x Class2→ Boolean
isRelated:Unidirectional-3 x Class1 x Class2 → Boolean
AXIOMS t: TypeName; u: Unidirectional-4; col: Collection-Pair; c1:
Class1; c2: Class2; p: PAIR
get_role1(u) = <role name>
get_role2(u) = <role name>
getVisibility1(u) = <visibility>
getVisibility2(u) = <visibility>
frozen (u) = True
changeable (u) = False
addOnly (u) = False
getMult1 (u) = <multiplicity>
getMult2(u) = <multiplicity>
get_ Class2 (create (t, col)) = col
<n1> ≤ rightCardinality (u) ≤ <m1><n2> ≤ leftCardinality (u) ≤ <m2>
name (create (t, col)) = t
name(addlink (u, c1, c2)) = name (u)
isEmpty (create (t, col))= True
isEmpty (addlink (u, c1, c2)) = False
rightCardinality (create (t, col), c1) = rightSize (col, c1)
leftCardinality (create (t, col), c2) = leftSize (col, c2)
isRightLinked (create (t, col), c1) = relatedC (col, c1)
isLeftLinked (create (t, col), c2) = relatedC (col, c2)
END-RELATION
```

4. 2. 5. Aggregation

```
RELATION SCHEME AggregationIS-SUBTYPE-OF BinaryAssociation [Whole:
Class1, Part: Class2]
DEFERREDOPERATIONS
isPart: Aggregation x Whole x Part→ Boolean
isEmpty: Aggregation → Boolean
isLinkedWhole: Aggregation x Whole → Boolean
isLinkedPart: Aggregation x Part → Boolean
END-RELATION
```

4. 2. 6. Aggregation/ Simple/ 1 to 1 / not frozen

RELATION SCHEME Aggregation-1
-- aggregation/simple/ 1 to 1/not frozen
IS-SUBTYPE-OF Aggregation
GENERATED-BY create, add*Part***EFFECTIVETYPES** Aggregation-1
OPERATIONS
name, frozen, changeable, addOnly, get_role1, get_role2, getMult1, getMult2, getVisibility1, getVisibility2, is*Part*, isEmpty, isLinked-Whole, isLinkedPart
create: TypeName → Aggregation-1
add*Part*: Aggregation-1(a) x *Part (p)* x *Whole (w)* → Aggregation-1
pre: rightCardinality (a, w) < 1 and leftCardinality (a, p) < 1
get*Part*: Aggregation-1 (a) x Whole (w) → *Part***pre**: isLinkedWhole (a, w)
get*Whole*: Aggregation-1(a) x Part (p) → *Whole***pre**: isLinkedPart (a, p)
remove*Part*: Aggregation-1 (a) x *Whole* (w) x *Part* (p) → Aggregation-1
pre: isPart (a, w, p) and not addOnly (a) and not frozen (a)
rightCardinality: Aggregation-1 x *Whole* → Nat
leftCardinality: Aggregation-1 x *Part* → Nat
AXIOMS a: Aggregation-1; p, p1: *Part*; w, w1: *Whole*; t: TypeName
name (create (t)) = t
name (add*Part* (a, p, w)) = name (a)
frozen (a) = False
changeable (a) = True
add-Only (a) = <*True or False*>
getMult1 (a) = 1
getMult2 (a) = 1
get_role1 (a) = <*name-role1*>
get_role2 (a) = <*name-role2*>
getVisibility1 = <*visibility*>
getVisibility2 = <*visibility*>
get*Part* (add*Part* (a, p, w), w1) = if w = w1 then p else getPart (a, w1)
get*Whole* (add*Part* (a, p, w), p1) = if (p = p1) then w else getWhole (a, p1)
isPart (create (t), w, p) = False
is*Part* (addPart (a, p, w), w1, p1) = (w = w1 and p = p1) or isPart (a, w1, p1)
isEmpty (create (t)) = True
isEmpty (add*Part* (a, p, w)) = False
removePart (add*Part* (a, p, w), p1, w1) =
if (p = p1 and w = w1) then a else removePart (a, p1, w1)

```
isLinkedWhole (create (t), w) = False
isLinkedWhole (addPart (a, w, p), w1) = w = w1 or isLinkedWhole (a,
w1)
isLinkedPart (create(t), p) = False
isLinkedPart (addPart (a, w, p), p1) = (p = p1) or isLinkedPart (a,
p1)
0 ≤ righCardinality (a, w) ≤ 1
0 ≤ leftCardinality (a, p) ≤ 1
righCardinality (create (t), p1) = 0
leftCardinality (create (t), w1) = 0
righCardinality (addPart (a, p, w), w1) =
if w = w1 then 1 else righCardinality (a, w1)
leftCardinality (addPart (a, p, w), p1) =
if p = p1 then 1 else leftCardinality (a, p1)
```
END-RELATION

4. 2. 7. Aggregation /Simple/ 1 to M / not frozen

RELATION SCHEME Aggregation-2
--aggregation/simple/1 to M/not frozen
IMPORTS C-*Part*: *Collection* [*Part*]
IS-SUBTYPE-OF Aggregation
GENERATED-BY create, add*Part***EFFECTIVETYPES** Aggregation-2
OPERATIONS
name, frozen, changeable, addOnly, get_role1, get_role2, getMult1,
getMult2, getVisibility1, getVisibility2, is*Part*, isEmpty, isLinked-
Whole, isLinkedPart
create: TypeName → Aggregation-2
add*Part*: Aggregation-2 (a) x *Part* (p) x *Whole* (w) → Aggregation-2
pre: leftCardinality (a, p) < 1 and righCardinality (a, w) < <*M*> and
not isPart (a, w, p)
get*Part*: Aggregation-2 (a) x Whole (w) → C-*Part***pre**: isLinkedWhole
(a, w)
get*Whole*: Aggregation-2 (a) x Part (p) → *Whole***pre**: isLinkedPart (a,
p)
rightCardinality: Aggregation-2 x *Whole* → Nat
leftCardinality: Aggregation-2 x *Part* → Nat
remove*Part*: Aggregation-2 (a) x *Whole* (w) x *Part* (p) → Aggregation-2
pre: isPart (a, w, p) and not addOnly (a) and not frozen (a)
AXIOMS a: Aggregation-2; p, p1: *Part*; w, w1: *Whole*; t: TypeName
name (create (t)) = t
name (add*Part* (a, p, w)) = name (a)
frozen (a) = False
changeable (a) = True

```
add-Only(a) = <True or False>
getMult1 (a) =1
getMult2 (a) = <M>
rightCardinality (create (t), w) = 0
rightCardinality (addPart (a, p, w), w1) =
if w = w1 then 1+ rightCardinality (a, w1) else rightCardinality (a,
w1)
leftCardinality (create (t), p) = 0
leftCardinality (addPart (a, p, w), p1) = if p = p1 then 1 else
leftCardinality (a, p1)
get_role1(a) = <name-role1>
get_role2 (a) = <name-role2>
getVisibility1= <visibility>
getVisibility2= <visibility>
getPart (addPart (a, p, w), w1) =
if (w = w1) then add (getPart (a, w1), p) else getPart (a, w1)
getWhole (addPart (a, p, w), p1) = if (p = p1) then w else getWhole
(a, p1)
isPart (create (t), w, p) = False
isPart (addPart (a, p, w), w1, p1) = (p = p1 and w = w1) or isPart
(a, w1, p1)
isEmpty (create (t)) = True
isEmpty (addPart (a, p, w)) = False
removePart (addPart (a, p, w), p1, w1) =
if (p = p1 and w = w1) then a else removePart (a, p1,w1)
isLinkedWhole (create (t), w) = False
isLinkedWhole (addPart (a, p, w), w1) = (w = w1) or isLinkedWhole
(a, w1)
isLinkedPart (create (t), p) = False
isLinkedPart (addPart (a, p, w), p1)= (p = p1) or isLinkedPart (a,
p1)
```
END-RELATION

4. 2. 8. Aggregation/ Simple/ N to M/not frozen

```
RELATION SCHEME Aggregation-3
--aggregation/simple/N to M/not frozen
IMPORTS C-Part: Collection [Part]
   C-Whole: Collection [Whole]
IS-SUBTYPE-OF Aggregation
GENERATED-BY create, addPart
EFFECTIVETYPES Aggregation-3
OPERATIONS
```

name, frozen, changeable, addOnly, get_role1, get_role2, getMult1, getMult2, getVisibility1, getVisibility2, is*Part*, isEmpty, isLinked-Whole, isLinkedPart

create: TypeName → Aggregation-3

add*Part*: Aggregation-3 x *Part (p)* x *Whole* (w) → Aggregation-3

pre: not isLinkedPart (a, p) and rightCardinality (a, w) < <*M*> and leftCardinality (a, p) < <*N*>

get*Part*: Aggregation-3 (a) x Whole (w) → C-*Part***pre**: isLinkedWhole (a, w)

get*Whole*: Aggregation-3 (a) x Part (p) → C-*Whole***pre**: isLinkedPart (a, p)

leftCardinality: Aggregation-3 x *Part* → Nat

rightCardinality: Aggregation-3 x *Whole* → Nat

remove*Part*: Aggregation-3 (a) x *Whole* (w) x *Part* (p) → Aggregation-3

pre: isPart (a, w, p) and not addOnly (a) and not frozen (a)

AXIOMS a: Aggregation-3; p, p1: *Part*; w,w1: *Whole*; t: TypeName

name (create (t)) = t

name (add*Part* (a, p, w)) = name(a)

frozen (a) = False

changeable (a) = True

add-Only (a) = <*True or False*>

getMult1 (a) = <*multiplicity*>

getMult2 (a) = <*multiplicity*>

rightCardinality (create (t), w) = 0

rightCardinality (add*Part* (a, p, w), w1) =

if w = w1 then 1+ rightCardinality (a, w1) else rightCardinality (a, w1)

leftCardinality (create (t), p) = 0

leftCardinality (add*Part* (a, p, w), p1) = if (p = p1) then 1+ left-Cardinality (a, p1)

   else leftCardinality (a, p1)

get_role1 (a) = <*name-role1*>

get_role2 (a) = <*name-role2*>

getVisibility1 = <*visibility*>

getVisibility2 = <*visibility*>

isPart (create (t), p, w) = False

isPart (add*Part* (a, p, w), p1, w1) = (p = p1 and w = w1) or isPart(a, p1, w1)

get*Part* (add*Part* (a, p, w), w1) =

if (w = w1) then add (getPart (a, w1), p) else get*Part* (a, w1)

get*Whole* (add*Part* (a, p, w), p1) =

if (p = p1) then add (getWhole (a, p1), w) else get*Whole* (a, p1)

isEmpty (create (t)) = True

```
isEmpty (addPart (a, p, w)) = False
remove (addPart (a, p, w), p1, w1) =
if (p = p1 and w = w1) then a else remove (a, p1, w1)
isLinkedWhole (create (t), w) = False
isLinkedWhole (addPart (a, w, p), w1) = (w = w1) or isLinkedWhole
(a, w1)
isLinkedPart (create (t), p) = False
isLinkedPart (addPart (a, w, p), p1) = (p = p1) or isLinkedPart (a,
p1)
```
END-RELATION

4. 2. 9. Aggregation/Simple/1 to 1/frozen

RELATION SCHEME Aggregation-4
-- aggregation/simple/ 1 to 1/frozen
IS-SUBTYPE-OF Aggregation
GENERATED-BY create, addPart
EFFECTIVETYPES Aggregation-4
OPERATIONS
name, frozen, changeable, addOnly, get_role1, get_role2, getMult1,
getMult2, getVisibility1, getVisibility2, isPart, isEmpty, isLinked-
Whole, isLinkedPart
create: TypeName → Aggregation-4
addPart: Aggregation-4 (a) x *Part (p)* x *Whole (w)* → Aggregation-4
pre: not isPart (a, w, p)
getPart: Aggregation-4 (a) x Whole (w) → *Part***pre**: isLinkedWhole (a,
w)
getWhole: Aggregation-4 (a) x Part (p) → *Whole***pre**: isLinkedPart (a,
p)
AXIOMS a: Aggregation-4; p, p1: *Part*; w, w1: *Whole*; t: TypeName
name (create (t)) = t
name (addPart (a, p, w)) = name (a)
frozen (a) = True
changeable (a) = False
addOnly (a) = False
getMult1 (a) = 1
getMult2 (a) = 1
get_role1 (a) = <*name-role1*>
get_role2 (a) = <*name-role2*>
getVisibility1 = <*visibility*>
getVisibility2 = <*visibility*>
isPart (create (t), w, p) = False
isPart (addPart (a, p, w), w1, p1) = (w = w1 and p = p1) or isPart
(a, w1, p1)

getPart (addPart (a, p, w), w1) = if w = w1 then p else getPart (a, w1)

getWhole (addPart (a, p, w), p1) = if p = p1 then w else getWhole (a, p1)

isLinkedWhole (create(t), w1) = False

isLinkedWhole (addPart (a, w, p), w1) = (w = w1) or isLinkedWhole(a, w1)

isLinkedPart (create(t), p1) = False

isLinkedPart (addPart (a, w, p), p1)) = (p = p1) or isLinkedPart (a, p1)

isEmpty (create(t)) = True

isEmpty (addPart (a, p, w)) = False

END-RELATION

4. 2.10. Aggregation/ Simple/ 1 to M/ frozen

RELATION SCHEME Aggregation-5

-- aggregation/simple/ 1 to N1..N2/ frozen

IMPORTS C-*Part*: *Collection* [*Part*]

IS-SUBTYPE-OF Aggregation [C-*Part*: Part]

GENERATED-BY create, addPart

EFFECTIVETYPES Aggregation-5

OPERATIONS

name, frozen, changeable, addOnly, get_role1, get_role2, getMult1, getMult2, getVisibility1, getVisibility2, isPart, isEmpty, isLinked-Whole, isLinkedPart

create: TypeName → Aggregation-5

addPart: Aggregation-5 (a) x *C-Part (cp)* x *Whole (w)* → Aggregation-5

pre: rightCardinality (a, w) < 1 and <n1> < size (cp)< <n2>

getPart: Aggregation-5 (a) x Whole (w) → C-*Part***pre**: isLinkedWhole (a, w)

get*Whole*: Aggregation-5 (a) x Part (p) → *Whole***pre**: isLinkedPart (a, p)

rightCardinality: Aggregation-5 x Whole → Nat

leftCardinality: Aggregation-5 x Part → Nat

AXIOMS a: Aggregation-5; cp, cp1: C-*Part* ; w, w1: *Whole* ; t: Type-Name

name (create (t)) = t

name (addPart (a, p, w)) = name (a)

frozen (a)= True

changeable (a) = False

addOnly (a) = False

getMult1 (a) =1

getMult2 (a) = <*M*>

```
get_role1 (a) = <name-role1>
get_role2 (a) = <name-role2>
getVisibility1 = <visibility>
getVisibility2 = <visibility>
isPart (create (t), w, p) = False
isPart (addPart (a, cp, w), w1, cp1) = (w = w1 and cp = cp1) or is-
Part (a, w1, cp1)
getPart (addPart (a, cp, w), w1) = if (w = w1) then cp else getPart
(a, w1)
getWhole (addPart (a, cp, w), p1) =
if includes (cp, p1) then w else getWhole (a, p1)
isPart (create (t), w1, p1) = False
isPart(addPart(a,cp,w),w1,cp1) = (w = w1 and cp = cp1) or isPart (a,
w1, p1)
isLinkedWhole (create (t), w1) = False
isLinkedWhole (addPart (a, w, cp), w1) = (w = w1) or isLinkedWhole
(a, w1)
isLinkedPart (create (t), cp1) = False
isLinkedPart (addPart (a, w, cp), cp1))= (cp = cp1) or isLinkedPart
(a, cp1)
isEmpty (create (t)) = True
isEmpty (addPart (a, cp, w)) = False
rightcardinality (create (t), w) = 0
rightCardinality (addPart (a, cp, w), w1) =
if (w=w1) then size (cp) else righCardinality (a, w1)
leftcardinality (create (t), w) = 0
leftCardinality (addPart (a, cp, w), w1) =
if (w = w1) then size (cp) else leftCardinality (a, w1)
```
END-RELATION

4. 2. 11. Aggregation/simple/1to n1..n2/changeable

```
RELATION SCHEME Aggregation-6
-- aggregation/simple/1to n1..n2/changeable
IMPORTS C-Part: Collection [Part]
IS-SUBTYPE-OF Aggregation [C-Part: Part; undefine: isPart]
GENERATED-BY create, addPartEFFECTIVETYPES Aggregation-6
OPERATIONS
name, frozen, changeable, addOnly, get_role1, get_role2, getMult1,
getMult2, getVisibility1, getVisibility2, isEmpty, isLinkedPart, is-
LinkedWhole
create: TypeName → Aggregation-6
addPart: Aggregation-6 (a) x C-Part (cp) x Whole (w) → Aggregation-6
pre: changeable (a) and <n1> ≤ size (cp) ≤ <n2>
```

```
rightCardinality: Aggregation-6 x Whole → Nat
leftCardinality: Aggregation-6 x Part → Nat
removePart: Aggregation-6 (a) x Whole (w) x Part (p) → Aggregation-6
pre: isPart (a, w, p) and not addOnly (a)
getPart: Aggregation-6 (a) x Whole (w) → C-Part (p)
pre: isLinkedWhole (a, w)
getWhole: Aggregation-6 (a) x Part (p) → Wholepre: isLinkedPart (a,
p)
isPart: Aggregation-6 x Whole x Part → Boolean
```

AXIOMS a: Aggregation-6; p, p1: *Part*; w, w1: *Whole*; t: TypeName;
cp: C-Part

```
name (create (t)) = t
name (addPart (a, cp, w)) = name (a)
frozen (a) = False
changeable (a) = True
addOnly (a) = <True or False>
getMult1 (a) = 1
getMult2 (a)= <n1>..<n2>
rightCardinality (create (t), w) = 0
rightCardinality (addPart (a, cp, w), w1) =
if (w = w1) then size (cp) else rightCardinality (a, w1)
leftCardinality (create (t), w) = 0
leftCardinality (addPart (a, cp, w), p1) =
if includes (cp, p1) then 1 else leftCardinality (a, w1)
get_role1 (a) = <name-role1>
get_role2 (a) = <name-role2>
getVisibility1= <visibility>
getVisibility2= <visibility>
getWhole (addPart (a, cp, w), p1) =
if includes (cp, p1) then w else getWhole (a, p1)
getPart (addPart (a,c p, w), w1) = if (w = w1) then cp else getPart
(a, w1)
isPart (create (t), w, p) = False
isPart (addPart(a, cp, w), w1, p1) =
includes (cp, p1) and (w = w1) or isPart (a, w1, p1)
isEmpty (create (t)) = True
isEmpty (addPart (a, cp, w)) = False
remove (addPart (a, cp, w), p1, w1) =
if (includes (cp, p1) and w = w1) then addPart (create (t), delete
(cp, p1), w)
   else remove (a, p, w1)
isLinkedWhole (create (t), w1) = False
isLinkedWhole (addPart (a, cp, w), w1)= (w = w1) or isLinkedWhole
```

```
(a, w1)
isLinkedPart (create (t), p1) = False
isLinkedPart (addPart(a, cp, w), p) = includes (cp, p) or isLinked-
Part (a, p)
```
END-RELATION

4. 2. 12. Aggregation/ 1 to n1..n2 /ordered/frozen

RELATION SCHEME Aggregation-7
```
--aggregation/simple/1to n1..n2/ordered/frozen
```
IMPORTS C-*Part*: Sequence [*Part*] [create-s: create]
IS-SUBTYPE-OF Aggregation [C-*Part*: *Part*]
GENERATED-BY create, add*Part***EFFECTIVETYPES** Aggregation-7
OPERATIONS
```
name, frozen, changeable, addOnly, get_role1, get_role2, getMult1,
getMult2, getVisibility1, getVisibility2, isPart, isEmpty, isLinked-
Whole, isLinkedPart
create: TypeName → Aggregation-7
addPart: Aggregation-7(a) x C-Part (cp) x Whole (w) → Aggregation-7
```
pre:$<n1> \leq$`size (cp)` $\leq$ `<n2> and not isLinkedWhole (a, w)`
```
rightCardinality: Aggregation-7 x Whole → Nat
leftCardinality: Aggregation-7 x Part → Nat
getPart: Aggregation (a) x Whole (w) → C-Part (p)
```
pre: `isLinkedWhole (a, w)`
```
getWhole: Aggregation (a) x Part (p) → Whole
```
pre: `isLinkedPart (a, p)`
AXIOMS `a: Aggregation-7; p, p1: Part; w, w1: Whole; t: TypeName; cp:`
`C-Part`
```
name (create (t)) = t
name (addPart (a, cp, w)) = name (a)
frozen (a)= True
changeable (a) = False
addOnly (a) = True
getMult1 (a) = 1
getMult2 (a) = <n1>..<n2>
rightCardinality (create (t), w) = 0
rightCardinality (addPart (a, cp, w), w1) =
if includes(cp, w1) then 1 else leftCardinality (a, w1)
rightCardinality (create (t), w) = 0
leftCardinality (addPart (a, cp, w), p1) =
if includes (cp, p1) then 1 else leftCardinality (a, p1)
get_role1(a) = <name-role1>
get_role2(a) = <name-role2>
getVisibility1 = <visibility>
getVisibility2 = <visibility>
```

getPart (addPart(a, cp, w), w1) = if (w = w1) then cp else getPart (a, w1)

getWhole (addPart (a, cp, w), p)=
if includes (cp, p) then w else getWhole (a, p)

isPart (create (t), p) = False

isPart (addPart (a, cp, w), p1, w1) =
(includes (cp, p1) and (w = w1)) or isPart (a, p1, w1)

isLinkedWhole (create (t), w) = False

isLinkedWhole (addPart (a, cp, w), w1) = (w = w1) or isLinkedWhole (a, w1)

isLinkedPart (create(t), w) = False

isLinkedPart (addPart (a, cp, w), p) = includes (cp, p) or isLinkedPart (a, p)

END-RELATION

4. 2. 13. Aggregation/ Composition/ 1..1

RELATION SCHEME Composition-1
--composition/simple/ 1..1/not frozen
IS-SUBTYPE-OF Aggregation
GENERATED-BYcreate, addEFFECTIVETYPES Composition-1
OPERATIONS
name, frozen, changeable, addOnly, get_role1, get_role2, getMult1, getMult2, getVisibility1, getVisibility2, getPart, getWhole, isPart, isEmpty, isLinkedPart, isLinkedWhole

create: TypeName → Composition-1

addPart: Composition-1(c) x Part (p) x Whole (w) → Composition-1
pre: rightCardinality(a, w) <1 and leftCardinality (a, p) < 1

removePart: Composition-1 (a) x Whole (w) x Part (p) → Composition-1
pre: isLinkedPart (a, w, p) and not addOnly (a) and not frozen (a)

leftCardinality: Composition-1 x Part → Nat

rightCardinality: Composition-1 x Whole → Nat

getPart: Composition-1(c) x Whole (w) → Part
pre: isLinkedWhole (c, w)

getWhole: Composition-1(c) x Part (p) → Whole
pre: isLinkedPart (c, p)

AXIOMS a: Composition-1; p, p1: Part; w, w1: Whole; t: TypeName

name (create (t)) = t

name (addPart (a, p, w)) = name (a)

frozen (a) = False

changeable (a) = True

add-Only (a) = <True or False>

getMult1 (a) = 1

getMult2 (a) = 1

```
get_role1 (a) = <name-role1>
get_role2 (a) = <name-role2>
getVisibility1= <visibility>
getVisibility2= <visibility>
getPart (addPart (a, p, w)) = if w = w1 then p else getPart (a, w1)
getWhole (addPart (a, p, w), p1)) = if (p = p1) then w else getWhole
(a, p1)
isPart (create(t), p1) = False
isPart (addPart (a, p, w), w1, p1) = (w = w1 and p = p1) or isPart
(a, w1, p1)
isEmpty (create (t)) = True
isEmpty (addPart (a, p, w)) = False
remove (addPart (a, p, w), p1, w1) =
if (p = p1 and w = w1) then a else remove (a, p1, w1)
isLinkedPart (create(t), p) = False
isLinkedPart (addPart (a, w, p), p1) = (p = p1) or isLinkedPart (a,
p1)
isLinkedWhole (create (t), p) = False
isLinkedWhole (addPart (a, w, p), w1) = (w = w1) or isLinkedWhole
(a, w1)
leftCardinality (create (t), p) = 0
leftCardinality (addPart (a, w, p), p1) = if (p = p1) then 1 else
leftCardinality (a, p1)
```
END-RELATION

4. 14. Composition / Simple/ 1 to M/ not frozen

```
RELATION SCHEME Composition-2
--composition / simple / 1..M / not frozen
IMPORTS C-Part: Collection [Part]
IS-SUBTYPE-OF Aggregation
EFFECTIVETYPES Composition-2
OPERATIONS
name, frozen, changeable, addOnly, get_role1, get_role2, getMult1,
getMult2, getVisibility1, getVisibility2, isPart, isEmpty, isLinked-
Part, isLinkedWhole
create: TypeName → Composition-2
addPart: Composition-2 (a) x Part (p) x Whole (w) → Composition-2
pre: leftCardinality (a, p) < 1 and not isPart (a, p, w) and right-
Cardinality (a, w) < <M>
rightCardinality: Composition-2 x Whole → Nat
leftCardinality: Composition-2 x Part → Nat
removePart: Composition-2 (a) x Whole (w) x Part (p) → Composition-2
pre: isPart (a, w, p) and not addOnly (a) and not frozen (a)
```

```
getPart: Composition (c) x Whole (w) → C-Part
```
pre: isLinkedWhole (c, w)
```
getWhole: Composition-2 (c) x Part (p) → Whole
```
pre: isLinkedPart (c, p)
AXIOMS a: Composition-2; p, p1: *Part*; w, w1: *Whole*; t: TypeName
```
name (create (t)) = t
name (addPart (a, p, w)) = name (a)
frozen (a) = False
changeable (a) = True
addOnly (a) = <True or False>
getMult1 (a) =1
getMult2 (a) = <M>
rightCardinality (create (t), w) = 0
rightCardinality (addPart (a, p, w), w1) =
if w = w1 then 1+ rightCardinality (a, w1) else rightCardinality (a, w1)
leftCardinality (create (t), p) = 0
leftCardinality (addPart (a, p, w), p1) = if p = p1 then 1 else
leftCardinality (a, p1)
get_role1 (a) = <name-role>
get_role2 (a) = <name-role>
getVisibility1 = <visibility>
getVisibility2 = <visibility>
isPart (create(t), p, w)= False
isPart (addPart (a, p, w), p1, w1) = (p = p1 and w = w1) or isPart
(a, p1, w1)
getPart (addPart (a, p, w), w1) =
if w = w1 then then includes (getPart (a, w1), p) else getPart (a,
w1)
getWhole (addPart (a, p, w), p1) = if p = p1 then w else getWhole
(a, p1)
isEmpty (create (t)) = True
isEmpty (addPart (a, p, w)) = False
remove (addPart (a, p, w), p1, w1) =
if (p = p1 and w = w1) then a else remove (a, p1, w1)
isLinkedPart (create (t), p1) = False
isLinkedWhole (create (t), w1) = False
isLinkedPart (addPart (a, w, p), p1) = (p = p1) or isLinkedPart (a,
p1)
isLinkedWhole (addPart (a, w, p), w1) = (w = w1) or isLinkedWhole
(a, w1)
```
END-RELATION

4. 15. Bidirectional / 1 to 1

RELATION SCHEME Bidirectional-1
IS-SUBTYPE-OF BinaryAssociation
GENERATED-BY create, addLink
EFFECTIVE
name, frozen, changeable, addOnly, get_role1, get_role2, getMult1,
getMult2, getVisibility1, getVisibility2
create: Typename → Bidirectional-1
addLink: Bidirectional-1(b) x *Class1(c1)* x *Class2(c2)* → Bidirection-al-1
pre: rightCardinality (b, c1) < 1 and leftCardinality (b, c2) < 1 and
not isRelated (a, c1, c2)
isEmpty: Bidirectional-1 → Boolean
isRightLinked: Bidirectional-1 x *Class1* → Boolean
isLeftLinked: Bidirectional-1 x *Class2* → Boolean
rightCardinality: Bidirectional-1 x *Class1* → Nat
leftCardinality: Bidirectional-1 x *Class2* → Nat
get*Class1*: Bidirectional-1(a) x *Class1* (c1) → *Class2***pre**: isRight-Linked (a,c1)
get*Class2*: Bidirectional-1(a) x *Class2* (c2) → *Class1***pre**: isLeftLinked (a, c2)
remove: Bidirectional-1 (a) x *Class1* (c1) x *Class2* (c2) → Bidirec-tional-1
pre: isRelated (a, c1, c2)
isRelated: Bidirectional-1 x Class1 (c1) x Class2 (c2) → Boolean
AXIOMS a: Bidirectional-1; c1, cc1: *Class1*; c2, cc2: *Class2*; t:
TypeName
name (create(t)) = t
name (add (a, c1, c2)) = name (a)
isEmpty (create(t) = True
isEmpty (addLink (a, c1, c2)) = False
frozen (a) = *<True or False>*
changeable (a) = *<True or False>*
addOnly (a) = *<True or False>*
get_role1 (a) = *<role name>*
get_role2 (a) = *<role name>*
getMult1(a) = *<multiplicity>*
getMult2 (a) = *<multiplicity>*
getVisibility1 (a) = *<visibility>*
getVisibility2 (a) = *<visibility>*
isRelated (create (t), c1, c2) = False
isRelated (addLink (a, c1, c2), cc1, cc2) =

```
(c1 = cc1 and c2 = cc2) or isRelated (a, cc1, cc2)
isRightLinked (create (t), c1) = False
isRightLinked (addLink (a, c1, c2), cc1) =
if c1= cc1 then True else isRightLinked (a,cc1)
isLeftLinked (create (t),c2) = False
isLeftLinked (addLink (a, c1, c2), cc2) =
if c2 = cc2 then True else isLeftLinked (a, cc2)
rightCardinality (create (t), c1) = 0
rightCardinality (addLink (a, c1, c2), cc1) =
if c1 = cc1 then 1 else rightCardinality (a, cc1)
leftCardinality (create (t), c1) = 0
leftCardinality (addLink (a, c1, c2), cc1) =
if c1= cc1 then 1 else leftCardinality (a, cc1)
getClass1(addLink (a, c1, c2), cc1) = if c1 = cc1 then c2 else
getClass1(a, cc1)
getClass2 (addLink (a, c1, c2), cc2) =
if c2 = cc2 then c2 else getClass2 (a, cc2)
remove (addLink (a, c1, c2), cc1, cc2) =
if (c1=cc1 and c2=cc2) then a else remove(a,cc1,cc2)
```
END-RELATION

4. 16. Bidirectional/ 1 to *

RELATION SCHEME Bidirectional-2
IMPORTS Collection-C2: Collection [Class2]
IS-SUBTYPE-OF BinaryAssociation
GENERATED-BY create, addLink
EFFECTIVEOPERATIONS
name, frozen, changeable, addOnly, get_role1, get_role2, getMult1,
getMult2, getVisibility1, getVisibility2
create: Typename→ Bidirectional-2
addLink: Bidirectional-2 (b) x *Class1 (c1)* x *Class2 (c2)* → Bidirec-
tional-2
pre: leftCardinality (b, c2) < 1 and not isRelated (a, c1, c2)
isEmpty: Bidirectional-2 → Boolean
isRightLinked: Bidirectional-2 x *Class1* → Boolean
isLeftLinked: Bidirectional-2 x *Class2* → Boolean
rightCardinality: Bidirectional-2 x *Class1* → Nat
leftCardinality: Bidirectional-2 x *Class2* → Nat
get*Class1*: Bidirectional-2 (a) x *Class1* (c1) → Collection-C2
pre: isRightLinked (a, c1)
get*Class2*: Bidirectional-2 (a) x *Class2* (c2) → *Class1***pre**:
isLeftLinked (a, c2)
remove: Bidirectional-2 (a) x *Class1* (c1) x *Class2* (c2) → Bidirec-

```
tional-2
pre: isRelated (a, c1, c2)
isRelated: Bidirectional-2 x Class1 (c1) x Class2 (c2) → Boolean
AXIOMS a: Bidirectional-2; c1, cc1: Class1; c2, cc2: Class2; t:
TypeName
name (create (t)) = t
name (add (a, c1, c2)) = name (a)
isEmpty (create (t)) = True
isEmpty (addLink (a, c1, c2)) = False
frozen (a) = <True or False>
changeable (a) = <True or False>
addOnly (a) = <True or False>
get_role1 (a) = <role name>
get_role2 (a) = <role name>
getMult1 (a) = <multiplicity>
getMult2 (a) = <multiplicity>
getVisibility1 (a) = <visibility>
getVisibility2 (a) = <visibility>
isRelated (create (t), c1, c2) = False
isRelated(addLink(a, c1, c2), cc1, cc2) =
(c1 = cc1 and c2 = cc2) or isRelated(a, cc1, cc2)
isRightLinked (create (t), c1) = False
isRightLinked (addLink (a, c1, c2), cc1) =
if c1 = cc1 then True else isRightLinked (a, cc1)
isLeftLinked (create (t), c2) = False
isLeftLinked (addLink (a, c1, c2), cc2) =
if c2 = cc2 then True else isLeftLinked (a, cc2)
rightCardinality (create (t), c1) = 0
rightCardinality(addLink (a, c1, c2), cc1) =
if c = cc1 then 1 + rightCardinality (a, cc1) else rightCardinality
(a, cc1)
leftCardinality (create (t), c2) = 0
leftCardinality(addLink (a, c1, c2), cc2) =
if c2 = cc2 then 1 else leftCardinality (a, cc2)
getClass2 (addLink (a, c1, c2), cc1) =
if c1 = cc1 then add (getClass2 (a, cc1), c2) else getClass2 (a,
cc1)
getClass1 (addLink (a, c1, c2), cc2) = if c2 = cc2 then c1 else
getClass1(a, cc2)
remove (addLink (a, c1, c2), cc1, cc2) =
if (c1 = cc1 and c2 = cc2) then a else remove(a, cc1, cc2)
isRelated (create (t), c1, c2) = False
isRelated(addLink(a, c1, c2), cc1, cc2) =
(c1= cc1 and c2 = cc2) or isRelated(a, cc1, cc2)
END-RELATION
```

4. 17. Bidirectional/ * to *

RELATION SCHEME Bidirectional-3
IMPORTS Collection-C1:Collection [Class1], Collection-C2: Collection [Class2]
IS-SUBTYPE-OF BinaryAssociation
GENERATED-BY create, addLink
EFFECTIVE
name, frozen, changeable, addOnly, get_role1, get_role2, getMult1, getMult2, getVisibility1, getVisibility2
create: Typename → Bidirectional-3
addLink: Bidirectional-3 (b) x *Class1(c1)* x *Class2 (c2)* → Bidirectional-3
pre: not isRelated (a, c1, c2)
isEmpty: Bidirectional-3 → Boolean
isRightLinked: Bidirectional-3 x *Class1* → Boolean
isLeftLinked: Bidirectional-3 x *Class2* → Boolean
rightCardinality: Bidirectional-3 x *Class1* → Nat
leftCardinality: Bidirectional-3 x *Class2* → Nat
get*Class2*: Bidirectional-3 (a) x *Class1* (c1) → Collection-C2
pre: isRightLinked (a, c1)
get*Class1*: Bidirectional-3 (a) x *Class2* (c2) → Collection-C1
pre: isLeftLinked (a, c2)
remove: Bidirectional-3 (a) x *Class1* (c1) x *Class2* (c2) → Bidirectional-3
pre: isRelated (a, c1, c2)
isRelated: Bidirectional-3 x Class1 (c1) x Class2 (c2) → Boolean

AXIOMS a: Bidirectional-3; c1,cc1: *Class1*; c2,cc2:*Class2*; t:TypeName
name (create (t))= t
name (add (a, c1, c2)) = name (a)
isEmpty (create(t))= True
isEmpty (addLink (a, c1, c2)) = False
frozen (a) = *<True or False>*
changeable (a) = *<True or False>*
addOnly (a) = *<True or False>*
get_role1 (a) = *<role name>*
get_role2 (a) = *<role name>*
getMult1(a) = *<multiplicity>*
getMult2 (a) = *<multiplicity>*
getVisibility1 (a) = *<visibility>*
getVisibility2 (a) = *<visibility>*
isRelated (create (t), c1, c2) = False
isRelated (addLink (a, c1, c2), cc1, cc2) =

```
(c1 = cc1 and c2 = cc2) or isRelated(a, cc1, cc2)
isRightLinked (create (t), c1) = False
isRightLinked (addLink(a, c1, c2), cc1) =
if c1 = cc1 then True else isRightLinked (a, cc1)
isLeftLinked (create (t), c2) = False
isLeftLinked (addLink (a, c1, c2), cc2) =
if c2 = cc2 then True else isLeftLinked (a, cc2)
rightCardinality (create (t), c1) = 0
rightCardinality (addLink (a, c1, c2), cc1) =
if c1 = cc1 then 1 + rightCardinality (a, cc1) else rightCardinality
(a, cc1)
leftCardinality (create (t), c2) = 0
leftCardinality (addLink (a, c1, c2), cc2) =
if c2 = cc2 then 1 + leftCardinality (a, cc2) else
leftCardinality(a, cc2)
getClass2 (addLink (a, c1, c2), cc1) =
if c1 = cc1 then add (getClass2 (a, cc1), c2) else getClass2 (a, cc1)
getClass1 (addLink (a, c1, c2), cc2) =
if c2 = cc2 then add (getClass1(a, cc2), c2) else getClass1 (a, cc2)
remove (addLink (a, c1, c2), cc1, cc2) =
if (c1 = cc1 and c2 = cc2) then a else remove (a, cc1, cc2)
```
END-RELATION

4. 18. Bidirectional / * to *

RELATION CLASS Bidirectional-4
IMPORTS Collection-C2: Collection [*Class2*]
   Collection-C1:Collection [*Class1*]
IS-SUBTYPE-OF BinaryAssociation
GENERATED-BY create, addlink
EFFECTIVE
name, create, frozen, changeable, addOnly, get_role1, get_role2,
getMult1, getMult2, getVisibility1, getVisibility2, isRelated
create: Typename → Bidirectional-4
addlink: Bidirectional-4 (b) x *Class1 (c1)* x *Class2 (c2)* → Bidirec-
tional-4
pre: rightCardinality (b, c1) < < *m1*> and leftCardinality (b, c2) <
<*m2*>
isEmpty: Bidirectional-4 → Boolean
isRightLinked: Bidirectional-4 x *Class1* → Boolean
isLeftLinked: Bidirectional-4 x *Class2* → Boolean
rightCardinality: Bidirectional-4 x *Class1* → Nat
leftCardinality: Bidirectional-4 x *Class2* → Nat
link1: Bidirectional-4 (a) x *Class1* (c1) → Collection-C2

pre: isRightLinked (a, c1)
link2: Bidirectional-4 (a) x *Class2* (c2) → Collection-C1
pre: isLeftLinked (a, c2)
remove: Bidirectional-4 (a) x *Class1* (c1) x *Class2* (c2) → Boolean
pre: isRelated (a, c1, c2)
AXIOMS a: Bidirectional-4; c1, cc1: *Class1*; c2, cc2: *Class2*; t:
TypeName
isEmpty (create (t)) = True
isEmpty (addlink (a, c1, c2)) = False
frozen(a) = *<True or False>*
changeable (a) = *<True or False>*
addOnly (a) = *<True or False>*
get_role1 (a) = *<role name>*
get_role2 (a) = *<role name>*
getMult1 (a) = *<multiplicity>*
getMult2 (a) = *<multiplicity>*
getVisibility1 (a) = *<visibility>*
getVisibility2 (a) = *<visibility>*
isRelated (create (t), c1, c2) = False
isRelated (addlink (a, c1, c2), cc1, cc2) =
(c1 = cc1 and c2 = cc2) or isRelated (a, cc1, cc2)
isRightLinked (create (t), c1) = False
isRightLinked (addlink1(a, c1, c2), cc1) =
if c1= cc1 then True else isRightLinked (a, cc1)
isLeftLinked (create (t), c2) = False
isLeftLinked (addlink2 (a, c1, c2), cc2) =
if c2 = cc2 then True else isLeftLinked (a, cc2)
rightCardinality (create (t), c1) = 0
rightCardinality (addlink1(a, c1, c2), cc1) =
if c1 = cc1 then 1+ rightCardinality (a, cc1) else rightCardinality
(a, cc1)
leftCardinality (create (t), c1) = 0
leftCardinality (addlink2 (a, c1, c2), cc1) =
if c1 = cc1 then 1 + leftCardinality (a, cc1) else leftCardinality
(a, cc1)
link1(addlink1(a, c1, c2), cc1) =
if c1 = cc1 then includes (link1(a), c2) else link1(a, cc1)
link2 (addlink2 (a, c1, c2), cc2) =
if c2=cc2 then includes(link2 (a), c1) else link2 (a, cc2)
remove1(addlink1(a, c1, c2), cc1, cc2) =
if (c1 = cc1 and c2 = cc2) then a else remove1(a, cc1, cc2)
remove2 (addlink2 (a, c2, c1), cc2, cc1) =
if (c2 = cc2 and c1 = cc1) then a else remove2(a, cc2, cc1)
END-RELATION

4. 19. Bidirectional/n1..n2 to m1..m2

RELATION SCHEME Bidirectional-5
IMPORTS *Class1, Class2,*
PAIR: Cartes-Product [*Class1, Class2*] [create-pair: create],
Collection-Links: *Collection* [PAIR] [create-c2: create],
Collection-C2: Collection [*Class2*], Collection-C1: Collection [*Class1*]
IS-SUBTYPE-OF BinaryAssociation
GENERATED-BY create, addlink
EFFECTIVEOPERATIONS
name, create, frozen, changeable, addOnly, get_role1, get_role2, getMult1, getMult2, getVisibility1, getVisibility2, is-related
create: Typename x Collection-Links (l) → Bidirectional-5
addlink: Bidirectional-5 (b) x *Class1 (c1)* x *Class2 (c2)* → Bidirectional-5
pre: rightCardinality (b, c1) < < *m1*> and leftCardinality (b, c2) < <*m2*>
isEmpty: Bidirectional-5 → Boolean
isRightLinked: Bidirectional-5 x *Class1* → Boolean
isLeftLinked: Bidirectional-5 x *Class2* → Boolean
rightCardinality: Bidirectional-5 x *Class1* → Nat
leftCardinality: Bidirectional-5 x *Class2* → Nat
link1: Bidirectional-5 (a) x *Class1 (c1)* → Collection-C2
pre: isRightLinked (a, c1)
link2: Bidirectional (a) x *Class2 (c2)* → Collection-C1
pre: isLeftLinked (a, c2)
remove: Bidirectional (a) x *Class1 (c1)* x *Class2 (c2)* → Boolean
pre: isRelated (a, c1, c2)

AXIOMS a: Bidirectional; c1, cc1: *Class1*; c2, cc2: *Class2*; t: Type-Name;
col: Collection-Link
isEmpty (create (t, cl)) = isEmpty (cl)
isEmpty (addlink (a, c1, c2)) = False
frozen (a) = <*True or False*>
changeable (a) = <*True or False*>
addOnly (a) = <*True or False*>
get_role1 (a) = <*role name*>
get_role2 (a) = <*role name*>
getMult1 (a) = <*multiplicity*>
getMult2 (a) = <*multiplicity*>
getVisibility1 (a) = <*visibility*>
getVisibility2 (a) = <*visibility*>

```
is-related (create (t, empty), c1, c2) = False
is-related(create (t, add(cl,e)), c1, c2) =
if select1 (e) = c1 and select2 (e) = c2 then TRUE
   else is-related (create (t, cl), c1, c2)
isRelated (addlink (a, c1, c2), cc1, cc2) =
(c1= cc1 and c2 = cc2) or isRelated (a, cc1, cc2)
isRightLinked (create (t, empty), c1) = False
isRightLinked (create (t, add (col, e)), c1) =
if select1(e) =c1 then TRUE else isRighLinked (create (t, col), c1)
isRightLinked (addlink1(a, c1, c2), cc1) = if c1 = cc1 then True
   else isRightLinked (a, cc1)
isLeftLinked (create (t, empty), c2) = False
isLeftLinked (addlink2 (a, c1, c2), cc2) = if c2 = cc2 then True
   else isLeftLinked (a, cc2)
isLeftLinked (create (t, add (col, e)), c2) =
if select2 (e) = c1 then TRUE else isLeftLinked (create (t, col),
c2)
rightCardinality (create (t, empty), c1) = 0
righCardinality (create (t, add (col, e)), c1) =
if select1(e) = c1 then 1+ rightCardinality (col, c1)
rightCardinality (addlink1(a, c1, c2), cc1) =
if c1 = cc1 then 1+ rightCardinality (a, cc1) else rightCardinality
(a, cc1)
leftCardinality (create (t, empty), c1) = 0
leftCardinality (create (t, add (col, e)), c1) =
if select1 (e) = c1 then 1+ leftCardinality (col, c1) else leftCar-
dinality (a, cc1)
if c1 = cc1 then 1 + leftCardinality (a, cc1) else leftCardinality
(a, cc1)
link1 (addlink1 (a, c1, c2), cc1) =
if c1= cc1 then includes (link1(a), c2) else link1(a, cc1)
link2 (addlink2 (a, c1, c2), cc2) =
if c2 = cc2 then includes (link2 (a), c1) else link2 (a, cc2)
remove1 (addlink1 (a, c1, c2), cc, cc2) =
if (c1 = cc1 and c2 = cc2) then a else remove1(a, cc1, cc2)
remove2 (addlink2 (a, c2, c1), cc2, cc1) =
if (c2 = cc2 and c1 = cc1) then a else remove2 (a, cc2, cc1)
```

END-RELATION

Appendix C:
Transformation Rule System

THE OBJECT CONSTRAINT LANGUAGE: AN OVERVIEW

This Appendix describes all the constructs of the Object Constraint Language (OCL) with which we can write constraints in MOF metamodels. A detailed description may be found at (OCL, 2006).

OCL was developed as a business modeling language within the IBM Insurance division and has its roots in the SYNTROPY method. It is a semi-formal language that remains easy to read and write.

OCL enables one to describe constraints on object oriented models and other object modeling artifacts. A constraint is a restriction on one or more values of (part of) an object oriented model or system. The OCL expressions are written in the context of UML diagrams and in general, specify invariant conditions that must hold for the system being modeled or queries over objects described in a model. For instance, in UML static diagrams, OCL expressions are linked to classifiers with their properties and relationships. In this context, classifiers can be classes, interfaces, primitive types and packages.

All classifiers of UML diagrams as well as attributes, association-ends, method and operations are considered valid types in OCL expressions. OCL expressions do not have side effects; i.e. their evaluation cannot alter the state of the corresponding executing system.

Next, OCL constructs linked to Essential OCL are described.

DOI: 10.4018/978-1-61520-649-0.ch017

Context Specification

OCL expressions are written in the context of instances of specific types. The context of an expression within an UML model can be specified through a context declaration at the beginning of the respective OCL expression.

In an OCL expression the reserved word *self* is used to refer to the contextual instance.

Invariants

An invariant is a constraint associated with a Classifier that is referred to as a type, and it must be true for all instances of that type at any time. Invariants are written in a context declaration followed as the name of the type. The *self* keyword can be dropped if the context is clear.

Package Context

If it is necessary to specify explicitly in which package, due to the package in which the Classifier belongs is not clear from the environment, we can use the package context. Invariants, preconditions and post-condition constraints can be enclosed between "package" and "endpackage" statements as follows:

```
Package Package::SubPackage
context X
inv: ...some invariant...
context X::operationName (...)
pre:...some precondition...
post:...some postcondition...
endpackage
Objects and Properties
```

OCL expressions can refer to Classifiers, e.g. types, classes, interfaces, associations (acting as types) and data types. All attributes, association-ends, methods and operations without side effects that are defined on these types can be used in OCL expressions. Operations and methods are defined to be side effect free if the *isQuery* attribute of an operation is True. A property can be one of: an attribute, an association-end, an operation with *isQuery* being true and a method with *isQuery* being true

The value of a property of an object is written in an OCL expression by a dot followed by name of the property.

An operation can be specified in OCL by means of preconditions and postconditions as follows:

```
Typename:: OperationName (parameter1:Type1,...): ReturnType
pre:_ some expression of self and parameter1
post: Result = _ some function of self and parameter1
```

self can be used in the expression to refer to the object on which an operation was called and the name *Result* is the name of the returned object, if there is any. The names of the *parameter (parameter1,...)* can also be used in the expression.

The value of a property in a postcondition is the value upon completion of the operation. To refer to the value of a property at the start of the operation, the property name has a postfix with "@" followed by the keyword "pre". Other predefined constraints can appear: *changeable*, *addOnly* and *frozen* in attributes and, *ordered*, *changeable*, *addOnly*, *frozen*, *xor* and *subset* in associations.

Navigations that are Derived from Associations

An association can be navigated from a specific object to other objects connected by the association and their properties. The syntax for expressing navigations uses the role of the association-end as follows:

```
object.rolename
```

If the role name does not appear in the UML diagram, the convention is to use the name of the association-end class.

The expression *object.rolename* refers to a collection of objects. OCL provides the predefined collection types *Collection*, *Set*, *Bag*, and *Sequence*. They are used to specify the exact results of navigation through associations in class models. They have a large number of predefined operations on them. Properties of collection are accessed by an arrow "- >" followed by the name of the property:

```
collection - > operationName
```

Properties can be combined to make more complicated expressions. Due to an OCL expression always evaluates to a specific object of a specific type, it is possible always apply another property to the result to get a new result value. Thus, each OCL expression can be evaluated left-to-right.

Pathnames for Packages

Within MOF metamodels, types are organized in packages. A package pathname prefix enables referring to types in other packages. The syntax is a package name followed by a double colon

```
Packagename::Typename
```

This usage of pathnames is transitive and can also be used for packages within packages:

```
Packagename1::Packagename2::TypeName
```

Accessing Overridden Properties of Supertypes

Whenever properties are redefined within a type, the property of the supertypes can be accessed using the *oclAsType ()* operation. *T.oclAsType()* evaluates the object as *oclType*

In OCL, a number of basic types are predefined. The most basic types are *Boolean*, *Integer*, *Real*, *String*, *Enumerate* and *Tuple*. OCL defines a number of operations on these predefined types.

Also, OCL provides a hierarchy of collection types including *Collection*, *Set*, *Bag*, *OrderedSet* and

Sequence.

If the name does not appear in the diagram, is associated by convention the name of the class association-end.

All types must conform in a valid expression. A type *t1* conforms to a type *t2* when an instance of *t1* can be substituted at each place where an instance of *t2* is expected. The basic type conformance rules are the following ones:

- Each type conforms to each of its supertypes
- Type conformance is transitive: if *t1* conforms to *t2*, and *t2* conforms to *t3*, then *t1* conforms to *t3*.

Predefined Types Collections

Collection is the abstract supertype whose subtypes are *Set*, *OrderedSet*, *Bag* and *Sequence*. All operations on collections are denoted by the following syntax:

```
<collection>-> <operation>
```

OCL Collections are automatically flattened; that is, a collection never contains collections but contains only simple objects.

OCL defines standard operations on collections such as *size, count, includes, includesAll, isEmpty* and *notEmpty*. Also, OCL provides many operations on the collection types that allow us to iterate over its elements. They are *select, reject, collect, exists, forall* and *iterate*. These operations take each element and evaluate an expression on them. Following, we describe these operations.

The *select* and *reject* operations specify a selection of a special subset from a specific collection. The *select* operation gets the subset of all elements of the collection for which the expression evaluates to True. The syntax of the select operation looks in three different forms:

```
collection -> select (v: Type |boolean-expression-with-v)
collection -> select (v |boolean-expression-with-v)
collection -> select (boolean-expression)
```

The first form declares an iterator variable called v. The type of this iterator variable is declared as Type. The second form is a shorthand notation, in which the type of the iterator variable is omitted. The third form is the shortest one. It can be used only if an explicit reference to the iterator is not needed in the expression

The *reject* operation is identical to the select operation, but with *reject* we get the subset of all elements of the collection for which the expression evaluates to False.

The syntax of the select operation looks also in three different forms:

```
collection -> reject (v: Type | boolean-expression-with-v)
collection -> reject (v | boolean-expression-with-v)
collection -> reject (boolean-expression)
```

The *collect* operation specify a collection which is derived from some other collection, but which contains different objects from the original collection (i.e, it does not return sub-collections as a *select* or *reject* operation). The syntax of the select operation comes in three different forms:

```
collection -> collect (v: Type | expression-with-v)
collection -> collect (v | expression-with-v)
collection -> collect (expression)
```

Because navigation through many objects is very common, OCL provides a shorthand notation for the collect operation. For any property name that is defined as a property on the objects in the collection, the following two expressions are equivalents:

```
collection.propertyname (par1, par2,…)
collection -> collect (propertyname (par1, par2,…))
```

The *exists* operation in OCL allows specifying a Boolean expression, which must hold for at least one element in the collection. The syntax for the *exists* operation is as follows:

```
collection -> exists (v: Type | Boolean-expression-with-v)
collection -> exists (v | Boolean-expression-with-v)
collection -> exists (Boolean-expression)
```

The *iterate* operation is the more generic so that operations *reject, select, forAll, exists, collect* can be described in terms of the *iterate* operation. The syntax of the iterate operation is as follows:

```
collection -> iterate (elem: T; acc: T = <expression> |  expression-
with-elem-and-acc)
```

The variable *elem* is an iterator; the variable *acc* is an accumulator. *acc* gets an initial value <expression>. The *iterates* operation iterates over the elements of the collection and the *expression-with-elem-and-acc* is evaluated and its value is assigned to *acc*. The value of *acc* is built up during the iteration of the collection.

The result of the *iterate* operation can be calculated as is shown in the following pseudocode:

```
iterate (elem: T; acc: T2 = value)
{ acc = value;
for (Enumeration e = collection.elements (); e.hasMoreElements ();)
{
elem= e.nextElement ();
acc = <expression-with-elem-acc>
}
return acc;
}
```

FROM OCL TO NEREUS: A SYSTEM OF TRANSFORMATION RULES

Rule	OCL NEREUS
R1	v (variable) v (variable)
R2	Type -> operationName (paramater1: Type1, parameter2: Type2,...): ReturnType operationName: Type x Type1 x. Type2 x ...-> ReturnType
R3	Type::operationName (parameter1: Type1, parameter2: Type2,...): ReturnType operationName: Type x Type1 x Type2 X ...-> ReturnType
R4	collection -> operationName (expr: OCLBooleanExpr, parameter1: Type1,...): ReturnType operationName: Collection x (*Elem* -> Boolean) x Type1 x ...-> ReturnType
R5	collection -> operationName (expr: OCLExprType, parameter1: Type1,...): ReturnType operationName: Collection x (*Elem* -> Type) x Type1 x ...-> ReturnType
R6	v. operationName (parameters) operationName (*Translate*_{NEREUS} (v),*Translate*_{NEREUS} (parameters))
R7	self.operationName (parameters) operationName (c, *Translate*_{NEREUS} *(parameters))* *with [c| ->self]*
R8	Type::operationName (parameters): ReturnType operationName = expression operationName (c, *Translate*_{NEREUS} (parameters)) = *Translate*_{NEREUS}(expression)) *with [c|->self]*
R9	V -> operationName (parameters) operationName (*Translate*_{NEREUS} (v), *Translate*_{NEREUS} (parameters))
R10	v.attributeName attributeName (v)
R11	**context** AssociationName object.roleName **AXIOMS** a: AssociationName get_roleName (a, object) *with [a| ->Assoc]*
R12	expression.operationName operationName (*Translate*_{Nereus} (expression))
R13	Expression1 binaryOperator expression2 *Translate*_{Nereus} (expression1)*Translate*_{Nereus} (binaryOperator) *Translate*_{Nereus} (expression2) *Translate*_{Nereus} (binaryOperator) (*Translate*_{Nereus} (expression1), *Translate*_{Nereus}(expression2))
R14	unaryOperator expression *Translate*_{Nereus} (unaryOperator) *Translate*_{Nereus} (expression)
R15	**if** booleanExpression **then** expression1 **else** expression2 **endif** **IF***Translate*_{Nereus} (booleanExpression) **THEN***Translate*_{Nereus} (expression1) **ELSE***Translate*_{Nereus}(expression2)

R16	**let** v: Type = expression1 **in** expression2-with-v
	LET
	v =*Translate*_{Nereus} (expression1)
	IN
	*Translate*_{Nereus} (expression2-with -v)
	END-LET
	*Translate*_{Nereus}(expression2-with -v)
	WHERE
	v =*Translate*_{Nereus} (expression1)
	END-WHERE
R17	Collection -> operationName (v:Element| boolean-expr-with-v)
	operationName::= forAll ⏐exists
	OPERATIONS
	operationName: Collection x (Element -> Boolean) -> Boolean
	AXIOMS
	…
	LET
	OPERATIONS
	f: Element -> Boolean
	AXIOMS v: Element
	f (v)= *Translate* _{NEREUS} (boolean-expr-with-v)
	IN
	operationName (collection, f)
	END-LET
	--
	operationName (collection, f)
	WHERE
	OPERATIONS
	f: Element -> Boolean
	AXIOMS v: Element
	f (v)= *Translate* _{NEREUS} (boolean-expr-with-v)
	END-WHERE
	Shorthand notation
	operationName (v) (collection, [f (v)])
R18	Collection -> operationName (v |boolean-expr-with-v)
	operationName::= forAll ⏐exists
	Collection [Element]
	OPERATIONS
	operationName: Collection x (Element-> Boolean) -> Boolean
	AXIOMS…
	LET
	OPERATIONS
	f: Element -> Boolean
	AXIOMS v: Element
	f (v)= *Translate* _{NEREUS} (boolean-expr-with-v)
	IN
	operationName (collection, f)
	END-LET
	--
	operationName (collection, f)
	WHERE
	OPERATIONS
	f: Element -> Boolean
	AXIOMS v: Element
	f(v)= *Translate* _{NEREUS} (boolean-expr-with-v)
	END-WHERE
	--
	Shorthand notation
	operationName (v) (collection, [f (v)])

R19	Collection -> operationName (v |boolean-expr) operationName::= forAll │exists *Collection [Element]* **OPERATIONS** operationName: Collection x (Element-> Boolean)-> Boolean **AXIOMS...** **LET** **OPERATIONS** f: Element -> Boolean **AXIOMS v: Elem** f(v)= *Translate* $_{NEREUS}$ (boolean-expr) **IN** operationName (collection, f) **END-LET** -- operationName (collection, f) **WHERE** **OPERATIONS** f: Element -> Boolean **AXIOMS v: Elem** f (v)= *Translate* $_{NEREUS}$ (boolean-expr) **END-WHERE** --- *Shorthand notation* operationName (v) (collection, [f (v)])
R20	Collection -> forAll (v1, v2 |boolean-expr-with-v1-and-v2) *Collection [Element]* Collection -> forAll (v1|forAll (v2, boolean-expr-with-v1-and-v2))
R21	Collection -> operationName (v: Element | boolean-expr-with-v) operationName::= select │ reject **OPERATIONS** operationName: Collection x (Element -> Boolean) -> Collection **AXIOMS** **LET OPERATIONS** f: Element -> Boolean **AXIOMS v: Element** f (v)= *Translate* $_{NEREUS}$ (boolean-expr-with-v) **IN** operationName (collection, f) **END-LET** operationName (collection, f) **WHERE** **OPERATIONS** f: Element -> Boolean **AXIOMS v: Element** f (v)= *Translate* $_{NEREUS}$ (boolean-expr-with-v) **END-WHERE** --- *Shorthand notation* operationName (v) (collection, [f (v)])

R22	Collection-> operationName (v |boolean-expr-with-v) operationName::= select | reject *Collection[Element]* **OPERATIONS** operationName: Collection x (Element-> Boolean)-> Collection **AXIOMS** **LET OPERATIONS** f: Element -> Boolean **AXIOMS v: Element** f (v)= *Translate$_{NEREUS}$*(boolean-expr-with-v) **IN** operationName (collection, f) **END-LET** operationName (collection, f) **WHERE** **OPERATIONS** f: Element -> Boolean **AXIOMS v: Element** f (v)= *Translate$_{NEREUS}$* (boolean-expr-with-v) **END-WHERE** -- *Shorthand notation* operationName (v) (collection, [f (v)])
R23	Collection-> operationName (boolean-expr) operationName::= select | reject *Collection [Element]* **OPERATIONS** operationName: Collection x (Element-> Boolean) -> Collection **AXIOMS** **LET OPERATIONS** f: Element -> Boolean **AXIOMS v: Element** f (v)= *Translate$_{NEREUS}$* (boolean-expr) **IN** operationName (collection, f) **END-LET** operationName (collection, f) **WHERE** **OPERATIONS** f: Element -> Boolean **AXIOMS v: Element** f (v)= *Translate$_{NEREUS}$*(boolean-expr) **END-WHERE** --- *Shorthand notation* operationName (v) (collection, [f (v)])

R24	Collection -> collect (v: Element | expression-with-v) *Let Type(expression-with-v) be S* **OPERATIONS** collect: Collection x (Element ->Boolean) -> Collection **AXIOMS** **LET** **OPERATIONS** f: Element -> S **AXIOMS v: Element** f (v)= *Translate* $_{NEREUS}$ (expr-with-v) **IN** collect (collection, f) **END-LET** collect (collection, f) **WHERE** **OPERATIONS** f: Element -> S **AXIOMS v: Element** f (v)= *Translate NEREUS* (expr-with-v) **END-WHERE** -- *Shorthand notation* Collect (v) (collection, [f (v)])
R25	Collection -> collect (v: Element | expression-with-v) *Let Type(expression-with-v) be S* *Collection [Element]* **OPERATIONS** collect: Collection x (Element ->Boolean) -> Collection **AXIOMS** **LET** **OPERATIONS** f: Element -> S **AXIOMS v: Element** f (v)= *Translate NEREUS* (expr-with-v) **IN** collect (collection, f) **END-LET** collect (collection, f) **WHERE** **OPERATIONS** f: Element -> S **AXIOMS v: Element** f (v)= *Translate NEREUS* (expr-with-v) **END-WHERE** -- *Shorthand notation* Collect (v) (collection, [f (v)])

R26	Collection -> collect (v: Element | expression-with-v) *Let Type(expression-with-v) be S* *Collection [Element]* **OPERATIONS** collect: Collection x (Element ->Boolean) -> Collection **AXIOMS** **LET** **OPERATIONS** f: Element -> S **AXIOMS v: Element** f (v)= *Translate* $_{NEREUS}$ (expr-with-v) **IN** collect (collection, f) **END-LET** collect (collection, f) **WHERE** **OPERATIONS** f: Element -> S **AXIOMS v: Element** f (v)= *Translate* $_{NEREUS}$ (expr-with-v) **END-WHERE** -- *Shorthand notation* Collect (v)(collection, [f (v)])
R27	collection -> iterate (v: Element; acc: Type = exp | expression-with-v-and-acc) **OPERATIONS** iterate: Collection x (Element x Acc: ANY) x -> Acc) -> Acc **AXIOMS** **LET** **OPERATIONS** f: Element x Type -> Type base: -> Type **AXIOMS v: Element; acc: Type** f (v, acc)=*Translate*$_{NEREUS}$(expr-with-v-and-acc) base = *Translate* $_{NEREUS}$ (exp) **IN** iterate (collection, f, base) **END-LET** iterate (collection, f, base) **WHERE** **OPERATIONS** f: Element x Type -> Type base: -> Type **AXIOMS v: Element; acc: Type** f (v, acc)=*Translate*$_{NEREUS}$ (expr-with-v-and-acc) base = *Translate* $_{NEREUS}$ (exp) **END-WHERE**
R28	Type::operationName (par1: Type1,...): ReturnType **pre**: expression-with-self - or-attribute-or--par1..pari operationName: Type (t) x Type1(t1) x...x TypeI (ti)-> ReturnType **pre**: *Translate*$_{NEREUS}$ (expression-with-self -or-attribute-or--par1..pari) *with [self| -> t; attribute| -> attribute(t); par1 | ->t1;...pari | ->ti]*
R29	Type::operationName (par1: Type1,...): ReturnType **post**: expression-with-self -or-attribute-or self **OPERATIONS** *Translate*$_{NEREUS}$(Type::operationName (par1: Type1,...): ReturnType **AXIOMS** Translate$_{NEREUS}$ (expression-with-self -or-attribute@pre-or result) With [self| ->t ; *attribute@pre* | -> *attribute (t) ; result | -> operationName (t, par1,..)]*

R30	Collection → operationName (parameterList): Boolean **post:** result = collection → forAll (elem: Element | bool-expr-with-elem) **OPERATIONS** *Translate*$_{NEREUS}$ *(*collection → operationName (parameterList): Boolean) **AXIOMS c: Collection; elem: Element; ...** operationName (create, parameterList)= TRUE operationName (add(c,elem), parameterList) = operationName (c,parameterList) AND *Translate*$_{NEREUS}$ (bool-expr-with-elem)
R31	Collection → operationName (parameterList): Boolean **post:** result = collection → exists (elem: Element | boolean-expression-with-elem) **OPERATIONS** *Translate*$_{NEREUS}$(collection → operationName (parameterList): Boolean) **AXIOMS c: Collection; elem: Element; ...** operationName (create, parameterList)= FALSE operationName (add(c,elem), parameterList) = operationName (c, parameterList) OR *Translate*$_{NEREUS}$ (boolean-expression-with-elem)
R32	Sequence → operationName (parameterList): Boolean **post**: result = Sequence { 1 ..sequence → size } → forAll (index: Integer | boolean-expr-with-index) **OPERATIONS** *Translate*$_{NEREUS}$ (sequence → operationName (parameterList): Boolean) **AXIOMS s: Sequence; index:Nat; ...** operationName (s, parameterList) = (1 ≤ index ≤ size (s)) **implies** *Translate*$_{NEREUS}$ (boolean-expr-with-index)
R33	Sequence { 1 .. sequence → size } → forAll (index: Integer | boolean-expr-with-index) **AXIOMS s: Sequence; index: Nat; ...** (1 ≤ index ≤ size(s)) implies *Translate*$_{NEREUS}$ (boolean-expr-with-index)
R34	Collection -> operationName (t1:T1; t2: T2;...): Boolean **post:** result = collection -> iterate (elem: Element; acc: Boolean = exp | bool-expr-with-elem-and-acc) **OPERATIONS** *Translate*$_{NEREUS}$ (collection -> operationName (t1:T1; t2: T2;...): Boolean) **AXIOMS c: Collection; elem: Element; t1:T1; t2:T2** operationName (create, t1, t2,..) = *Translate*$_{NEREUS}$ (exp) operationName (add (c, elem), t1, t2,.....) = *Translate*$_{NEREUS}$ (bool-expr-with-elem-and-acc) *With [acc |-> operationName (c, t1, t2,...)]*

R35	collection -> operationName (t1: T1; t2: T2;...): returnType **post:** result = collection -> iterate(elem:Element; acc: Type = exp | expr-with-elem-and-acc) **OPERATIONS** *Translate$_{NEREUS}$* (collection -> operationName (t1:T1; t2: T2;...): returnType) **AXIOMS c: Collection; t1: T1; t2: T2,** **LET** **OPERATIONS** g: Element x Type -> Type base: -> Type **AXIOMS e: Element; acc:Type** g (e, acc) = *Translate$_{NEREUS}$* (expr -with-elem-and-acc) base = *Translate$_{NEREUS}$* (expr) **IN** operationName (c, t1, t2,...) = iterate (c, g, base) **END-LET** **AXIOMS c: Collection; t1:T1; t2:T2,** operationName (c, t1, t2,...) = iterate (c, g, base) **WHERE** **OPERATIONS** g: Element x Type -> Type base: -> Type **AXIOMS e: Element; acc:Type** g (e, acc) = *Translate$_{NEREUS}$* (expr -with-elem-and-acc) base = *Translate$_{NEREUS}$* (expr) **END-WHERE**
R36	sequence → operationName (t1: T1, t2: T2, ..): returnType **post:** result = sequence → iterate (elem: Element; acc: Type = expr | expr-with-elem-and-acc) **OPERATIONS** *Translate$_{NEREUS}$* (sequence → operationName (t1:T1,t2:T2, ..): returnType) **AXIOMS s: Sequence ; elem: Element; t1: T1; t2: T2,...** operationName (create, t1,t2, ...) = *Translate$_{NEREUS}$* (expr) operationName (add (s, elem), t1, t2,.....) = *Translate$_{NEREUS}$* (expr-with-elem-and-acc) *with [acc |-> operationName (s, t1, t2,...)]*
R37	bag → operationName (t1: T1, t2: T2, ..): returnType **post:** result = bag → iterate (elem: Element; acc: Type = expr | expr-with-elem-and-acc) **OPERATIONS** *Translate$_{NEREUS}$* (bag→operationName (t1:T1, .): returnType) **AXIOMS b: Bag; elem: Element; t1:T1; t2:T2,...** operationName (create, t1, t2,..) = *Translate$_{NEREUS}$* (expr) operationName (add (b, elem), t1, t2,.....) = *Translate$_{NEREUS}$* (expr-with-elem-and-acc) *With [acc|->operationName (b, t1, t2,...)]*

R38	Collection -> operationName (t1:T1; t2: T2;...): returnType **post:** result = collection -> iterate (elem:Element; acc: Type = exp | expr-with-elem-and-acc) **OPERATIONS** *Translate* _{NEREUS} (collection -> op (t1:T1; t2: T2;...): returnType) **AXIOMS c: Collection ; t1: T1; t2: T2;...** **LET** **OPERATIONS** g: Element x Type -> Type base: -> Type **AXIOMS elem: Element; acc: Type** g (elem, acc) = *Translate* _{NEREUS} (expr -with-elem-and-acc) base = *Translate* _{NEREUS} (expr) **IN** operationName (c, t1, t2,...) = iterate (c, g, base) **END-LET** -- **AXIOMS c: Collection ; t1: T1; t2: T2;...** operationName (c, t1, t2,...) = iterate (c, g, base) **WHERE** **OPERATIONS** g: Element x Type -> Type base: -> Type **AXIOMS elem: Element; acc:Type** g (elem,acc) = *Translate* _{NEREUS} (expr -with-elem-and-acc) base = *Translate* _{NEREUS} (expr) **END-WHERE**
R39	sequence → operationName (t1: T1,t2: T2, ..): returnType **post:** result = sequence →iterate (elem: Element; acc: Type = expr | expr-with-elem-and-acc) **OPERATIONS** *Translate*_{NEREUS} (sequence → operationName (t1: T1, t2: T2, ..): returnType) **AXIOMS s: Sequence; elem: Element; t1:T1; t2: T2, ...** operationName (create, t1, t2,..) = *Translate*_{NEREUS} (expr) operationName (add (s, elem), t1, t2,.....) = *Translate*_{NEREUS} (expr-with-elem-and-acc) *with [acc |-> operationName (s, t1, t2,...)]*
R40	bag → operationName (t1: T1,t2: T2, ..): returnType **post:** result = bag → iterate (elem: Element; acc: Type = expr | expr-with-elem-and-acc) **OPERATIONS** *Translate*_{NEREUS} (bag→operationName (t1:T1, ..):returnType) **AXIOMS b: Bag; elem: Element; t1: T1; t2: T2,...** operationName (create, t1, t2,..) = *Translate*_{NEREUS} (expr) operationName (add (b, elem), t1, t2,.....) = *Translate*_{NEREUS} (expr-with-elem-and-acc) *With [acc|->operationName (b, t1, t2,...)]*
R41	set → operationName (t1: T1, t2: T2, ..): returnType **post:** result = set →iterate (elem: Element; acc: Type = expr | expr-with-elem-and-acc) **OPERATIONS** *Translate*_{NEREUS} (set→operatioName (t1:T1, t2: T2, ..): returnType) **AXIOMS s: Set; elem: Elem; t1:T1; t2:T2,...** operationName (create, t1,t2,..) = *Translate*_{NEREUS} (expr) operationName (add (s, elem), t1, t2,..) = *Translate*_{NEREUS} (expr-with-elem-and-acc) *with [acc |->operationName (excluding (s, e), t1, t2,...)]*

R42	T → operationName (parameterList): returnType **post**: result binary-operator expr **OPERATIONS** *Translate*$_{NEREUS}$ (T → operationName (parameterList): returnType) **AXIOMS t: T, ...** operationName (t, parameterList) *Translate*$_{NEREUS}$(binary-operator) *Translate*$_{NEREUS}$(expr)
R43	T → operationName (parameterList): returnType **post**: result -> iteratorOperation (iteratorExpression) **OPERATIONS** *Translate*$_{NEREUS}$ (T → operationName (parameterList): returnType) **AXIOMS t: T, ...** iteratorOperation(operationName (t, parameterList), *Translate*$_{NEREUS}$ (iteratorExpression)
R44	T → operationName (parameterList): returnType **post**: expression1 = expression2 **OPERATIONS** *TranslateNEREUS* (T → operationName (parameterList): returnType) **AXIOMS** *Translate*$_{NEREUS}$ (expression1) = *Translate*$_{NEREUS}$(expression2)
R45	T → operationName (parameterList): returnType **post**: expression **OPERATIONS** *Translate*$_{NEREUS}$ (T → operationName (parameterList): returnType) **AXIOMS** *Translate*$_{NEREUS}$ (expression)
R46	T-> operationName (v:Type | bool-expr-with-v) OperationName::= forAll | exists | select | reject T::= Collection|Set|OrderedSet|Bag operationName (v) (*Translate*$_{NEREUS}$ (T), [*Translate*$_{NEREUS}$ (bool-expr-with-v)])
R47	T -> collect (v: type | v.property) collect (v)(*Translate*$_{NEREUS}$ (T), [*Translate*$_{NEREUS}$ (v.property)])
R48	c.property (Shorthand notation) c -> collect (property) collect (v) (*Translate*$_{NEREUS}$ (c), [*Translate*$_{NEREUS}$ (property)])
R49	T -> iterate (e: Element; acc: Type = expr | boolean-expr-with-e) Iterate (v) (*Translate*$_{NEREUS}$ (T), [*Translate*$_{NEREUS}$ (boolean-expr-with-e)], [*Translate*$_{NEREUS}$(expr)])
R50	Set {} createSet OrderedSet {} createOrderedSet Sequence {} createSequence Bag {} createBag Set { e1,e2,...,ei} Including (including (... (including (createSet, ei),..., e2), e1)) OrderedSet {e1,e2,...,ei} Including (including (...(including (createOrderedSet, ei), ...,e2),e1)) Sequence {e1,e2,...,ei} Including (including (...(including (createSequence, ei),..., e2), e1)) Bag {e1,e2,...,ei} Including (including (...(including (createBag, ei),..., e2), e1))
R51	Packagename::rolename Packagename::rolename

R52	Let v be enum (e1,e2, ...,ei,..)
	v = # ei
	v = #ei

Appendix D:
Design Pattern Metamodels

Appendix D describes three metamodels for the Observer pattern: a PSM metamodel based on the Eiffel platform, a PSM metamodel based on a Java platform and a ISM metamodel based on the Java platform.

D.1. EIFFEL-PSM OBSERVER METAMODEL

Description of the Metaclasses

AssocEndEffectiveObserver

Description
This end-association connects an association ObserverSubject, of which is member, with an EffectiveObserver.

Generalizations

- AssociationEnd (from PSM-Eiffel)

DOI: 10.4018/978-1-61520-649-0.ch018

Figure 1. Eiffel PSM observer metamodel

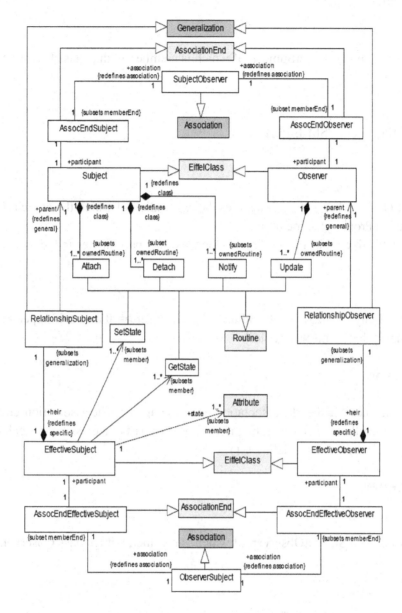

Associations

- association: ObserverSubject [1] It denotes the association of which this end-association is member. It redefines Property::association.
- participant: EffectiveObserver [1] It denotes the class that participates in the association.

Constraints

[1]   It has a multiplicity n1..n2 (n1>= 0 and n2>=1) self.lower >= 0 **and** self.upper >= 1

AssocEndEffectiveSubject

Description

It connects an association ObserverSubject, of which is member, with a class EffectiveSubject.

Generalizations

- AssociationEnd (from PSM-Eiffel)

Associations

- association: ObserverSubject [1] It denotes the association of which the association-end is member. It redefines Property::association.
- participant: EffectiveSubject [1] It denotes the class that participates in the association.

Constraints

[1] It has a multiplicity n1..n2 (n1>= 0 and n2>=1) self.lower >= 0 **and** self.upper >=1
[2] It must be navigable self.isNavigable()

Additional operations

[1] isNavigable denotes whether the association-end is navigable. The association-end is member of a binary association then, to be navigable, it must be own part of a class. isNavigable(): Boolean isNavigable() = **not** self.class -> isEmpty()

AssocEndObserver

Description

It connects an association SubjectObserver, of which is member, with a class Observer.

Generalizations

- AssociationEnd (from PSM-Eiffel)

Associations

- association: SubjectObserver [1] It denotes the association of which this association-end is member. It redefines Property::association.
- participant: Observer [1] It denotes the class that participates in the association.

Constraints

[1] It has a multiplicity n1..n2 (n1>= 0 and n2>=1) self.lower >= 0 **and** self.upper >= 1
[2] It must be navigable. self.isNavigable()

AssocEndSubject

Description

It connects an association SubjectObserver, of which is member, with a class Subject.

Generalizations

- AssociationEnd (from PSM-Eiffel)

Associations

- association: SubjectObserver[1] It denotes the association of which this association-end is member. It redefines Property::association.
- participant: Subject [1] It denotes the class that participates in the association.

Constraints

[1]   It has a multiplicity n1..n2 (n1>= 0 and n2>=1). self.lower >= 0 **and** self.upper >=1

Attach

Description

It defines a routine that is declared by Subject.

Generalizations

- Routine (from PSM-Eiffel)

Associations

- subject: Subject [1] It denotes the class that declares this routine. It redefines Routine::class.

Constraints

[1]   This routine changes the state of the subject. **not** self.isQuery
[2]   This routine has a non-empty set of parameters being one of them an input parameter (direction = #in) whose type is Observer. self.ownedParameter -> notEmpty () **and** self.ownedParameter -> select (par | par.direction = #in **and** par.type = oclIsKindOf (Observer)) -> size () = 1
[3]   Its visibility must be public. self.visibility = #public

Detach

Description
It defines a routine that is declared by Subject.

Generalizations

- Routine (from PSM-Eiffel)

Associations

- subject: Subject [1] It denotes the class that is declared by this routine. It redefines Routine::class.

Constraints

[1] This routine changes the state of the subject. not self.isQuery
[2] It has a non-empty set of parameters being one of them an input parameter whose type is Observer. self.ownedParameter -> notEmpty () **and** self.ownedParameter -> select (par | par.direction = #in **and** par.type = oclIsKindOf (Observer)) -> size () = 1
[3] Its visibility must be public. self.visibility = #public

EffectiveObserver

Description
This metaclass specifies the features that a class with the behavior of an effective observer must have in the model of the pattern *Observer*.

Generalizations

- EiffelClass (from PSM-Eiffel)

Associations

- assocEndEffectiveObserver: AssocEndEffectiveObserver[1] It denotes the association-end of the association ObserverSubject in which this classifier participates.
- relationshipObserver:RelationshipObserver[1] It denotes a generalization where EffectiveObserver takes the role of heir. It is a subset of Classifier::generalization.

Constraints

[1] Instances of effective observers should not be a deferred class. not self.isDeferred

EffectiveSubject

Description
This metaclass specifies the features that must have a class taking the role of effective subject in the model of the Observer pattern.

Generalizations

- EiffelClass (from PSM-Eiffel)

Associations

- assocEndEffectiveSubject:AssocEndEffectiveSubject [1] It denotes the association-end of the association ObserverSubject in which this classifier participates.
- getState: GetState [1..*] Every instance of EffectiveSubject must have one or more operation instances of GetState. They can be own or inherited. It is a subset of NameSpace::member.
- relationshipSubject:RelationshipSubject [1] It denotes a generalization where EffectiveSubject takes the role of heir. It is a subset of Classifier::generalization.
- setState: SetState [1..*] Every instance of EffectiveSubject must have one or more operation instances of SetState. They can be own or inherited. It is a subset of NameSpace::member.
- state: Attribute [1..*] It specifies a non-empty set that contains all attributes of EffectiveSubject. They can be own or inherited. It is a subset of NameSpace::member.

Constraints

[1]   Instances of effective subjects should not be a deferred class. not self.isDeferred

GetState

Description
It defines a routine member of EffectiveSubject. It specifies a service that can be required from another object.

Generalizations

- Routine (from PSM-Eiffel)

Associations
No additional associations.

Constraints

[1]   It is not a deferred routine and does not change the state of the subject not self.isDeferred and self. isQuery

[2] The state should return to the subject, therefore within the set of arguments must have at least one parameter whose address is out or return. self.ownedParameter -> notEmpty () **and** self.owned-Parameter -> select (par | par.direction = #return **or** par.direction = #out) -> size () >= 1

[3] Its visibility must be public. self.visibility = #public

Notify

Description
It defines a routine that is declared by Subject.

Generalizations

- Routine (from PSM-Eiffel)

Associations

- Subject: Subject [1] It denotes the class that is declared by this routine. It redefines Routine::class.

Constraints

[1] This routine does not change the subject state. self.isQuery
[2] Its visibility must be public. self.visibility = #public

Observer

Description
This metaclass specifies the features that must have every class taking the role of observer in the model of the Observer pattern in the Eiffel platform.

Generalizations

- EiffelClass (from PSM-Eiffel)

Associations

- assocEndObserver: AssocEndObserver [1] It denotes the association-end of the association SubjectObserver in which this class participates.
- update: Update [1..*] Every instance of Observer must have at least one routine instance of Update. It is a subset of EiffelClass::ownedRoutine.

Constraints
No additional constraints.

ObserverSubject

Description
This metaclass specifies a binary association between instances of EffectiveObserver and Effective-Subject.

Generalizations

*   Association (from Kernel)

Associations

*   assocEndEffectiveObserver:AssocEndEffectiveObserver [1] It represents a connection with the class EffectiveObserver. It is a subset of Association::memberEnd.
*   assocEndEffectiveSubject:AssocEndEffectiveSubject [1] It represents a connection with the class EffectiveSubject. It is a subset of Association::memberEnd.

Constraints

[1]   It has two association-ends. self.memberEnd -> size () =2

RelationshipObserver

Description
This class specifies the inheritance relation (Generalization) between an observer (Observer) and an effective observer (EffectiveObserver) in the model of the Observer pattern.

Generalizations

*   Generalization (from Kernel)

Associations

*   heir: EffectiveObserver [1] It denotes the element that takes the role of heir in the relation. It redefines Generalization::specific.
*   parent: Observer [1] It denotes the element that takes the role of parent in the relation. It redefines Generalization::general.

Constraints
No additional constraints.

RelationshipSubject

Description
This metaclass specifies an inheritance relation (Generalization) between a subject (Subject) and an effective subject (EffectiveSubject) in the model of the *Observer* pattern.

Generalizations

- Generalization (from Kernel)

Associations

- heir: EffectiveSubject [1] It denotes the element that takes the role of heir in the relation. It redefines Generalization::specific.
- parent: Subject [1] It denotes the element that takes the role of parent in the relation. It redefines Generalization::general.

Constraints
No additional constraints.

SetState

Descriptions
It defines a routine member of EffectiveSubject. It specifies a service that can be required from another object.

Generalizations

- Routine (from PSM-Eiffel)

Associations
No additional associations.

Constraints

[1] It is not a deferred routine and modifies the state of the subset. **not** self.isDeferred **and not** self.isQuery
[2] The set of arguments is non-empty and one of them must be an input parameter. self.ownedParameter -> notEmpty () **and** self.ownedParameter ->select (par | par.direction= #in) -> size () >=1
[3] Its visibility must be public. self.visibility = #public

Subject

Description
This metaclass specifies the features that must have an Eiffel class taking the role of subject in the model of the Observer pattern in the Eiffel platform.

Generalizations

- EiffelClass (from PSM-Eiffel)

Associations

- assocEndSubject: AssocEndSubject [1] It denotes the association-end of the association SubjectObserver in which this class participates.
- attach: Attach [1..*] Every instance of Subject must have at least a routine instance of Attach. It is a subset of Subconjunto de EiffelClass::ownedRoutine.
- detach: Detach [1..*] Every instance of Subject must have at least a routine instance of Detach. It is a subset of EiffelClass::ownedRoutine.
- notify: Notify[1..*] Every instance of Subject must have at least a routine instance of Notify. It is a subset of EiffelClass::ownedRoutine.

Constraints
No additional constraints.

SubjectObserver

Description
This metaclass specifies a binary association between the instances Subject and Observer.

Generalizations

- Association (from Kernel)

Associations

- assocEndObserver: AssocEndObserver [1] It represents a connection with the class Observer. It is a subset of Association::memberEnd.
- assocEndSubject:AssocEndSubject [1] It represents a connection with the class Subject. It is a subset of Association::memberEnd.

Constraints

[1]   It has two association-ends. self.memberEnd -> size () =2

Update

Description

It defines the routine that is declared by the Observer specifying the required services by another object.

Generalizations

- Routine (from PSM-Eiffel)

Associations

- observer: Observer [1] It denotes the class that declares this operation. It is a subset of Routine::ownedRoutine.

Constraints

[1] It is a routine that does not change the observer state. self.isQuery
[2] Its visibility must be public. self.visibility = #public

D.2. JAVA-PSM OBSERVER METAMODEL

Description of Metaclasses

AssocEndConcreteObserver

Description

This association-end connects an association ObserverSubject, of which is member, with a ConcreteObserver.

Generalizations

- AssociationEnd (from PSM-Java)

Associations

- association: ObserverSubject [1] It denotes the association of which this association-end is member. It redefines Property::association
- participant: ConcreteObserver [1] It denotes the classifier that participates in the association.

Figure 2. Java PSM observer metamodel

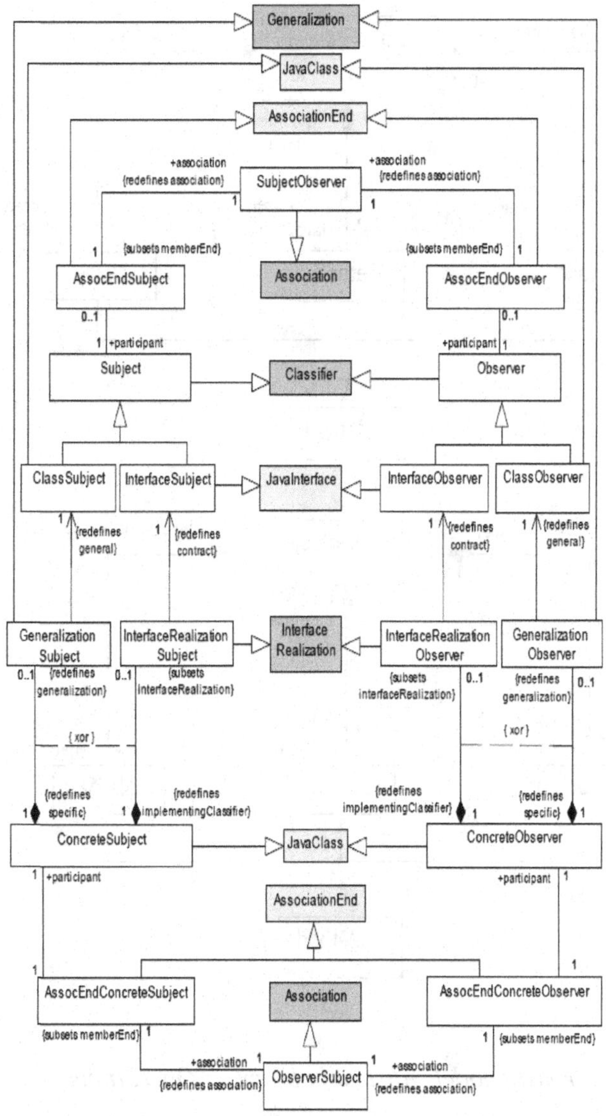

Constraints

[1] It has a multiplicity n1..n2 (n1 >= 0 and n2 >= 1). self.lower >= 0 **and** self.upper > 0

AssocEndConcreteSubject

Description

This association-end connects an association ObserverSubject, of which is member, with a class ConcreteSubject.

Figure 3. Java PSM observer metamodel: Abstract subject: Operations

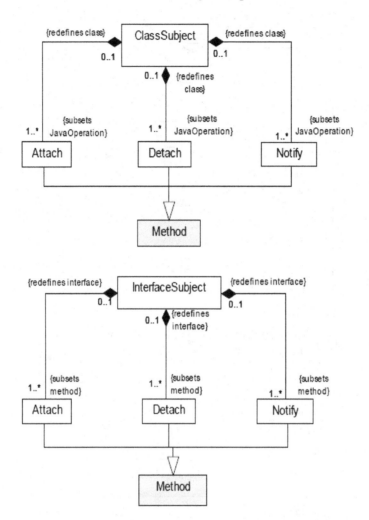

Figure 4. Java PSM observer metamodel: Abstract observer: Operations

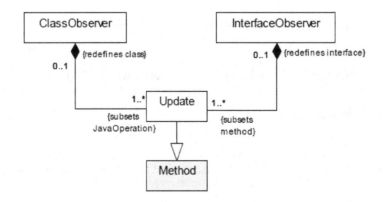

Figure 5. Java PSM observer metamodel: Concrete subject: Attributes and operations

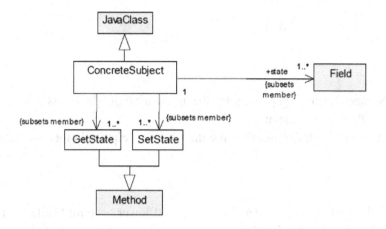

Generalizations

• AssociationEnd (from PSM-Java)

Associations

• association: ObserverSubject [1] It denotes the association of which this association-end is member. It redefines Property::association.
• participant: Concretesubject [1] It denotes the classifier that participates in the association.

Constraints

[1]   It has a multiplicity n1..n2 (n1 >= 0 and n2 >= 1). self.lower >= 0 **and** self.upper > 0
[2]   It is navigable. self.isNavigable ()

Additional operations

[3]   The observer operation isNavigable determines whether this association-end is navigable. Due to it is member of a binary association, to be navigable must be an own association-end of a class. isNavigable(): Boolean isNavigable() = **not** self.class -> isEmpty ()

AssocEndObserver

Description
It connects an association SubjectObserver, of which is member, with a class Observer.

Generalizations

- AssociationEnd (from PSM-Java)

Associations

- association: SubjectObserver [1] It denotes the association of which this association-end is member. It redefines Property::association.
- participant: Observer [1] It denotes the classifier that participates in the association.

Constraints

[1]   It has a multiplicity n1..n2 (n1 >= 0 and n2 >=1). self.lower >= 0 **and** self.upper > 0

[2]   It must be navigable self.isNavigable ()

AssocEndSubject

Description

It connects an association SubjectObserver, of which is member, with a class Subject.

Generalizations

- AssociationEnd (from PSM-Java)

Associations

- association: SubjectObserver [1] It denotes the association of which this association-end is member. It redefines Property::association.
- participant: Subject [1] It denotes the classifier that participates in the association.

Constraints

[1]   It has a multiplicity n1..n2 (n1 >= 0 and n2 >= 1). self.lower >= 0 **and** self.upper > 0

Attach

Description

It defines a method that is declared by a subject.

Generalizations

- Method (from PSM-Java)

Associations

- classSubject: ClassSubject [0..1] It denotes the class declaring this method. It redefines JavaOperation::class.
- interfaceSubject: InterfaceSubject [0..1] It denotes the interface declaring this method. It redefines Method::interface.

Constraints

[1] This method changes the subject state. **not** self.isQuery

[2] This method has a non-empty set of parameters, being one of them an input parameter whose type is Observer. self.ownedParameter -> notEmpty () **and** self. ownedParameter -> select (param | param.direction= #in **and** param.type = oclIsKindOf(Observer)) -> size () = 1

[3] Its visibility must be public. self.visibility = #public

ClassObserver

Description

A metaclass ClassObserver specifies the features that must have a Java class taking the role of observer in the model of the Observer pattern.

Generalizations

- Observer, JavaClass (from PSM-Java)

Associations

- update: Update [1..*] Every instance of ClassObserver must have at least a method instance of Update. It is a subset of JavaClass::javaOperation.

Constraints

No additional constraints.

ClassSubject

Description

This metaclass specifies the features that must have a Java class taking the role of subject in the model of the pattern *Observer*.

Generalizations

- Subject, JavaClass (from PSM-Java)

Associations

- attach: Attach [1..*] Every instance of ClassSubject has at least a method instance of Attach. It is a subset of JavaClass:: javaOperation.
- detach: Detach [1..*] Every instance of ClassSubject has at least a method instance of Detach. It is a subset of JavaClass:: javaOperation.
- notify: Notify[1..*] Every instance of ClassSubject has at least a method instance of Notify. It is a subset of JavaClass:: javaOperation.

Constraints

No additional constraints.

ConcreteObserver

Description

This metaclass specifies the features that must have a Java class with the behavior of a concrete observer in the model of the pattern *Observer*.

Generalizations

- JavaClass (from PSM-Java)

Associations

- assocEndConcreteObserver:AssocEndConcreteObserver [1] It denotes the association-end of the association ObserverSubject in which this classifier participates.
- generalizationObserver: GeneralizationObserver [0..1] It denotes a generalization where ConcreteObserver takes the role of child (specific). It redefines Classifier::generalization.
- interfaceRealizationObserver:InterfaceRealizationObserver [0..1] It denotes an interface realization where ConcreteObserver takes the role of the classifier implementing the contract (implementingClassifier). It is a subset of BehavioredClassifier::interfaceRealization.

Constraints

[1] An instance of a concrete observer can not be an abstract class. **not** self.isAbstract
[2] If an instance of a concrete observer participates in an interface realization, then it must be a BehavioredClassifier. self.interfaceRealizationObserver -> notEmpty () **implies** self.oclIsKindOf (BehavioredClassifier))

ConcreteSubject

Description

This metaclass specifies the features that must have a class taking the role of subject in the model of the *Observer* pattern.

Generalizations

- JavaClass (from PSM-Java)

Associations

- assocEndConcreteSubject:AssocEndConcreteSubject [1] It denotes the association-end of the association ObserverSubject in which this classifier participates.
- generalizationSubject:GeneralizationSubject [0..1] It denotes a generalization where ConcreteSubject takes the role of child (specific). It redefines Classifier::generalization.
- getState: GetState [1..*] Every instance of ConcreteSubject must have one or more method instances of GetState. They may be own or inherited. It is a subset of NameSpace::member.
- interfaceRealizationSubject:InterfaceRealizationSubject [0..1] It denotes an interface realization where ConcreteSubject takes the role of the classifier implementing the contract (implementingClassifier). It is a subset of BehavioredClassifier::interfaceRealization.
- setState: GetState [1..*] Every instance of ConcreteSubject must have one or more method instances of SetState. They may be own or inherited. It is a subset of NameSpace::member.
- state: Field [1..*] It specifies a non-empty set of all attributes of ConcreteSubject. They may be own or inherited. It is a subset of NameSpace::member.

Constraints

[1]   An instance of the concrete subject can not be an abstract class. **not** self.isAbstract
[2]   If an instance of a concrete subject participates in an interface realization, then it must be a BehavioredClassifier. self.interfaceRealizationSubject -> notEmpty () **implies** self.oclIsKindOf (BehavioredClassifier))

Detach

Description
It defines a method that is declared by a subject.

Generalizaciones

- Method (from PSM-Java)

Associations

- classSubject: ClassSubject [0..1] It denotes the class that declares this method. It redefines JavaOperation::class.
- interfaceSubject: InterfaceSubject [0..1] It denotes the interface that declares this method. It redefines Method::interface.

Constraints

[1]   This method changes the subject state. **not** self.isQuery

[2]   This method has a non-empty set of parameters being one of them an input parameter of type Observer. self.ownedParameter -> notEmpty () **and** self.ownedParameter -> select (param | param. direction= #in **and** param.type = oclIsKindOf (Observer)) -> size() = 1

[3]   Its visibility must be public. self.visibility = #public

GeneralizationObserver

Description

This metaclass specifies a generalization between an observer (ClassObserver) and a concrete observer (ConcreteObserver) in the model of the pattern *Observer*.

Generalizations

*   Generalization (from Kernel)

Associations

*   classObserver: ClassObserver [1] It denotes the general element of this relation. It redefines Generalization::general.
*   concreteObserver: ConcreteObserver [1] It denotes the specific element of this relation. It redefines Generalization::specific.

Constraints

No additional constraints.

GeneralizationSubject

Description

This metaclass specifies a generalization between a subject (ClassSubject) and a concrete subject (ConcreteSubject) in the model of the *Observer* pattern.

Generalizations

*   Generalization (from Kernel)

Associations

*   classSubject: ClassSubject [1] It denotes the general element of this relation. It redefines Generalization::general.
*   concreteSubject: ConcreteSubject [1] It denotes the specific element of this relation. It redefines Generalization::specific.

Constraints

No additional restrictions.

GetState

Description

It defines a method that is member of ConcretetSubject. It specifies a service that can be required from another object.

Generalizations

*   Method (from PSM-Java)

Associations

No additional associations.

Constraints

[1]   It is an observer and concrete method. self.isQuery **and not** self.isAbstract
[2]   Because it has to return the state of the subject, the set of parameters should not be empty and at least, must have one of them whose direction is out or return. self.ownedParameter -> notEmpty () **and** self.ownedParameter ->select (par | par.direction= #return **or** par.direction = #out) -> size () >=1
[3]   Its visibility must be public. self.visibility = #public

InterfaceObserver

Description

The metaclass InterfaceObserver specifies the features that must have a Java interface taking the role of abstract observer in the model of the Observer pattern.

Generalizations

*   Observer, JavaInterface (from PSM-Java)

Associations

*   update: Update [1..*] Every instance of InterfaceObserver must have at least one operation instance of Update. It is a subset of JavaInterface::method.

Constraints

No additional constraints.

InterfaceSubject

Description

This metaclass specifies the features that must have a Java interface taking the role of abstract subject in the model of the pattern *Observer*.

Generalizations

- Subject, JavaInterface (from PSM-Java)

Associations

- attach: Attach [1..*] Every instance of InterfaceSubject must have at least a method instance of Attach. It is a subset of JavaInterface::method.
- detach: Detach [1..*] Every instance of InterfaceSubject must have at least a method instance of Detach. It is a subset of JavaInterface::method.
- notify: Notify [1..*] Every instance of InterfaceSubject must have at least a method instance of Notify. It is a subset of JavaInterface::method.

Constraints

No additional constraints.

InterfaceRealizationObserver

Description

This metaclass specifies an interface realization between an abstract observer (InterfaceObserver) and a concrete observer (ConcreteObserver) in the model of the pattern *Observer*.

Generalizations

- InterfaceRealization (from Kernel)

Associations

- concreteObserver: ConcreteObserver [1] It denotes the element implementing the contract in this relation. It redefines InterfaceRealization::implementingClassifier.
- interfaceObserver: InterfaceObserver [1] It denotes the element that defines the contract in this relation.It redefines InterfaceRealization::contract.

Constraints

No additional constraints.

InterfaceRealizationSubject

Description
This metaclass specifies an interface realization between an abstract subject (InterfaceSubject) and a concrete subject (ConcreteSubject) in the model of the pattern *Observer*.

Generalizations

*   InterfaceRealization (from Kernel)

Associations

*   concreteSubject: ConcreteSubject [1] It denotes the element implementing the contract in this relation. It redefines InterfaceRealization::implementingClassifier.
*   interfaceSubject: InterfaceSubject [1] It denotes the element that defines the contract in this relation. It redefines InterfaceRealization::contract.

Constraints
No additional constraints.

Notify

Description
It defines a method that is declared by the subject.

Generalizations

*   Method (from PSM-Java)

Associations

*   classSubject: ClassSubject [0..1] It denotes the class that declares the method. It redefines JavaOperation::class.
*   interfaceSubject: InterfaceSubject [0..1] It denotes the interface that declares this method. It redefines Method::interface.

Constraints

[1]   It is a method that changes the subject state. self.isQuery
[2]   Its visibility is public. self.visibility = #public

Observer

Description

An observer is a specialized classifier that specifies the features of observers in the model of the pattern *Observer*. It is an abstract metaclass.

Generalizations

*   Classifier (from Kernel)

Associations

*   assocEndObserver:AssocEndObserver [0..1] It denotes the association-end of the association SubjectObserver in which this classifier participates.

Constraints

No additional constraints.

ObserverSubject

Description

This metaclass specifies a binary association between two instances of Observer and Subject.

Generalizations

*   Association (from Kernel)

Associations

*   assocEndConcreteObserver:AssocEndConcreteObserver [1] It represents a connection with the classifier ConcreteObserver. It is a subset of Association::memberEnd.
*   assocEndConcreteSubject:AssocEndConcreteSubject [1] It represents a connection with the classifier ConcreteSubject. It is a subset of Association::memberEnd.

Constraints

[1]   It has two association-ends. self.memberEnd -> size () = 2

SetState

Description

It defines an operation that is member of ConcreteSubject. It specifies a service that can be required from another object.

Generalizaciones

- Method (from PSM-Java)

Associations
No additional associations.

Constraints

[1] It is a concrete method that modify the subject state. **not** self.isAbstract **and not** self.isQuery
[2] It has a non-empty set of parameters and one of them, at least must be an input parameter. self. OwnedParameter -> notEmpty () **and** self.OwnedParameter -> select (param | param.direction = #in) -> size () >= 1
[3] Its visibility must be public. self.visibility = #public

Subject

Description
This metaclass is a specialized classifier that specifies the features that must have instances taking the role of subject in the model of the pattern Observer. It is an abstract metaclass.

Generalizations

- Classifier (from Kernel)

Associations

- assocEndSubject: AssocEndSubject [0..1] It denotes the association-end of the association SubjectObserver in which the classifier participates.

Constraints
No additional constraints.

SubjectObserver

Description
This metaclass specifies a binary association between two classifiers: Subject y Observer.

Generalizations

- Association (from Kernel)

Associations

- assocEndObserver: AssocEndObserver [1] It represents a connection with the classifier Observer. It is a subset of Association::memberEnd.
- assocEndSubject: AssocEndSubject [1] It represents a connection with the classifier Subject. It is a subset of Association::memberEnd.

Constraints

[1] It has two association-ends. self.memberEnd -> size () = 2

Update

Description

It defines a method that is declared by an observer. This method specifies a service that can be required by another object.

Generalizations

- Method (from PSM-Java)

Associations

- classObserver: ClassObserver [0..1] It denotes the class that declares this operation. It redefines JavaOperation::class.
- interfaceObserver: InterfaceObserver [0..1] It denotes the interface that declares this operation. It redefines Method::interface.

Constraints

[1] It is a method that does not change the observer state. self.isQuery
[2] Its visibility must be public. self.visibility = #public

D. 3. JAVA-ISM OBSERVER METAMODEL

Description of the Metaclasses

AddLink

Description

It defines a method that is declared by an instance of the class SubjectObserverAssociation.

Figure 6. Java ISM observer metamodel

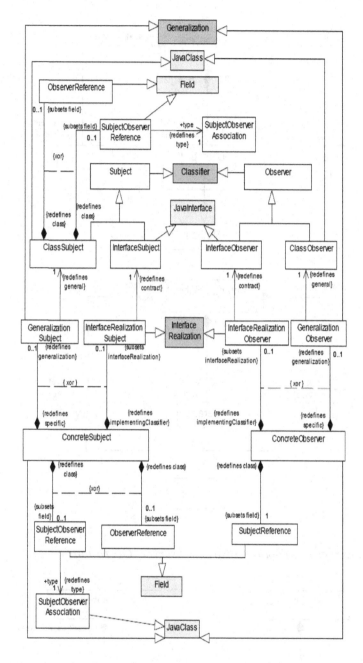

Generalizations

- Method (from ISM-Java)

Associations

- subjectObserverAssociation:SubjectObserverAssociation [1] It denotes the class that declares this method. It redefines JavaOperation::class.

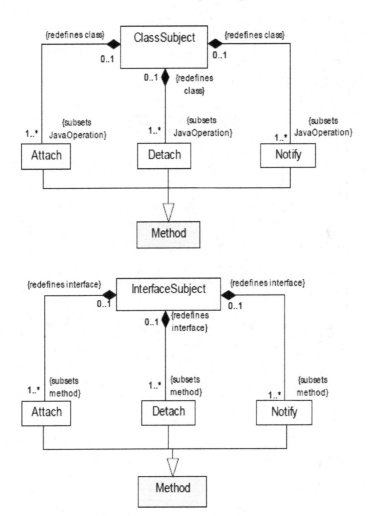

Figure 7. Java ISM observer metamodel: Abstract subject: Operations

Figure 8. Java ISM observer metamodel: Abstract observer: Operations

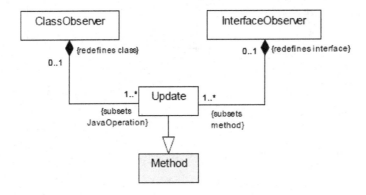

Figure 9. Java ISM observer metamodel: Concrete subject: Operations and attributes

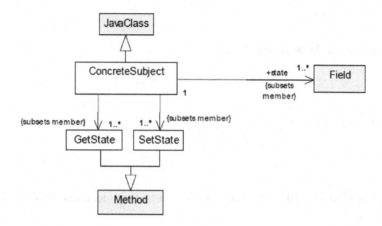

Figure 10. Java ISM observer metamodel: SubjectObserverAssociation: Operations

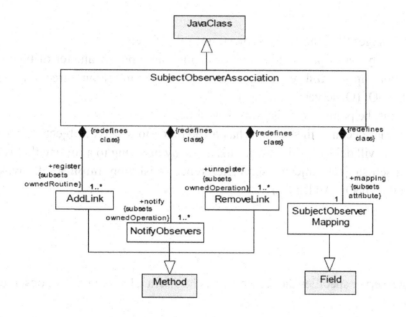

Constraints

[1] This method changes the state of the instance defining it. **not** self.isQuery

[2] It has a non-empty set of parameters being one of them an input parameter. self.parameter -> notEmpty () **and** self. parameter -> select (param | param.direction = #in **and** param.type = oclIs-KindOf (Observer)) -> size () = 1

[3] Its visibility must be public. self.visibility = #public

Attach

Description
It defines a method that is declared by a subject.

Generalizations

- Method (from ISM-Java)

Associations

- classSubject: ClassSubject [0..1] It denotes the class that declares this method. It redefines JavaOperation::class.
- interfaceSubject: InterfaceSubject [0..1] It denotes the interface that declares this method. It redefines Method::interface.

Constraints

[1] This method changes the state of the subject. **not** self.isQuery

[2] It has a non-empty set of parameters, one of them is an input parameter of type Observer. self. parameter -> notEmpty () **and** self. parameter -> select (param | param.direction = #in **and** param. type = oclIsKindOf (Observer)) -> size () = 1

[3] Its visibility must be public. self.visibility = #public

[4] If the subject that declares this routine has a reference to a class SubjectObserverAssociation, then this routine will delegate this task to this class, by invoking to a routine that is an instance of AddLink. **not** self.subject.subjectObserverReference -> isEmpty **implies** self.invokedRoutine -> exists (r | r.oclIsTypeOf (AddLink))

ClassObserver

Description
A metaclass ClassObserver specifies the features of a class Java taking the role of observer in the model of a pattern *Observer*.

Generalizations

- Observer, JavaClass (from ISM-Java)

Associations

- update: Update [1..*] Every instance of ClassObserver must have at least a method instance of Update. It is a subset of JavaClass::javaOperation.

Constraints

No additional constraints.

ClassSubject

Description

This metaclass specifies the features that must have a Java class taking the role of subject in the model of the pattern Observer.

Generalizations

- Subject, JavaClass (from ISM-Java)

Associations

- attach: Attach [1..*] Every instance of ClassSubject has at least a method instance of Attach. It is a subset of JavaClass::javaOperation.
- detach: Detach [1..*] Every instance of ClassSubject has at least a method instance of Detach. It is a subset of JavaClass::javaOperation
- notify: Notify [1..*] Every instance of ClassSubject has at least a method instance of Notify. It is a subset of JavaClass::javaOperation.
- observerReference: ObserverReference [0..1] It denotes the attribute that allows the subject to maintain a reference to its observers. It is a subset of JavaClass::field.
- subjectObserverReference:SubjectObserverReference [0..1] It denotes the attribute, which is a reference to a class that maintains the relation subject-observers. It is a subset of JavaClass::field.

Constraints

No additional constraints.

ConcreteObserver

Description

This metaclass specifies the features that must have a Java class with the behavior of a concrete observer in the model of the pattern Observer.

Generalizations

- JavaClass (de ISM-Java)

Associations

- generalizationObserver: GeneralizationObserver [0..1] It denotes a generalization where ConcreteObserver takes the role of child (specific). It redefines Classifier::generalization.

- interfaceRealizationObserver: InterfaceRealizationObserver [0..1] It denotes an interface realization where ConcreteObserver takes the role of the classifier implementing the contract. It is a subset of BehavioredClassifier::interfaceRealization.
- subjectReference: SubjectReference [0..1] It denotes a reference to subjects that are observed by the observer. It is a subset of JavaClass::field.

Constraints

[1]   An instance of a concrete observer can not be an abstract class. **not** self.isAbstract

[2]   If an instance of a concrete observer participates in an interface realization, then it must be a BehavioredClassifier. self.interfaceRealizationObserver -> notEmpty () **implies** self.superClass -> exists (c | c.oclIsTypeOf (BehavioredClassifier))

ConcreteSubject

Description
This metaclass specifies the features that must have a class taking the role of concrete subject in the model of the pattern *Observer*.

Generalizations

- JavaClass (from ISM-Java)

Associations

- generalizationSubject: GeneralizationSubject [0..1] It denotes a generalization where ConcreteSubject takes the role of child (specific). It redefines Classifier::generalization.
- getState: GetState [1..*] Every instance of ConcreteSubject must have one or more method instances of GetState. They can be own or inherited. It is a subset of NameSpace::member.
- interfaceRealizationSubject: InterfaceRealization [0..1] It denotes an interface realization where ConcreteSubject takes the role of the classifier implementing the contract (implementingClassifier). It is a subset of BehavioredClassifier::interfaceRealization.
- observerReference: ObserverReference [0..1] It denotes the attribute that allows the subject to maintain a reference to its observers. It is a subset of JavaClass::field.
- setState: GetState [1..*] Every instance of ConcreteSubject must have one or more method instances of SetState. They can be own or inherited. It is a subset of NameSpace::member.
- state: Property [1..*] It specifies a non-empty set of all attributes of ConcreteSubject. They can be own or inherited. It is a subset of NameSpace::member.
- subjectObserverReference: SubjectObserverReference [0..1] It denotes the attribute, which is a reference to a class maintaining the relation subject-observers. It is a subset of JavaClass::field.

Constraints

[1]   An instance of a concrete subject can not be an abstract class. **not** self.isAbstract

[2] If an instance of a concrete subject participates in an interface realization, then it must be a BehavioredClassifier. self.interfaceRealizationSubject -> notEmpty () **implies** self.superClass -> exists (c | c.oclIsTypeOf (BehavioredClassifier))

[3] If an instance of a concrete subject is subclass of ClassSubject, it will inherit the field ObserverReference or the field subjectObserverReference, therefore it does not need to declare any references to its observers. On the contrary, if it implements the interface InterfaceSubject, then it must declare a field whose type is ObserverReference or SubjectObserverReference to maintain information of its observers. **not** self.generalizationSubject -> isEmpty () **implies** self.observerReference -> isEmpty () **and** self.subjectObserverReference -> isEmpty () and **not** self.interfaceRealizationSubject -> isEmpty () **implies not** self.observerReference -> isEmpty () **xor not** self.observerReference -> isEmpty ()

Detach

Description

It defines a method that is declared by a subject.

Generalizations

- Method (from ISM-Java)

Associations

- classSubject: ClassSubject [0..1] It denotes the class that declares this method. It redefines JavaOperation::class.
- interfaceSubject: InterfaceSubject [0..1] It denotes the interface that declares this method. It redefines Method::interface.

Constraints

[1] This method changes the subject state. **not** self.isQuery

[2] It has a non-empty set of parameters being one of them an input parameter whose type is Observer. self.parameter -> notEmpty () **and** self.parameter ->select (param | param.direction = #in **and** param.type = oclIsKindOf(Observer)) -> size () = 1

[3] Its visibility must be public. self.visibility = #public

[4] If the subject that declares this routine has a reference to a SubjectObserverAssociation class, this routine will delegate its task to this class, by invoking to a routine instance of RemoveLink. **not** self.subject.subjectObserverReference -> isEmpty () **implies** self.invokedRoutine->exists (r | r.oclIsTypeOf (RemoveLink))

GeneralizationObserver

Description
This metaclass specifies a generalization between an abstract observer (ClassObserver) and a concrete observer (ConcreteObserver) in the model of the pattern O*bserver*.

Generalizations

•   Generalization (from Kernel)

Associations

•   classObserver: ClassObserver [1] It denotes the general element of this relation. It redefines Generalization::general.
•   concreteObserver: ConcreteObserver [1] It denotes the specific element of this relation. It redefines Generalization::specific.

Constraints
No additional constraints.

GeneralizationSubject

Description
This metaclass specifies a generalization between an abstract subject (ClassSubject) and a concrete subject (ConcreteSubject) in the model of the pattern *Observer*.

Generalizations

•   Generalization (from Kernel)

Associations

•   classSubject: ClassSubject [1] It denotes a general element of this relation. It redefines Generalization::general.
•   concreteSubject: ConcreteSubject [1] It denotes the specific element of this relation. It redefines Generalization::specific.

Constraints
No additional constraints.

GetState

Description
This metaclass specifies a generalization between an abstract subject (ClassSubject) and a concrete subject (ConcreteSubject) in the model of the pattern *Observer*.

Generalizations

- Method (from ISM-Java)

Associations
No additional associations.

Constraints

[1] It is an observer and concrete method. self.isQuery **and not** self.isAbstract

[2] As it must return the subject state, the set of parameters must not be empty, and at least, one of the parameters must have a direction equal to *out* or *return*. self.parameter -> notEmpty () **and** self. parameter -> select (par | par.direction = #return **or** par.direction = #out) -> size () >=1

[3] Its visibility must be public. self.visibility = #public

InterfaceObserver

Description
An InterfaceObserver specifies the features that must have a Java interface taking the role of abstract observer in the model of the pattern *Observer*.

Generalizations

- Observer, JavaInterface (from ISM-Java)

Associations

- update: Update [1..*] Every instance of InterfaceObserver has at least an operation instance of Update. It is a subset of JavaInterface::method.

Constraints
No additional constraints.

InterfaceSubject

Description
This metaclass specifies the features that must have a Java interface taking the role of abstract subject in the model of a pattern *Observer*.

Generalizations

- Subject, JavaInterface (from ISM-Java)

Associations

- attach: Attach [1..*] Every instance of InterfaceSubject has at least a method instance of Attach. It is a subset of JavaInterface::method.
- detach: Detach [1..*] Every instance of InterfaceSubject has at least a method instance of Detach. It is a subset of JavaInterface::method.
- notify: Notify[1..*] Every instance of InterfaceSubject has at least a method instance of Notify. It is a subset of JavaInterface::method.

Constraints
No additional constraints.

InterfaceRealizationObserver

Description
This metaclass specifies an interface realization between an abstract observer (InterfaceObserver) and a concrete observer (ConcreteObserver) in the model of the pattern *Observer*.

Generalizations

- InterfaceRealization (from Kernel)

Associations

- concreteObserver: ConcreteObserver [1] It denotes the element that implements the contract in this relation. It redefines InterfaceRealization::implementingClassifier.
- interfaceObserver: InterfaceObserver [1] It denotes the element that defines the contract in this relation. It redefines InterfaceRealization::contract.

Constraints
No additional constraints.

InterfaceRealizationSubject

Descriptions
This metaclass specifies an interface realization between an abstract subject (InterfaceSubject) and a concrete subject (ConcreteSubject) in the model of the pattern *Observer*.

Generalizations

- InterfaceRealization (from Kernel)

Associations

- concreteSubject: ConcreteSubject [1] It denotes the element that implements the contract in this relation. It redefines InterfaceRealization::implementingClassifier.
- interfaceSubject: InterfaceSubject [1] It denotes the element that defines the contract in this relation. It redefines InterfaceRealization::contract.

Constraints
No additional constraints.

Notify

Description
It defines a method that is declared by a subject.

Generalizations

- Method (from ISM-Java) Associations
- classSubject: ClassSubject [0..1] It denotes the class that declares this method. It redefines JavaOperation::class.
- interfaceSubject: InterfaceSubject [0..1] It denotes the interface that declares this method. It redefines Method::interface.

Constraints

[1] It is a method that does not change the subject state. self.isQuery
[2] Its visibility must be public. self.visibility = #public
[3] If the subject that declares this routine has a reference to a SubjectObserverAssociation class, this routine will delegate its task to this class by invoking this routine instance of NotifyObserver. **not** self.subject.subjectObserverReference -> isEmpty **implies** self.invokedRoutine -> exists (r | r.oclIsTypeOf(NotifyObserver))

NotifyObservers

Description
It defines a method that is declared by an instance of SubjectObserverAssociation.

Generalizations

- Method (from ISM-Java)

Associations

- subjectObserverAssociation:SubjectObserverAssociation [1] It denotes the class that declares this method. It redefines JavaOperation::class.

Constraints

[1] This is a method that does not change the state of the instance that defines it. self.isQuery
[2] Its visibility must be public. self.visibility = #public

Observer

Description
An observer is a specialized classifier that specifies a classifier whose role is observer in the model of the pattern *Observer*. It is an abstract metaclass.

Generalizations

- Classifier (from Kernel)

Associations
No additional associations.

Constraints
No additional constraints.

ObserverReference

Description
This field represents a reference to observers of a subject.

Generalizations

- Field (from ISM-Java)

Associations

- subject: Subject [1] It denotes the class that declares this field. It redefines Field::class.

Constraints

[1] The type of this field must correspond to some of the collections of the Java library. self.type. oclIsKindOf (JavaCollection) **and** self.type.parameter -> size () = 1 **and** self.type.parameter. ownedParameteredElement.oclIsTypeOf (Observer)

[2] Its visibility must be private or protected. self.visibility = #private **or** self.visibility = #protected

RemoveLink

Description
It defines a method that is declared by an instance of SubjectObserverAssociation.

Generalizations

*   Method (from ISM-Java)

Associations

*   subjectObserverAssociation:SubjectObserverAssociation [1] It denotes the class that declares this method. It redefines JavaOperation::class.

Constraints

[1] This method changes the state of instances defining it. **not** self.isQuery
[2] It has a non-empty set of parameters being one of them an input parameter whose type is observer. self.parameter -> notEmpty() **and** self.parameter -> select (param | param.direction = #in **and** param.type = oclIsKindOf (Observer)) -> size () = 1
[3] Its visibility must be public. self.visibility = #public

SetState

Description
It defines an operation member of ConcreteSubject. It specifies a service that can be required from another object.

Generalizations

*   Method (from ISM-Java)

Associations
No additional associations.

Constraints

[1] This is a method that is concrete and modifies the state of the subject. **not** self.isAbstract **and not** self.isQuery
[2] It has a non-empty set of parameters being at least one of them an input parameter. self.parameter -> notEmpty () **and** self.parameter ->select (param | param.direction = #in) -> size () >= 1
[3] Its visibility must be public. self.visibility = #public

Subject

Description

This metaclass specifies a specialized classifier that takes the role of subject in the model of the pattern *Observer*. It is an abstract metaclass.

Generalizations

- Classifier (from Kernel)

Associations

No additional associations.

Constraints

No additional constraints.

SubjectObserverAssociation

Description

This metaclass specifies the features of the class that maintains the relation between a subject and its observers.

Generalizations

- JavaClass (from ISM-Java)

Associations

- mapping: SubjectObserverMapping [1] It specifies an own attribute. It is a subset of JavaClass::field.
- notify: NotifyObservers [1..*] It specifies an own operation. It is a subset of JavaClass::method.
- register: AddLink [1..*] It specifies an own operation. It is a subset of JavaClass::method.
- unregister: RemoveLink [1..*] It specifies an own operation. It is a subset of JavaClass::method.

Constraints

No additional constraints.

SubjectObserverMapping

Description

This metaclass specifies the class attribute SubjectObserverAssociation, that maintains the mapping between a subject and its observers.

Generalizations

- Field (from ISM-Java)

Associations

- subjectObserverAssociation: SubjectObserverAssociation [1] It denotes the class that declares this attribute. It redefines Field::Class.

Constraints

[1] Its visibility must be private or protected. self.visibility = #private **or** self.visibility = #protected

SubjectObserverReference

Description

This attribute is a reference to a class SubjectObserverAssociation, which maintain the relation between a subject and its observers.

Generalizations

- Field (from ISM-Java)

Associations

- subject: Subject [1] It denotes the class that declares this attribute. It redefines Attribute:: class.
- type: SubjectObserverAssociation [1] It refers to the type of this attribute. It redefines Attribute::type.

Constraints

No additional constraints.

Update

Description

It defines a method that is declared by an observer which specifies a service that is required by another object.

Generalizations

- Method (from ISM-Java)

Associations

- classObserver: ClassObserver [0..1] It denotes the class that declares this operation. It redefines JavaOperation::class.
- interfaceObserver: InterfaceObserver [0..1] It denotes the interface that declares this operation. It redefines Method::interface.

Constraints

[1]   This is a method that does not change the state of the observer. self.isQuery

[2]   Its visibility must be public. self.visibility = #public

About the Author

Liliana Favre is a full professor of Computer Science at Universidad Nacional del Centro de la Provincia de Buenos Aires in Argentina. She is also a researcher of CIC (Comisión de Investigaciones Científicas de la Provincia de Buenos Aires). Her current research interests are focused on model driven development, model driven architecture and formal approaches, mainly on the integration of algebraic techniques with MDA-based processes. She has been involved in several national research projects about formal methods and software engineering methodologies. Currently she is research leader of the Software Technology Group at Universidad Nacional del Centro de la Provincia de Buenos Aires. She has published several book chapters, journal articles and conference papers. She has acted as editor of the book *UML and the Unified Process*.

Index

A

abstract interpretation 207, 215, 216, 217
abstraction 107, 199, 200, 202, 204, 206, 222, 226
abstraction levels 2, 3, 10, 11, 18, 26
abstract syntax tree (AST) 4, 206
activity diagrams 199, 204
adaptability 115
AGG visual programming environment 51, 77, 79
architectural levels 4
architectural specifications 98
Architecture-Driven Modernization (ADM) Task Force 201, 238
architectures 1, 4, 12, 16, 27
AssEndComponent property 163, 165, 166, 169, 170, 171, 173, 186, 187, 188, 189
assertion language 111
assertions 111
ASSOCIATES clause 109
Association component 80, 81, 83, 93, 107, 108, 109, 110
associations 34, 35, 36, 37, 80, 81, 83
axioms 98

B

Bag type 84, 95
basic specification 98, 99
Boolean basic type 84, 87, 88, 89, 91, 92, 93, 94, 95, 96
Boolean expressions 111
BOX_ scheme 80, 82, 90
business rules 1, 2, 31
byte code 1

C

class diagrams 199, 200, 201, 202, 204, 207, 208, 214, 215
classes 34, 35, 36, 37, 38, 39, 40, 41, 42, 43, 44, 45, 46
classical compiler techniques 199, 207
class invariant assertions 111
ClassObserver 127, 130, 136, 142, 150
class parameters 107
ClassSubject 127, 128, 130, 131, 133, 142, 150, 151
code 1, 2, 3, 4, 5, 6, 7, 8, 9, 10, 11, 12, 15, 16, 17, 20, 26
collaboration diagram 199, 208
Collection specification 100
combining operators 98
common algebraic language 98
common algebraic specification language (CASL) 98, 99, 100, 102, 103, 105, 106, 111, 253, 267
common warehouse metamodel (CWM) 17, 22, 24, 32, 50, 77, 255
complete algebraic specifications 107
complete MOF (CMOF) metamodel 52
component 107, 108, 109, 112
component-based reuse 115
Component-Composite-Generalization relationship 162, 163
Component-Leaf-Generalization relationship 162
component libraries 115
Component pattern 162, 163, 164, 165, 166, 167, 168, 169, 170, 171, 172, 173, 174, 175, 176, 183, 184, 186, 187, 188, 189, 190

component quality model 117

Composite-Component-Assoc relationship 162

Composite pattern 161, 162, 163, 164, 165, 166, 167, 168, 169, 170, 171, 172, 173, 174, 175, 176, 177, 178, 179, 180, 181, 182, 183, 184, 185, 187, 188, 189

computation independent model (CIM) 6, 16, 18, 19, 232, 242, 253, 254, 255

computer aided software engineering (CASE) 10, 13, 115, 156, 158, 201, 202, 203, 226, 227, 243, 244, 245, 249, 250, 252

ConcreteObserver 121, 125, 128, 130, 132, 134, 142, 150, 151, 153

ConcreteSubject metaclass 121, 122, 125, 129, 130, 131, 133, 134, 135, 142, 151, 153

constraints 98

CORBA middleware 15, 24, 31, 32

Core language 52, 73, 74

D

data abstraction 102

data encapsulation 102

data flow graph 201, 208, 209, 210, 211

data mining 201

data reverse technologies 201

data types 35, 36

data warehouse 201

DEFERRED clause 107

design 1, 2, 3, 5, 6, 10, 13, 15, 17, 22, 27, 30, 31

design patterns 1, 6, 115, 116, 117, 119, 156

design pattern techniques, evolution of 116

design recovery 2

design views 1

diagram interchange specifications 8

domain specific language (DSL) 8, 11, 31, 35, 204, 232, 233

dynamic analysis 200, 201, 204, 205, 206, 207, 208, 211, 212, 213, 214, 215

E

Eclipse generative modeling tools (EclipseG-MT) 204

Eclipse Modeling framework 51

Eclipse open source framework 204, 227

EffectiveObserver abstract class 138

EffectiveSubject abstract class 138

Eiffel code 107

Eiffel contracts 107

Eiffel language 107, 108, 109, 111, 112, 117, 119, 120, 136, 137, 138, 144, 149, 150

Eiffel libraries 109

Eiffel platform 136, 137, 149, 150

Eiffel-PSM Observer Metamodel 396

essential MOF (EMOF) metamodel 52, 74, 75, 76, 232

EssentialOCL 232

evolution system techniques 49

extension operators 98

Extract Composite refactoring rule 161, 162, 163, 170, 174, 182, 183, 184, 185

F

first-order logic 98

formal specifications 11, 159, 160, 199, 203, 204, 205

forward engineering 2, 3, 6, 7, 9, 10, 16, 17, 49, 158, 159, 243, 245, 249, 250, 252

free specifications 98, 100

Fujaba Tool Suite project 204

G

generated specifications 98, 100

Graph Transformation platform 204

H

heuristics 107, 112

Hide operator 100

high-level architecture 201

high-level views 1

I

implementation component model (ICM) 262

implementation level 109

implementation pieces 115

implementation specific abstraction levels 158

implementation specific model (ISM) 7, 8, 9, 11, 16, 18, 26, 34, 39, 41, 43, 115, 116, 117, 118, 119, 120, 140, 141, 142, 143, 144, 159, 160, 183, 204, 205, 206, 218, 219, 220, 221, 222, 225, 226, 232, 233

IMPORTS clause 107
incomplete algebraic specifications 107
industrial software development environments 159
INHERITS keyword 107
instantiating schemes 107
Integer basic type 84
interaction diagrams 199, 201, 204, 208
Interaction Pattern Specification (IPS) 117
ISM-C++ Metamodel 278, 316
ISM-Eiffel Metamodel 278, 294
ISM-Java Metamodel 278, 305

J

JavaClass 218, 219, 220, 221, 222
Java-ISM Observer Metamodel 420
Java platform 119, 120, 136, 137, 138, 139, 140, 141, 142, 143, 144, 157
Java program 211, 214
Java-PSM Observer Metamodel 406
Java source code 159
Java statements 209, 210

L

Leaf pattern 162, 163, 165, 166, 167, 168, 169, 171, 172, 173, 175, 183, 184, 187, 188, 189
legacy code 1, 5
legacy systems 1, 2, 10, 17
loose specifications 98, 100

M

MDA-based CASE tools 115
MDA-based object oriented reverse engineering 199
MDA-based processes 49
MDA-based software development processes 49
MDA-based tools 273
MDA reverse engineering 231, 232
MDA technical issues 115
megamodels 115, 116, 117, 118, 119
membership equational logic (MEL) 51
metaclasses 116, 120, 121, 122, 127, 128, 129, 130, 132, 133, 134, 135, 137, 139, 142, 162, 163, 168, 170, 173

meta-metamodels 243, 252
metamodel-based refactorings 160
metamodeling 49, 51, 52, 116, 117, 157,
metamodeling patterns 257
metamodeling techniques 199, 204
metamodel notation 37
metamodels 4, 7, 8, 9, 10, 11, 12, 16, 17, 19, 20, 21, 22, 23, 24, 25, 26, 27, 28, 29, 30, 31, 34, 35, 37, 38, 39, 40, 41, 43, 45, 46, 49, 51, 52, 53, 76, 78, 115, 116, 117, 118, 119, 120, 121, 122, 124, 136, 137, 138, 139, 140, 141, 142, 143, 144, 145, 149, 150, 151, 159, 160, 161, 162, 174, 192, 194, 196, 200, 204, 205, 206, 207, 218, 219, 220, 221, 222, 224, 225, 243, 245, 246, 247, 248, 249, 250, 251, 252
metamodel transformations 161
meta object facility (MOF) metamodel 8, 9, 10, 11, 12, 14, 16, 17, 18, 19, 22, 23, 24, 25, 26, 27, 28, 29, 30, 31, 33, 34, 35, 36, 37, 45, 46, 47, 49, 51, 52, 53, 54, 59, 76, 77, 79, 80, 81, 83, 84, 85, 97, 158, 160, 161, 162, 196, 197, 198, 200, 204, 205, 206, 218, 219, 221, 222, 228, 232, 233, 234, 235
meta-patterns 158, 161, 162
mining software repositories (MSR) 201
model-driven approaches 257
model driven architecture (MDA) 6, 7, 8, 9, 10, 11, 12, 13, 14, 15, 16, 17, 18, 19, 21, 22, 32, 34, 35, 49, 51, 52, 53, 77, 78, 115, 116, 117, 118, 119, 120, 143, 145, 157, 158, 159, 160, 161, 197, 199, 200, 201, 202, 203, 204, 205, 206, 211, 212, 213, 214, 227, 228, 229, 196, 231, 232, 233, 234, 235, 228, 236, 237, 238, 242, 243, 244, 245, 247, 248, 249, 250, 251, 252, 253
model driven development (MDD) 6, 11, 16, 200, 201, 203, 253
models 3, 6, 7, 8, 9, 10, 11, 12, 14, 15, 16, 17, 18, 19, 20, 21, 22, 25, 26, 27, 28, 29, 30, 31, 33, 34, 35, 37, 46, 158, 159, 160, 162, 170, 174, 197
-driven architecture
   formalization of processes 247

driven architecture (MDA) 242–252
-driven development (MDD) 245
model transformations 115, 116, 117, 143, 144,
       243, 245, 250, 251, 252
MOMENT framework 200

N

NEREUS 258, 259
NEREUS classes 107
NEREUS constructions 107
NEREUS metamodeling language 11, 49, 52,
       53, 54, 55, 56, 57, 58, 59, 60, 61, 65, 67,
       69, 72, 75, 80, 81, 83, 84, 85, 86, 87, 88,
       89, 90, 92, 95, 97, 98, 99, 100, 102, 107,
       108, 112, 113, 116, 150, 154, 158, 160,
       185, 189, 190, 191, 196, 205, 224, 225,
       233, 332, 333, 334, 336, 337, 338, 339,
       350, 353, 355
NEREUS specifications 107

O

object constraint language (OCL) 6, 8, 10, 14,
       16, 18, 19, 25, 28, 29, 33, 35, 37, 38, 45,
       47, 158, 174, 178, 183, 184, 190, 193,
       196, 199, 203, 204, 205, 207, 213, 214,
       219, 221, 222, 225, 228, 232, 233, 234,
       242, 243, 244, 245, 247, 248, 250, 251,
       252, 254, 332, 333, 335, 336, 337, 338,
       344, 345, 352, 354, 355, 381, 382, 383,
       384, 385, 386
object diagram 199, 202, 204, 208
object flow graph 5
Object Management Group (OMG) 6, 8, 10,
       11, 14, 15, 16, 17, 21, 24, 25, 28, 30, 31,
       32, 33, 34, 38, 47, 201, 204, 228, 229,
       238, 253
object-oriented code 107, 199, 200, 204, 206,
       208, 213, 227
object-oriented languages 5, 107, 108
object-oriented program model 207, 214
object-oriented programs 212
Observer abstract class 116, 118, 120, 121,
       122, 123, 124, 125, 126, 127, 128, 129,
       130, 131, 132, 133, 134, 135, 136, 137,
       138, 139, 140, 141, 142, 143, 144, 145,
       146, 148, 149, 150, 152, 154, 155

Observer components 120
Observer design pattern 116
Observer pattern metamodel 118, 120, 121,
       122, 130, 131, 132, 135, 136, 137, 139,
       149
ObserverReference 141, 142
OCL basic types 84
OCL specifications 80, 83, 84
operations 98, 99, 100, 102, 105
operation signatures 111

P

package diagram 199, 201, 202, 204, 208
PackageObserver Metamodel 150
Packages 35, 37
packages diagrams 80
parameters 117, 127, 130, 135, 144, 145, 147,
       148, 149, 150
partial functions 98, 99
Participates associaton 111
pattern solutions 116, 117
perfective model evolution 158
person and meeting (P&M) class diagram 85,
       91, 96, 97, 111
platform component description (PDM) 20
platform independent abstraction levels 158
platform independent component model
       (PICM) 262
platform independent model (PIM) 6, 8, 9, 10,
       11, 16, 18, 19, 20, 46, 47, 115, 116, 117,
       118, 119, 120, 121, 122, 137, 139, 144,
       146, 147, 148, 149, 150, 154, 155, 158,
       159, 160, 161, 183, 190, 199, 200, 203,
       204, 205, 206, 232, 233, 235, 253
platform specific abstraction levels 158
platform specific component model (PSCM)
       262
platform specific model (PSM) 7, 8, 9, 11, 16,
       18, 20, 34, 46, 115, 116, 117, 118, 119,
       120, 136, 137, 138, 139, 140, 141, 144,
       145, 146, 148, 149, 150, 154, 155, 158,
       159, 160, 161, 199, 200, 203, 204, 205,
       206, 207, 218, 219, 220, 221, 222, 225,
       232, 233, 235, 253, 255
polymorphism 212
postcondition assertions 111, 112

postconditions 117, 150, 154
precondition assertions 111
preconditions 117, 144, 148, 154, 155
predicates 98, 99
private operation visibility 100
protected operation visibility 100
PSM-Eiffel 137, 154
PSM-Eiffel Metamodel 278
PSM-Java Metamodel 278, 284
public operation visibility 100

Q

query, view, transformation (QVT) metamodel 8, 14, 17, 28, 29, 30, 33, 45, 47, 51, 52, 73, 74, 75, 79, 203, 204, 243, 256
QVT-Core 232

R

rational unified process (RUP) 21, 22, 27
Real basic type 84
realization sub-component 108
reengineering 2, 3, 4, 5, 6, 9, 10
refactoring 158, 159, 160, 161, 162, 163, 169, 170, 174, 182, 183, 184, 185, 189, 190, 191, 192, 193, 194, 196, 197, 244, 245, 247, 251, 252
refactoring techniques 159, 160
refinements 117, 118, 120, 150, 154
Relation language 52, 73, 74
renaming operators 98
requirements 1, 2, 3, 6, 18, 21
restructuring 2
reusability 115
reusable components 115, 117, 119
reusable infrastructure 49
reusable schemes 80
reverse engineering 1, 2, 3, 4, 5, 6, 9, 10, 11, 12, 13, 14, 17, 20, 26, 49, 53, 158, 159, 199, 200, 201, 202, 203, 204, 205, 206, 208, 213, 214, 215, 218, 222, 226, 231, 232, 233, 234, 235, 243, 244, 245, 249, 252
role-based modeling language (RBML) 116
round-trip engineering 49

S

sequence diagram 199, 222
Sequence type 84, 91
Set type 84, 93, 94, 95
slicing techniques 4
software artifacts 1, 2, 3, 8, 35, 199, 201
software evolution 236, 237, 238, 239
software language engineering 235
software process engineering 235
software process engineering metamodel (SPEM) 17, 21, 24, 27, 33
software quality 116
sorts 98, 99
source code 1, 3, 4, 6, 7, 10, 12, 16, 199, 201, 202, 203, 204, 206, 207, 208, 214
source metamodel 160, 161, 162, 163, 180, 181, 182, 183, 185
specification techniques, formal 49, 50, 51, 52, 53, 56, 77, 79
specification techniques, semiformal 49, 50
state diagrams 199, 201, 202, 204, 205, 208, 215, 216, 217, 222
static analysis 4, 5, 10, 12, 200, 202, 204, 205, 206, 207, 208, 211, 212, 213, 214
stereotypes 51
Story Diagrams 204
Story Driven Modeling 204
String basic type 84, 90, 92, 93, 95
structural pattern specification (SPS) 117
structured specifications 98, 99
subclass 161, 163, 165, 166, 168, 169, 171, 173, 174, 183
Subject abstract class 120, 121, 126, 127, 128, 129, 132, 134, 135, 136, 137, 138, 151, 152
SubjectObserverAssociation 143, 144
SubjectObserverMapping 143
SubjectObserverReference 141, 142
subsorts 98, 99
superclass 161, 165, 166, 168, 171, 173, 174, 183
SYNTROPY method 381
system entities lifecycle 199, 204
system functionality 231
system processes 199, 204

T

target metamodel 160, 161, 162, 163, 180, 181
taxonomy of associations 108
traceability 1, 12
transformation processes 80
transformation rules 80, 84, 85, 95, 107
transformation rule system 381, 382, 383, 384,
    385, 386, 387, 388, 389, 390, 391, 392,
    393, 394, 395
transformations 107, 109, 116, 117, 143, 144,
    149, 150, 154, 155, 157
trivial translation 107
trusted components 157,

U

UML CASE tools 202, 203
UML class diagrams 80, 161, 163
UML diagrams 205
UML Infrastructure 232
UML models 159, 197

UML static diagrams 381
unified modeling language (UML) 6, 8, 10,
    14, 15, 16, 17, 18, 19, 20, 21, 22, 23, 24,
    25, 26, 27, 30, 31, 32, 33, 34, 35, 36, 37,
    46, 49, 50, 193, 196, 197, 198, 199, 200,
    202, 203, 204, 205, 207, 208, 213, 214,
    218, 221, 222, 224, 227, 229, 232, 234,
    242, 243, 244, 245, 247, 248, 249, 250,
    251, 252, 254, 267

V

validation 116
verification 116

X

XML metadata interchange (XMI) 15, 23, 25,
    30, 33, 204, 257

Z

Z language 50